Essential Presidential Prayers and Texts

A Roman Missal Study Edition and Workbook

Daniel J. Merz

Abbot Marcel Rooney, OSB

Nihil Obstat
Very Reverend Daniel A. Smilanic, JCD
Vicar of Canonical Service
September 20, 2011

Imprimatur
Reverend Monsignor John F. Canary, STL, DMIN
Vicar General
Archdiocese of Chicago
September 20, 2011

The *Nihil Obstat* and *Imprimatur* are declarations that the material is free from doctrinal or moral error, and thus is granted permission to publish in accordance with c. 827. No legal responsibility is assumed by the grant of this permission. No implication is contained herein that those who have granted the *Nihil Obstat* and *Imprimatur* agree with the content, opinions, or statements expressed.

Anna Belle O'Shea pointed the presidential prayers.

Graziano Marcheschi provided proclamation tips for the Triduum and commentary for the Solemn Blessing for the Easter Vigil.

The commentary for the Tones for the Presidential Prayers was provided by Michael S. Driscoll. That commentary originally appeared in *The Order of Mass: A Roman Missal Study Edition and Workbook*, by Michael S. Driscoll and J. Michael Joncas © 2011, Archdiocese of Chicago: Liturgy Training Publications.

Printed in the United States of America.

ISBN: 978-1-61671-037-8

PTSSF

To Conception Abbey,
who taught me to love
the liturgy and the Word.

Contents

Introduction

It is, by now, a well-known and established phrase: *lex orandi . . . lex credendi* (the law of praying [establishes/grounds] the law of believing). The orations, Prefaces, and blessings of the third edition of *The Roman Missal* embody the law of praying for Catholics of the Roman Rite, and this commentary attempts to draw out some of their underlying law of believing. These prayers have had a quite varied history. Some were written by theologian Popes in the fifth century, others by theologians in the twentieth century, and the rest by a host of dedicated and spiritual writers in between. All were focused on expressing the Paschal Mystery in language inspired by scripture, grounded in theology, and applied through image and metaphor.

This work, *Essential Presidential Prayers and Texts: A Roman Missal Study Edition and Workbook*, a companion volume to *The Order of Mass: A Roman Missal Study Edition and Workbook,* by Fathers Michael S. Driscoll and Jan Michael Joncas, digs into the scripture, theology, and imagery of the prayers with great zeal, attempting to open up some of this euchological richness for the reader. There is a twofold reason behind this effort. First, to help the priest who prays the prayers (and all who hear them) to do so with a deeper understanding of their language and theology. It is hoped that this work may even contribute toward a deeper grasp of the spirituality within these prayers. Secondly, to serve as a source of inspiration for preaching on the liturgy. The homilist at Mass is not limited to preaching on the Lectionary readings proclaimed during the Liturgy of the Word. He also has the opportunity to preach on any of the liturgical texts or themes of the day. These commentaries, for the most part, do not attempt to give concrete application of the spirituality or theology of the texts, but simply to bring that spirituality and theology into relief, to present a host of inspired themes from which a homilist may choose (and himself, then, give application of them to his flock).

The prayers are translations of the Latin. Some of the original Latin texts belong to a more or less integral cultural background, for example, ancient Roman and patristic linguistic patterns. Some of the texts come from later medieval society, and some derive from a more contemporary linguistic and cultural milieu. This temporal and cultural span among the prayers poses challenges for translators, because the same word may be used differently from one prayer to the next, depending on its history. The present commentary, however, has more pastoral aspirations, and the exegesis of these prayers does not go into their origin or editorial history. Where possible, the scriptural allusions within the prayers have been provided. Knowing how the Church has interpreted scripture in these liturgical texts can be a most fruitful exercise in learning to think with the Church. Coming to grasp some of the theology behind the prayers is learning to speak and pray with the Church. Theology may be defined as a word (including the Word) of God, about God and to God. To immerse oneself deeply enough in theology is to begin to see the world and life from a new perspective, a divine perspective. This commentary hopes to contribute to just such a perspective.

An Interior Participation

Commentators on the revised translation of *The Roman Missal* have noted that the new style of prayers will require some preparation both to pray them well (this is the first order of importance) and to proclaim them well (also clearly important, but of a second order). Spending time with these prayers in *lectio divina,* or spiritual reading, is highly recommended. This could be preparation not only for Holy Mass, but sessions of the Rite of Christian Initiation of Adults or other faith formation sessions the parish may offer. The idea is to let this prayer of the Church work its way into the heart and help to shape the prayer that is offered at the altar of the heart. Then, when prayer is offered at the altar in the church, there will be a deep interior participation that gives witness of a living liturgy with authentic dialogue—both human and divine.

A certain surrender is required here. On the one hand, both priest and laity are asked to make this prayer of the Church their own and to pray it with integrity. On the other hand, it can happen that the priest or member of the laity is struggling with doubt or temptation, and the prayer of the Church feels distant at best. In such moments, "integrity" must run deeper than feelings, and the act of surrender must become more than mere words. It becomes a real act of faith grounded in love, which takes one beyond feelings and into duty, commitment, and sacrifice. Over time, one begins to understand that the prayer of the Church is not mere words, but truly a sacrifice, and when offered sincerely, a *sacrificium laudis*, a sacrifice of praise.

On the second order of proclaiming the texts, proclamation tips have been provided. The word "tips" is used advisedly. There is not one way to proclaim these prayers. This will vary to some extent depending on the heart of the offerer or the needs of the assembly. The tips are provided simply to emphasize key phrases in the context of the whole prayer. The new translations are often a single sentence that highlight the unity and integrity of the prayer. As the texts are prayed, the whole of the prayer should be borne in mind. Roman prayers are often characterized as sober, concise, and concrete. When seen in relation to some of the prayers of the Eastern Churches, their sobriety and conciseness become quite evident. Nonetheless, the prayers are no less complex and profound, and care will be needed to pray and proclaim them well.

It is this author's hope that priest celebrants who make use of this resource will consult it as part of their homily preparation and general preparation. We have become accustomed to seeking liturgical themes from the scripture readings of the day. With this resource, perhaps we will become accustomed to seeking themes also from the liturgical prayer texts of the day. May this commentary be one more help (grace) in the continuing renewal of the Sacred Liturgy, which is ever ancient and ever new. May it be for you a Word of God, about God and to God.

Rev. Daniel J. Merz

Chanting Our Prayers

The sounds of the choir at our parish and the Latin chants the priest sang are strong memories from my childhood. The rhythm of the chants and the beauty of the choir enhanced my prayer at Mass. As I moved into adulthood, it was such a blessing to participate more fully in the liturgy; and as a musician, in the sung liturgy. Some of my deepest moments of prayer at Eucharist are from those liturgies with their glorious sharing of the sung prayer between choir, cantor, a singing presider and the assembly. At those times, I sense the nobility to which the *Constitution on the Sacred Liturgy* refers in article 113:

> A liturgical service takes on a nobler aspect when the rites are celebrated with singing, the sacred ministers take their parts in them, and the faithful actively participate.

The implementation of the third edition of *The Roman Missal* is an opportunity for renewing this full participation at liturgy that includes the lifting of one's voice in song. It is especially important for the priest celebrant to give leadership to the singing at Mass. As *Sing to the Lord: Music in Divine Worship* (STL), 19, states:

> The importance of the priest's participation in the Liturgy, especially by singing, cannot be overemphasized. The priest sings the presidential prayers and dialogues of the Liturgy according to his capabilities, and he encourages sung participation in the liturgy by his own example, joining in the congregational song.

"According to his capabilities" is a key phrase in this quote; my experience is that many people underestimate their capability to sing. How, then, to inspire priest celebrants to use this study edition and workbook to discover the fullest capability possible in singing the liturgy? No less than an embodiment of singing from the heart with an attitude of joy will call forth the fullness of the assembly's response. The following story emphasizes the depth to which sung prayer reaches.

Vulnerability in Song

When I was a much younger cantor, information on a seminar came across my work desk. It targeted music therapists and was being held at a local hospital. Its title, "Music and Healing," piqued my interest, so I signed up to attend, despite having no background in music therapy. I do not remember the presenter's name, although it was clear he was well known in music therapy circles. The entire stage was set up with the musical instruments he used with clients. With a volunteer therapist, the presenter demonstrated the process and the instruments. As a cantor, I was fascinated by his comment that the very last thing he would consider inviting the clients to use to express what they were dealing with was their voice. This invitation came only after weeks, or even months, of therapy sessions in which either percussive instruments or instruments that made more lyrical sounds were used. There is such a vulnerability in using one's voice in song, said the therapist.

It affected me deeply to realize that, each time I ministered as a cantor at a liturgy, I was inviting people in the assembly to use their voices. These were people who might be going through a divorce, who might be worried about a sick parent, who might have a teenager struggling with addiction to drugs—any number of difficulties that would make opening up and using their voice in song a struggle. From that moment, I knew so much more clearly how vital it was for me to encourage the assembly to find its voice, to empower each person to find healing in singing. If we can become more vulnerable to one another and to God by letting go of our fears, our embarrassment, our doubts, our angers, our inhibitions, and our hurts, we will be able to sing, and we will be changed. That change, of course, will come from God. As STL, 2, states:

> A cry from deep within our being, music is a way for God to lead us to the realm of higher things. As St. Augustine says, "Singing is for the one who loves." Music is therefore a sign of God's love for us and of our love for him.

A Partnership with Parish Musicians

How does one move, then, from the desire to sing well to singing to one's full capability? Commitment, conviction for the task, and rehearse, rehearse, rehearse. The pages of this study edition and workbook are designed to make it easier for the priest to sing the chant once the musical pattern of the chant is learned. Following this introduction to the music portion of the book are the Tones for the Presidential Prayers, as provided in Appendix I of *The Roman Missal*. The commentary on those pages, written by Michael S. Driscoll, was excerpted from *The Order of Mass: A Roman Missal Study Edition and Workbook*.

This book provides proclamation texts and texts with the pointing of the simple tones of the presidential prayers on facing pages. (Margin space is provided for making notes on the singing of the chants.) Pointing the text is a way of indicating the word or syllable on which the pitch moves. Chant is sung speech, so most of the text is sung on one pitch, with movement to other pitches within a very small range. The pointing provided in this book divides the prayer texts into three sections: A, B, and C. A set pattern begins and ends each section of the prayer text, and pointers help focus where the pitches change within the pattern of the chant. A different method for providing pointers is used at the end of each section. The three methods are consistent throughout:

- The pitch movement at the end of the A section is indicated by bolded and underlined text.
- The pitch movement at the end of the B section is indicated by bolded text.
- The pitch movement at the end of the C section is indicated by bolded and italicized text.

Chant is best pitched in the voice's mid-range. The liturgical musician can help the priest celebrant establish his best mid-range pitch and teach him the chant patterns based on that beginning pitch. The priest celebrant is highly encouraged to call upon the talents and gifts of the parish music director while preparing to sing the liturgy. Before beginning to sing the chant, however, it is best to spend rehearsal time with the parish musician for an understanding of the pointers in the texts and how the movement in the pitch heightens the flow of the chant. Although chant is fluid and without a set beat, it contains a pulse that becomes familiar with repeated use. For a first practice, it might be good to go through one Sunday in the workbook together with the parish musician, with the musician chanting the prayers so that the pointers highlighting the movement in the chant pattern can be recognized. Such sessions will help the priest become familiar with the sound of the chant patterns. Taping solo rehearsals will be beneficial, allowing the individual to notice improvements and where work still needs to be done. It is important for the priest to hear how well his chanting keeps the integrity of the pitch relationship. This is an essential grounding that is critical, because once the sound of the chant pattern is well established, it is fairly easy to apply from prayer to prayer.

The time spent in rehearsal with the musician, which ensures that the chant pattern and personalized beginning pitch are locked into the voice, will be worth it. The consistent use of the established mid-range pitch will mean that its sound will become available interiorly, so that even without the musician, the chant can be pitched confidently and the pattern sung to lead into the assembly's response. The pitch of the chant should be neither too low nor too high, so that the assembly can comfortably respond to the chanted prayer.

Often the suggestions in the margins for the spoken word will be helpful for the sung word as well. It will benefit the priest to first speak the prayer before chanting it, paying attention to pauses and emphases. This can be done even before meeting with the parish musician. Of course, just as the spoken word needs to be articulated well so as to be understood by the assembly, the same is true for the chanted word. Particular attention needs to be given to singing the beginning and ending of words, to vowel sounds and consonants. After becoming acquainted and comfortable with the text, the pitch, and the chant pattern, the focus can be on pacing and the best places to breathe within the chant. Are the same words emphasized in the chant as in the spoken prayer? The liturgical musician can make suggestions or affirm natural emphases of words or phrases.

Clarity of pitch, the chant pattern, the pulse of the chant, articulation, breathing, and the words or syllables to emphasize are all part of the rehearsal with the parish musician. Time spent in preparation allows the priest to be freed up enough musically to pray the chanted prayers.

The musician and priest can decide together how best to approach rehearsals. Much will depend on how often the liturgy is sung. Will it be every Sunday or only for special occasions and feasts? That decision will help determine if a regular weekly rehearsal is needed to attain a strong comfort level with the chants; or if several rehearsals in the weeks prior to each liturgical season, with the focus on only certain texts, are required. Keep in mind that "Great importance should therefore be attached to the use of singing in the celebration of the Mass. . . . Every care should be taken that singing not be absent in celebrations that occur on Sundays and on Holydays of Obligation" (GIRM, 40).

Besides the parish music director, cantors in the parish can be helpful to the priest. If the music director is not available at times, perhaps a cantor can substitute for rehearsal support. Cantors can offer tips regarding their practice patterns in preparation for ministering. Often there is a(n) (Arch)diocesan School for Cantors. The National Association of Pastoral Musicians offers a track for cantors at its annual convention. The same principles taught at these schools can be applied for the presider. In addition, musical scores of chants and recordings can be downloaded from NPM's website (www.npm.org). The CD, *Learning the Chants of the Missal, Part II: Presidential Prayers and Texts,* published by Liturgy Training Publications, is another invaluable tool for becoming acquainted with the chant tones. Remember that pitches vary and that the pitch on the CD or downloaded music may not be the particular mid-range pitch that an individual has established. Listening to the music chants between pratices with the parish musician will solidify the work done in the sessions and will immerse the singer in the sound of the chant pattern. The mid-range pitch used to begin the chant does not matter; maintaining the relationship between the pitches does.

Rooting Prayer in Hearts and Minds

The pointed texts in this book, the work with the musician, and listening to chanted music will help priests make sung prayer their own and convey meaning to the assembly. Chanted prayer allows a different kind of participation than spoken prayer. The assembly listens differently. To chant the prayer well slows it down and allows it to better root itself in hearts and minds. Over time this will affect the assembly's response. The hope is that with time, each parish community and each parishioner will become the song as a sign of God's presence among us.

Denise La Giglia

Denise La Giglia, a pastoral musician and spiritual director, is the co-author of *The Liturgical Flutist* (GIA) and has published several meditational CDs. She is a former program director for both the Office for Divine Worship for the Archdiocese of Chicago and GIA Publications, Inc., and member of the staff at the Institute for Spiritual Leadership, Chicago. Her master of arts degree in pastoral studies is from Loyola University Chicago.

From the Editor

Rev. Daniel J. Merz, SLD, and Abbot Marcel Rooney, OSB, the authors of *Essential Presidential Prayers and Texts: A Roman Missal Study Edition and Workbook*, bring academic, liturgical, and pastoral experience to their reflections on the prayers of the Mass.

Father Merz is the associate director of the United States Conference of Catholic Bishops' Secretariat of Divine Worship. Prior to his position at the Bishops' Conference, he was the vice rector and dean of students at Conception Seminary College, Conception, Missouri, where he taught Latin and liturgy. Father Merz is a priest of the Diocese of Jefferson City, Missouri, and chaired the Diocesan Liturgical Commission there from 2007 to 2011. He earned his licentiate in sacred liturgy in 1999 and his doctorate in sacred liturgy in 2011 from the Pontifical Institute of Liturgy at Sant' Anselmo in Rome. For two years he served as associate pastor at the Cathedral of St. Joseph in Jefferson City.

His homilies and reproducible bulletin articles appear in *Preparing Your Parish for the Revised Roman Missal: Homilies and Reproducibles for Faith Formation* © 2010 Liturgy Training Publications. He has published two articles in *Liturgical Ministry* (one on the Liturgy of the Eucharist in the revised *General Instruction of the Roman Missal*, Summer 2003; the other on priestly spirituality in the Eucharistic Prayer, Summer 2005).

Abbot Rooney is in the process of founding a Pastoral Institute of Sacred Liturgy, Music and Art in the Diocese of Madison, Wisconsin. The former Abbot Primate of the Benedictine Order has taught in the doctoral program at the Pontifical Institute of Liturgy in Rome, at Conception Seminary, and assisted the Congregation for Divine Worship in Rome and served as adviser to the U.S. Bishops' Committee on Liturgy.

He earned a licentiate in sacred theology in 1975 and a doctorate in sacred theology in 1976 from the Pontifical Institute of Liturgy. His master of arts degree in music is from the Eastman Conservatory of Music, Rochester, New York. He has served as the pastor of St. John the Baptist Church, Brinkley, Arkansas, and St. Francis Church, Forrest City, Arkansas.

Father Merz wrote the commentaries and proclamation tips for Advent, Lent, Easter Time, and Ordinary Time. Abbot Rooney wrote the chant tips for the Prefaces; the commentary, and chant and proclamation tips, for the Solemnities of the Lord and the Feasts and Solemnities in the Proper of Saints, as well as the chant tips and commentary for the Triduum. In addition to the commentaries and tips on the prayers in this book, the authors have provided commentaries and tips to the Prefaces that are within the Order of Mass. The url, www.StudyThePresidentialTexts.com, where the Prefaces can be found are indicated on Sundays, solemnities, and feasts throughout the book.

Periodically in this resource, a homily follows the commentary on the Preface. Those homilies may be linked directly to the day or to an aspect of the saint honored on that day. Often the homilies examine a part of the liturgy: "'When We Eat This Bread . . . : Glory in Humble Service,'" focuses on the second Memorial Acclamation in light of the reading from 1 Corinthians at the Evening Mass of the Lord's Supper; "Food for the Journey," on the Solemnity of the Body and Blood of Christ, reflects on the readings for Year A of that solemnity, considering our lifelong journey of living in union with Jesus; and on the Nativity of St. John the Baptist, the homily "The Lamb of God: Our Way to Redemption" provides exegesis on the words that John the Baptist used to herald Christ. You may not want to use the homilies verbatim, but you can always adapt them to the needs of your parish. The homilies are excerpted from *Preparing Your Parish for the Revised Roman Missal: Homilies and Reproducibles for Faith Formation* © 2010, Liturgy Training Publications and www.RevisedRomanMissal.org.

May this resource bring you to a more profound appreciation of the prayers of our liturgy.

Mary G. Fox

Tones for the Presidential Prayers

Solemn Tone

All the presidential prayers in the Missal (Collects, Prayers over the Offerings, Prayers after Communion) may be pointed for use with the solemn tone according to the following formula. The reciting tone is preceded by one "G" (before ascending to "A"), including after the Flex. At every cadence, whether a Flex or a Full Stop, the grave (\) indicates where to descend to "G," and the acute (/) indicates where to ascend back to "A." The grave at the Flex may or may not fall on the the text accent, depending on the textual accent pattern. The grave at the Full Stop is always applied to the second to last syllable before the final accent, without respect to the accentuation of that syllable. When the Eucharistic Prayer is sung according to the tone in the Missal, the Prayer over the Offerings must be sung according to the solemn tone.

Pointing a text eliminates the need for providing musical notation. It also ensures that the speech quality of the text receives priority. The text is delivered, for the most part, on a reciting tone, and only two notes are used. Begin on the note below the reciting tone and move immediately to the reciting tone. At a logical point halfway though the sentence, a pause, or flex, is added. This is marked by a backward slash, indicating a return to the lower note. Immediately using that note, resume the text. At the end of the sentence, a backward (grave) and forward (acute) slash, indicate descent and return to the reciting tone. The slashes may be regarded as pointing to the direction of the melody. The conclusion is formulaic and intended to cue the assembly to sing their **Amen**. Note that there are a couple of variations for the close. In the first form of the Trinitarian formula, we anticipate the verbs as being addressed directly to God. In the second case, we speak about God in the third person plural, since we are talking about three persons. This formulation seems strange at first glance, but with study and practice, will flow easily.

The simpler conclusion makes the prayer **Through Christ our Lord**.

These pages offer Priest Celebrants a way to chant any or all of the presidential prayers using certain chant formulas. The musical rules for this application are not difficult, and once the formulaic tones are learned, anything can be sung. But a few words about chant, in general, are appropriate here.

Chant is a simple form of sung speech. Originally, chant was used for projecting the voice in a large space during worship. Without microphones, the scriptures and prayers were chanted so that the sound would carry more effectively. (Song carries better than speech.) This practice continued through Jesus's day and even to today in synagogues and churches. The Jewish method of chant was adopted by the early Church. Later, chant became appreciated for its beauty and was further developed as another way to sing and praise God.

The difficulty today is that many people claim to be non-singers. Africans are fond of saying that if you can speak, you can sing. So singing shouldn't be a deal breaker if you are able to talk.

Here, then, are some thoughts about chant to provide you with confidence. Historically, the word "chant" is derived from the French *chantre* (singing; song), but has become, in English, a polysemous catch-all that depends greatly on the context of its use for precise meaning and nuance.

In modern music, only two modes or scales are in general use: the major scale (very upbeat) and the minor scale (more subdued); whereas in chant, eight modes (according to the Medieval theory) allow for greater nuance. In this respect, the resource-

Or:

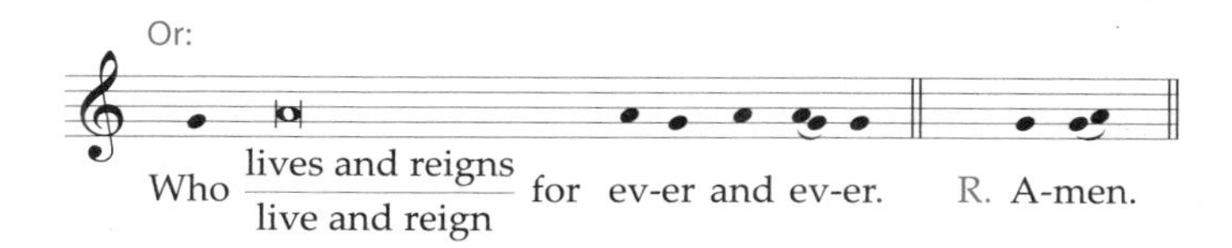

Collect (First Sunday of Advent)

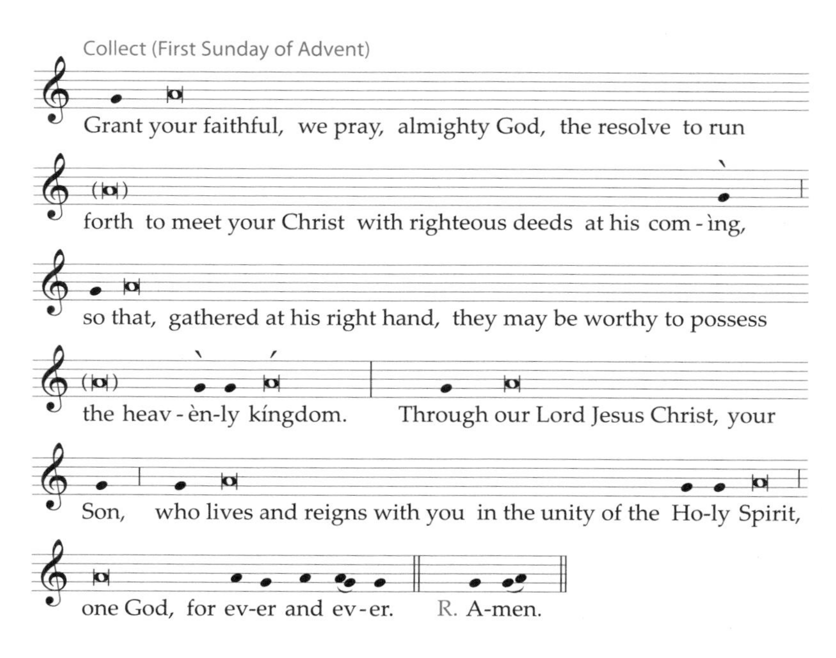

Prayer over the Offerings (The Epiphany of the Lord, The Mass During the Day)

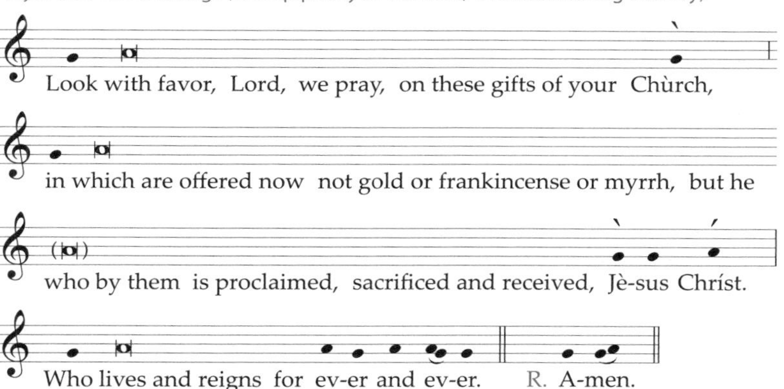

Note the final words receive a special cadence, signaling that one has come to the end of the prayer and cuing the assembly to respond with **Amen.**

In this Collect, one full sentence and a Trinitarian formula close the prayer. Note the two vertical bar lines separating the sentence from the Trinitarian formula and another between the closing formula and the **Amen**. These full vertical lines signify full stops. In the full sentence, a number of commas are in the text, but they are not all treated in the same manner. In the first line, the commas set off the addressee, and thus are not observed, per se. After the word **coming**, however, the main clause is complete and a breath should be taken before moving to the purpose clause marked by the words **so that**. **Kingdom** marks the end of the full sentence, so take a big breath here before moving to the Trinitarian close.

The Epiphany text is pointed in such a manner that a pause, or flex, is taken after the word **Church**, since this completes the thought in the first phrase but is not the end of the sentence. The second line amplifies on **Church**, with **Jesus Christ** marking the full stop. The conclusion flows from the sentence and terminates in the usual manner.

fulness and variety of plainsong chant outstrip modern music in terms of nuance.

A notion of what music should sound like is the great enemy of chant. Stylings heard on the radio or even in classical music need to be disregarded. To begin to understand chant, therefore:

- forget vibrato,
- forget bar lines,
- forget jazzy inflections,
- forget singing in a punctuated note-by-note manner,
- forget holding out long notes that build to dramatic cut-offs,
- most of all, forget your singing personality and spin.

Chant is sung as a prayer that is spoken privately—with self-surrender, deference, and humility. It differes from spoken prayer in that it uses music. If you can remember that, the rest will fall into place.

To prepare to chant, think of yourself praying in private, but audibly. Now add notes and move them up and down. Your style is always *legato*. The chant is the same—always smooth and extended. If you break the *legato* in the middle of a phrase, the spell will be broken. This is especially important with moving notes on one syllable.

In two short sentences, let me suggest the most common notions of chant: (1) it is distinct from song and speech; (2) it is the equivalent of "intone," that is to say, it is not tuneful. Yet, the word "chant" also is used to describe Gregorian plainsong, which, though it includes passages that are

A second tone called "simple" is also provided. Curiously, the simple tone is more complex than the solemn tone but still not that difficult. As the solemn tone fluctuates around two tones (reciting tone and lower neighbor), the simple tone revolves around two tones that are a third apart. The underlying scheme for the tones is generally bipartite—the sentence is divided into two halves. In the first half, an intonation formula leads to a reciting tone that is followed by a cadence (mediant). If the first half of the phrase is sufficiently long, the line is inflected (flex) before proceeding to the mediant. The second half may begin with another intonation, return to a reciting tone, and end with a final cadence (full stop). On the mediant, one passes to the lower note through a passing tone, returning immediately to the reciting tone, thus cuing the hearer that more is to follow. At the end of the sentence, the melody descends a fifth, thus indicating aurally that the sentence is finished. Applying these principles to the same Collect (Epiphany), we see that **Church** is the flex point, whereas, the mediant is **frankincense or myrrh**. Note that the back slash is placed over the note where the one begins to move—two syllables before the final accent.

The system of pointing is a brilliant way to sing grammar and punctuation and thus communicate meaning.

Simple Tone

The presidential prayers (Collects, Prayers over the Offerings, Prayers after Communion) may also be sung according to the simple tone, which follows.

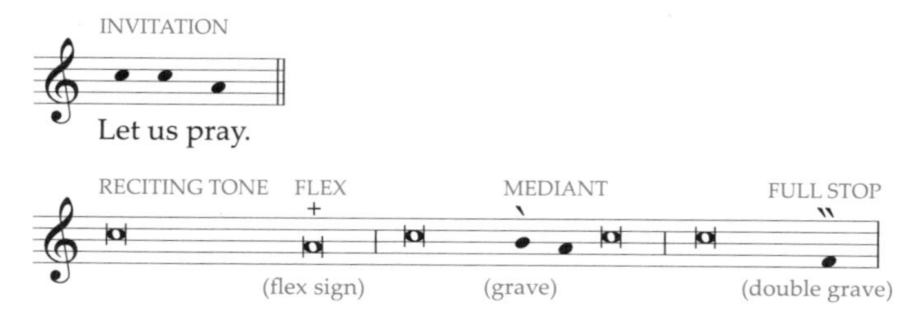

For the Flex and Full Stop, the pointing depends upon where the accent falls. When the final syllable is accented, a flex (+) sign or double grave (\\) is to be given to it. When the final syllable is not accented, this syllable is sung on the Reciting Tone and the flex sign or double grave is to be placed so as to indicate where one descends for the non-accented syllable(s). Examples:

For the Mediant cadence, the grave (\) is placed two syllables before the final accent, without respect to the accentuation of these two syllables.

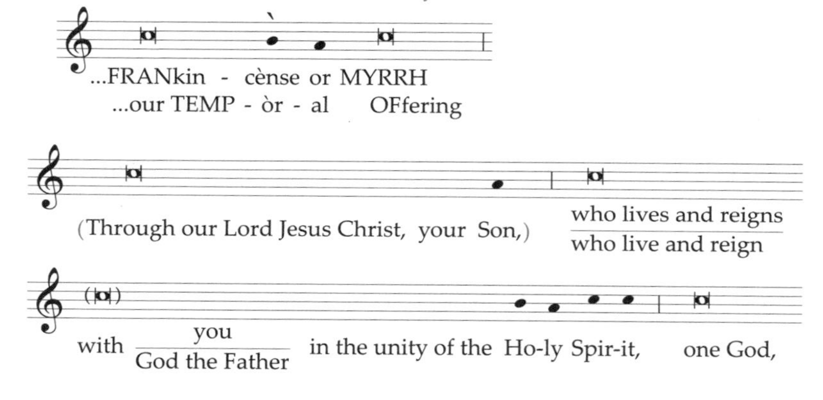

"intoned," is arguably rife with flowing and even "tuneful" melodies. Where, then, is the line between chant and song, and what is chant's relationship to other musical terms, such as "intone"?

It also must be understood that, in plainsong, the notation is not, and was never meant to indicate, absolute pitch. Rather, the pitch is relative to the person singing. So the singer chooses a comfortable pitch within the singing range and builds the melody around this. It must, therefore, be well understood that the notes read on the stave (the five lines) are to be sung at the pitch that is within the compass of the singer(s), according to the size of the building, and the special character of the piece. The instructions indicate the notes "G" and "A." It might be more beneficial to translate these into solfege terminology and call these "sol" and "la." Thus, one would simply choose a comfortable tone in the middle of the vocal range and sing up the scale, "do-re-mi-fa-sol-la." "La" is your reciting tone and "sol" is the start and return. Another way to approach this is to find a note in the middle of your range (not too low, otherwise the chant will sound muddy) and make that tone the starting tone; then sing from "do" to "re" and "re" will be the reciting tone.

Finally, a word must be said about the vertical lines punctuating the music. In modern notation, these are called bar lines, and the notes fit within these lines to measure out the music. In plainchant, however, normal speech patterns govern the flow of the music; therefore, the music is not fit between the bar lines.

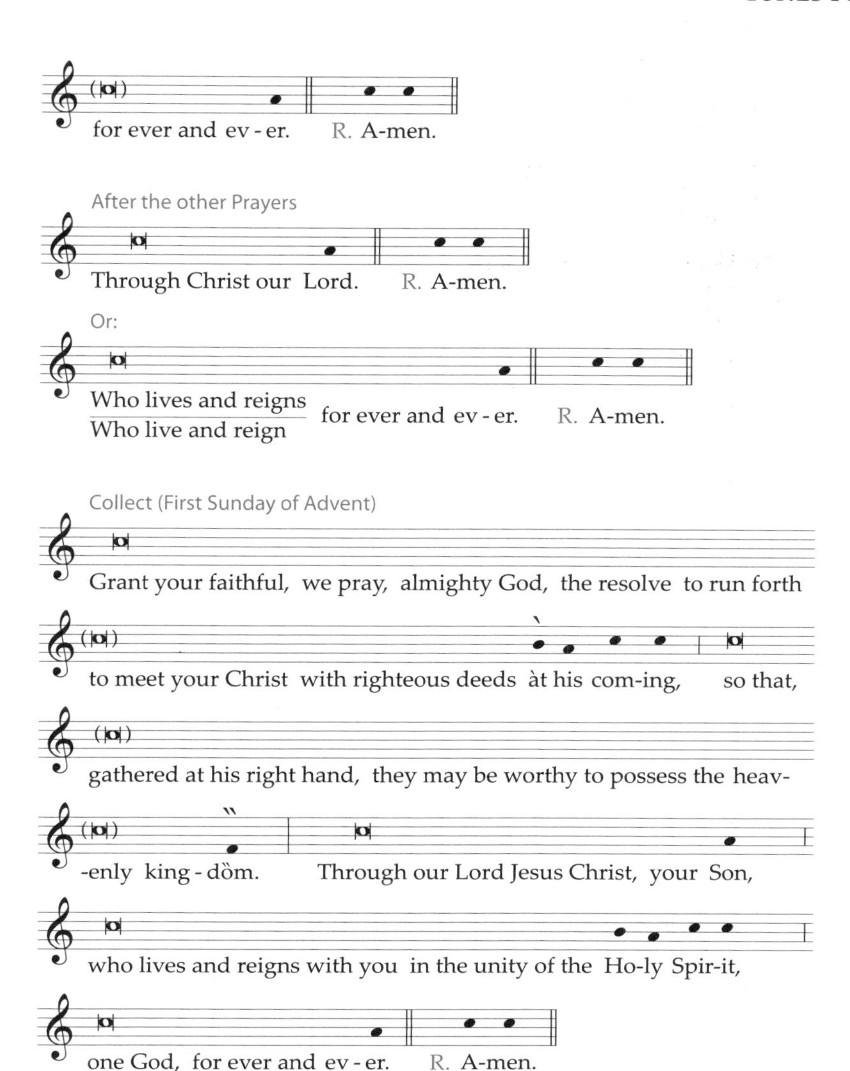

Note the two closing formulas. The first is Trinitarian with two variations. In the first variation, the Trinity is directed in the second person, whereas, in the second variation, God is spoken about in the third person. Therefore, the ajustment must be made with the verb **lives** and **live**. The second formula is made **Through Christ our Lord** without reference to the other persons of the Trinity.

Applying the simple tone to the Collect on which the solemn tone was demonstrated (First Sunday in Advent), we note that the long first half of the sentence is broken with a flex. The flex is the aural equivalent of a comma. The second half of the praise marks the result that is hoped for (**so that**). The sentence ends on the word **kingdom** and the leap downward is a clear indication that the end has been reached. In the Trinitarian conclusion, the appropriate adjustment has been made to the verbs (lives) and (reigns). Just before the full stop, the melody moves on the words **Holy Spirit**, giving a clear indication that the end is coming, marked by the fifth leap downward, thus cuing the assembly for the **Amen**.

Full and double bars mark the end of a significant phrase. They are treated as full stops and preceded by a slight *ritardando*. Half bars mark less significant sections; breaths may be taken, but the rhythm should not be significantly interrupted. Quarter bars mark shorter musical phrases. The rhythm should not be interrupted, and breathing, if needed, should steal time from the note preceding the bar line.

Full bar lines also serve as musical rests. Following the bar line, time is added using rests that are equal in value to either a single or double pulse (where the note receives a single pulse, equivalent to an eighth note). The value of the rest depends on the rhythm of the phrase following the bar line. To review, a full vertical line in a double set of vertical lines means to pause and take a breath. This marks the completion of a sentence or a full thought. A half-bar usually divides a long line into smaller bite-size portions. A short breath can certainly be taken at the half-bar, provided that it does not hinder the intelligibility of the text. The text reigns supreme. Finally, sometimes a short vertical line on the top line of the stave punctuates the music. These are called quarter-lines. Think of these as commas. A short lift or pause can help in making the text understandable without necessitating a breath.

Finally, we will discuss pointing a text. Musical notation does not need to be added to chant a text. The system offered in these pages uses forward and backward slashes that can be written above the words as a cue for when to move. Simple and solemn tones are provided that

Let us look now at how an Offertory prayer is pointed. The sentence is divided into two parts with the conclusion added immediately after the full stop. Since the first phrase is sufficiently long, we add a flex on the word **us**, pausing with a breath before moving to the mediant. Since the mediant does not fall on a period, we simply lift (or breathe, if necessary) before moving to the second part, ending on the word **redemption**. The concluding formula is very simple, made **through Christ our Lord**, without any mention of the Trinity. Since this phrase is so brief, it can be moved into directly after the full stop.

Applying the simple tone to the Offertory prayer for Epiphany, we again note the bipartite division of the sentence. The flex marks the word **Church**, subdividing the first half into two halves. The second half moves directly without breath to the full stop. A full vertical line comes after the word **Christ**, thus a breath is taken.

prescribe the intervals, or the distance, between the notes. A limited number of notes are involved; thus you should experience little consternation once you catch on to the formulas and the system of pointing a text. The flex is the intermediate pause in a long sentence. The backward slash points down—indicating the direction of the melody. The full stop uses a back slash followed by a forward slash, again pointing first down, then back up. The simple tone, in addition to the flex and full stop, provides a mediant stop. The intervals are a little different from the solemn tones but quite manageable.

Advent

FIRST SUNDAY OF ADVENT

Collect

Pause briefly after **faithful** but not after **we pray**, which goes with **almighty God** (perhaps lower the voice slightly for **we pray, almighty God**).The next two lines go together. Pause after **so that**.

Grant your faithful, we pray, almighty God,
the resolve to run forth to meet your Christ
with righteous deeds at his coming,
so that, gathered at his right hand,
they may be worthy to possess the heavenly Kingdom.
Through our Lord Jesus Christ, your Son,
who lives and reigns with you in the unity of the Holy Spirit,
one God, for ever and ever.

Prayer over the Offerings

This is a tone of humble petition. Do not pause until after **O Lord**. Emphasize **your gifts** and **you grant**. Make a brief pause after **us**. Raise the voice slightly for **devoutly**. Contrast **here below** with **eternal redemption**.

Accept, we pray, O Lord, these offerings we make,
gathered from among your gifts to us,
and may what you grant us to celebrate devoutly here below
gain for us the prize of eternal redemption.
Through Christ our Lord. *

Prayer after Communion

Proclaim **mysteries** with richness and depth. **In which we have participated** strikes a note of incredulous awe—that we have been so privileged. **Walk amid passing things** is what we do as pilgrims. Give due emphasis to **to love** but more stress to **things of heaven**. Do the same with **hold fast** and **what endures**.

May these mysteries, O Lord,
in which we have participated,
profit us, we pray,
for even now, as we walk amid passing things,
you teach us by them to love the things of heaven
and hold fast to what endures.
Through Christ our Lord. **

* Use Preface I of Advent in the Order of Mass. Commentary, and proclamation and chant tips, for the Preface can be found at *www.StudyThePresidentialTexts.com/Prefaces* and in *The Order of Mass: A Roman Missal Study Edition and Workbook*, pages 24–25.

** You may use the Solemn Blessings for Advent in the Order of Mass, page 166 in *The Order of Mass: A Roman Missal Study Edition and Workbook*.

Collect: Anything we do that is of eternal value is only so through God's granting it. The Collect is offered for God's "faithful," the baptized. The Mass includes prayers for the whole world, but the Mass is efficacious for the faithful. The "resolve" the prayer requests refers to strength of will, the moral core of the human heart. It is not what we know, but how we choose to act. The prayer presents an image of the faithful running (by means of "righteous deeds") toward Christ, who is "coming" (Advent) toward us. "Righteous" is an important scriptural word; it signifies right relationships, so this prayer implies that our "deeds" must uphold the human value of all we meet. In the Christian life, we don't stroll casually toward Christ. When we see him, we long for him—and run toward him. If we keep our eyes fixed on the coming Christ, then we will be formed into his chosen people, already in this world, gathered at his right hand. Only then are we worthy to receive the heavenly kingdom (we can't "build the city of God"—that is purely God's work).

Prayer over the Offerings: The prayer's emphasis is twofold. First, all that we offer is already God's gift to us. This is why the Church speaks of the "duty" to give thanks to God, because we have nothing that we have not received. The difficulty arises in what we sometimes do with what we have received, which makes it necessary to ask the Lord to "accept" it. He will not accept what we have perverted from its proper use or dignity. The word "offerings" (in Latin, *munera*) is an immensely important liturgical word, with biblical resonances of

The space below is for your notes.

Refer to pages viii–x for an explanation of the pointing of the chants and to page xii for the Tones for the Presidential Prayers from *The Roman Missal.*

Pointed Text

Collect

B Grant your faithful, we pray, almighty God,
the resolve to run forth to meet your Christ
with righteous deeds **at** his coming,
C so that, gathered at his right hand,
they may be worthy to possess the heavenly King***dom***.
Through our Lord Jesus Christ, your Son,
who lives and reigns with you in the unity of the Holy Spirit,
one God, for ever and ever.

Prayer over the Offerings

A Accept, we pray, O Lord, these offerings we make,
gathered from among your gifts to **us**,
B and may what you grant us to celebrate devoutly **here** below
C gain for us the prize of eternal redemp***tion***.
Through Christ our Lord.

Prayer after Communion

A May these mysteries, O Lord,
in which we have participated,
profit us, we **pray**,
B for even now, as we walk amid **pass**ing things,
C you teach us by them to love the things of heaven
and hold fast to what en***dures***.
Through Christ our Lord.

sacrifice, mission, and grace. The "offerings" speak of God's gift (grace), which bestows on us a responsibility to act (mission), and this action is ultimately offered back to God (sacrifice). The second emphasis is on the mysterious interplay between our actions in time and the eternal effects of what we do "here below," but only by God's grace, in heaven. Advent and Christmas are so important: they renew our opportunity to experience more deeply the eternal "prize" that is made real for us in such events repeated in time.

Prayer after Communion: "Mysteries" refer to divine transcendent realities. Mysteries are the eternal made present in time. Here "mysteries" refer specifically to the Eucharist just celebrated, but each Eucharist memorializes the Paschal Mystery of Christ from his Incarnation to his coming in glory. These are the realities in which we participate every time we offer the liturgy in the Church. The prayer asks that these mysteries may "profit" us. The Latin (*prosint*) literally means "may they be for us" or "may they act on [our] behalf."

The mysteries of Christ are to become our mysteries, at work within us. They work to transform us into Christ, such that he lives ever more fully in and through us. Thus, the twofold consequence of having participated in these mysteries—learning to love the things of heaven and holding fast to what endures (literally, to "what is coming")—is epitomized in Christ's having walked the earth "amid passing things." Christ teaches us how the things of earth are intended to whet our appetite for the things of heaven.

SECOND SUNDAY OF ADVENT

Collect

Almighty and merciful God,
may no earthly undertaking hinder those
who set out in haste to meet your Son,
but may our learning of heavenly wisdom
gain us admittance to his company.
Who lives and reigns with you in the unity of the Holy Spirit,
one God, for ever and ever.

Place emphasis on the **might** in **Almighty** but more so on **merciful**. Enunciate **earthly undertaking hinder** with deliberateness, almost staccato-like. Pick up the pace a little with **set out in haste**. Express joy at **learning of heavenly wisdom**, because it leads to **admittance to his company**. Express this with wonder.

Prayer over the Offerings

Be pleased, O Lord, with our humble prayers and offerings,
and, since we have no merits to plead our cause,
come, we pray, to our rescue
with the protection of your mercy.
Through Christ our Lord. *

Be pleased is the cry to God from our need. Convey more longing than confidence. Place more emphasis on **prayers** than **humble** and then on **offerings** as related yet distinct. The next clause is matter of fact. **Come**, the Advent connection, should be hope-filled. **Rescue** is a word of hope. Fill **mercy** with gratitude and delight.

Prayer after Communion

Replenished by the food of spiritual nourishment,
we humbly beseech you, O Lord,
that, through our partaking in this mystery,
you may teach us to judge wisely the things of earth
and hold firm to the things of heaven.
Through Christ our Lord. **

Proclaim **Replenished** with fullness of gratitude in the gift. Stress **spiritual**. **Partaking in this mystery** is distinct and of a piece. The last two lines are nicely paralleled: **judge wisely the things of earth** and **hold firm to the things of heaven**.

* Use Preface I of Advent in the Order of Mass. Commentary, and proclamation and chant tips, for the Preface can be found at *www.StudyThePresidentialTexts.com/Prefaces* and in *The Order of Mass: A Roman Missal Study Edition and Workbook*, pages 24–25.

** You may use the Solemn Blessings for Advent in the Order of Mass, page 166 in *The Order of Mass: A Roman Missal Study Edition and Workbook*.

Collect: "Earthly undertaking" might refer to pursuits or trials and sufferings that come through the actions of others or as a result of external events (e.g., natural disasters, disease, or crime). This may suggest why God is addressed as "almighty" and "merciful": we exercise no real power in our undertakings, for the Lord is all-mighty, and our choices may hinder us—thus leaving us in need of mercy. From Baptism, the Christian should hasten toward Christ. The Latin *in tui occúrsum Fílii festinántes* (meaning literally, "hastening in the course of your Son") suggests that we are traveling the path marked out by Christ. The only path to the Father is through the Son. Describing wisdom as "heavenly" contrasts it strongly with the "street smarts" of the world ("earthly undertakings"). This stresses that earthly learning does not avail for attaining the company of Christ. The Latin *consortes* (translated as "admittance to his company") is more intimate, implying a personal, fraternal, or even spousal participation.

Prayer over the Offerings: No human being is without merit in some capacity, and yet how seldom we call to mind that none of our merits stands for anything before God. Our only hope is to plead not our merits but Christ's coming with mercy—our greatest protection in this world and the next. Keeping this in mind will indeed lend humility to our prayers and offerings.

Pointed Text

Collect

B Almighty and merciful God,
may no earthly undertaking hinder those
who set out in haste to **meet** your Son,
C but may our learning of heavenly wisdom
gain us admittance to his com***pa***ny.
Who lives and reigns with you in the unity of the Holy Spirit,
one God, for ever and ever.

Prayer over the Offerings

A Be pleased, O Lord, with our humble prayers and of**fe**rings,
B and, since we have no merits to **plead** our cause,
C come, we pray, to our rescue
with the protection of your mer***cy***.
Through Christ our Lord.

Prayer after Communion

A Replenished by the food of spiritual nourishment,
we humbly beseech you, O **Lord**,
B that, through our partaking **in** this mystery,
C you may teach us to judge wisely the things of earth
and hold firm to the things of hea***ven***.
Through Christ our Lord.

The space below is for your notes.

Refer to pages viii–x for an explanation of the pointing of the chants and to page xii for the Tones for the Presidential Prayers from *The Roman Missal.*

Prayer after Communion: Post-communion prayers are inherently bold: after having received so abundantly in the Eucharist, we ask for more. Thus, these prayers should always be uttered with humble gratitude. The "food" of Holy Communion, received and digested in the body, is nonetheless primarily "spiritual nourishment." Bodily food for spiritual nourishment affirms the oneness of body and soul; what we do in one affects the other. "Partaking" can imply physical eating, but also intellectual and spiritual sharing or participation. The Eucharistic "mystery" of which we partake encompasses Christ in his entirety, from his eternal being in the Trinity, through his Incarnation, to his Second Coming. From Christ's cosmic perspective, we can gain wisdom about what matters in life. *Perpendere* (translated here as "to judge") means "to weigh," as on a scale. Saint Paul speaks of storing up while on earth a "weight of glory" in heaven (2 Corinthians 4:17). The choices we make and the attitudes we form on earth will be judged in the light of "things of heaven." The worldly amass earthly clutter, but those nourished spiritually judge by a different standard. They use the things of earth as a means to grow in love for those of heaven.

THIRD SUNDAY OF ADVENT

Collect

Place equal emphasis on **faithfully** and **await**. **Enable us** is the key petition proclaiming God's sovereignty and our dependence. While stressing **joys**, especially stretch out **so great a salvation**, though without too much energy, almost hushed. Pray **with solemn worship and glad rejoicing** distinctly but matter-of-factly.

O God, who see how your people
faithfully await the feast of the Lord's Nativity,
enable us, we pray,
to attain the joys of so great a salvation
and to celebrate them always
with solemn worship and glad rejoicing.
Through our Lord Jesus Christ, your Son,
who lives and reigns with you in the unity of the Holy Spirit,
one God, for ever and ever.

Prayer over the Offerings

Emphasize **sacrifice**, **worship**, and **unceasingly**. Draw out **unceasingly**. Pause briefly after **to complete**. Speak **begun in sacred mystery** with the understanding and inflection that another clause is coming. Draw out with emphasis **powerfully**. Add a final stress on **your saving work** while drawing out **saving** a bit.

May the sacrifice of our worship, Lord, we pray,
be offered to you unceasingly,
to complete what was begun in sacred mystery
and powerfully accomplish for us your saving work.
Through Christ our Lord. *

Prayer after Communion

Give more stress to **mercy** than **implore**. Bring out that the sustenance is **divine**. Use a rising voice on **cleanse** and a lowered voice on **faults**. Stress **coming** in its Advent content/theme.

We implore your mercy, Lord,
that this divine sustenance may cleanse us of our faults
and prepare us for the coming feasts.
Through Christ our Lord. **

* Use Preface I or II of Advent in the Order of Mass. Commentary, and proclamation and chant tips, for the Preface can be found at *www.StudyThePresidentialTexts.com/Prefaces* and in *The Order of Mass: A Roman Missal Study Edition and Workbook*, pages 24–27.

** You may use the Solemn Blessings for Advent in the Order of Mass, page 166 in *The Order of Mass: A Roman Missal Study Edition and Workbook.*

Collect: The biblical background to this prayer lays significant stress on our awaiting the coming of salvation; more precisely, awaiting it with faith (like the good servant in Luke who was faithful in small matters). This is difficult for those who are intent upon accomplishing things for themselves. But salvation is not something any person can accomplish alone. The most one can do is be receptive when it comes. Awaiting in faith implies such receptivity. This is not to say that our work in this world has no importance; indeed, Saint Paul wrote that those who would not work should not eat (2 Thessalonians 3:10). Rather, it means that salvation is entirely dependent on the work of Christ—including the "work" of his birth as man—and our task is patience and faith. The "joys" (*gaudia*) that are awaited and hoped for echo the traditional theme of the Third Sunday of Advent (*Gaudete*). In fact, the prayer asserts that the Mass is our attempt to celebrate fittingly the joys of this salvation. We pray for a great gift and already give thanks in anticipation of it.

Prayer over the Offerings: The key for understanding this prayer is its central phrase: "to complete what was begun in sacred mystery." This refers to the institution of the Eucharist, and more broadly the Paschal Mystery. The phrase "was begun" is literally "instituted" (*instituta* in Latin). The unceasing "sacrifice of worship" refers to Christ's eternal offering of himself in the Spirit before the Father, but in the liturgy we enter into Christ's worship through that same Spirit. Christ's sacrificial mystery is brought to fulfillment in us. "Sacrifice" lit-

Pointed Text

The space below is for your notes.

Refer to pages viii–x for an explanation of the pointing of the chants and to page xii for the Tones for the Presidential Prayers from *The Roman Missal.*

Collect

B O God, who see how your people
faithfully await the feast of the **Lord's** Nativity,
C enable us, we pray,
to attain the joys of so great a salvation
and to celebrate them always
with solemn worship and glad rejoic***ing***.
Through our Lord Jesus Christ, your Son,
who lives and reigns with you in the unity of the Holy Spirit,
one God, for ever and ever.

Prayer over the Offerings

A May the sacrifice of our worship, Lord, we **pray**,
B be offered to **you** unceasingly,
C to complete what was begun in sacred mystery
and powerfully accomplish for us your saving ***work***.
Through Christ our Lord.

Prayer after Communion

B We implore your **mer**cy, Lord,
C that this divine sustenance may cleanse us of our faults
and prepare us for the coming ***feasts***.
Through Christ our Lord.

erally means something that "makes holy." This worship makes us holy because it is Christ's worship, a "saving work." His life was a "work" of submission to the Father. The "work" of the Holy Spirit was raising Christ to glory. Our "work" is similarly to empty ourselves, letting go of all personal desire that is other than Christ. If we submit to that kind of "sacrifice," the Holy Spirit will raise us to glory with Christ. This is what the Spirit will "powerfully accomplish for us." We do well never to forget that Christ is wholly "for us."

Prayer after Communion: The fruits of the Eucharist are understood here in a sacrificial sense. The "cleansing" is the effect of Christ's sacrifice on the Cross and Resurrection. The Latin *expiatos*, or "cleanse," is a strictly sacrificial term. It is a past participle, which means that the prayer foresees the Christian as having been cleansed from faults prior to arriving at the "coming feasts." The "divine sustenance" (*subsidia*, plural in Latin) comprises the ways that the Eucharist serves to prepare us to battle evil both from within and without (*subsidia* was originally a military term for reinforcements). The *Catechism of the Catholic Church* states that the Eucharist "is a remedy to free us from our daily faults" (#1436). The prayer pleads that in the "mercy" of God the "divine sustenance" received in Communion may strengthen us to work for conversion. The cleansing action of Communion serves to "prepare us for the coming feasts." The Church holds that the way to prepare for a feast is through fasting and penance, which are intended to stimulate conversion.

FOURTH SUNDAY OF ADVENT

Collect

Emphasize **pour**, **grace**, and **hearts**. Pray **was made known** and **by the message of an Angel** with a touch of awe. **Passion** and **Cross** should be steady and deliberate. This is what we have to offer: our suffering. The final line gives the hope-filled reason for enduring something like the Cross.

Pour forth, we beseech you, O Lord,
your grace into our hearts,
that we, to whom the Incarnation of Christ your Son
was made known by the message of an Angel,
may by his Passion and Cross
be brought to the glory of his Resurrection.
Who lives and reigns with you in the unity of the Holy Spirit,
one God, for ever and ever.

Prayer over the Offerings

Be subtle, but realize in proclamation the parallel between **gifts laid upon your altar** and **power**, which filled the **womb**. The main verb to stress is **sanctify**; it is the heart of the prayer.

May the Holy Spirit, O Lord,
sanctify these gifts laid upon your altar,
just as he filled with his power
the womb of the Blessed Virgin Mary.
Through Christ our Lord. *

Prayer after Communion

Imbue **pledge** with hope-filled confidence. Stress the eternal character of this redemption. Let a hint of anticipation come through with an emphasis on **ever nearer** and **all the more eagerly**. **Worthy celebration** should be restrained and sober with the primary emphasis on **mystery**.

Having received this pledge of eternal redemption,
we pray, almighty God,
that, as the feast day of our salvation draws ever nearer,
so we may press forward all the more eagerly
to the worthy celebration of the mystery of your Son's Nativity.
Who lives and reigns for ever and ever. **

* Use Preface II of Advent in the Order of Mass. Commentary, and proclamation and chant tips, for the Preface can be found at *www.StudyThePresidentialTexts.com/Prefaces* and in *The Order of Mass: A Roman Missal Study Edition and Workbook*, pages 26–27.

** You may use the Solemn Blessings for Advent in the Order of Mass, page 166 in *The Order of Mass: A Roman Missal Study Edition and Workbook*.

Collect: The Angel Gabriel applied the title "full of grace" to Mary, and this prayer reformulates his message on behalf of the faithful, begging the Lord to fill us, too, with his grace. The prayer asks that what was done for Mary may be done for us. What the Angel revealed to Mary, he also revealed to us. As Mary was brought to glory through the Passion and Cross of her son, so it was promised that we should come to glory if we enter into Christ's Passion and Cross. In this prayer, we see the sweep of the Paschal Mystery from Incarnation to Resurrection. We cannot separate the mystery of Christ into segments. In his glory, we encounter the incarnate one, the crucified, and the risen one. The mystery is one. The Incarnation of the Son reveals an important change in the way we are to view one another—no longer according to the "flesh" but in light of the new creation in Christ. Lastly, "was made known" (*cognovimus*) implies a personal knowledge of Christ, a knowledge of the heart (pour your grace into our hearts). The encounter must be personal.

Prayer over the Offerings: A main activity of the Holy Spirit in the world is sanctification. To be made holy literally means to be set apart or designated. Ritually, this is what happens when the gifts are laid upon the altar. They are set apart from all other bread and wine for a particular purpose. When people are "set apart," it means they have been established in a new relationship. When people enter into a relationship, they become unique to each other. When the Holy Spirit sanctifies someone, he brings that person into relationship

Pointed Text

Collect

A Pour forth, we beseech you, O Lord,
your grace into our **hearts**,
B that we, to whom the Incarnation of Christ your Son
was made known by the message **of** an Angel,
C may by his Passion and Cross
be brought to the glory of his Resurrec***tion***.
Who lives and reigns with you in the unity of the Holy Spirit,
one God, for ever and ever.

Prayer over the Offerings

A May the Holy Spirit, O **Lord**,
B sanctify these gifts laid u**pon** your altar,
C just as he filled with his power
the womb of the Blessed Virgin Ma***ry***.
Through Christ our Lord.

Prayer after Communion

A Having received this pledge of eternal redemp**tion**,
B we pray, almighty God,
that, as the feast day of our salvation draws **e**ver nearer,
C so we may press forward all the more eagerly
to the worthy celebration of the mystery of your Son's Nati***vi***ty.
Who lives and reigns for ever and ever.

The space below is for your notes.

Refer to pages viii–x for an explanation of the pointing of the chants and to page xii for the Tones for the Presidential Prayers from *The Roman Missal.*

with the divine, and that relationship makes the person forever unique to God, forever holy. The Holy Spirit "sanctified" the womb of the Blessed Virgin by filling it with "his power," the Son of God, thus establishing an intimate and unique relationship, a particular "holiness." Only one person is the Mother of God according to the flesh. The prayer begs that the same "power" fill the gifts placed on the altar as it filled the womb of Mary—and ultimately fills those who offer the gifts.

Prayer after Communion: "Pledge," here referring to Holy Communion, elsewhere designates the Holy Spirit given in our hearts at Baptism (Ephesians 1:13–14); thus, the prayer reminds us of the spiritual nature of this food and its Trinitarian character. Christ is always made present to us only through the Holy Spirit: he was conceived by the Spirit, lived in the power of the Spirit, was raised from the dead by the Spirit, and now is made sacramentally present by the Spirit. The "pledge" is the appetizer to the full-course banquet in the Kingdom. It is this "pledge" that strengthens us to "press forward," now toward Christmas and ultimately toward heaven. The "drawing nearer" of salvation renews our hope in the "mystery" of new birth: Christ's nativity, but also our birth into his body, which is the true reason for this celebration. This is the "feast day of our salvation"; the Incarnation has salvific power for us. Christmas is not so much history as mystery: it is less the commemoration of Christ's birth in time than the celebration of his birth in us and our birth into him.

Christmas Time

THE NATIVITY OF THE LORD

At the Vigil Mass

This Mass is used on the evening of December 24, either before or after First Vespers (Evening Prayer I) of the Nativity.

Collect

Place a parallel emphasis on **gladden** and **wait in hope**. Proclaim **joyfully** peacefully and with sober excitement. Place some stress on **just as** and **also** to bring out the parallel between **Redeemer** and **Judge**. **Confidently** should convey confidence. Proclaim **comes again** with confidence and anticipation.

O God, who gladden us year by year
as we wait in hope for our redemption,
grant that, just as we joyfully welcome
your Only Begotten Son as our Redeemer,
we may also merit to face him confidently
when he comes again as our Judge.
Who lives and reigns with you in the unity of the Holy Spirit,
one God, for ever and ever.

Prayer over the Offerings

Proclaim **As we look forward** with joyful anticipation. Place some emphasis on **coming** to underline the not-yet nature of this celebration. With stress on **serve** and a slight pause after **you**, raise the voice for **all the more eagerly**. The rest of the prayer has a rhythm of four phrases: **in them**, **make manifest**, **the beginnings**, and **our redemption**. Don't give **knowing** prominence (it is not in the Latin).

As we look forward, O Lord,
to the coming festivities,
may we serve you all the more eagerly
for knowing that in them
you make manifest the beginnings of our redemption.
Through Christ our Lord. *

Prayer after Communion

The main cry of the prayer is **Grant**. The main petition is **new vigor**. Put loving emphasis on **Only Begotten Son**. Proclaim **heavenly mystery** with solemnity, even mystic intensity.

Grant, O Lord, we pray,
that we may draw new vigor
from celebrating the Nativity of your Only Begotten Son,
by whose heavenly mystery we receive both food and drink.
Who lives and reigns for ever and ever. **

* Select from Preface I, II, or III of the Nativity of the Lord in the Order of Mass. Commentary, and proclamation and chant tips, for the Preface can be found at *www.StudyThePresidentialTexts.com/Prefaces* and in *The Order of Mass: A Roman Missal Study Edition and Workbook*, pages 28–35. If Eucharistic Prayer I is used, the proper form of the Communicantes is prayed from the Order of Mass. It is found in *The Order of Mass: A Roman Missal Study Edition and Workbook*, page 129.

** You may use the Solemn Blessing for the Nativity of the Lord in the Order of Mass, pages 166–167 in *The Order of Mass: A Roman Missal Study Edition and Workbook.*

Collect: This prayer evinces a theme of "already-not yet." It proclaims that we "wait in hope for our redemption," yet the prayer's scriptural background (Luke 1:68) tells that God has already come to his people with redemption. It proclaims that we "joyfully welcome / . . . our Redeemer," and yet we also await his coming as Judge. The time of the Church is the time of the Sacraments (i.e., Real Presence) but not its fullness. Christ's coming brought Truth, but our mortal nature still needs to be transformed into that Truth. The more we open our hearts to him as Redeemer, the less we need to fear him as Judge. The Latin behind "gladden" and "joyfully" (*laetificas* and *laeti*) comes from the same root. This "gladdening" or "joy" is the public, social joy of the community. This prayer also proclaims that God's action in our lives, provided we "wait in hope," will be to gladden us. He does not simply make us wait but provides us with a foretaste of joy in these celebrations. The surest sign of the presence of the Holy Spirit is joy.

Prayer over the Offerings: In this vigil Mass we are still "looking forward" both to the full feast of Christmas and to the full feast of heaven. The reference to the "coming festivities," likewise, asserts that the real feasting is yet to come. Every vigil has at its heart an eschatological outlook—it is an awaiting, a longing for the coming dawn when the true morning star will rise in our hearts (2 Peter 1:19). The Church's wisdom teaches us to prepare for a feast with penitence, then to prolong the celebration once it has arrived. This is in stark

The space below is for your notes.

Refer to pages viii–x for an explanation of the pointing of the chants and to page xii for the Tones for the Presidential Prayers from *The Roman Missal*.

Pointed Text

Collect

A O God, who gladden us year by year
as we wait in hope for our redemp**tion**,
B grant that, just as we joyfully welcome
your Only Begotten Son as **our** Redeemer,
C we may also merit to face him confidently
when he comes again as our ***Judge***.
Who lives and reigns with you in the unity of the Holy Spirit,
one God, for ever and ever.

Prayer over the Offerings

B As we look forward, O Lord,
to the com**ing** festivities,
C may we serve you all the more eagerly
for knowing that in them
you make manifest the beginnings of our redemp***tion***.
Through Christ our Lord.

Prayer after Communion

A Grant, O Lord, we **pray**,
B that we may draw new vigor
from celebrating the Nativity of your Only Be**got**ten Son,
C by whose heavenly mystery we receive both food and ***drink***.
Who lives and reigns for ever and ever.

contrast with modern society, which anticipates Christmas but ends it abruptly on December 26. Being redeemed prompts us to more eager service. Redemption means the overcoming of selfishness such that the "I" is no longer regarded. There is no "I want," but only the gift of self in greater love. This gift is revealed in the liturgy, which teaches, but more importantly, transforms us. The "coming festivities" are the sacramental foretaste of that fullness of redemption when our union in loving service will be complete.

Prayer after Communion: The prayer asks for "new vigor," which is expected to result from the celebration of Christ's birth. The word "celebrating" translates the Latin *recensita*, which literally means "mulled over"; it refers not to the current liturgy, but to all those that have gone before during Advent. The understanding is that for four weeks we have pondered the riches of the Incarnation, gaining nourishment and "new vigor." The prayer does not specify the hoped-for object of this new vigor, but coming at the end of the liturgy, just before the sending forth, it bears a strong suggestion of mission and evangelization. This implies that the new vigor is intended for sharing the spiritual insights garnered here with all we will meet. This prayer makes two further points. First, the Nativity of Christ is a heavenly mystery, and thus a part of the Paschal Mystery of redemption and on par with Easter. Second, the worthy celebration of this mystery strengthens us in our journey of faith. This feast carries within it the power of redemption.

Treat the first phrase like a complete sentence with a period **after December**. Using a cursive style of singing from that point on, sing **when ages beyond number** as a new sentence. Make a slight pause at **world**, so as to clearly articulate **when God . . . .** Try not to break or breathe at **earth** but hold the word slightly and go right from **and formed** to the end of the phrase. Hold slightly **-ness** of **likeness**, pausing briefly.

Articulate carefully **century upon century**. Hold very briefly **Flood;** try not to breathe or break there but continue with **as a sign**. Hold and take a breath after **peace**.

Pause slightly after both **Abraham** and **faith** (holding only to articulate carefully) to respect the commas. Try to continue without a break until the end of **Chaldees**—hold the last syllable slightly and take a breath.

Try to keep the entire phrase **thirteenth . . . Egypt** together as one thought, holding only the last syllable. Take a breath there.

The Nativity of Our Lord Jesus Christ

from the *Roman Martyrology*

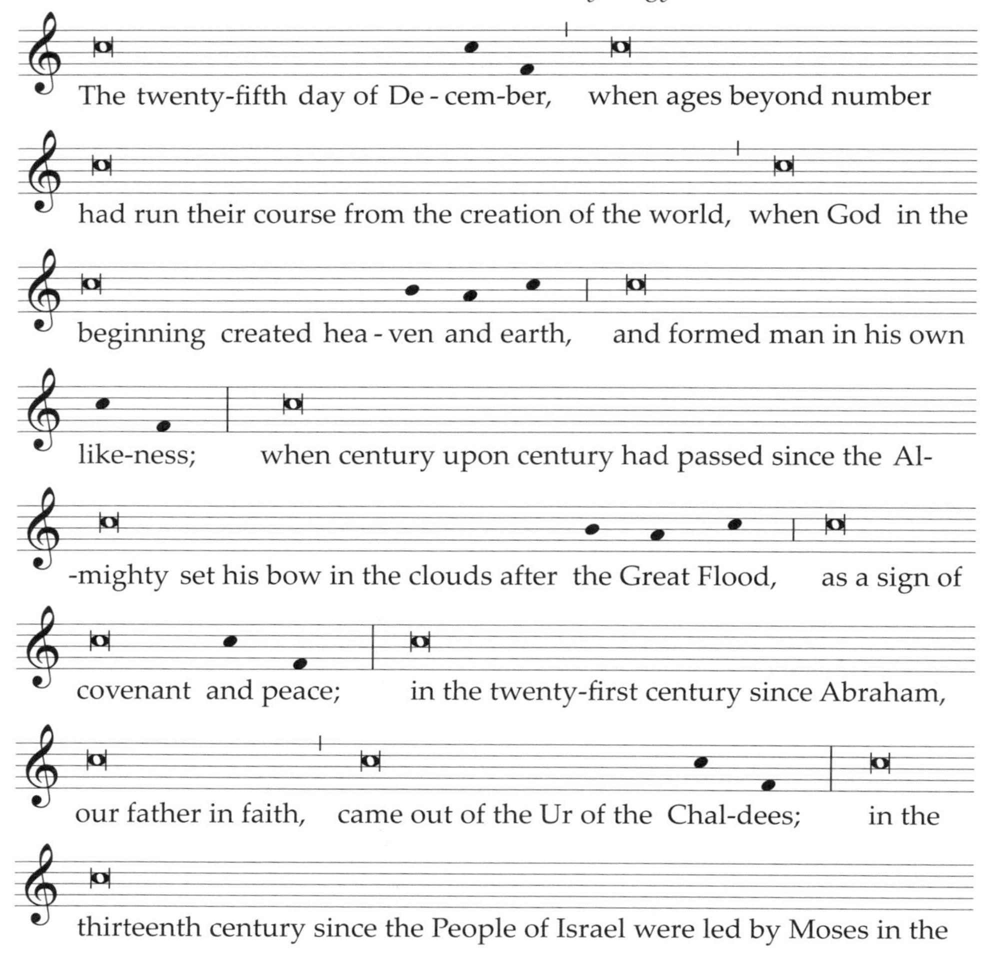

Christmas Proclamation: The Christmas Proclamation situates the birth of Christ among various events of sacred and secular history—in this way professing Christ as Lord of both. It may be sung or proclaimed during the Liturgy of the Hours or before the beginning of the Mass during the Night. It may not replace any part of the Mass. According to circumstances, the proclamation may be sung or recited at the ambo by a Deacon, cantor, or reader.

The opening lines make the immediate connection between God's work of creation "in the beginning" and his work of creation with the Incarnation. A second important connection is that God "formed man in his own likeness." That "likeness" (*imago*) was the Son with a view toward the Incarnation. The "bow" that the Almighty set in the clouds refers to the rainbow, which was understood as the bow (as in "bow and arrows") of the Divine, resplendent and magnificent. Setting his bow in the clouds was his promise to cease waging war against humanity in the flood. It was the first "covenant" that God made with humanity following the Fall. Salvation history is said to begin with the call of Abraham (*Catechism of the Catholic Church*, #1080), who is named "our father in faith." Abraham is the official beginning of the Judaeo-Christian faith (and in some sense, one could include the Muslim faith as well, which claims Abraham as its father). Just as Moses led the people of Israel out of slavery in Egypt, so Christ led all believers out of slavery to sin and death. The anointing

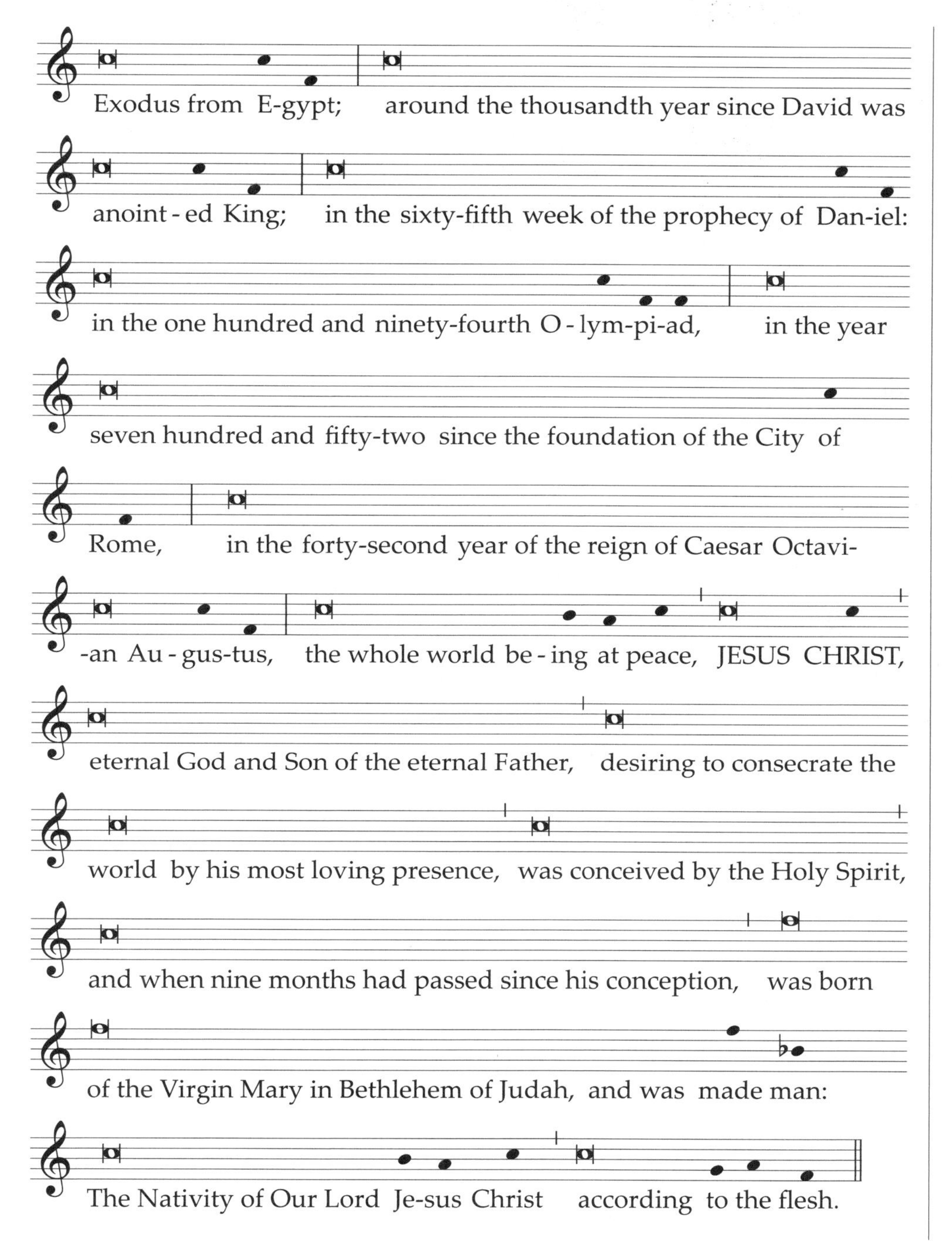

Keep together the phrase **around . . . King**, holding only **King** and pausing briefly there. Treat the next three phrases the same way. Try to keep each phrase together until the comma, at which point the syllable can be slightly held, and a very short breath taken.

Begin to slow down the phrase, **in the forty-second year . . . .** At the end, hold the last syllable. Do not take a long breath there but try to convey the sense of momentum for the next phrase. Slow down that phrase very noticeably, articulating each syllable as a means of doing so. Articulate each syllable of **JESUS CHRIST** carefully and slowly. Keep the phrase **eternal God . . .** rather slow, but not as slow as **JESUS CHRIST**. Return to the cursive style with the phrases **desiring . . .** and **was conceived**. Slow down the phrase **and when nine . . .** to prepare for the culmination. That culmination begins with raising the voice a fourth at **was born**. Slow this entire phrase, elongating **-dah** of **Judah** slightly, and at the end, holding **man**.

Sing the last phrase slowly and solemnly, as it ties to the opening phrase. Articulate carefully **Je-sus Christ**. Do not hold **Christ** but finish the thought with **according to the flesh** sung slowly and solemnly.

in kingship of David by the prophet Samuel prefigures Christ's anointing as priest, prophet, and king by the Holy Spirit. The prophecy of Daniel refers to Daniel 9:24–27. There, the Angel Gabriel explains to Daniel that in 70 weeks of years (490 years), "transgression will stop and sin will end, guilt will be expiated, / Everlasting justice will be introduced / . . . / and a most holy will be anointed." This has been taken to refer to the Crucifixion and Resurrection of Christ, and approximately five weeks of years before that would be his birth. The Olympiad refers to the Greek culture that was dominant throughout the known world at the time, and the founding of Rome recalls the Roman influence for Western culture. There is an irony to the proclamation that under Caesar the world was at "peace" because Caesar fought many wars and killed many people, enslaving many others. Caesar's peace was not the peace of God, which was born on this night. It is as though, in the midst of the usual wars, the world took a breath in awe of the birth of true Peace. This Peace desired "to consecrate the world by his most loving presence." "Most loving" is the Latin superlative *piissimo*, which refers to the relationship between a parent and child. Christ came to make the world holy through the way he would live and love as Son to the Father, even to dying on the Cross. The birth of Christ is the fulfillment of sacred and secular history.

THE NATIVITY OF THE LORD

At the Mass during the Night

Collect

Use solemnity with this line and give due emphasis to **radiant**, **splendor**, and **true** more than **light**. **Mysteries of his light** is a way of saying "mysteries of Christ," referring to the Sacraments. Stress **mysteries** strongly. Parallel **light on earth** with **gladness in heaven**. Draw out **delight** with a measure of solemn joy.

O God, who have made this most sacred night
radiant with the splendor of the true light,
grant, we pray, that we, who have known the mysteries of his light on earth,
may also delight in his gladness in heaven.
Who lives and reigns with you in the unity of the Holy Spirit,
one God, for ever and ever.

Prayer over the Offerings

Pronounce **oblation** as **ob-lation**, and stress **feast** as the point of rest for that clause. The central element of the prayer is the **most holy exchange**. Place less emphasis on **we may be found** and more on **likeness of Christ**. With a very brief pause after **nature**, express **united to you** with a mixture of awe and joy.

May the oblation of this day's feast
be pleasing to you, O Lord, we pray,
that through this most holy exchange
we may be found in the likeness of Christ,
in whom our nature is united to you.
Who lives and reigns for ever and ever. *

Prayer after Communion

The key words and phrases are: **gladdened**, **Redeemer's Nativity**, **honorable way of life**, and **union with him**.

Grant us, we pray, O Lord our God,
that we, who are gladdened by participation
in the feast of our Redeemer's Nativity,
may through an honorable way of life become worthy of union with him.
Who lives and reigns for ever and ever. **

* Select from Preface I, II, or III of the Nativity of the Lord in the Order of Mass. Commentary, and proclamation and chant tips, for the Preface can be found at *www.StudyThePresidentialTexts.com/Prefaces* and in *The Order of Mass: A Roman Missal Study Edition and Workbook*, pages 28–33. If Eucharistic Prayer I is used, the proper form of the Communicantes is prayed from the Order of Mass. It is found in *The Order of Mass: A Roman Missal Study Edition and Workbook*, page 129.

** You may use the Solemn Blessing for the Nativity of the Lord in the Order of Mass, pages 166–167 in *The Order of Mass: A Roman Missal Study Edition and Workbook*.

Collect: "This most sacred night" (*sacratissimam noctem*) calls to mind the collect for Thursday of Holy Week that mentions "this most sacred Supper" (*sacratissimam cenam*). The parallels are many between the birth of Christ and his "birth" on the Eucharistic Table. The collect twice mentions "light": "the splendor of the true light" (*lumen*) and "the mysteries of his light" (*lux*). The Latin makes a distinction between *lux*, which seems to refer to the divine himself (the Latin has "mysteries of the light" without the pronoun "his"), and *lumen*, which seems to refer to the revelation, salvation, and glory that comes to us from the light (*lux*). The "most sacred night" is radiant with the "splendor" of true light, that is, true revelation or salvation. Salvation will be fulfilled in the Cross and Resurrection, but already here, its splendor radiates. We know the Light (Christ) through his mysteries, that is, the Sacraments of revelation. The prayer closes with the connection between knowing his Sacraments on earth and delighting in his gladness in heaven.

Prayer over the Offerings: The opening petition for the "oblation" to be pleasing refers initially to the "oblation" on the altar, but includes the offerings of all present. Ultimately, the gifts on the altar include the lives of the assembly. After this petition, three key words should be highlighted. The first is "exchange" (*commercia*), referring to the most fundamental law of free relationships: give and take must be from both parties. How awesome it is that God enters this give and take with us, freeing us from slavery to sin.

The space below is for your notes.

Refer to pages viii–x for an explanation of the pointing of the chants and to page xii for the Tones for the Presidential Prayers from *The Roman Missal.*

Pointed Text

Collect

A O God, who have made this most sacred night
radiant with the splendor of the true **light**,
B grant, we pray, that we, who have known the mysteries of his **light** on earth,
C may also delight in his gladness in hea***ven***.
Who lives and reigns with you in the unity of the Holy Spirit,
one God, for ever and ever.

Prayer over the Offerings

A May the oblation of this day's feast
be pleasing to you, O Lord, we **pray**,
B that through this most holy exchange
we may be found in the like**ness** of Christ,
C in whom our nature is united to ***you***.
Who lives and reigns for ever and ever.

Prayer after Communion

A Grant us, we pray, O Lord our **God**,
B that we, who are gladdened by participation
in the feast of our Redee**mer's** Nativity,
C may through an honorable way of life become worthy of union with ***him***.
Who lives and reigns for ever and ever.

The second is "likeness" (*forma*), which recalls both Adam and Eve having been created in the likeness of God and Christ having emptied himself of that likeness to die on the Cross, thereby restoring our likeness. The third is "nature" (*substantia*), sharing the same root as "consubstantial," the term used in the Creed. If we empty ourselves like Christ, we will find our "likeness" restored and the consequent "exchange" will unite us substantially in our "nature" to Christ.

Prayer after Communion: The phrase "gladdened by participation / in the feast of our Redeemer's Nativity" is slightly different in the Latin; a more literal rendering would be, "we rejoice to frequent the Nativity of our Redeemer." "We rejoice" is *gaudemus*, the Advent word for interior gladness. The Latin states that we frequent the birth, the mystery of the Incarnation, not only its celebration. *Frequentare* also means "to come close." We rejoice because we can once again draw close to the birth of Christ. The prayer's petition is "grant us to become worthy of union" with Christ. The key for explaining how this is possible is "way of life" (*conversationibus*). Benedictine monks make a vow of *conversatio*, sometimes translated as "conversion of morals." The implication is that our joyful participation in the Redeemer's birth is an essential step in the refashioning (rebirthing) of our nature in his image. The new life born this night is the "honorable way of life" that we hope to lead. This is why we are gladdened: the impossible "way of life" has become possible.

THE NATIVITY OF THE LORD

At the Mass at Dawn

Collect

Linger slightly on **new** to explode into **radiance**. Do not to pause too much after **incarnate Word**, because **light of faith** is tied to it. Stress the parallel between **minds** and **deeds**.

Grant, we pray, almighty God,
that, as we are bathed in the new radiance of your incarnate Word,
the light of faith, which illumines our minds,
may also shine through in our deeds.
Through our Lord Jesus Christ, your Son,
who lives and reigns with you in the unity of the Holy Spirit,
one God, for ever and ever.

Prayer over the Offerings

Mysteries of the Nativity goes together. Without overdoing, give some stress to **this day**. Bring out the parallel between **just as** and **so**. Take a brief pause after **man**, with another brief pause after **confer on us** to give reverent emphasis to **what is divine**.

May our offerings be worthy, we pray, O Lord,
of the mysteries of the Nativity this day,
that, just as Christ was born a man and also shone forth as God,
so these earthly gifts may confer on us what is divine.
Through Christ our Lord. *

Prayer after Communion

Stress **with fullness of faith** as though it refers to Christ. Draw out **hidden depths** and slow down on **ever more and more**.

Grant us, Lord, as we honor with joyful devotion
the Nativity of your Son,
that we may come to know with fullness of faith
the hidden depths of this mystery
and to love them ever more and more.
Through Christ our Lord. **

* Select from Preface I, II, or III of the Nativity of the Lord in the Order of Mass. Commentary, and proclamation and chant tips, for the Preface can be found at *www.StudyThePresidentialTexts.com/Prefaces* and in *The Order of Mass: A Roman Missal Study Edition and Workbook*, pages 28–33. If Eucharistic Prayer I is used, the proper form of the Communicantes is prayed from the Order of Mass. It is found in *The Order of Mass: A Roman Missal Study Edition and Workbook*, page 129.

** You may use the Solemn Blessing for the Nativity of the Lord in the Order of Mass, pages 166–167 in *The Order of Mass: A Roman Missal Study Edition and Workbook*.

Collect: This prayer is rendered difficult both by the complexity of the prayer and by the translation. The "new radiance" (*nova luce*) is not *lumen*, which implies revelation, but *lux*, which is closer to divinity. It is not that there is a "new" divinity, but that the divinity of the Word is new in its incarnate form, which enables us to have a share in that divinity: "we are bathed" in it. The translation implies that the "light of faith" illumines our minds and shines through our deeds, but the Latin, with no mention of light, states that the Word "illumines our minds" through faith and so shines through our deeds. This is important: the actor in all of this is the Word made flesh, and not some reflection of him. We are bathed in the Word himself. We are illumined by him. And it is the Word that makes our deeds salutary and effective. Being "bathed" in the divine light that is the Word is a purifying and sanctifying experience. The divine light burns away all that is not pure. The manifold imagery of light is fitting for the Mass at Dawn, with the rising sun on the horizon.

Prayer over the Offerings: The offerings (*munera*) of bread and wine are set parallel to the mysteries of Christ's Nativity. "This day" (*hodiernae*) reminds us that this mystery is present in the "today" that is Jesus Christ (Hebrews 13:8). The offerings are earthly but will become divine in the Eucharistic Prayer. In the Nativity, the Word becomes earthly. The "mysteries" are spelled out as referring primarily to his dual nature. We behold his humanity but with faith can perceive his divinity "shining forth." The prayer presupposes the neces-

The space below is for your notes.

Refer to pages viii–x for an explanation of the pointing of the chants and to page xii for the Tones for the Presidential Prayers from *The Roman Missal*.

Pointed Text

Collect

A Grant, we pray, almighty **God**,
B that, as we are bathed in the new radiance of your incarnate Word,
the light of faith, which illu**mines** our minds,
C may also shine through in our ***deeds***.
Through our Lord Jesus Christ, your Son,
who lives and reigns with you in the unity of the Holy Spirit,
one God, for ever and ever.

Prayer over the Offerings

A May our offerings be worthy, we pray, O Lord,
of the mysteries of the Nativity this **day**,
B that, just as Christ was born a man and also shone **forth** as God,
C so these earthly gifts may confer on us what is di***vine***.
Through Christ our Lord.

Prayer after Communion

A Grant us, Lord, as we honor with joyful devotion
the Nativity of your **Son**,
B that we may come to know with full**ness** of faith
C the hidden depths of this mystery
and to love them ever more and ***more***.
Through Christ our Lord.

sity of faith to perceive such realities. The prayer closes with the petition that the "earthly gifts" (*terra substantia*) may bring us the gift of divinity. The translation misses an important connection apparent in the Latin. *Substantia* (in the singular) refers primarily to the human nature of Christ and only secondarily to the earthly gifts being offered. The petition recalls the *admirabile commercium*, the exchange of God's becoming man that man might share in God. By implication, the Eucharistic gifts embody this exchange.

Prayer after Communion: This unusual post-Communion prayer makes no explicit mention of the gift received in Holy Communion. Attention is focused on the gift received in the bread from heaven made flesh. The joy of "joyful devotion" is *laeta*, which refers to the public joy of this communal celebration of Christmas as opposed to the restrained Advent joy (*gaudium*). The verb "come to know" is deliberately progressive, meaning that this knowledge is too much to be grasped at once. It must be assimilated through meditation and conversion. "The hidden depths of this mystery" refers to God's plan of self-revelation, unfolded partially in creation and history, but "with fullness" in Christ's coming. Specifically in this feast, "mystery" refers to Christ's birth; believers must seek grace (God's "granting") to let its inner reality permeate the Christian's heart and work. The translation of "love them ever more and more" falls short of the Latin, which has "to love them ever more and more with the fire of charity," referring to the divine charity revealed in Christ.

THE NATIVITY OF THE LORD

At the Mass during the Day

Collect

Express awe with **wonderfully**, and delighted awe with **still more wonderfully**. **Dignity** is an important word, but **human nature** is also important. Both need stress. Stress **divinity of Christ**, then be subdued for **humbled himself to share in our humanity**.

O God, who wonderfully created the dignity of human nature
and still more wonderfully restored it,
grant, we pray,
that we may share in the divinity of Christ,
who humbled himself to share in our humanity.
Who lives and reigns with you in the unity of the Holy Spirit,
one God, for ever and ever.

Prayer over the Offerings

Pronounce **oblation** as **ob-lation**; pronounce **solemn day** with solemnity. Try to stress that God is the primary actor in **you manifested**. Draw out **wholly** and stress **your sight**. Again, linger on **fullness**. Christ fulfills all previous rites of **worship** in himself.

Make acceptable, O Lord, our oblation on this solemn day,
when you manifested the reconciliation
that makes us wholly pleasing in your sight
and inaugurated for us the fullness of divine worship.
Through Christ our Lord. *

Prayer after Communion

The central phrase is **Savior of the world**; linger on it. Proclaim **born this day** with some insistence. Stress the **divine** of **divine generation**. Pause after **giver** and be deliberate with **even of immortality**. Express it with awe.

Grant, O merciful God,
that, just as the Savior of the world, born this day,
is the author of divine generation for us,
so he may be the giver even of immortality.
Who lives and reigns for ever and ever. **

* Select from Preface I, II, or III of the Nativity of the Lord in the Order of Mass. Commentary, and proclamation and chant tips, for the Preface can be found at *www.StudyThePresidentialTexts.com/Prefaces* and in *The Order of Mass: A Roman Missal Study Edition and Workbook*, pages 28–33. If Eucharistic Prayer I is used, the proper form of the Communicantes is prayed from the Order of Mass. It is found in *The Order of Mass: A Roman Missal Study Edition and Workbook*, page 129.

** You may use the Solemn Blessing for the Nativity of the Lord in the Order of Mass, pages 166–167 in *The Order of Mass: A Roman Missal Study Edition and Workbook*.

Collect: The dignity of our human nature (*substantia*) is linked to our having been created in the image of God. With the Incarnation, God restores that image in Christ completely by means of his Death, Resurrection, and Pentecost, thus opening the way to restoration for humanity. This is why we can sing in the Exsultet "O happy fault": our state after the "restoration" is greater than before. This restoration is a glorification culminating in sharing in the nature of God. The phrase "humbled himself to share in our humanity" is a reminder of the lowliness of human nature: It cannot compare with the divine dignity. The Latin uses two words for the English "share." Our "share" in divinity is *consortes,* which is a union like that of husband and wife, where two people form a union of persons. But, Christ's "share" in humanity is *particeps*, which, in this context, might imply a union in substance or nature. We become the intimate partners of God, but he becomes a member of the human race itself.

Prayer over the Offerings: The petition is simple: "make acceptable our oblation." No human offering on its own can be a fitting gift for the divine; thus the prayer must ask that divine power make it so. It is freeing to know that no pressure is on us to make our gift worthy of God. We can only offer our best and beg the Lord's mercy to make up for what is lacking. Giving the petition this form is an expression of the theology of the day. Christ is our reconciliation with the Father. We can strive to please God in many ways, but only Christ,

The space below is for your notes.

Refer to pages viii–x for an explanation of the pointing of the chants and to page xii for the Tones for the Presidential Prayers from *The Roman Missal.*

Pointed Text

Collect

A O God, who wonderfully created the dignity of human nature
and still more wonderfully restored **it**,
B grant, we pray,
that we may share in the divini**ty** of Christ,
C who humbled himself to share in our human***i***ty.
Who lives and reigns with you in the unity of the Holy Spirit,
one God, for ever and ever.

Prayer over the Offerings

A Make acceptable, O Lord, our oblation on this solemn **day**,
B when you manifested the reconciliation
that makes us wholly pleasing **in** your sight
C and inaugurated for us the fullness of divine wor***ship***.
Through Christ our Lord.

Prayer after Communion

A Grant, O merciful **God**,
B that, just as the Savior of the world, born this day,
is the author of divine genera**tion** for us,
C so he may be the giver even of immortal***i***ty.
Who lives and reigns for ever and ever.

by virtue of his twofold nature, is "wholly pleasing." We must thus join ourselves to Christ. The prayer makes a nice play on words when God "manifested" to us his Son, who, in turn, makes us pleasing in God's "sight." God reveals Jesus to us, and Jesus shows us to God in Jesus himself. The "fullness of divine worship" is also Christ himself. In becoming visible, he manifests the fullness of divinity and offers on our behalf the fullness of worship. Both our reconciliation and our worship take place "through him, and with him, and in him."

Prayer after Communion: Though not explicitly noting that Holy Communion has been received, immortality is a focus. Holy Communion is understood as a pledge of immortality. Christ is Savior precisely as "author of divine generation." This "divine generation" is our new birth in Baptism, which begets in us divine life. The Incarnation is the source and foundation for the exchange of natures that brings us eternal life. As the divine life spreads by the power of faith and Baptism, Christ is recognized more and more as Savior of the world. The only petition of the prayer is a plea that the adopted sonship given in Baptism be for all eternity. The phrase "born this day" expresses the Church's joy-filled insistence on the reality, the truth of God made flesh, the reality of the full humanity of Christ. The prayer is thoroughly imbued with words suggestive of birth: "born," "author," "generation," and even "giver" (*largitor*). Such expressions tie in with the Communion received, which works to bring Christ to birth in each of us who receive him.

THE HOLY FAMILY OF JESUS, MARY AND JOSEPH

Feast

Collect

O God, who were pleased to give us
the shining example of the Holy Family,
graciously grant that we may imitate them
in practicing the virtues of family life and in the bonds of charity,
and so, in the joy of your house,
delight one day in eternal rewards.
Through our Lord Jesus Christ, your Son,
who lives and reigns with you in the unity of the Holy Spirit,
one God, for ever and ever.

Put stress on **shining example**. Say **graciously grant that we may imitate them** humbly and in a subdued manner. A threefold emphasis is on **virtues of family life** (pause), **and in the bonds of charity**, and **and so, in the joy of your house**. Draw out both **delight** and **eternal**.

Prayer over the Offerings

We offer you, Lord, the sacrifice of conciliation,
humbly asking that,
through the intercession of the Virgin Mother of God and Saint Joseph,
you may establish our families firmly in your grace and your peace.
Through Christ our Lord. *

Pause after **Lord** and stress the **sacrifice of conciliation**, referring to the offerings on the altar. Place less emphasis on **through** than on **intercession** and be measured with **Virgin Mother of God** and **Saint Joseph**. Stress **firmly**, **grace**, and **peace**.

Prayer after Communion

Bring those you refresh with this heavenly Sacrament,
most merciful Father,
to imitate constantly the example of the Holy Family,
so that, after the trials of this world,
we may share their company for ever.
Through Christ our Lord. **

Pause slightly after **you**, to bring out the delight in **refresh**. Emphasize **constantly** with the idea of perseveringly, without giving up hope. In stressing **trials of this world**, be careful not to overdo it. **Trials** should evoke a sentiment of patient endurance. With rising voice and greater joy, proclaim **share their company** (pause) **for ever**.

* Select from Preface I, II, or III of the Nativity of the Lord in the Order of Mass. Commentary, and proclamation and chant tips, for the Preface can be found at *www.StudyThePresidentialTexts.com/Prefaces* and in *The Order of Mass: A Roman Missal Study Edition and Workbook*, pages 28–33. If Eucharistic Prayer I is used, the proper form of the Communicantes is prayed from the Order of Mass. It is found in *The Order of Mass: A Roman Missal Study Edition and Workbook*, page 129.

** You may use the Solemn Blessing for the Nativity of the Lord in the Order of Mass, pages 166–167 in *The Order of Mass: A Roman Missal Study Edition and Workbook*.

Collect: On the surface, this prayer is potentially ambivalent. One might think that all we have to do to arrive at "eternal rewards" is to follow the "example" of the Holy Family. But there is more to it. God gives us this example, but he also must "grant" us, through his grace alone ("graciously"), the capacity both to follow their example and to reach "eternal rewards." The word for "delight" (*fruamur*) is normally used for people (to delight in or enjoy someone for their own sake). Here the delight is in "eternal rewards"—God himself. This prayer has two main points: the virtues of family life sealed with the bonds of charity, and the joys (indeed, eternal rewards) of God's house: "Better one day in your courts / than a thousand elsewhere" (Psalm 84:11). The word for joy is rather the exuberant communal joy (*laetitia*) that comes in reaching the goal, which is ultimately the household and family of heaven. In one sense, practicing these domestic virtues and living in the bonds of charity is to be "in the joy" of God's house.

Prayer over the Offerings: The Latin *placationis* ("conciliation") conveys the sense that only one offering is perfectly pleasing, perfectly pure (in a word, perfect), and that is Christ's. The English "conciliation" evokes its root sense of having everything in its proper place. We offer the sacrifice that aligns things properly, that brings order and peace to chaos. The Latin does not strictly make the request "through the intercession," but rather "following upon their intercession" or more literally "with their prayers coming between." This dis-

Pointed Text

Collect

A O God, who were pleased to give us
the shining example of the Holy Fam**i**ly,
B graciously grant that we may imitate them
in practicing the virtues of family life and in the **bonds** of charity,
C and so, in the joy of your house,
delight one day in eternal re***wards***.
Through our Lord Jesus Christ, your Son,
who lives and reigns with you in the unity of the Holy Spirit,
one God, for ever and ever.

Prayer over the Offerings

A We offer you, Lord, the sacrifice of concilia**tion**,
B humbly asking that,
through the intercession of the Virgin Mother of God **and** Saint Joseph,
C you may establish our families firmly in your grace and your ***peace***.
Through Christ our Lord.

Prayer after Communion

A Bring those you refresh with this heavenly Sacrament,
most merciful Fa**ther**,
B to imitate constantly the example of the **Ho**ly Family,
C so that, after the trials of this world,
we may share their company for e***ver***.
Through Christ our Lord.

The space below is for your notes.

Refer to pages viii–x for an explanation of the pointing of the chants and to page xii for the Tones for the Presidential Prayers from *The Roman Missal*.

tinction is worth noting because it avoids the mistaken notion that God could be compelled by the intercession of the Saints or that we could limit God as to how he may answer our petition, i.e., only through another's intercession. By invoking the Virgin as "Mother of God" in making the petition, the prayer employs the greatest (and most powerful) treasure available to the human race. The "peace" mentioned here is not an earthly detente or even fraternity. It is "your peace"—the kind of peace shared in the heavenly Communion.

Prayer after Communion: To be refreshed is to be given new life, new strength to face whatever difficulties may lie ahead. The Latin behind "refresh" (*reficis*) could be translated as "remake." The heavenly Communion that we share in the Eucharist so refreshes us that we become more and more a new creation in Christ. With this fresh strength, fresh grace of the Sacrament, we are enabled to imitate the "example of the Holy Family." The Latin for "example" is in the plural, implying that there are many ways to imitate the Holy Family. The Church intends to inspire the same holiness, peace, and fraternity as was evident in Nazareth. The "trials of this world" alludes to the scriptural parable of the sower, where worldly cares and anxieties suffocate faith. Those "in the world" are rightly concerned with finding worldly means to provide for their families, but the temptation is to make the priorities of the world our priorities. The Christian family is called to deal with the world with our eyes fixed on the heavenly company, with which we hope "to deal" forever.

January 1

The Octave Day of the Nativity of the Lord [Christmas]

SOLEMNITY OF MARY, THE HOLY MOTHER OF GOD

Collect

Place matching emphasis on **fruitful virginity** and **Blessed Mary**. Mary is blessed because of her fruitful virginity. Pause after **Mary**. Pause after **we pray** to draw out **experience**, and pause slightly after **of her**. Place more emphasis on **worthy** than on **we**. The key phrase to stress is **author of life**. This is whom we want to receive. The prayer should end strongly with **Son**.

O God, who through the fruitful virginity of Blessed Mary
bestowed on the human race
the grace of eternal salvation,
grant, we pray,
that we may experience the intercession of her,
through whom we were found worthy
to receive the author of life,
our Lord Jesus Christ, your Son.
Who lives and reigns with you in the unity of the Holy Spirit,
one God, for ever and ever.

Prayer over the Offerings

Do not pause after **grant to us** but speak the entire line as one thought clause. Do not pause much, if at all, after **that**. Slow down on **glory**, **beginnings**, and **grace**, and rest on **grace** before continuing. Pause after **one day**. Be careful not to lower your voice on **completion**. Keep the voice strong, as though the completion is a beginning.

O God, who in your kindness begin all good things
and bring them to fulfillment,
grant to us, who find joy in the Solemnity of the holy Mother of God,
that, just as we glory in the beginnings of your grace,
so one day we may rejoice in its completion.
Through Christ our Lord. *

Prayer after Communion

Stress **heavenly** and pause briefly after **Sacrament** to emphasize **with joy**. Be deliberate with **blessed ever-Virgin Mary Mother of your Son and Mother of the Church**.

We have received this heavenly Sacrament with joy, O Lord:
grant, we pray,
that it may lead us to eternal life,
for we rejoice to proclaim the blessed ever-Virgin Mary
Mother of your Son and Mother of the Church.
Through Christ our Lord. **

* Use Preface I of the Blessed Virgin Mary in the Order of Mass. Commentary, and proclamation and chant tips, for the Preface can be found at *www.StudyThePresidentialTexts.com/Prefaces* and in *The Order of Mass: A Roman Missal Study Edition and Workbook*, pages 82–83.

** You may use the Solemn Blessing for the Blessed Virgin Mary in the Order of Mass, page 174 in *The Order of Mass: A Roman Missal Study Edition and Workbook*.

Collect: In Mary, virginity and motherhood come together. The fruit of Mary's virginity is the God-man who is the "grace of eternal salvation." Mary's virginity was the essential effect of her Immaculate Conception: true virginity is not merely physical integrity, but integrity of body and soul as well. This unity is broken in the rest of us by sin. Thus, Mary's true virginity enabled her to receive the Holy Spirit so fully that she became mother yet remained virgin. The Collect makes a bold petition: that we may experience Mary's intercession—the intercession of a mother caring for her children. Inasmuch as we are all born into her Son in Baptism, she is mother to us. The prayer closes, naming the "Son" as the "author of life." At Christmas, the beginning of our life is born. In Mary, the whole human race "received" the author of life. The challenge of this Collect is for us to open our lives to receive Mary's Son still today. Laying aside our sins (in this sense, becoming virginal), we create the space for the new and eternal life that comes from the Son.

Prayer over the Offerings: This prayer celebrates the unmerited and even unexpected gifts we receive from God. This is why we "find joy" in this feast. Mary's virgin motherhood and the "beginnings of grace" that are in her son are wholly of God. It is essential that we be willing to accept an unmerited gift—not always an easy task. The prayer goes on, however, to say that "all good things" are of God, and we are encouraged to understand and celebrate them as such. The "completion" of this grace is not the Death and Resurrection of

The space below is for your notes.

Refer to pages viii–x for an explanation of the pointing of the chants and to page xii for the Tones for the Presidential Prayers from *The Roman Missal.*

Pointed Text

Collect

A O God, who through the fruitful virginity of Blessed Mary
bestowed on the human race
the grace of eternal salva**tion**,
B grant, we pray,
that we may experience the interces**sion** of her,
C through whom we were found worthy
to receive the author of life,
our Lord Jesus Christ, your ***Son***.
Who lives and reigns with you in the unity of the Holy Spirit,
one God, for ever and ever.

Prayer over the Offerings

A O God, who in your kindness begin all good things
and bring them to fulfill**ment**,
B grant to us, who find joy in the Solemnity of the holy Mo**ther** of God,
C that, just as we glory in the beginnings of your grace,
so one day we may rejoice in its comple***tion***.
Through Christ our Lord.

Prayer after Communion

A We have received this heavenly Sacrament with joy, O **Lord**:
B grant, we pray,
that it may lead us to e**ter**nal life,
C for we rejoice to proclaim the blessed ever-Virgin Mary
Mother of your Son and Mother of the ***Church***.
Through Christ our Lord.

Christ, but rather the completion of Christ's mystery in each of us. This is a prayer of petition for the present and the future. We recall the beginnings of grace in Mary's womb precisely to prompt us to petition for that beginning of grace, or rather its completion, in us. It is important that we be aware of God's grace at work in our lives so that we can cooperate with it. To cooperate is to "glory" in it. In other words, we cooperate by letting God's love make us beautiful (glorious), just as he did the Virgin Mary.

Prayer after Communion: Remember that the "Sacrament" contains all the mysteries celebrated on this feast. That is what "we have received." The fundamental "joy" of receiving this "Sacrament" is that it is a pledge to us of "eternal life." This "joy" connotes the shared public experience of celebrating in communion with others; a further reason for joy in the Sacrament is that we receive it in communion with the whole Church. The verb phrase "we rejoice" is *gloriamur* in Latin—"we glory." This implies that we are enriched by proclaiming the mystery of this feast, which is also our mystery. The end of the prayer reminds us that the joy of this feast is not just something that happened to Mary and Christ, but what is happening to us. The Latin employs two words for "mother." The first is *Genetrix*, taken from the Council of Ephesus and meaning "Bearer." The second is *Mater*, meaning "mother." The first term communicates Mary's motherhood of Christ's divinity as well as his humanity; the second proclaims our participation in the reality of Christ's sonship.

THE EPIPHANY OF THE LORD

Solemnity

At the Vigil Mass

This Mass is used on the evening of the day before the Solemnity, either before or after First Vespers (Evening Prayer I) of the Epiphany.

Collect

Exult in the word **splendor**, which is a synonym for Christ. Give equal emphasis to **your** and **majesty**. Pause after **may**, so as to emphasize **pass through**. Draw out the contrast between **this world** and **eternal home**.

May the splendor of your majesty, O Lord, we pray,
shed its light upon our hearts,
that we may pass through the shadows of this world
and reach the brightness of our eternal home.
Through our Lord Jesus Christ, your Son,
who lives and reigns with you in the unity of the Holy Spirit,
one God, for ever and ever.

Prayer over the Offerings

Proclaim **offerings** with the understanding that it includes our lives. Draw out **Only Begotten Son** but don't pause after **Son**. Pause briefly after **to you**, so as to emphasize **praise** and bring out the parallel with **eternal salvation**.

Accept we pray, O Lord, our offerings,
in honor of the appearing of your Only Begotten Son
and the first fruits of the nations,
that to you praise may be rendered
and eternal salvation be ours.
Through Christ our Lord. *

Prayer after Communion

Be somewhat subdued with the first two lines in order to stress **star of your justice**. Put more emphasis on **bright in our minds**. Linger on **true treasure**, then pause briefly. Pause again briefly after **consist**.

Renewed by sacred nourishment,
we implore your mercy, O Lord,
that the star of your justice
may shine always bright in our minds
and that our true treasure may ever consist in our confession of you.
Through Christ our Lord. **

* Use the Preface of the Epiphany in the Order of Mass. Commentary, and proclamation and chant tips, for the Preface can be found at *www.StudyThePresidentialTexts.com/Prefaces* and in *The Order of Mass: A Roman Missal Study Edition and Workbook*, pages 34–35.

** You may use the Solemn Blessing for the Epiphany of the Lord in the Order of Mass, page 168 in *The Order of Mass: A Roman Missal Study Edition and Workbook*.

Collect: The "splendor" of God's majesty is Christ, and the "light" of Christ is the gift of faith by which we walk: "shed its light" renders the Latin verb *illustret*, which means to illuminate or radiate. The light of faith, revealed on this day, does not eradicate the "shadows of this world" but enables us to "pass through" them without fear. This is what it means to hope. The light of faith enables us to trust in the promise of a future homeland, and this hope gives us courage to continue walking amidst the shadows. The "splendor" shines internally where the darkening of the world's day cannot reach. If we are illumined from within by God's grace, then all the external trials and persecutions that come to us in life will be seen in their "proper light"—that is, from the proper perspective, which is the perspective of heaven, where this interior splendor will become the "brightness" of eternity. Our inner grace will then be manifest in all creation, and vice versa. In heaven, the internal and the external will become one and never again be an occasion of deception.

Prayer over the Offerings: The word *munera*, translated here as "offerings," is multivalent; it includes the sense that these offerings are our protection, our inspiration, our duty, and our gift of service. The word "appearing" (*apparitione* in Latin) means that we must not limit the revelation of this feast only to what we can see. No one has ever "seen" God (1 John 4:12), but his appearing in the sacrament of human flesh and blood made his Real Presence manifest to human senses. The "first fruits of the nations" are the Wise

The space below is for your notes.

Refer to pages viii–x for an explanation of the pointing of the chants and to page xii for the Tones for the Presidential Prayers from *The Roman Missal*.

Pointed Text

Collect

A May the splendor of your majesty, O Lord, we **pray**,
B shed its light u**pon** our hearts,
C that we may pass through the shadows of this world
and reach the brightness of our eternal ***home***.
Through our Lord Jesus Christ, your Son,
who lives and reigns with you in the unity of the Holy Spirit,
one God, for ever and ever.

Prayer over the Offerings

A Accept we pray, O Lord, our of**fer**ings,
B in honor of the appearing of your Only Begotten Son
and the first fruits **of** the nations,
C that to you praise may be rendered
and eternal salvation be ***ours***.
Through Christ our Lord.

Prayer after Communion

A Renewed by sacred nour**ish**ment,
B we implore your mer**cy**, O Lord,
C that the star of your justice
may shine always bright in our minds
and that our true treasure may ever consist in our confession of ***you***.
Through Christ our Lord.

Men, in whom we must see ourselves; we can even identify on some level with their giving of gifts. We, too, must make a journey of faith to recognize his appearing in our hearts. Every liturgy incorporates an exchange of gifts between God and us. This prayer identifies that exchange as the praise we render to God for the eternal salvation he bestows on us. We do well, however, not to consider this an even exchange. Our gift of praise in no way requires the return gift of salvation. Both are free.

Prayer after Communion: The Eastern Church draws a parallel between the Incarnation of Christ and his transubstantiation in the Eucharist. Christ was born into our flesh, and he is "born" into bread and wine on the altar at Mass. Just as the Incarnation "renewed" human nature, so does reception of Holy Communion renew us. The "star of justice" plays on the passage from Malachi 4:12 that speaks of the "sun of justice." Both refer to Christ, whose light brings inner warmth and healing and revelation, guiding us in our journey of faith, shining "bright in our minds," keeping us warm when the chills of doubt blow, and giving us hope when the darkness weighs upon us. This star "shines bright" with the light of revelation, which includes by its nature the light of love. Christianity is the fire and warmth of a relationship that enables us to see all creation in a new and wonderful light. The "treasure" of the Wise Men is a symbolic confession of the Christ child's identity and destiny. Our "true treasure" lies in a similar confession that ties our identity and destiny to his.

THE EPIPHANY OF THE LORD

At the Mass during the Day

Collect

Draw out **Only Begotten Son** and stress **revealed** as the key concept of this feast.

Stress **know you** and pause after **by faith**. Linger on **behold the beauty** and proclaim with awe **sublime glory**.

O God, who on this day
revealed your Only Begotten Son to the nations
by the guidance of a star,
grant in your mercy
that we, who know you already by faith,
may be brought to behold the beauty of your sublime glory.
Through our Lord Jesus Christ, your Son,
who lives and reigns with you in the unity of the Holy Spirit,
one God, for ever and ever. *

Prayer over the Offerings

Without lessening the volume, lower the pitch of the voice slightly on **favor** as a kind of plea. Pause after **now** and go slowly on each of the gifts. Raise the voice on **he** and pause slightly. Speak each verb slowly and distinctly. Pause after **received** in order to make a proclamation of **Jesus Christ**.

Look with favor, Lord, we pray,
on these gifts of your Church,
in which are offered now not gold or frankincense or myrrh,
but he who by them is proclaimed,
sacrificed and received, Jesus Christ.
Who lives and reigns for ever and ever. **

Prayer after Communion

Stress **heavenly** and linger slowly on **always** and **everywhere**. Take a quick breath after **perceive**. Proclaim **revere with true affection** with tenderness. Proclaim **mystery** with a sense of awe. Be somewhat firm with **willed us**.

Go before us with heavenly light, O Lord,
always and everywhere,
that we may perceive with clear sight
and revere with true affection
the mystery in which you have willed us to participate.
Through Christ our Lord. ***

* The Epiphany Proclamation, located on page 30–31, may be proclaimed after the Gospel.

** Use the Preface for the Epiphany of the Lord in the Order of Mass. Commentary, and proclamation and chant tips, for the Preface can be found at *www.StudyThePresidentialTexts.com/Prefaces* and in *The Order of Mass: A Roman Missal Study Edition and Workbook*, pages 34–35.

*** You may use the Solemn Blessing for the Epiphany of the Lord in the Order of Mass, *The Order of Mass: A Roman Missal Study Edition and Workbook*, page 168.

Collect: The "revelation" of this solemnity is primarily the revelation of God's Son to "the nations," but the Collect also "reveals" God's mastery over nature in manifesting his Son "by the guidance of a star." God's twofold revelation allows the prayer to refer to the "beauty of your sublime glory." The Latin *speciem*, meaning "beauty," refers to the face. The beauty of the face is less a matter of features than that we communicate personal interchange by means of the face. It is difficult to objectify someone when we look them in the eyes and speak face to face; hence, the beauty of the face. Through the Incarnation, God has a face in which we may see his glory that should be reflected in our faces. The disfigurement of Christ's face in his Passion reveals the corruption of sin that lies beneath our exterior "beauty." In this sense, Christ's Passion was like the lancing of a wound, which allowed the healing and refashioning of our "beauty" into his "sublime glory." The Latin for "sublime glory," *celesitudinis*, literally means "heights"—God's beauty is higher than the stars.

Prayer over the Offerings: The Latin behind "look" (*intuere*) means "to gaze into." This prayer asks the Lord to gaze into the Church's gifts and to see what they will become: Christ, and our lives in Christ. Our gifts are acceptable only insofar as they are offered through Christ. When the Father looks upon the assembly of believers, he sees only his Son, thanks to our baptism in his Son. The Father's gaze perceives each of us in his Son and his Son in each of us. The "gifts" become offerings when they are offered in the liturgy. Each of the Magi's

The space below is for your notes.

Refer to pages viii–x for an explanation of the pointing of the chants and to page xii for the Tones for the Presidential Prayers from *The Roman Missal*.

Pointed Text

Collect

A O God, who on this day
revealed your Only Begotten Son to the nations
by the guidance of a **star**,
B grant in your mercy
that we, who know you alrea**dy** by faith,
C may be brought to behold the beauty of your sublime glo***ry***.
Through our Lord Jesus Christ, your Son,
who lives and reigns with you in the unity of the Holy Spirit,
one God, for ever and ever.

Prayer over the Offerings

A Look with favor, Lord, we pray,
on these gifts of your **Church**,
B in which are offered now not gold or frankin**cense** or myrrh,
but he who by them is proclaimed,
C sacrificed and received, Jesus ***Christ***.
Who lives and reigns for ever and ever.

Prayer after Communion

B Go before us with heavenly light, O Lord,
always and **e**verywhere,
C that we may perceive with clear sight
and revere with true affection
the mystery in which you have willed us to parti***ci***pate.
Through Christ our Lord.

gifts mentioned here corresponds characteristically to a subsequent verbal participle: myrrh "proclaims" the death of Christ, and calls us to die in Christ; frankincense is burned up as a priestly "sacrifice," calling us to make our lives "a sacrificial offering to God for a fragrant aroma" (Ephesians 5:2); and gold signifies the one whom we "receive" as our king in Holy Communion who was sacrificed and died for us, calling us to rule our lives with the golden rule of charity.

Prayer after Communion: The "heavenly light" (*caelesti lumine*) is the light of faith, the reflection of God who is "always and everywhere." This light gives us "clear sight" to discern reality (the Body and Blood) behind appearance (the bread and wine) and so to honor that reality. Discerning the Body of Christ in the Eucharist helps us to "revere" the body of Christ that is our brothers and sisters in the Church (1 Corinthians 11:29). The light of faith strengthens our heart, enabling us to perceive others' actions with compassion. Thus, the anguish we might feel from another is transformed into compassion for his insecurities. With clearer sight, we perceive not from ours but from the other's perspective; when I forget myself, then the quirks of others are no longer annoyances, and quirks become irrelevant as I perceive the other more clearly in the light of faith. Then I will be able to revere others "with true affection." The "mystery in which you have willed us to participate" at the end of the prayer refers to Christ's command to "do this in memory of me."

The Announcement of Easter and the Moveable Feasts

On the Epiphany of the Lord, after the singing of the Gospel, a Deacon or cantor, in keeping with an ancient practice of Holy Church, announces from the ambo the moveable feasts of the current year according to this formula:

Treat **Know** with respect for the comma in the text. At the end of the next words, respect the comma, but keep the voice singing on to **that, as we**. Broaden **Lord Jesus Christ**. Treat **so** as if a comma were after it, setting off **by leave of God's mercy**, holding the last syllable slightly, and then going on to **we announce**. Slow this phrase noticeably. Try not to break or breathe before **the joy**. Treat **the** lightly, so as to accent strongly **joy**. Hold **-tion** of **Resurrection**, and slow noticeably the last of the phrase with its elaborate melodic development on **Savior**. Do not pause after singing the name of the month, but continue directly with **will fall**. Articulate carefully **Ash Wednesday**. Do not hold the last syllable long, but continue the sense by going on with **and** (treat lightly so as to put the emphasis on the next words) **the beginning**. If possible, do not hold **fast**, but continue directly—even though the voice drops to "la"—with **of the most**. Slow noticeably **Lenten season** with its elaborate melodic development. Hold slightly the name of the month, but do not breathe; rather, continue with **you will celebrate**. Hold **Day** slightly, after broadening **with joy Easter Day**. If necessary, take a short breath after **Day** and continue with **the Paschal**. Treat the elaborate melodic development at the end of the phrase as has been indicated before. Again,

From at least the Council of Trent through the Pontifical of 1962, this Proclamation was used only, it seems, at Pontifical Masses on Epiphany. In the post-conciliar reforms, a revised *Pontificale* was never issued and this Proclamation was overlooked for a long time. Liturgy Training Publications published an English version of it in the 1970s and 1980s, and in 1989, the U.S. Bishops' Conference petitioned and received the *recognitio* from Rome for an official version, which was published in the 1994 and 2004 Sacramentary Supplement. The Proclamation was then included, for the first time, in the third edition of the *Missale Romanum* and a new translation is now published in *The Roman Missal*, 2010.

Theologically, this Proclamation emphasizes the unity and integrity of the Paschal Mystery. Even though we stretch that mystery across an entire liturgical calendar, we must not mentally separate the Christ child from the Christ crucified. This is why, for example, depictions of the infant Christ usually show him strangely adult like, not quite an infant at all. It is the artist's way of demonstrating the whole of the mystery in the kernel of Christmas. Epiphany is the feast of the manifestation of this Christ to the world. The Church sees it as fitting, therefore, on this day to proclaim to the world the major events of Christ's saving mystery. At the start, the birth of Christ is recalled in the same line as his Resurrection, and both mysteries evoke joy in his disciples. The joy of the Resurrection is announced "by leave of God's mercy." The Latin verb here trans-

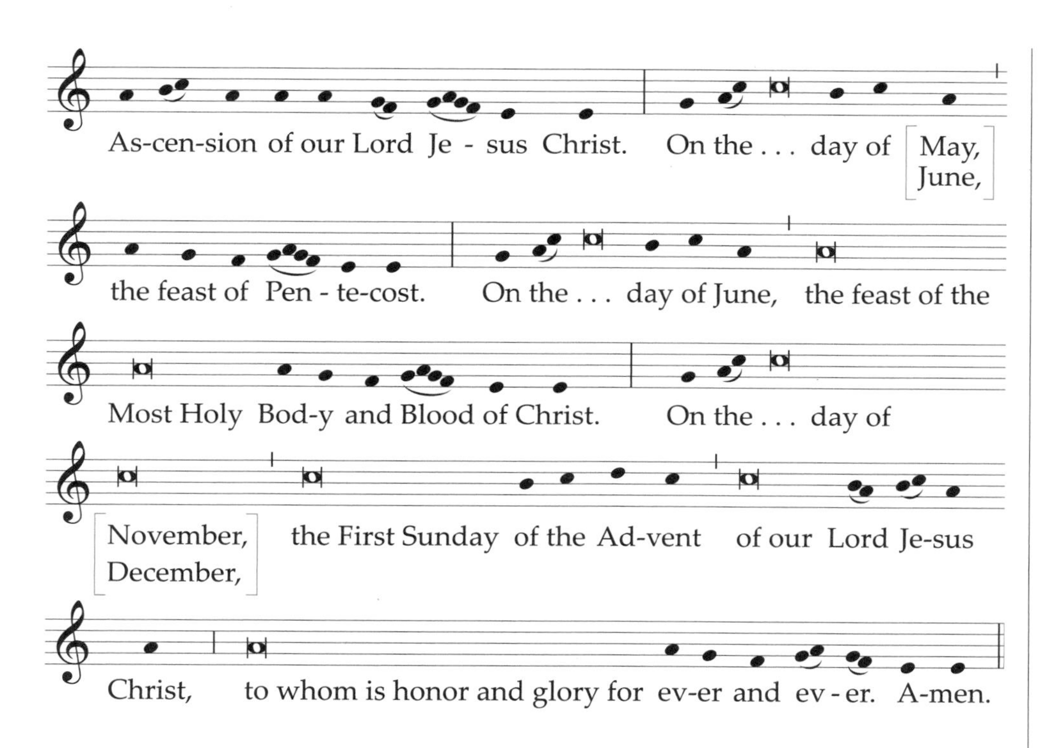

hold slightly the name of the month in the next phrase, but do not breathe; rather, continue with **will be**. Follow earlier tip for handling the end of the phrase, **Lord Jesus Christ**.

The announcement of **Pentecost** and the **Body and Blood of Christ** in the next two phrases follows the tips given above for the other feasts. In the last phrase of the Announcement, hold the last syllable of the month, but do not break the voice, before continuing with **the First Sunday**. Note the text: **of the Advent**. Do not hold -**vent** in **Advent**, but continue with **of our Lord**. Lengthen **Christ**, and, if possible, do not breathe there, but rather continue with **to whom is honor**. Slow and broaden the ending noticeably, holding -**er** in the final **ever** and making a slight break in the voice, before concluding with **Amen**—with both syllables being held.

lated as "by leave" is *annuente*, which literally means "by his nod." In the Greek poem the "Iliad," Zeus commits himself to fulfilling another's request by "nodding" or bowing his head. It is the expression of the divine will to act on behalf of humanity. In the Proclamation, the divine will is expressed in his "mercy." It is God's mercy which gives us the joy of "our Savior."

The dates that follow begin with Ash Wednesday, called "the beginning of the fast." Following his Baptism, Christ's ministry began with keeping the fast that Adam and Eve had broken. The announcement of Easter Day is called the "Paschal feast" (the Latin is literally "the holy Passover"), and once again, joy (*gaudio*) is mentioned. Both the Ascension and Pentecost are included as key feasts of recapitulation and spiritualization. The feast of the Most Holy Body and Blood reveals the fruit of the Resurrection, Ascension, and Pentecost, namely, the gift of the Eucharist in the life of the Church. The Proclamation closes with the announcement of the First Sunday of Advent, which, coming last, emphasizes the eschatological character of Advent. This is the feast of the Second Coming of Christ, "to whom is honor and glory for ever and ever. Amen."

THE BAPTISM OF THE LORD

Feast

Where the Solemnity of the Epiphany is transferred to Sunday, if this Sunday occurs on January 7 or 8, the Feast of the Baptism of the Lord is celebrated on the following Monday.

Collect

Without rushing, do not pause after **ever-living God**, but go right into **who**. Pause for the clauses that follow. In the next two clauses, place the emphasis on **when** and **as,** and proclaim the rest of the clause without a break. Go slowly and distinctly with **solemnly declared him your beloved Son**. Pause after **be** and emphasize **well pleasing**.

Almighty ever-living God,
who, when Christ had been baptized in the River Jordan
and as the Holy Spirit descended upon him,
solemnly declared him your beloved Son,
grant that your children by adoption,
reborn of water and the Holy Spirit,
may always be well pleasing to you.
Through our Lord Jesus Christ, your Son,
who lives and reigns with you in the unity of the Holy Spirit,
one God, for ever and ever.

Or:

Emphasize **very flesh**. Stress the contrast between **inwardly** and **outwardly**. Pause briefly after **inwardly** in order to give due weight to **transformed**.

O God, whose Only Begotten Son
has appeared in our very flesh,
grant, we pray, that we may be inwardly transformed
through him whom we recognize as outwardly like ourselves.
Who lives and reigns with you in the unity of the Holy Spirit,
one God, for ever and ever.

Prayer over the Offerings

Pause briefly after **brought**. Stress **revealing** and **beloved**. Emphasize **transformed** and give equal weight to both **sacrifice** and **him**. Raise the voice for **in his compassion**.

Accept, O Lord, the offerings
we have brought to honor the revealing of your beloved Son,
so that the oblation of your faithful
may be transformed into the sacrifice of him
who willed in his compassion
to wash away the sins of the world.
Who lives and reigns for ever and ever.

Collect: The first three lines of this prayer following the address recall the three essential elements of Christ's baptism: water, the Holy Spirit, and the declaration that he is the "beloved Son." The next three lines petition that this mystery of Christ pass into each of us. The good news is our share in Christ's life through the gift of the Spirit. Since this prayer is primarily about sonship, we should consider what it means to be beloved sons and daughters of the Father. First, it means we are loved—"you are my beloved Son." Second, it means we are to be receptive of the Father's gifts—above all, the Holy Spirit, but also suffering. Third, we are to be nurtured by the Father, who feeds us with the body and blood of Christ. Fourth, we belong to the Father: even when others may abandon us, he will never abandon us—"I have carved you on the palms of my hands" (Isaiah 49:15–16). Fifth, it means we are to be free (Matthew 17:24; Luke 15:29–32). Lastly, it means we are heirs to the kingdom of the Father (Romans 8:17). All these are qualities of sonship.

Alternative Collect: The baptism of Christ celebrates an epiphany, a manifestation. The emphasis is on the reality of Christ's humanity: he "appeared in our very flesh." The Latin is "in the substance of our flesh," thus connecting the expression with the Creed's "consubstantial" and the Eucharist's "transubstantiation." The one who has so appeared is called God's "Only Begotten Son." In this feast the Father's voice is heard declaring Christ to be his "beloved Son."

The space below is for your notes.

Refer to pages viii–x for an explanation of the pointing of the chants and to page xii for the Tones for the Presidential Prayers from *The Roman Missal.*

Pointed Text

Collect

A Almighty ever-living God,
who, when Christ had been baptized in the River Jordan
and as the Holy Spirit descended upon him,
solemnly declared him your beloved **Son**,
B grant that your children by adoption,
reborn of water and the **Ho**ly Spirit,
C may always be well pleasing to ***you***.
Through our Lord Jesus Christ, your Son,
who lives and reigns with you in the unity of the Holy Spirit,
one God, for ever and ever.

Or:

B O God, whose Only Begotten Son
has appeared in our, **ve**ry flesh
C grant, we pray, that we may be inwardly transformed
through him whom we recognize as outwardly like our***selves***.
Who lives and reigns with you in the unity of the Holy Spirit,
one God, for ever and ever.

Prayer over the Offerings

A Accept, O Lord, the offerings
we have brought to honor the revealing of your beloved **Son**,
B so that the oblation of your faithful
may be transformed into the sacri**fice** of him
C who willed in his compassion
to wash away the sins of the ***world***.
Who lives and reigns for ever and ever.

"Son" is an essential title for Jesus, demonstrating his identity and ours. "Only Begotten Son" defines completely who Jesus is—the Son who has received everything from his Father. It delineates his relationship with the Father, who has many "sons" by creation and by adoption, but one who is Only-Begotten. The heart of the prayer is the petition for inward transformation. The Son took our nature to refashion it in his image. Humanity is spiritually disfigured, and Christ takes on our nature to bring us into his transformed nature.

Prayer over the Offerings: Now that we, the faithful, have been nourished by the sacred gift of Communion in the liturgy, we have the strength we need to entreat God's mercy as we turn to face the outside world. The Eucharist gives us the communion with God that makes it possible for us to beg his mercy successfully in the world. Notice that "faithfully listening" is not in the past tense but the present, meaning that the faithful listening refers not to what we have done during the Mass, but what we will do in the world. Listening to Christ, not just in the liturgy but in the world as well, is what enables us to be Christians in every moment of our lives. It is noteworthy that in the Baptism event, the voice "listened to" was the Father's, but here we are told to listen to the Son, just as the Father commanded on the mountain of the Transfiguration (Matthew 17:5). The mysteries of Christ are all one. The Baptism, the Transfiguration, the Nativity, the Passion and Death, are one mystery in the one Christ, and are best understood in relation to one another.

Bring out the accent on **be** in **The Lord be with you.** In the next phrase, make a strong accent on **Lift**, and slow both notes of **hearts**. In the third dialogue, move to the word **thanks** before accenting, and hold that word slightly to give it emphasis. Broaden both notes of **Lord**, and hold **God**.

Sing this proclamation cursively in a reciting tone. In **salvation**, do not hold **-va**; only broaden the two notes slightly. Hold **-tion**. **Always** and **everywhere** require a slight broadening and clear enunciation. The accent of the phrase falls on **thanks**, which should be held briefly. In the next phrase, clearly make three phrases of the text, by respecting the commas after **Lord** and **Father** and the period at **God**.

Do not lengthen or pause at **Jordan**, but only at **Baptism**. Pause very briefly at **so that** to make the sense of the coming phrases clearer. Briefly hold on the **-en** of **heaven**. Hold slightly on **-lieve** of **believe**, but with no break there. Broaden **Word . . . us** before taking a break and breath. Make a slight hold on **dove** in the next phrase. No hold or pause after **Servant**. Make the break after holding **-ness** of **gladness**, but do not make this long because of the sense, which demands continuing to the next phrase. Broaden the last four words of the sentence.

Preface: The Baptism of the Lord.

Preface: The Baptism of the Lord

A long history of salvation is associated with the waters of the Jordan River (Joshua 3:4–4:24; 2 Kings 2:8, 14; 2 Kings 5:9–14; Psalm 114:3–5). They serve as the boundary between desert and Promised Land, between disease and healing, between slavery and freedom. Christ is washed in the Jordan to cleanse our leprosy of sin; he sanctifies the waters so that they might sanctify us and enable us to cross over into the freedom of his kingdom. This mystery at the Jordan reveals a "new Baptism," as opposed to the baptism of the Jews or of John the Baptist or even the ritual washing that every observant Jew had to perform to be made ritually clean (Numbers 19). In his new Baptism, Christ is the fulfillment of all of these Old Testament references. The "signs and wonders" (*miris mysteriis*) refer to Christ's sanctifying the waters, to the voice coming down from heaven, and to the descent of the Spirit in the "likeness of a dove" (Matthew 4:16), a symbol of purity and peace. Peace means reconciliation, fractured relationships made whole. In Christ's Baptism, we see all of the essential elements in Christian Baptism, including the revelation of the Trinity, and the actions whereby we sinners are sanctified, are reconciled in peace to God, and become children of the Father by adoption. The Preface identifies the "voice" from above as the sign that makes possible our faith in the Incarnation—that Jesus is the beloved Son of the Father. For the Christian, this would be the voice of conscience, which is awakened in Baptism by the indwelling of the Holy Spirit. *Gaudium*

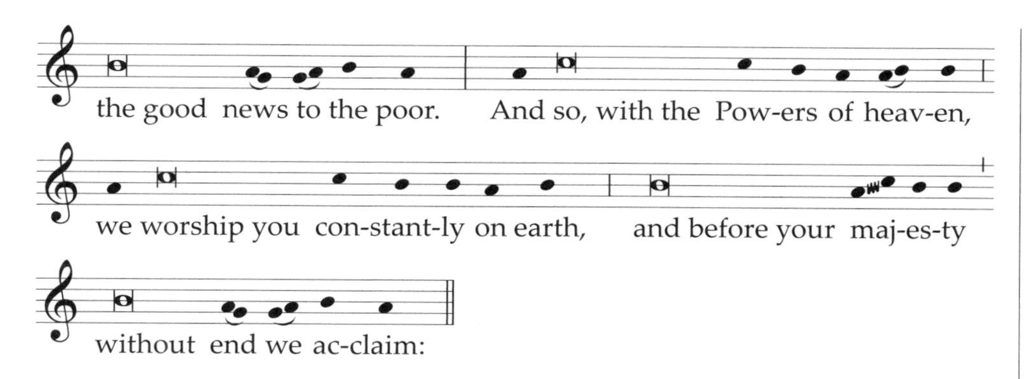

Slight pause after **And so**. Respect the commas, but try to keep this section together, without big breaks for breaths. Broaden the last phrase, especially on **majesty**. Slow **we ac-**, and put emphasis on **-claim**, so as to evoke the response **Holy, Holy, Holy . . . .**

Holy, Holy, Holy Lord God of hosts . . .

Text without music:

V. **The Lord be with you.**
R. And with your spirit.

V. **Lift up your hearts.**
R. We lift them up to the Lord.

V. **Let us give thanks to the Lord our God.**
R. It is right and just.

It is truly right and just, our duty and our salvation,
always and everywhere to give you thanks,
Lord, holy Father, almighty and eternal God.

Emphasize **truly**, **duty**, and **salvation**.

For in the waters of the Jordan
you revealed with signs and wonders a new Baptism,
so that through the voice that came down from heaven
we might come to believe in your Word dwelling among us,
and by the Spirit's descending in the likeness of a dove
we might know that Christ your Servant
has been anointed with the oil of gladness
and sent to bring the good news to the poor.

Slightly pause after **For**. Give some restrained enthusiasm to **signs and wonders** and stress strongly **new**. Emphasize and pause after **voice**; do the same with **heaven**; and again with **Word**, followed by a slight pause to stress **dwelling**. In the next clause, pause slightly after **and**. The rest of the clause is measured but without pauses. Slightly pause after **know,** with strong emphasis on **Christ** and **Servant**. Proclaim **oil of gladness** with a measure of reverent nobility. When proclaiming **good news,** believe it.

And so, with the Powers of heaven,
we worship you constantly on earth,
and before your majesty
without end we acclaim:

Holy, Holy, Holy Lord God of hosts . . .

et Spes (*Pastoral Constitution on the Church in the Modern World*), 16, describes the conscience as the "most secret core and sanctuary of the human person. There they are alone with God whose voice echoes in their depths." It is the same voice that sounded above the waters at Jesus's Baptism and which calls to mind the words of the Psalmist: "The voice of the Lord is over the the waters, / the God of glory thunders, / the Lord, over the mighty waters. / The voice of the Lord is power; / the voice of the Lord is splendor" (Psalm 29:3–4). Jesus's anointing with power and the Spirit (Acts of the Apostles 10:38) brings "good news to the poor" (Luke 4:18). All of humanity, bound by sin, is "poor" and in need of that "good news," which is not Christ's Baptism in the Jordan, but our Baptism in Christ! The "oil of gladness" alludes to the Holy Spirit in Hebrews 1:9: "You loved justice and hated wickedness; / therefore God, your God, anointed you / with the oil of gladness above your companions." Other references are in Psalm 45:8 and Isaiah 61:3.

Pause after **entreat**, as though searching for the word. Proclaim **your mercy**, as though having found the perfect expression. Put the greater stress on **faithfully** and **Only Begotten**. Pause after **children** and speak slowly and deliberately **in name** and **in truth**.

Prayer after Communion

Nourished with these sacred gifts,
we humbly entreat your mercy, O Lord,
that, faithfully listening to your Only Begotten Son,
we may be your children in name and in truth.
Through Christ our Lord.

A Nourished with these sacred gifts,
we humbly entreat your mercy, O **Lord**,
B that, faithfully listening to your Only Be**got**ten Son,
C we may be your children in name and in ***truth***.
Through Christ our Lord.

Prayer after Communion: Now that we, the faithful, have been nourished by the sacred gift of Communion in the liturgy, we have the strength we need to "entreat" God's mercy as we turn to face the outside world. The Eucharist gives us the communion with God that makes it possible for us to beg his mercy successfully in the world. Notice that "faithfully listening" is not in the past tense but the present, meaning that the faithful listening refers not to what we have done during the Mass, but to what we will do in the world. Listening to Christ in the liturgy and in the world is what enables us to be not merely nominal, Sunday-morning Christians, but Christians in every moment of our lives. It is noteworthy that in the Baptism event, the voice "listened to" was the Father's, but here we are told to listen to the Son, just as the Father commanded on the mountain of the Transfiguration. ("This is my beloved Son in whom I am well pleased; listen to him" [Matthew 17:5].) The mysteries of Christ are all one. The Baptism, the Transfiguration, the Nativity, the Passion and Death, are one mystery in the one Christ, and are best understood in relation to one another.

Lent

ASH WEDNESDAY

Minor emphasis and slight pause with **begin**. Stress **holy fasting**, slowly and distinctly, to set fasting apart from mere discipline. Say **campaign of Christian service** with the determined resolution of a field commander. Proclaim **take up battle against spiritual evils** with some urgency. Pause after **we may be armed** (spoken again with resolution) to stress the weapons: **self-restraint**.

Collect *

Grant, O Lord, that we may begin with holy fasting
this campaign of Christian service,
so that, as we take up battle against spiritual evils,
we may be armed with weapons of self-restraint.
Through our Lord Jesus Christ, your Son,
who lives and reigns with you in the unity of the Holy Spirit,
one God, for ever and ever.

The Liturgy of the Eucharist

The prayer begins with three couplets: **solemnly offer**, **annual sacrifice**, and **beginning of Lent**. Add a hint of pleading to **entreat**. Do not pause after **that** but briefly after **away from** to emphasize **harmful pleasures**. Do not pause after **and** or **worthy** but pause after **sins**. Stress **devoutly**. Pause to emphasize **Passion** and **Son**.

Prayer over the Offerings

As we solemnly offer
the annual sacrifice for the beginning of Lent,
we entreat you, O Lord,
that, through works of penance and charity,
we may turn away from harmful pleasures
and, cleansed from our sins, may become worthy
to celebrate devoutly the Passion of your Son.
Who lives and reigns for ever and ever. **

Pause briefly after **received**. Emphasize **Sacrament** and **sustain**. Without too much emphasis, parallel **to you** and **for us**. Give greater stress to **pleasing** and draw out the words **healing remedy**.

Prayer after Communion

May the Sacrament we have received sustain us, O Lord,
that our Lenten fast may be pleasing to you
and be for us a healing remedy.
Through Christ our Lord.

Pause briefly after **Pour out** to emphasize **spirit of compunction**. Rest humbly on **bow**. Raise the voice in reverence for **majesty**. Speak **mercy** with kindness. Pause after **merit**. Stress **rewards you promise**. Pray last line with humble resolve.

Prayer over the People

For the dismissal, the Priest stands facing the people and, extending his hands over them, says this prayer:

Pour out a spirit of compunction, O God,
on those who bow before your majesty,
and by your mercy may they merit the rewards you promise
to those who do penance.
Through Christ our Lord.

Collect: A powerful wisdom is at work in this Collect. Spiritual evils are the most dangerous menace we can face. (Jesus said, "Do not be afraid of those who kill the body but cannot kill the soul" [Matthew 10:28].) Against this greatest of all evils, the greatest weapon we have is "holy fasting," emptying ourselves. The wisdom is that the more we rely on ourselves, the less we rely on God. The language of the Collect is metaphorical militarism, but the "battle" is not to attack the enemy, but to "restrain" ourselves. The enemy seems to be our fallen nature, which needs to be brought into submission to the spirit (Romans 8:1–13). Fasting is not limited to food, but can include the curbing of any desires. It is called "holy" to distinguish it from dieting or mere discipline for worldly gain. Instead of military service, this campaign (the whole time of Lent) is Christian through and through. We empty ourselves of pride, grudges, jealousy, etc., in order to serve others in true charity. The greatest battle of the Christian is to restrain our appetites, to empty ourselves to make room for God.

Prayer over the Offerings: The adverb "solemnly" captures the tone for this prayer and for the day. A "solemn" feast (*sollemnis* is related to *sollus,* meaning "whole" and to *salvus,* meaning "safe") calls for complete attention and dedication, implying an importance that is a matter of life and death. This "solemn offering" intends to help us "turn away from harmful pleasures" and "to celebrate devoutly the Passion." The realization of "harm" and of the need to celebrate Christ's Passion confirms that this offering is a matter of life

Pointed Text

Collect

A Grant, O Lord, that we may begin with holy fasting
this campaign of Christian ser**vice**,
B so that, as we take up battle against spir**i**tual evils,
C we may be armed with weapons of self-re***straint***.
Through our Lord Jesus Christ, your Son,
who lives and reigns with you in the unity of the Holy Spirit,
one God, for ever and ever.

The Liturgy of the Eucharist

Prayer over the Offerings

A As we solemnly offer
the annual sacrifice for the beginning of Lent,
we entreat you, O **Lord**,
B that, through works of penance and **char**ity,
C we may turn away from harmful pleasures
and, cleansed from our sins, may become worthy
to celebrate devoutly the Passion of your ***Son***.
Who lives and reigns for ever and ever.

Prayer after Communion

B May the Sacrament we have received sustain **us**, O Lord,
C that our Lenten fast may be pleasing to you
and be for us a healing re***me***dy.
Through Christ our Lord.

* The Distribution of Ashes takes the place of the Penitential Act.

** Use either Preface III or IV of Lent in the Order of Mass. Commentary, and proclamation and chant tips, for the Preface can be found at *www.StudyThePresidentialTexts.com/Prefaces* and in *The Order of Mass: A Roman Missal Study Edition and Workbook*, pages 40–43.

The space below is for your notes.

Refer to pages viii–x for an explanation of the pointing of the chants and to page xii for the Tones for the Presidential Prayers from *The Roman Missal*.

and death. Our "penance" is intended to help us "turn away from" the non-essential. Works of "charity" are a positive turning toward the good and the essential. We should never simply abstain from evil, but must exchange evil for good. Note that our "penance and charity" do not cleanse us from sins. This is what is called a divine passive—the passive verb "cleansed" means that the active agent is God. The adverb "devoutly" means that the celebration of the Passion must be personal—Christ dying in us and we dying in him.

Prayer after Communion: The "Sacrament" received in this Mass includes the whole mystery of Christ's life, Death, and Resurrection. Only this Paschal Mystery enables human works such as the "Lenten fast" (the Latin is plural "fastings") to be efficacious. Here the Mystery enables our fast to be both "pleasing" to God and "a healing remedy" for us. When our actions are pleasing to God, they draw us closer to him, which heals the divisions in our lives. Saint Paul was clear that his first priority was to please God (Galatians 1:10). It is important to consider how fasting is a "healing." Adam and Eve broke the fast in the garden and our humanity became mortally wounded. Christ, on the other hand, kept a fast at the beginning of his ministry and began the healing of our sickness. Fasting reminds us that we are dependent, and that we are ultimately dependent not on the "food" of this world, but on God. Our Lenten fast, then, becomes a "healing remedy" insofar as it is united with Christ and leads us to deeper reliance on God.

Blessing and Distribution of Ashes

After the Homily, the Priest, standing with hands joined, says:

Linger on **humbly** as the key attitude. Say **God our Father** together.

Raise the voice slightly with **abundance** and **grace**.

Dear brethren (brothers and sisters), let us humbly ask God our Father
that he be pleased to bless with the abundance of his grace
these ashes, which we will put on our heads in penitence.

After a brief prayer in silence, and, with hands extended, he continues:

Pause after **O God**. Raise the voice slightly and pause after **humility**. Stress **forgiveness**. Speak the petition **lend your merciful ear . . .** with energy, stressing **merciful**. Emphasize and pause after **kindness**. Slow down through **grace of your blessing** but do not pause until **servants**. The Sign of the Cross is made over the ashes (the grace will be poured upon the people through the sign of the ashes). Pause after **that**. Raise the voice and slow down for **minds made pure**. Primary emphasis is given to **Paschal Mystery**.

O God, who are moved by acts of humility
and respond with forgiveness to works of penance,
lend your merciful ear to our prayers
and in your kindness pour out the grace of your ✠ blessing
on your servants who are marked with these ashes,
that, as they follow the Lenten observances,
they may be worthy to come with minds made pure
to celebrate the Paschal Mystery of your Son.
Through Christ our Lord.
R. Amen.

Blessing and Distribution of Ashes: Humility is the key both in the introduction and in the prayer. The Latin for "abundance" (*ubertas*) comes from the word for breast (*uber*). God's grace nourishes us as an infant ("Oh, that you may suck fully of the milk of her comfort, / That you may nurse with delight at her abundant breasts!" [Isaiah 66:11]), but we must admit our helplessnesses as freely as an infant, too. Such "acts of humility" move God to come near us (the Latin for "are moved" is *flecteris,* meaning to bend down). God is eager to forgive and heal if we but show any sign of repentance ("works of penance"). The introduction states that the ashes will be blessed and they are afterward sprinkled with holy water, but the blessing names the faithful, "your servants," as the recipients of the "grace of blessing." The ashes are the means for the real blessing given to God's people. The purpose of the blessing (i.e., with being marked with ashes) is to "purify our minds"—the goal of the time of Lent, so that we may celebrate the Paschal Mystery worthily at Easter Time. We "celebrate" that Mystery most worthily when it is alive in our daily living. Our "acts of humility" and "works of penance" serve to unite us to the dying of Christ so that we may come to share in his rising as well.

Conversion is the main theme of Lent, both as preparation for Baptism and renewal of it. The prayer names God as desirous of conversion. The signs that we can give of such a conversion are the acknowledgment of our lowliness ("we are but ashes") and our "steadfast observance

Or:

O God, who desire not the death of sinners,
but their conversion,
mercifully hear our prayers
and in your kindness be pleased to bless ✠ these ashes,
which we intend to receive upon our heads,
that we, who acknowledge we are but ashes
and shall return to dust,
may, through a steadfast observance of Lent,
gain pardon for sins and newness of life
after the likeness of your Risen Son.
Who lives and reigns for ever and ever.
R. Amen.

Raise the voice slightly with **death**. Pause briefly after **sinners**. Emphasize **conversion**. Stress **mercifully**. Do not pause long after **prayers**. Pause after **and** to put **in your kindness** together. Stress **but ashes** and **dust**. Keep the parallel rhythm between **pardon for sins** and **newness of life**. Draw out **likeness** and **Risen**.

of Lent" (the Latin has "zeal for lenten exertions"). Our "work" is to acknowledge and be zealous—the difference in the Latin is important, because it makes clear that we do not "gain pardon" and "newness" as the result of our successful "observance of Lent" but rather by the "zeal" of our observance. The key is desire for God, not achievement. The latter belongs to God alone. Actually, the "pardon" and "newness" are dependent on God's "merciful" hearing and "blessing" of the ashes. By admitting, however, our lowly status (dust and ashes), we open ourselves to his mercy and blessing, so that we may be raised to the glorious "likeness" of Christ, who has glorified our "dust" in his Resurrection. Although the word "likeness" recalls the original creation of man in the "image and likeness" of God, the prayer proclaims that this likeness is "newness" of life. The Resurrection does not merely restore us to the state of Adam and Eve, but raises us to a yet closer divine "likeness."

FIRST SUNDAY OF LENT

Collect

Proclaim **Grant** with authority yet reverence. Give emphasis to **holy Lent**. Raise the voice with **riches** and pause briefly before continuing with equal energy for **hidden in Christ**. Speak **worthy conduct** soberly and pause. Go slowly with **pursue their effects**.

Grant, almighty God,
through the yearly observances of holy Lent,
that we may grow in understanding
of the riches hidden in Christ
and by worthy conduct pursue their effects.
Through our Lord Jesus Christ, your Son,
who lives and reigns with you in the unity of the Holy Spirit,
one God, for ever and ever.

Prayer over the Offerings

Speak **right dispositions** slowly and distinctly, pausing briefly before and after **O Lord, we pray**. Keep the voice raised, coming down only with **offerings**. Pause after **them** and stress **beginning**, **venerable**, and **sacred time**.

Give us the right dispositions, O Lord, we pray,
to make these offerings,
for with them we celebrate the beginning
of this venerable and sacred time.
Through Christ our Lord.

Prayer after Communion

Speak **renewed** with energy. Raise the voice equally for **heavenly**. Proclaim the three couplets with a measure of rhythm: gentle with the first, energetic with the second, and steadfast with the third. Pause after **O Lord** and **learn**. Speak the line as a plea. Sound a note of longing with **to hunger for Christ**. Emphasize and pause after **true**. Be strong for **living**. Show energy with **strive to live**. Stress **every**. Slow and distinct for **which proceeds from your mouth**.

Renewed now with heavenly bread,
by which faith is nourished, hope increased,
and charity strengthened,
we pray, O Lord,
that we may learn to hunger for Christ,
the true and living Bread,
and strive to live by every word
which proceeds from your mouth.
Through Christ our Lord.

Prayer over the People

Stress and pause after **bountiful blessing**. Speak **O Lord, we pray**, together. Pause after **hope**. Stress **may grow**. Pause after **virtue**. Stress **be strengthened**. Without pausing, emphasize **eternal redemption**.

May bountiful blessing, O Lord, we pray,
come down upon your people,
that hope may grow in tribulation,
virtue be strengthened in temptation,
and eternal redemption be assured.
Through Christ our Lord.

Collect: The first word communicates clearly that all things lie in God's power to "grant." God is asked to "grant" two requests. First, "to grow in understanding of the riches hidden in Christ" and second, to "pursue their effects" in our lives. To grow in understanding is also to grow in appreciation of the work that Christ has done to foster in us a greater attitude of gratitude and reverence. Our "worthy conduct" (*conversatio*—which means a conversion of morals) is not of our doing, but the result of what Christ has done in us. The prayer names Lent as a "holy" time. More literally, the Latin has "exercises of the Lenten sacrament/mystery." This brings out more directly the participation of Lent in the Paschal Mystery of Jesus, as well as the hard work (exercises) to which we are called. The "hidden riches" of Christ is a reminder that there is more to reality than what meets the eye. The flesh of Christ was the sacrament of his divinity. Behind the symbols of our Sacraments we can experience hidden riches of spirit and life, and of divinity.

Prayer over the Offerings: To understand the "right dispositions" to have, we must remember that the context of this prayer is the First Sunday of Lent, which is the beginning of Lent proper. Our attitude, then, must be Lenten, which was explained in the Collect as plunging deeper into the hidden riches of Christ's mystery and seeking to change one's life to be in accord with Christ. It is important to note that our work consists in "disposing" ourselves for what God will do. This is an essential action of the Christian. "These offerings" are the

Pointed Text

Collect

A Grant, almighty God,
through the yearly observances of holy **Lent**,
B that we may grow in understanding
of the riches hid**den** in Christ
C and by worthy conduct pursue their ef***fects***.
Through our Lord Jesus Christ, your Son,
who lives and reigns with you in the unity of the Holy Spirit,
one God, for ever and ever.

Prayer over the Offerings

B Give us the right dispositions, O Lord, we pray,
to make these **of**ferings,
C for with them we celebrate the beginning
of this venerable and sacred ***time***.
Through Christ our Lord.

Prayer after Communion

A Renewed now with heavenly bread,
by which faith is nourished, hope increased,
and charity streng**thened**,
B we pray, O Lord,
that we may learn to hunger for Christ,
the true and **liv**ing Bread,
C and strive to live by every word
which proceeds from your ***mouth***.
Through Christ our Lord.

The space below is for your notes.

Refer to pages viii–x for an explanation of the pointing of the chants and to page xii for the Tones for the Presidential Prayers from *The Roman Missal.*

symbol of our inner dispositions. Through the Eucharistic Prayer, they will be wholly conformed to the mystery that is Christ. The more we offer ourselves through them, the more we, too, will share in that conformation. Lent is both venerable and sacred as the ancient way of preparing our hearts for the Triduum and the Easter celebrations. It is the time to renew our baptismal promises and deepen our commitment to renouncing whatever remains of sin and to opening our lives more fully to the gift of the Holy Spirit.

Prayer after Communion: The three theological virtues, without which one cannot have the life of God, are mentioned as gifts received through reception of Holy Communion. This connects the reception of Communion with receiving the life of God (John 6:53–57). The three foundational pillars of the Chrisitan life are fostered in the Eucharist. The fasting of Lent is ultimately intended to lead us to hunger for Christ, who is the most satisfying food of all. As the Word of the Father, he is "every word that comes forth from the mouth of God" (Matthew 4:4). Nowhere does the prayer imply that the Communion received is satisfying in a physical way. To the contrary, this "heavenly bread" both renews or refreshes and at the same time awakens deeper desires for fulfillment. Saint Augustine wrote that, by desiring, our capacity for God is enlarged. This Communion stirs up desire, or "hunger," for Christ, thereby serving to stretch our heart. Our work is to "strive," while having the proper disposition. Christ will fill us, then, with truth and life.

Bring out the accent on **be** in **The Lord be with you.** In the next phrase, make a strong accent on **Lift**, and slow both notes of **hearts**. In the third dialogue, move to the word **thanks** before accenting, and hold that word slightly to give it emphasis. Broaden both notes of **Lord**, and hold **God**.

Sing this proclamation cursively in a reciting tone. In **salvation**, do not hold **-va**; only broaden the two notes slightly. Hold **-tion**. Slightly broaden and clearly enunciate **always** and **everywhere**. The accent of the phrase falls on **thanks**, which should be held briefly. In the next part, clearly make four phrases of the text, by respecting the commas after **Lord**, **Father**, and **God**.

At the end of the first phrase, hold **food** only briefly but continue with **he consecrated**. Hold **fast**. Without taking a breath, continue with **the pattern**. Broaden **Lenten observance**, holding the last syllable. Slight pause at **and** to bring out the sense of the coming phrase. Hold briefly **-pent** of **serpent**, but do not pause there, rather continue with the sense by going on to **taught us**.

Slight pause at **that**. Broaden the text at **Paschal Mystery**. Do not hold that last syllable long, because the sense calls for continuing with **we might pass**. Broaden the **-ternal paschal feast**, pausing and taking a breath there.

Preface: The Temptation of the Lord
Jesus is the new Adam. The first Adam rejected a life of dependence on "every word that comes from the mouth of God" (Matthew 4:4), believing rather that his life could be dependent on bread alone. Jesus begins his ministry by keeping the fast that Adam broke. In doing this, Jesus reestablished the "pattern" of salvation as dependence on God. Christ taught us to overturn the snares of the devil by the manner of his fasting and by his use of God's word. Leaven acts as a corrupting agent, which is why leavened bread (or fermented wine) was never allowed to touch the altar in the Jewish Temple, because no agent of corruption should have contact with the altar of the living God. Malice is singled out as a corrupting vice. In 1 Corinthians 5:8, Saint Paul contrasts it with "sincerity." The devil is a liar (John 8:44) and tempts us by posing half-truths to lead us to despair. In the ancient world, to bake leavened bread involved continuity with the past (dough from a previous loaf would be kneaded in the new loaf—thus, guaranteeing the presence of leaven), hard work (it was necessary to knead the dough) and patience (waiting for it to rise). On the other hand, dough without leaven represents haste, a break with the past, simplicity, inactivity, powerlessness (inability to rise) and a lack of labor (no kneading). In 1 Corinthians 5:7–8, Saint Paul is speaking in the negative, which is why he invokes the unleavened image. He asks us to fast from wickedness and remember the oppression of our sinful past, just as Israel is called to do in the Passover. In a number of biblical

Pause slightly after **And so**. Respect the commas, but try to keep this section together, without big breaks for breaths. Broaden the last phrase, especially on **praise**. Slow **we ac-**, and put emphasis on **-claim**, so as to evoke the response **Holy, Holy, Holy . . . .**

Holy, Holy, Holy Lord God of hosts . . .

Text without music:

V. **The Lord be with you.**
R. And with your spirit.

V. **Lift up your hearts.**
R. We lift them up to the Lord.

V. **Let us give thanks to the Lord our God.**
R. It is right and just.

It is truly right and just, our duty and our salvation,
always and everywhere to give you thanks,
Lord, holy Father, almighty and eternal God,
through Christ our Lord.

Emphasize **truly**, **duty**, and **salvation**.

By abstaining forty long days from earthly food,
he consecrated through his fast
the pattern of our Lenten observance
and, by overturning all the snares of the ancient serpent,
taught us to cast out the leaven of malice,
so that, celebrating worthily the Paschal Mystery,
we might pass over at last to the eternal paschal feast.

And so, with the company of Angels and Saints,
we sing the hymn of your praise,
as without end we acclaim:

Holy, Holy, Holy Lord God of hosts . . .

Speak **forty long days** slowly and deliberately. Emphasize **consecrated**. Stress and pause after **pattern**. Raise the voice on **our** to communicate what we must do. Pause after **and**. Speak **snares of the ancient serpent** with a measure of disdain. Raise the voice for **cast out** and put more emphasis on **malice** than on **leaven**. Without pausing after **so that**, draw out **worthily the Paschal Mystery**. Be deliberate in pronouncing **pass over**. Raise the voice with **eternal**. Be hopeful with **paschal feast**.

passages, leaven is used as a symbol for wickedness and sin (because of its connection with decay). We maintain the use of unleavened bread in the Eucharist for the biblical symbolism of purity and the call to break from sin. It is a sign of ourselves needing to be emptied of wickedness in order to be transformed into Christ through the invocation of the Holy Spirit during the Eucharistic Prayer. In this Preface, there is also a wonderful word play on "Paschal," a Hebrew word that is also translated as "Passover." If we celebrate worthily the "Paschal" (Passover) Mystery, then we, too, can "pass over" with Christ—who passed over from death to life—and reach the eternal "paschal" (Passover) feast, where the life to which Christ has passed over will be our food.

SECOND SUNDAY OF LENT

Pause after **O God**. Speak **commanded** with authority, pausing after **us**. Emphasize **listen** and **beloved Son**. Speak **inwardly by your word** with reverence. Pause briefly after **that**. Proclaim **spiritual sight made pure** with strong desire. Speak **may rejoice** with some energy and **behold your glory** with awe.

Collect

O God, who have commanded us
to listen to your beloved Son,
be pleased, we pray,
to nourish us inwardly by your word,
that, with spiritual sight made pure,
we may rejoice to behold your glory.
Through our Lord Jesus Christ, your Son,
who lives and reigns with you in the unity of the Holy Spirit,
one God, for ever and ever.

Pause after **sacrifice** and again after **we pray**. Proclaim **cleanse** with confident pleading. Proclaim **sanctify** with confident joy. Pause briefly after **faithful** and again after **mind**. Emphasize **paschal** with reverence.

Prayer over the Offerings

May this sacrifice, O Lord, we pray,
cleanse us of our faults
and sanctify your faithful in body and mind
for the celebration of the paschal festivities.
Through Christ our Lord.

Raise the voice and draw out **glorious**. The second line is oriented toward **to you, O Lord**. Without pausing after **allowing us**, dip the voice and change the pace a bit for **while still on earth**. Stress **partakers** and **things of heaven**.

Prayer after Communion

As we receive these glorious mysteries,
we make thanksgiving to you, O Lord,
for allowing us while still on earth
to be partakers even now of the things of heaven.
Through Christ our Lord.

Speak gently, yet linger on **Bless**. Pause after **faithful**. Raise the voice on **blessing**. Stress **for ever**. Pause after **Gospel** and **always desire**. Draw out **always**. Pray **at last attain** with a measure of relieved joy. Speak **that glory** deliberately, then pause. Raise the voice with **beauty**. Do not drop voice on **Body**. Do not overdo **to the amazement of his Apostles**.

Prayer over the People

Bless your faithful, we pray, O Lord,
with a blessing that endures for ever,
and keep them faithful
to the Gospel of your Only Begotten Son,
so that they may always desire and at last attain
that glory whose beauty he showed in his own Body,
to the amazement of his Apostles.
Through Christ our Lord.

Collect: This Collect is inspired by the accounts of the Transfiguration, in which the voice of the Father named Jesus as his "beloved Son" and "commanded" Peter, James, and John to "listen" to him. The Collect proclaims that the words of the Father were addressed to "us," who must always be students in relation to Jesus. The heart of the prayer is the petition to be nourished "inwardly by your word." Notice the parallel between "your beloved Son" and "your word." The more we are pastured on the word of God, the more our conversion and growth are effected. This is about transformation—one might say "transfiguration." The purification of "spiritual sight" means the removal of all obstacles that hinder us from seeing the purity that is God—in other words, the removal of all worldly attachments until we are attached not even to our earthly life but to God alone. The "work" which we do in this prayer is all receptivity: listen, be nourished, be made pure, rejoice, and behold. We are to let the glory of Christ purify us and transform us into his likeness.

Prayer over the Offerings: The imagery of "sacrifice" calls to mind the Old Testament sacrifices "that can never take away sins" (Hebrews 10:11), but also the sacrifice of Christ, which fulfills them (Hebrews 10:12). In the sacrifice of Christ, his shed blood "cleanse(s) us of our faults" (Revelation 7:14). "This" sacrifice will be consecrated (offered) in the Eucharistic Prayer. In the Communion banquet that follows, the faithful will be both cleansed by the Body of Christ ("we have been consecrated through the offering of the body

Pointed Text

Collect

A O God, who have commanded us
to listen to your beloved **Son**,
B be pleased, we pray,
to nourish us inwardly **by** your word,
C that, with spiritual sight made pure,
we may rejoice to behold your glo***ry***.
Through our Lord Jesus Christ, your Son,
who lives and reigns with you in the unity of the Holy Spirit,
one God, for ever and ever.

Prayer over the Offerings

A May this sacrifice, O Lord, we **pray**,
B cleanse us of our faults
and sanctify your faithful in bo**dy** and mind
C for the celebration of the paschal festi***vi***ties.
Through Christ our Lord.

Prayer after Communion

B As we receive these glorious mysteries,
we make thanksgiving to **you**, O Lord,
C for allowing us while still on earth
to be partakers even now of the things of hea***ven***.
Through Christ our Lord.

The space below is for your notes.

Refer to pages viii–x for an explanation of the pointing of the chants and to page xii for the Tones for the Presidential Prayers from *The Roman Missal*.

of Jesus" [Hebrews 10:10]), and sanctified, made holy, by the blood of Christ ("you who once were far off have become near by the blood of Christ"; [Ephesians 2:13]). To become holy means to be set apart for God. In Christ's blood, the faithful have drawn near to God; they have been set apart from this world. This twofold action of cleansing from faults and sanctifying for relationship is what enables the faithful to join in Christ's Paschal festivities of passing over from death into eternal life.

Prayer after Communion: That "we receive . . . glorious mysteries" into ourselves is amazing. What makes them "glorious" is the working of the Holy Spirit who has transubstantiated the bread and wine into "these glorious mysteries." Glory is an experience that lifts one higher, nearer to God. The reception of Holy Communion fills us with the life of God, which changes us if we let it. Such a gift fills us with thanksgiving—the Latin expresses this a bit stronger: "We are diligent to return thanks." The experience of Communion impels us, gnaws at us, troubles us until we respond appropriately. This prayer also acknowledges that we share in the heavenly reality, while still belonging to the earth. The prayer highlights that the main "work" of the Christian is to "receive." The "things of heaven" refer to the gifts of the Holy Spirit that are communicated to us through the Sacraments. Notice how the prayer ends in the key of heaven, which is where every good prayer should take us. Many of the Prayers after Communion finish with an eschatological flourish.

Bring out the accent on **be** in **The Lord be with you**. In the next phrase, make a strong accent on **Lift**, and slow both notes of **hearts**. In the third dialogue, move to the word **thanks** before accenting, and hold that word slightly to give it emphasis. Broaden both notes of **Lord** and hold **God**.

Sing this proclamation cursively in a reciting tone. In **salvation**, do not hold **-va**; only broaden the two notes slightly. Hold **-tion**. Slightly broaden and clearly enunciate **always** and **everywhere**. The accent of the phrase falls on **thanks**, which should be held briefly. In the next part, clearly make four phrases of the text, by respecting the commas after **Lord**, **Father**, and **God**.

Make a slight lengthening of **Death** and continue without a breath.

Lengthen **-ry** of **glory** and pause briefly. Hold slightly **-ets** of **prophets**. Continue with **that the Passion**. Broaden the phrase **glory of the Resurrection**.

Pause slightly after **And so**. Respect the commas, but try to keep this section together without big breaks for breaths.

Preface: The Transfiguration of the Lord
This Preface boldly proclaims that the Death of Christ was a path to glory and not shameful. It is precisely in Christ's humbling himself by embracing his "coming Death" that the Father shows his approval in the Transfiguration. It is in humility that the power and glory of God can be "manifested." Humility enables God to act. He cannot act with pride, because pride is ultimately empty air. The language implies that this glory that Christ revealed, however, was always with him. In the Transfiguration, the Father simply removes the veil hiding his divinity within the flesh of Christ. In the Eastern Churches, the Transfiguration is seen as an apt icon of the power which acts upon the bread and wine in the Holy Eucharist. On the mountain, the flesh of Christ, ordinary earthly matter, becomes glorified and reveals Jesus as beloved Son of the Father. Similarly, in the Eucharistic Prayer, bread and wine become the glorified Body and Blood of Christ. This Preface and day also powerfully proclaim the unity of the Old and the New Testaments. In other words, everything that happened in the Old Testament was an anticipation of Christ, either explicitly or, at least, in the sense that the Word, who was coming into the world, was the hidden desire behind all other desires that were driving the Old Testament figures. Some people at the time of Christ believed that only the Law was canonical. Jesus reveals clearly on the mount that the prophets are equally inspired. A reflection of this "canonical" prophecy continued in the early Church

Broaden the last phrase, especially on **majesty**. Slow **we ac-**, and put emphasis on **-claim**, so as to evoke the response **Holy, Holy, Holy . . . .**

Holy, Holy, Holy Lord God of hosts . . .

Text without music:

V. **The Lord be with you.**
R. And with your spirit.

V. **Lift up your hearts.**
R. We lift them up to the Lord.

V. **Let us give thanks to the Lord our God.**
R. It is right and just.

Emphasize **truly**, **duty**, and **salvation**.

It is truly right and just, our duty and our salvation,
always and everywhere to give you thanks,
Lord, holy Father, almighty and eternal God,
through Christ our Lord.

Pause after **For**. Emphasize **coming Death** with somber anticipation. Pause briefly after **mountain**. Express the next phrase with amazement, drawing out **glory**. Pause briefly after **to show**. Express some wonder with the phrase **even by . . . .** Parallel **Passion** and **glory**.

For after he had told the disciples of his coming Death,
on the holy mountain he manifested to them his glory,
to show, even by the testimony of the law and the prophets,
that the Passion leads to the glory of the Resurrection.

Pause after **And so**, proclaiming the rest with a hint of excitement and awe.

And so, with the Powers of heaven,
we worship you constantly on earth,
and before your majesty
without end we acclaim:

Holy, Holy, Holy Lord God of hosts . . .

and remains today a valid charism in the Church (1 Corinthians 12:10, 14:22). Prophecy is to proclaim truth about Christ, whether in parable, poem, prose, hymn, or any other variety of media. Christians can only read the Old Testament through the prism of Christ. And the main testimony of the Old Testament, according to the Preface, is that the Passion, the suffering of Christ, leads to glory. The Passion is a necessary prelude for us, because we must be emptied of this world in order to receive God's glory, which is the Holy Spirit. Suffering breaks our ties to earth and reveals the utter lack of power we ultimately have in this life. We, too, cannot skip sharing in the suffering of Christ if we hope to share in his Resurrection.

Prayer over the People: The scriptural background for this prayer is the Transfiguration, which explains the mention of glorious beauty revealed in Christ's own body. It is a good example of how beauty and glory are practically synonymous. The petition of the prayer is actually stronger in the Latin: "make them so adhere to the Gospel." The Latin word for "desire" (*suspirare*) means to sigh and long for. The sense is that being nourished on the Gospel (the Father's voice commanded us to listen to his beloved Son) will instill in us a longing for the glory Christ revealed in the Transfiguration. This is a marvelous insight to preach on because we all desire the beautiful.

THIRD SUNDAY OF LENT

Collect

Pause after **O God**. Stress **every mercy** and **all goodness**. Speak **fasting, prayer and almsgiving** slowly and distinctly. Without pausing, go slower for **graciously**. Proclaim **lowliness** humbly but matter of factly, and the same for the following clause. Raise the voice with **lifted up**.

O God, author of every mercy and of all goodness,
who in fasting, prayer and almsgiving
have shown us a remedy for sin,
look graciously on this confession of our lowliness,
that we, who are bowed down by our conscience,
may always be lifted up by your mercy.
Through our Lord Jesus Christ, your Son,
who lives and reigns with you in the unity of the Holy Spirit,
one God, for ever and ever.

Prayer over the Offerings

Pause briefly after **O Lord** and speak **sacrificial offerings** distinctly. The rhythmic stress of the next line falls on **we**, **beseech pardon**, and **own**. The last line has a two-beat rhythm on **take care** and **neighbor**.

Be pleased, O Lord, with these sacrificial offerings,
and grant that we who beseech pardon for our own sins,
may take care to forgive our neighbor.
Through Christ our Lord. *

Prayer after Communion

Stress **pledge**, **yet hidden**, and **heaven**. With only a brief pause after **heaven**, stress **are nourished** and proclaim **still on earth** deliberately. Do not pause until after **on high**. Give strong emphasis to **in mystery** and parallel that with **true completion**.

As we receive the pledge
of things yet hidden in heaven
and are nourished while still on earth
with the Bread that comes from on high,
we humbly entreat you, O Lord,
that what is being brought about in us in mystery
may come to true completion.
Through Christ our Lord.

Prayer over the People

Pause briefly after **Direct**. Speak **O Lord, we pray** together. Place the emphasis on **hearts**. Speak **kindness** with great gentleness, pausing briefly and continuing with the same gentle tone. Pause briefly after **abiding**. Stress **you** and **neighbor**. Raise the voice and linger a bit on **whole**.

Direct, O Lord, we pray, the hearts of your faithful,
and in your kindness grant your servants this grace:
that, abiding in the love of you and their neighbor,
they may fulfill the whole of your commands.
Through Christ our Lord.

* When the Gospel from Year A is not read, use either Preface I or II of Lent in the Order of Mass. Commentary, and proclamation and chant tips, for the Preface can be found at *www.StudyThePresidentialTexts.com/Prefaces* and in *The Order of Mass: A Roman Missal Study Edition and Workbook*, pages 36–39.

Collect: The word "author" is related to authority and authoritative. Mercy and goodness are "character traits," so to speak, for God. It is in the divine nature to be merciful, and "goodness" is one of the four transcendentals (along with truth, beauty, and oneness) that likewise belong to God. Every act of mercy or goodness that we may encounter in the world is a reflection of the divine nature of God. The three "remedies" for sin go hand in hand: fasting empties us to receive and reveals our dependence on God; prayer fosters the one essential relationship in our lives, invoking God's grace to fill our emptiness; and almsgiving consecrates our fasting and prayer as for others and, therefore, of God. A crucial aspect of being Christian is to be convicted of our sinfulness and fallen nature. The Blessed Mother proclaimed her "lowliness" and in the same breath how God's favor on her lowliness has made her blessed for all ages. When we embrace the truth of fallen humanity (revealed in our fasting), the God "of every mercy" responds graciously by raising us up.

Prayer over the Offerings: The Prayer over the Offerings is preparation for the "marvelous exchange" that occurs in the Eucharistic Prayer wherein the "sacrificial offerings" that we bring are united with the one great sacrifice of Christ and given to the Father, who, in turn, blesses them and returns them to us as the Body and Blood of his Son. The reason why the Lord can "be pleased" with what we bring is because we join ourselves and our offerings to Christ. The prayer also mentions another "exchange" that needs God's

Pointed Text

Collect

A O God, author of every mercy and of all goodness,
who in fasting, prayer and almsgiving
have shown us a remedy for **sin**,
B look graciously on this confession **of** our lowliness,
C that we, who are bowed down by our conscience,
may always be lifted up by your mer***cy***.
Through our Lord Jesus Christ, your Son,
who lives and reigns with you in the unity of the Holy Spirit,
one God, for ever and ever.

Prayer over the Offerings

A Be pleased, O Lord, with these sacrificial of**fer**ings,
B and grant that we who beseech pardon for **our** own sins,
C may take care to forgive our neigh***bor***.
Through Christ our Lord.

Prayer after Communion

A As we receive the pledge
of things yet hidden in heaven
and are nourished while still on earth
with the Bread that comes from on **high**,
B we humbly entreat **you**, O Lord,
C that what is being brought about in us in mystery
may come to true comple***tion***.
Through Christ our Lord.

The space below is for your notes.

Refer to pages viii–x for an explanation of the pointing of the chants and to page xii for the Tones for the Presidential Prayers from *The Roman Missal*.

blessing to be fruitful: as we receive pardon, we are empowered to forgive. The verb for "take care" means to be zealous for (*studeamus*). It calls to mind the sinful woman who washes the feet of Jesus with her tears. Her many sins are forgiven, which is why she is able to love "greatly." To show mercy, we must first be shown mercy. Children who never hear their parents seek forgiveness decide that they must be perfect and never learn the freedom of confessing faults and receiving forgiveness.

Prayer after Communion: The "pledge" is not the same as the "Bread . . . from on high." The former refers to the gift of the Holy Spirit, who is given to us in Baptism. In the world, however, the Spirit always seems to work sacramentally—at least in relation to flesh and blood human beings. Thus, the Spirit is received through the Sacrament of the Eucharist, the "Bread . . . from on high," which is Christ, risen and glorified in the Spirit. We are nourished by the Eucharist, through which the Spirit gives us a promise and even a foretaste of the glory of Christ that is still "hidden in heaven." The petition of the prayer seeks the "completion" of the pledge. Faith in God's word is what gives us hope that our pledge will be completed. The gift of the Holy Spirit that we already enjoy is nothing compared to being fully penetrated by that Spirit in the way that Christ is with the Resurrection. Even the charismatic gifts of the Spirit cannot compare with the impact of the Spirit on God's people when we are fully opened to the "mystery" that is now only beginning to act in us.

Bring out the accent on **be** in **The Lord be with you.** In the next phrase, make a strong accent on **Lift**, and slow both notes of **hearts**. In the third dialogue, move to the word **thanks** before accenting, and hold that word slightly to give it emphasis. Broaden both notes of **Lord**, and hold **God**.

Sing this proclamation cursively in a reciting tone. In **salvation**, do not hold **-va**; only broaden the two notes slightly. Hold **-tion**. Slightly broaden and clearly enunciate **always** and **everywhere**. The accent of the phrase falls on **thanks**, which should be held briefly.

At the end of the first phrase, hold **drink** slightly, and then continue without a break to **he had**. Hold **her** and pause briefly.

Hold **faith** slightly at the end of the next phrase, and then continue without a breath or break to **that he**.

Broaden **the fire of divine love**.

Slight pause after **And so**. Respect the commas, but try to keep the section together, without big breaks for breaths. Broaden the last phrase, especially on **praise**. Slow **we ac-**, and put emphasis on **-claim**, so as to

Preface: The Samaritan Woman
The patriarchs in Genesis were constantly digging wells. Moments of grace occur beside living wells, and moments of treachery beside dry wells. Genesis 16: God speaks to Hagar and encourages her at a well. Genesis 21: God points out a well to Hagar and her son Ishmael, saving them from death. Genesis 21: Abraham makes an oath of peace with his neighbors at a well. Genesis 24: Rebekah, the future wife of Isaac, is first met at a well. Genesis 26: the Philistines, the enemies of Israel, fill up all the wells of Abraham; a few verses later, Isaac reopens all the wells; and Isaac makes the same oath of peace with his neighbors by a well. Genesis 29: Jacob meets Rachel at a well. Genesis 37: Joseph is thrown into an "empty and dry" well to await being sold into slavery. These verses chronicle the thirst within human beings. The well is always a symbol of the divine wellspring. That is why the Philistines seek to fill them up—to cut off Isaac from his divine source. That is why an act of treachery to Joseph can only occur beside a well that is empty and dry. If we go through all of Scripture in search of wells, we reach the Gospel accounts. There we find the well beside which the Savior was resting, wearied by his journey, when a Samaritan woman came to draw water from it. It is beside the well that he waits for us. In the very places where we go to quench our thirst, he is present, and waits. Beside all the "wells" of our life, all the places where we go to find relief (bars, malls, sporting events, etc.), the Savior sits, asking us to satisfy our thirst by responding to his gift of faith. In the

Holy, Holy, Holy Lord God of hosts . . .

evoke the response **Holy, Holy, Holy . . . .**

Text without music:

V. **The Lord be with you.**
R. And with your spirit.

V. **Lift up your hearts.**
R. We lift them up to the Lord.

V. **Let us give thanks to the Lord our God.**
R. It is right and just.

It is truly right and just, our duty and our salvation,
always and everywhere to give you thanks,
Lord, holy Father, almighty and eternal God,
through Christ our Lord.

Emphasize **truly**, **duty**, and **salvation**.

For when he asked the Samaritan woman for water to drink,
he had already created the gift of faith within her
and so ardently did he thirst for her faith,
that he kindled in her the fire of divine love.

And so we, too, give you thanks
and with the Angels
praise your mighty deeds, as we acclaim:

Holy, Holy, Holy Lord God of hosts . . .

Pause after **For**. Proclaim **already created** and **gift of faith** as couplets with deliberate emphasis. Proclaim **ardently** with a bit of fire, **thirst** with a bit of desire and keep the voice slightly raised with **faith**. Stress **he** in contrast to **her**. Proclaim **fire of divine love** with energy and wonder. Pause after **And so**, proclaiming the rest with a hint of excitement and awe.

Preface, faith is not something that humans can create on their own. We cannot believe in one who has not revealed himself to us; but, once revealed, the gift must be embraced. This is why Christ "thirsts" for the faith, which he himself has created. Notice the play in the description of Christ "ardently" thirsting. He burns for water (faith) and then "kindles" the "fire of divine love." In accepting the gift of faith, we come to know the Lord. Deeper knowledge can lead to deeper love. Christ creates the gift of faith, which must be accepted, and he kindles the fire of divine love, which must be nurtured.

Prayer over the People: The petition to "direct" our hearts is an act of faith in both God's goodness and his wisdom. Morality is not something that can be voted on. Our task is to learn the nature that is given in our hearts and then to act in accord with that nature that has been given to us by God. We also have been given free will, and can choose what is good and is of our nature or decide on what is contrary to our nature, for example, to strike out against our neighbor. But to do this would lead us to frustration and vanity. "Abiding" in love comes from Jesus's command in the Gospel of John, a twofold command that begins with God and finds completion in the rest of creation. Our love will be rightly formed when it goes first to God.

FOURTH SUNDAY OF LENT

In this Mass, the color violet or rose is used. Instrumental music is permitted, and the altar may be decorated with flowers.

On this Sunday is celebrated the second scrutiny in preparation for the Baptism of the catechumens who are to be admitted to the Sacraments of Christian Initiation at the Easter Vigil.

Collect

Pause after **God** and **Word**. Stress **reconcile** and **yourself** and draw out **wonderful way**. Proclaim **prompt devotion** and eager **faith** with a parallel rhythm, pausing after **faith**. Speak **hasten** with energy, pausing only briefly before continuing. Proclaim **solemn celebrations** slowly and reverently.

O God, who through your Word
reconcile the human race to yourself in a wonderful way,
grant, we pray,
that with prompt devotion and eager faith
the Christian people may hasten
toward the solemn celebrations to come.
Through our Lord Jesus Christ, your Son,
who lives and reigns with you in the unity of the Holy Spirit,
one God, for ever and ever.

Prayer over the Offerings

Gentle emphasis on **with joy** (and a smile!) will capture the spirit of this prayer. Proclaim **eternal remedy** with joyful relief. Place emphasis on **faithfully** and keep the voice raised with **revere them**. Have only a hint of a pause after **to you** and more of a pause after **as is fitting**, keeping the voice again from dropping until the last clause **for the salvation of all the world**.

We place before you with joy these offerings,
which bring eternal remedy, O Lord,
praying that we may both faithfully revere them
and present them to you, as is fitting,
for the salvation of all the world.
Through Christ our Lord. *

* When the Gospel from Year A is not read, use either Preface I or II of Lent in the Order of Mass. Commentary, and proclamation and chant tips, for the Preface can be found at *www.StudyThePresidentialTexts.com/Prefaces* and in *The Order of Mass: A Roman Missal Study Edition and Workbook*, pages 36–39.

Collect: The scriptural background to this prayer is 2 Corinthians 5, in which Saint Paul writes of the "ministry of reconciliation" that God has entrusted to him and the other Apostles. There, Saint Paul states that God reconciled the world to himself through "Christ." The prayer changes Christ to "your Word" (*Verbum tuum*). In verse 19, Paul notes that the "message of reconciliation" has been entrusted to him. The Vulgate has *verbum reconciliationis*. Today's Preface mentions the "mystery of the incarnation" that has led the "human race" out of darkness. in Latin, the prayer literally states that God "worked" (*operaris*) the reconciliation of the human race. This is the *opus Dei*, the work of God, and we are ministers and messengers of it to others. The Collect continues, asking that all Christians may respond to this message "with prompt devotion and eager faith." Devotion means with personal investment, and faith means total investment. A true faith act is an act of the whole person, mind, heart, and body.

Prayer over the Offerings: The word for "joy" (*laetantes*) is a public, communal type of joy. We journey toward Easter and the renewal of baptismal faith as a Church, and our salvation comes to us as a Church. We cannot find reconciliation or healing apart from belonging to the Body of Christ. The "offerings" (*munera*) refer to the gifts of bread and wine, but more importantly to the lives of all those gathered. These lives will be blessed and united to the Body of Christ and, when given back to us, they bring the "eternal remedy" which is recon-

The space below is for your notes.

Refer to pages viii–x for an explanation of the pointing of the chants and to page xii for the Tones for the Presidential Prayers from *The Roman Missal*.

Pointed Text

Collect

A O God, who through your Word
reconcile the human race to yourself in a wonderful **way**,
B grant, we pray,
that with prompt devotion and **ea**ger faith
C the Christian people may hasten
toward the solemn celebrations to ***come***.
Through our Lord Jesus Christ, your Son,
who lives and reigns with you in the unity of the Holy Spirit,
one God, for ever and ever.

Prayer over the Offerings

A We place before you with joy these offerings,
which bring eternal remedy, O **Lord**,
B praying that we may both faithfully revere them
and present them to you, **as** is fitting,
C for the salvation of all the ***world***.
Through Christ our Lord.

ciliation/healing and communion with Christ. The Real Presence of Christ in these gifts is what prompts us to "revere them." The Latin prays that God will "perfect us" (*perficias*) by bringing us to revere them and then to "present them" to God "for the salvation of the world." Our healing must always reach out to the rest of the Body of Christ to whom we are intricately connected. Giving ourselves away—as God does in Christ—is our salvation. We give ourselves first to God and then, with his blessing, to all others we meet.

Bring out the accent on **be** in **The Lord be with you.** In the next phrase, make a strong accent on **Lift**, and slow both notes of **hearts**. In the third dialogue, move to the word **thanks** before accenting, and hold that word slightly to give it emphasis. Broaden both notes of **Lord** and hold **God**.

Sing this proclamation cursively in a reciting tone. In **salvation**, do not hold **-va**; only broaden the two notes slightly. Hold **-tion**. Slightly broaden and clearly enunciate **always** and **everywhere**. The accent of the phrase falls on **thanks**, which should be held briefly.

Do not hold or pause at **Incarnation**, but rather continue with **he has**. If possible, do not hold or pause at **darkness** but rather complete the sense/phrase by continuing with **into**. Articulate carefully the three syllables of **radiance**, and broaden **of the faith**, pausing slightly there. Hold **sin** at the end of the next phrase, but continue with **through** without a break. Similarly, try to hold together **regeneration** (while holding slightly the last syllable) and **to make**. Broaden **adopted children** and hold the last syllable before taking a breath.

Preface: The Man Born Blind

Before the Incarnation, there was a separation between God and humanity. All the events, symbols, and sacrifices of the Old Testament were unable to penetrate the interior of humanity. We could draw close to God, but never participate in his eternal life. The flood washed the surface of the earth, but the heart of man remained in sin until the Incarnation and the waters of Baptism cleansed us from within. The animal sacrifices were only a foreshadowing, perpetually renewed, until the sacrifice of Christ came that actually took away sin. With the Incarnation, a door is made wherein we enter the life of the Trinity through the flesh of Christ; or one could also say that the life of the Trinity entered our humanity. Nowhere in the Old Testament does anyone claim to be a temple of the Holy Spirit until Christ. The "radiance" that shines with faith refers to the experience of realizing that our life is shaped by, and finds ultimate meaning in, Christ. All our human aspirations suddenly make sense in Christ, the true man, and our grasping for meaning (walking in darkness) finds it. Through the Incarnation, we realize the extent of our former slavery, that our strivings were ultimately exercises in frustration. Saint Paul tells us that in light of the surpassing riches found in Christ, everything he had done before Christ was so much rubbish. The "ancient sin" refers to Adam and Eve's act of choosing themselves over God. The devil had tempted them to believe that their lives depended on "bread alone," which could make them equal to God and without need of him. We

Holy, Holy, Holy Lord God of hosts . . .

Slow **ac**- and put emphasis on -**claim**, so as to evoke the response **Holy, Holy, Holy . . . .**

Text without music:

V. **The Lord be with you.**
R. And with your spirit.

V. **Lift up your hearts.**
R. We lift them up to the Lord.

V. **Let us give thanks to the Lord our God.**
R. It is right and just.

It is truly right and just, our duty and our salvation,
always and everywhere to give you thanks,
Lord, holy Father, almighty and eternal God,
through Christ our Lord.

Emphasize **truly**, **duty**, and **salvation**.

By the mystery of the Incarnation,
he has led the human race that walked in darkness
into the radiance of the faith
and has brought those born in slavery to ancient sin
through the waters of regeneration
to make them your adopted children.

Pause at the end of the first two lines. Proclaim **radiance** with energy, drawing out the first syllable. Pause briefly after **those** and again after **sin**. Keep the voice raised with **regeneration**, pausing briefly before continuing. Stress **your**.

Therefore, all creatures of heaven and earth
sing a new song in adoration,
and we, with all the host of Angels,
cry out, and without end acclaim:

Holy, Holy, Holy Lord God of hosts . . .

are all born into this sin. Our lives are turned in on ourselves. We tend to see things from a rather self-centered perspective. Infants and young children are completely centered on themselves and cry whenever their will is frustrated (what makes them beautiful is not their "innocence" but their total dependence on others for survival). Through the waters of regeneration (Baptism), we are born anew as adopted children of the heavenly Father. In this new birth, we come to life not centered on ourselves, but on the other. As children of God by grace alone, we, too, realize our total dependence on our heavenly Father. The Christian life is marked by interdependence (it is communal) and by selflessness (it desires to give itself away).

Prayer after Communion

Pause after **O God**. Give emphasis to **everyone**, pausing briefly. Stress both **illuminate** and **hearts**. Do not pause until after **we pray**. Proclaim **splendor** with energy, and **grace** with tenderness. Pause briefly after **ponder**. Place emphasis on **worthy** and **pleasing**. Pause briefly after **love you** and proclaim **all sincerity** slowly and distinctly.

O God, who enlighten everyone who comes into this world,
illuminate our hearts, we pray,
with the splendor of your grace,
that we may always ponder
what is worthy and pleasing to your majesty
and love you in all sincerity.
Through Christ our Lord.

Prayer over the People

Pause briefly after **O Lord**. Speak **sustain the weak** with compassion. Stress **life** and proclaim **unfailing light** slowly and confidently. Pause hardly at all after **light** and stress **walk** and **shadow**. Speak **shadow of death** with sobriety. Proclaim **rescued by your mercy** with joyful relief. Pause briefly after **bring those**, then continue steadily until **every evil**. Raise the voice with hope for **highest good**.

Look upon those who call to you, O Lord,
and sustain the weak;
give life by your unfailing light
to those who walk in the shadow of death,
and bring those rescued by your mercy from every evil
to reach the highest good.
Through Christ our Lord.

Prayer after Communion: "Everyone" (*hominem*) refers to "man" in the generic sense. Christ is the true man "who comes into the world" (John 1:9). His coming was "enlightened" by the Holy Spirit, who made it possible for him to come to light in the Incarnation, in his ministry, and in his Resurrection. Every step of his incarnate life was filled with the radiance of the Spirit. Our hearts become illumined when we are incorporated into Christ. Lent is both preparation for Baptism and for its renewal. In Baptism, we receive the Holy Spirit, the "splendor of God's grace," who brings light to those in darkness. This gift of the Spirit, who is light, enables the Christian to ponder (*cogitare*) the true nature and purpose of life and to act in a worthy and pleasing manner. Such action can only come as a result of the working of the Holy Spirit. "Sincerity" literally is being "without the wax," a reference to the masks actors wore in the ancient world. The love here envisioned is love for the sake of the one loved. It is not an act to please and win approval.

Prayer over the People: The "look" of the Lord heartens those who are faltering. The "unfailing light" refers to the divinity itself (*Lux*), whose nature "gives life" and direction to those walking without purpose (i.e., "in the shadow of death"). The "highest good" is nothing other than the "unfailing light." We long to reach warmth, knowledge, insight, beauty, refreshment, and hope—all gifts that can be experienced when we walk from darkness into sunlight. The gifts of walking into the true Light, then, cannot even be imagined.

Pointed Text

Prayer after Communion

A O God, who enlighten everyone who comes into this world,
illuminate our hearts, we pray,
with the splendor of your **grace**,
B that we may always ponder
what is worthy and pleasing **to** your majesty
C and love you in all sincer*i*ty.
Through Christ our Lord.

The space below is for your notes.

Refer to pages viii–x for an explanation of the pointing of the chants and to page xii for the Tones for the Presidential Prayers from *The Roman Missal.*

FIFTH SUNDAY OF LENT

Collect

Stress **your**. Pause after **help**. Proclaim the rest of the line together. Stress **eagerly** and pause. Pause briefly after **same charity**. Raise the voice on **love** and let it drop some on **world**. Proclaim **Through . . . Son** with grateful sobriety. Pause after **Son**.

By your help, we beseech you, Lord our God,
may we walk eagerly in that same charity
with which, out of love for the world,
your Son handed himself over to death.
Through our Lord Jesus Christ, your Son,
who lives and reigns with you in the unity of the Holy Spirit,
one God, for ever and ever.

Prayer over the Offerings

Pause briefly after **Hear us**. Do not pause after **and**. Place emphasis on **instilled**, proclaiming it with wonder and authority. **Teachings** goes with **instilled** and should be proclaimed similarly. Speak **graciously** with tenderness and **purify** with energy and confident pleading. Proceed slowly and do not pause after **them**. Proclaim **working** with energy.

Hear us, almighty God,
and, having instilled in your servants
the teachings of the Christian faith,
graciously purify them
by the working of this sacrifice.
Through Christ our Lord. *

Prayer after Communion

Pause briefly after **We pray**. Do not put emphasis on **we** but rather on **always** and pause briefly after **be counted**. Raise the voice with some joy on **members of Christ**. Pause briefly after **Blood** and end strongly and peacefully with **communion**.

We pray, almighty God,
that we may always be counted among the members of Christ,
in whose Body and Blood we have communion.
Who lives and reigns for ever and ever.

Prayer over the People

Draw out **long**, which should be prayed with an awareness of our needs. Proclaim **mercy** with tenderness. Speak **and grant that what** together and keep the voice slightly raised. Place emphasis on **your prompting**. Pause briefly after **receive** and proclaim it with confidence.

Bless, O Lord, your people,
who long for the gift of your mercy,
and grant that what, at your prompting, they desire
they may receive by your generous gift.
Through Christ our Lord.

* When the Gospel from Year A is not read, use either Preface I or II of Lent in the Order of Mass. Commentary, and proclamation and chant tips, for the Preface can be found at *www.StudyThePresidentialTexts.com/Prefaces* and in *The Order of Mass: A Roman Missal Study Edition and Workbook*, pages 36–39.

Collect: The Latin for "help" is *opitulante*, which literally means to bring resources, strength, power, wealth. We lack the essential resources needed to love as God loves. God loves by giving himself away, even unto death. The scriptural background of John 3:16 has the Father loving the world, but the prayer shifts this to the Son. The union between Father and Son is such that whatever one loves, the other loves just as strongly. The word for "charity" (*caritate*) is the translation of the Greek *agape*, referring to self-giving love. The "help" which is sought in the prayer is to enable us to "walk eagerly in that same charity." We are called to take up our cross and follow him. The adverb "eagerly" describes the attitude of discipleship. We must find the motivation (the heart) that will enable us to sacrifice ourselves willingly, eagerly. This kind of attittude only arises from love. We will become true disciples when our hearts of stone are turned to flesh (Ezekiel 36:26). This is the work of the Holy Spirit: to renew our hearts and enable us to love as God loves.

Prayer over the Offerings: The opening words, "Hear us," are a plea for action from the Lord. For him, to "hear" is to respond. It is God who "instills" Christian "teachings." The word for "teachings" (*eruditionibus*) does not refer to doctrine in the sense of the deposit of faith, but rather to the process of taking away our unrefined nature—all that holds us back from becoming the true "man" in Christ Jesus. The main petition, "purify them," refers to purifying "your servants." This prayer envisions a process. First, the action of God must be requested.

Pointed Text

Collect

A By your help, we beseech you, Lord our **God**,
B may we walk eagerly in that same charity
with which, out of love **for** the world,
C your Son handed himself over to ***death***.
Through our Lord Jesus Christ, your Son,
who lives and reigns with you in the unity of the Holy Spirit,
one God, for ever and ever.

Prayer over the Offerings

A Hear us, almighty **God**,
B and, having instilled in your servants
the teachings of the **Chris**tian faith,
C graciously purify them
by the working of this sa***cri***fice.
Through Christ our Lord.

Prayer after Communion

A We pray, almighty **God**,
B that we may always be counted among the mem**bers** of Christ,
C in whose Body and Blood we have commu***nion***.
Who lives and reigns for ever and ever.

The space below is for your notes.

Refer to pages viii–x for an explanation of the pointing of the chants and to page xii for the Tones for the Presidential Prayers from *The Roman Missal.*

His "instilling" will only be the result of an openness and a request: "Hear us." The action of God is to teach and prepare us, shape and form us into his image—this is the purpose of the "teachings of the Christian faith." The final step is to "purify" or cleanse (*mundari*) us by the working of the sacrifice. The Eucharistic sacrifice makes present the mystery of the Cross, in which we are cleansed by the shedding of Christ's Blood. The "teachings" refer to the Liturgy of the Word and the purifying sacrifice refers to the Liturgy of the Eucharist.

Prayer after Communion: The "members of Christ" refer to the Church. The summit of communion for Christians is the ability to share the Eucharist together. Thus, although Catholics share a tremendous amoung of theology with the Othodox Churches, our communion remains incomplete until the bishops of each Church can share communion in the celebration of the Eucharist. This prayer pleads never to be separated from communion with Christ's body, the Church. If Christ is the "true man" (see the Preface), and the Church is his body, then to be separated from the Church is to be separated from Christ to some extent. The bond that unites Christians together is the Body and Blood of Christ. True communion with another human being will be found only when that communion is rooted in Christ. The union of marriage will be strongest and most complete when the spouses place their union as secondary to their union with Christ. The proper order is important. The verb "to be counted" (*numeremur*) implies a public accounting. There is an implicit

Bring out the accent on **be** in **The Lord be with you.** In the next phrase, make a strong accent on **Lift**, and slow both notes of **hearts**. In the third dialogue, move to the word **thanks** before accenting, and hold that word slightly to give it emphasis. Broaden both notes of **Lord**, and hold **God**.

Sing this proclamation cursively in a reciting tone. In **salvation**, do not hold **-va**; only broaden the two notes slightly. Hold **-tion**. **Always** and **everywhere** require a slight broadening and clear enunciation. The accent of the phrase falls on **thanks**, which should be held briefly.

Set off in the first phrase **true man** by careful articulation. It might be good to treat **Lazarus** as if there were a comma after the name, thus lengthening slightly. In the next phrase, parallel to the previous, set off **eternal God** by careful articulation. Hold slightly and breathe at **tomb**. Pause after **just as**. Hold briefly and take a quick break if necessary at **race**. Broaden and slow **mysteries to new life**.

reference to our membership of Christ being a public witness to rest of the world. This is fitting for the Prayer after Communion as the faithful prepare to go forth. They are charged to witness the joys of communion as experienced in this Eucharist.

Preface: Lazarus

As "true man," Jesus embraced all the emotions that are common to our human condition. Even though he knew that, in the power of his divinity, he would raise Lazarus from the dead, still, in his humanity, he was grieved and troubled by the tragedy of death and he expressed his grief in tears. Two great truths are related here. First, pastorally, the truth of a matter—in this case, the resuscitation of Lazarus—does not automatically overturn the emotions of a moment (e.g., though I know I must forgive another, the emotions of anger and hurt still need to be dealt with). To be "true man" is to embrace the whole of human existence, that we are body, mind, and heart. It also includes having the proper balance within oneself of these components. Harmony and balance are needed between my emotional life and my intellectual life, for example. In Jesus, there is a perfect harmony of the mental, emotional, and physical aspects of our human nature. Second, theologically, the tears of Jesus reveal both the weakness and the strength of humanity. In his humanity, he could only weep for Lazarus and the tragedy that is death. Our humanity alone cannot overturn death. It is precisely in showing our weakness, however, that strength from on high can be

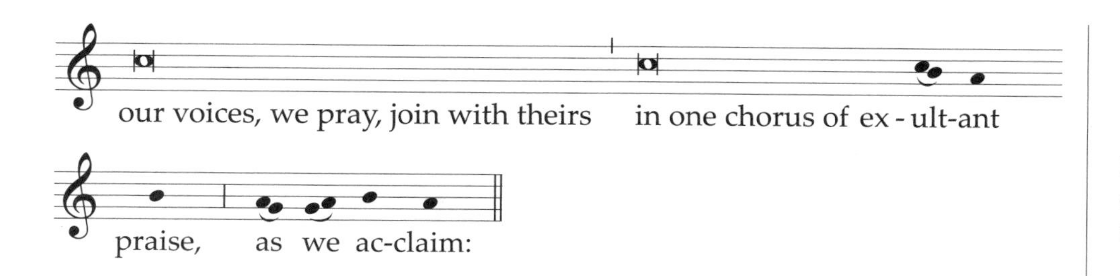

Broaden praise. Slow we -**ac** and put emphasis on -**claim**, so as to evoke the response **Holy, Holy, Holy . . . .**

Holy, Holy, Holy Lord God of hosts . . .

Text without music:

V. **The Lord be with you.**
R. And with your spirit.

V. **Lift up your hearts.**
R. We lift them up to the Lord.

V. **Let us give thanks to the Lord our God.**
R. It is right and just.

It is truly right and just, our duty and our salvation,
always and everywhere to give you thanks,
Lord, holy Father, almighty and eternal God,
through Christ our Lord.

Emphasize **truly**, **duty**, and **salvation**.

For as true man he wept for Lazarus his friend
and as eternal God raised him from the tomb,
just as, taking pity on the human race,
he leads us by sacred mysteries to new life.

Pause after **For**. Parallel **true man** and **eternal God**. Pause briefly after **true man** and again after **eternal God**. Speak **wept for Lazarus his friend** with compassion. Raise the voice in hope-filled awe with **raised**. Pronounce **just as** slowly and distinctly, pausing afterward. Proclaim **taking pity on the human race** with humble joy or relief. Place some emphasis on **us** and pause briefly. Give a parallel rhythm to **sacred mysteries** and **new life**.

Through him the host of Angels adores your majesty
and rejoices in your presence for ever.
May our voices, we pray, join with theirs
in one chorus of exultant praise, as we acclaim:

Holy, Holy, Holy Lord God of hosts . . .

evoked. The Preface continues by revealing that the same compassion ("pity") which Jesus expressed in the death of Lazarus, is also directed toward the rest of humanity. If we embrace our weaknesses, our tears, then he will take pity on us and lead us to "new life." The "true man" does not pretend to be more perfect than he is. We must realize that we are in need of "new life" and cry out for it, thus evoking Christ's compassion. This new life is different from the raising of Lazarus because of the "sacred mysteries" which intervene, referring to the Cross and Resurrection. The humanity of Christ has not been resuscitated, like Lazarus, but raised to eternity. Through the Paschal Mystery, we may be led to the same glorified life of Christ. We already experience the "sacred mysteries" in the liturgy, which plants in us the seeds of this new life. In the liturgy, our soul is nourished on the vision of Christ, and his mystery already begins to take root within us.

Prayer over the People: Those who long for mercy are aware of their need for it. This is the challenge to the Christian people. We are good at seeing another's need for mercy, but can struggle to see weaknesses in ourselves. The blessing takes this into account by stating that our desires come with God's "prompting." Sometimes the only way that we realize our need is to be overwhelmed by it. To embrace our need for mercy is to be open to God's "generous gift" of it.

Holy Week

PALM SUNDAY OF THE PASSION OF THE LORD

First Form: The Procession*

1. On this day the Church recalls the entrance of Christ the Lord into Jerusalem to accomplish his Paschal Mystery. Accordingly, the memorial of this entrance of the Lord takes place at all Masses, by means of the Procession or the Solemn Entrance before other Masses. The Solemn Entrance, but not the Procession, may be repeated before other Masses that are usually celebrated with a large gathering of people.

It is desirable that, where neither the Procession nor the Solemn Entrance can take place, there be a sacred celebration of the Word of God on the messianic entrance and on the Passion of the Lord, either on Saturday evening or on Sunday at a convenient time.

Proclaim these words slowly and deliberately, with solemnity and anticipatory joy in the voice. Follow the line breaks for pauses.

Dear brethren (brothers and sisters),
since the beginning of Lent until now
we have prepared our hearts by penance and charitable works.
Today we gather together to herald with the whole Church
the beginning of the celebration
of our Lord's Paschal Mystery,
that is to say, of his Passion and Resurrection.
For it was to accomplish this mystery
that he entered his own city of Jerusalem.
Therefore, with all faith and devotion,
let us commemorate
the Lord's entry into the city for our salvation,
following in his footsteps,
so that, being made by his grace partakers of the Cross,
we may have a share also in his Resurrection and in his life.

After the address, the Priest says one of the following prayers with hands extended.

Proclaim **ever-living** evenly. Speak **sanctify** with energy, while making the Sign of the Cross over the palm branches. Pause after **we**. Emphasize **Christ** and **King**, then raise the voice joyfully with **exultation**. Stress **eternal** and **him**. After the prayer, the palm branches are sprinkled with holy water in silence.

Let us pray.

A Almighty ever-living **God**,
B sanctify ✠ these branches **with** your blessing,
C that we, who follow Christ the King in exultation,
may reach the eternal Jerusalem through ***him***.
Who lives and reigns for ever and ever.
R. Amen.

Introductory address: This address highlights "penance and charitable works." Acts of penance are intended to empty us, so that we can share with others, but also to overturn our self-centered world. Charitable works are necessary to teach us what to do with our acts of penance. Our attitude is to be charitable, but our focus must be even more other-centered. As we join with Jesus as he begins to enter into the Paschal Mystery, we engage "the celebration" of that mystery. Jerusalem is described as Jesus's "own city," the city where he established our peace with God. Our "faith and devotion" are the best resources to bring in this week-long journey. We are to let Jesus enter our hearts, which, through Baptism, have become "his own city." His journey within us is a journey to make us "partakers" of his Cross, so that we might share his eternal life.

Prayer after the address: The titles for the divine stress God's omnipotence and life as Jesus prepares to undergo suffering and Death. Palm branches are a symbol of victory and honor. The divine blessing beseeched on the branches raises the symbolism to the victory that Christ accomplished over sin and death. With palm branches blessed, we are strengthened to "follow Christ" joyfully, "in exultation." The Latin behind "exultation" refers to a joy that causes one to leap in the air. It is related to the word for exile. The connotation seems to be the joy one feels at being set free from exile or slavery. In memory, the Christian assembly enters the historical Jerusalem with Christ. In mystery, Christ

Or:

A Increase the faith of those who place their hope in you, O God,
and graciously hear the prayers of those who call **on** you,
B that we, who today hold high these branchess
to hail Christ **in** his triumph,
C may bear fruit for you by good works accomplished in ***him***.
Who lives and reigns for ever and ever.
R. Amen.**

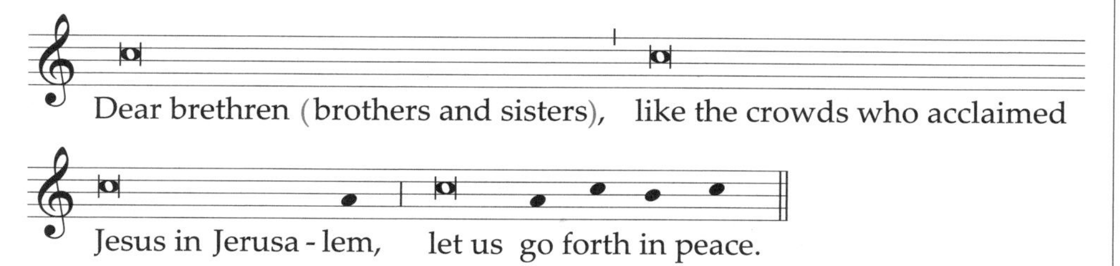

Dear brethren (brothers and sisters),
like the crowds who acclaimed Jesus in Jerusalem,
let us go forth in peace.

Or:

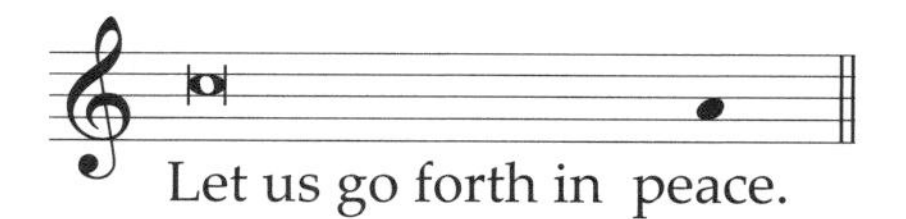

Let us go forth in peace.

In this latter case, all respond:

Pause briefly after **those** and raise the voice some with **hope**. Proclaim **graciously** gently, Pause after **we** and raise the voice for **high these branches**, pausing only briefly. Give equal emphasis to **Christ** and **triumph**. Place emphasis on **bear fruit** and pause after **for you**. Give equal emphasis to **accomplished in him**. After the prayer, the palm branches are sprinkled with holy water in silence.

* For the rubrics for the First Form: The Procession, the Second Form: The Solemn Entrance, and the Third Form: The Simple Entrance refer to Palm Sunday of the Passion of the Lord in *The Roman Missal*.

** The Gospel for the blessing of palms follows the Prayer of Blessings.

enters the "holy city" of the Church and our hearts. It is in the hope of entering the heavenly Jerusalem that we follow Christ with such joy to remember his suffering and to embrace ours. This hope is based in Christ. Our "following" and "reaching" can only occur "through him." We rejoice, suffer, die, and rise all "through him."

Optional prayer: In this triumphal procession into Jerusalem, the prayer notes the hope placed in Jesus. The prayer seeks an increase in faith to go with our hopes. The theological virtues are tied to each other. Each needs the others to be complete. Hope is born of our need for something from another, the reason our prayer "calls on" God and seeks a hearing. The "triumph" of Christ, which we herald by branches "held high," refers to his Passion and Resurrection. In the Resurrection of Christ, we are enabled to "bear fruit" in good works. Through his Resurrection, Christ pours his life into us, renewing our hope and courage to lay down our lives in service—the fruit of Christ's martyrdom.

Exhortation: The Church calls us through this exhortation to enter into the spirit of Palm Sunday. The Latin version exhorts us to imitate the crowds in the way they acclaimed Jesus, and separately says, "Let us go forth in peace." The English translation makes it seem that our main imitation of the crowds is the way they went forth in peace, but this is not the case. The crowds had not yet found the "peace" which Jesus effected in the Paschal Mystery. Their exultation was purely human.

Proclaim **Almighty** distinctly and **ever-living God** slowly and evenly. Pause briefly after **who**. Stress **example**. Speak **humility** with sincerity, pausing only an instant before continuing. Pause briefly after **Savior** to parallel **to take flesh** and **submit to the Cross**. Linger on **graciously grant** and pause briefly. Draw out **patient suffering**.

Collect

Almighty ever-living God,
who as an example of humility for the human race to follow
caused our Savior to take flesh and submit to the Cross,
graciously grant that we may heed his lesson of patient suffering
and so merit a share in his Resurrection.
Who lives and reigns with you in the unity of the Holy Spirit,
one God, for ever and ever.

Emphasize **Passion** and **Only Begotten Son**. Slowly proclaim **reconciliation**. Pause briefly after **with you**. Pause after **so that**. Raise the voice slightly with **not** and **own deeds**. Stress **yet** and pause briefly. Emphasize **sacrifice**. Proclaim **once for all** with determination and confidence. Slow down with **feel already**. Raise the voice with **effects**. Proclaim **mercy** with tenderness.

Prayer over the Offerings

Through the Passion of your Only Begotten Son, O Lord,
may our reconciliation with you be near at hand,
so that, though we do not merit it by our own deeds,
yet by this sacrifice made once for all,
we may feel already the effects of your mercy.
Through Christ our Lord.

Proclaim **Nourished** with gratitude. Stress the **sacred** of **sacred gifts**. Reverently pray the second line. Pause after **that**. Begin **just as** with energy. Stress **death**. Keep voice slightly raised with **Son**, pausing slightly. Place emphasis on **hope** and **believe**. To bring out the parallel, emphasize **so** and **Resurrection**. Proclaim the next line with expectant longing, stressing **lead**. Go slower and gentler with **to where you call**.

Prayer after Communion

Nourished with these sacred gifts,
we humbly beseech you, O Lord,
that, just as through the death of your Son
you have brought us to hope for what we believe,
so by his Resurrection
you may lead us to where you call.
Through Christ our Lord.

Pause after **Look** and **O Lord**. Bow the head at the name of Jesus. Speak **did not hesitate** with firm confidence and take a breath. Place the emphasis on **delivered**, **hands**, and **wicked**. Keep the voice raised on **wicked**. Speak **submit** with humility and proclaim **agony of the Cross** with sadness and gratitude.

Prayer over the People

Look, we pray, O Lord, on this your family,
for whom our Lord Jesus Christ
did not hesitate to be delivered into the hands of the wicked
and submit to the agony of the Cross.
Who lives and reigns for ever and ever.

Collect: "Example" (*documenta*) comes from the verb *doceo*, which means "to teach." The virtue of humility refers to the truth of our human nature. In submitting his flesh to the Cross, Christ was teaching us the truth about our nature. Our existence is centered on ourselves. Christ's "example of humility" was completely selfless. It does not "benefit" God to bring humanity into communion with him. Christ's Death on the Cross was completely for us, out of love for us. The prayer states that God "caused" Christ to take on flesh and submit to the Cross. This must be understood from the perspective of the Trinity, who is one. In the Father sending his only Son, he is sending himself. No separation exists between Father and Son. This is God submitting himself to suffering and death. The reference to "suffering" is qualified by "patient" and this is important, because it makes clear that our suffering must be accepted and embraced to be fully redemptive. This is how we "merit a share" in the glorified life that is beyond all suffering, and beyond all selfishness.

Prayer over the Offerings: The word for "reconciliation" is *placatio*, a difficult word to translate. Its root may come from *planus*, which describes the sea when calm and level. Literally, *placatio* means appeasement, but this rings in English ears like an angry God needing to be satisfied. The phrase is literally, "may your *placatio* be near to us." The context makes clear that the self-gift of Christ, his "example of humility," is pleasing to God. Jesus is the Father's "beloved Son with whom [he is] well-pleased" (Matthew 3:17; 17:5).

Pointed Text

Collect

A Almighty ever-living **God**,
B who as an example of humility for the human race to follow
caused our Savior to take flesh and submit **to** the Cross,
C graciously grant that we may heed his lesson of patient suffering
and so merit a share in his Resurrec***tion***.
Who lives and reigns with you in the unity of the Holy Spirit,
one God, for ever and ever.

Prayer over the Offerings

A Through the Passion of your Only Begotten Son, O Lord,
may our reconciliation with you be near at **hand**,
B so that, though we do not merit it by **our** own deeds,
C yet by this sacrifice made once for all,
we may feel already the effects of your mer***cy***.
Through Christ our Lord.

Prayer after Communion

A Nourished with these sacred gifts,
we humbly beseech you, O **Lord**,
B that, just as through the death of your Son
you have brought us to hope for what **we** believe,
C so by his Resurrection
you may lead us to where you ***call***.
Through Christ our Lord.

The space below is for your notes.

Refer to pages viii–x for an explanation of the pointing of the chants and to page xii for the Tones for the Presidential Prayers from *The Roman Missal*.

Precisely in his sacrifice, Jesus is the *placatio*, or "reconciliation," which is near to us. The "sacrifice made once for all" implies a sacrifice that is unique in all the world. What made it so unique was the completeness of his self-gift, his "emptying" himself (of both humanity and divinity, Philippians 2:7) unto death. Our "own deeds" will always fall short of this total gift. The beauty in this prayer is the bold statement that "already" in this life, we can "feel the effects" of Christ's gift. In the Eucharist, we gain a foretaste of his "mercy."

Prayer after Communion: The word "nourished" implies that "these sacred gifts" have satisfied our need. However, even in Communion, our soul-hunger is not quenched. In some ways, this foretaste of the heavenly banquet serves to arouse our hunger for God. Our soul is best "nourished" when its longing for God is aroused. Saint Augustine wrote that the more poignantly we desire God, the more our hearts become enlarged, giving us a greater capacity to receive God and to love others. The best nourishment for the soul leads to a deeper hunger for God. The prayer states that the Death of Christ brings hope to believers. He died without fear of death, but with confidence in God's promise (Hebrews 5:7). The Latin behind the last line slightly differs from the English translation, stating more literally, we may arrive toward where we strive or long. This ties in clearly with the virtue of hope, which is connected to longing for the realization of what we believe. Christ's Death teaches us not to fear death, and his Resurrection shows us where a faithful death will lead us.

Bring out the accent on **be** in **The Lord be with you**. In the next phrase, make a strong accent on **Lift**, and slow both notes of **hearts**. In the third dialogue, move to the word **thanks** before accenting, and hold that word slightly to give it emphasis. Broaden both notes of **Lord**, and hold **God**.

Sing this proclamation cursively in a reciting tone. In **salvation**, do not hold **-va**; only broaden the two notes slightly. The last syllable, **-tion**, should be held. **Always** and **everywhere** require a slight broadening and clear enunciation. The accent of the phrase falls on **thanks**, which should be held briefly. In the next sentence, clearly make four phrases of the text, by respecting the commas after **Lord**, **Father**, and **God**.

Make a slight hold on **-cent** of **innocent**, but do not breathe there. Hold **-ners** of **sinners** but if possible do not breathe there (if it is necessary to breathe, make it very quick). Slow and broaden **condemnation** through **guilty**. In the next phrase, hold **sins**, and if possible continue, without breathing, to **and his**. Slow and broaden the word **justification**, holding the last syllable.

In the concluding phrase, make a slight pause after **And so**. Respect the commas but try to keep this section together, without big breaks for breaths. Broaden the last phrase, especially on **praise**. Slow **we ac-**, and put emphasis on **-claim**, so as to evoke the **Holy, Holy, Holy . . . .**

Preface: The Passion of the Lord

The suffering of Christ is directly related to the sinfulness of humanity. In his Passion, he revealed the true ugliness of human nature under sin: cruel, self-serving, jealous, prideful, etc. In his Passion, Christ shows us humanity, though not yet glorified, still free from the selfishnesses of sin. This is what enables him to offer himself "willingly" because he did not consider himself, but only the need to redeem lost humanity. This Preface continually places before us our fallenness. We are "sinners," and "the guilty." We are grimed by "our sins" and in need of "justification." On this Sunday, when the Gospel account of the Passion is proclaimed in its entirety, the Church wants us to be fully aware of our complicity in evil and, thus; of our need for a Savior. A two-step process is highlighted in this Preface. First, our sins are "washed away." This is negative, the removal of what obstructs a relationship with God. Our attachment to the world and this life is cleansed. Second, the Resurrection brings us into "justification," or right relationship, with God. God cannot enter into relationship with someone who is a slave to sin. Only as free men and women can we enter into Communion with the Father. This is how the Old Testament sacrifices worked. First was the Trespass sacrifice, which symbolized the removal of sin (the blood of the animal, unblemished and representing the blood of the sinner, would be shed and given to God in the Temple). Next came there would be the Communion sacrifice, which symbolized the peace now enjoyed with God (the meat from the animal would

Holy, Holy, Holy Lord God of hosts . . .

Text without music:

V. **The Lord be with you.**
R. And with your spirit.

V. **Lift up your hearts.**
R. We lift them up to the Lord.

V. **Let us give thanks to the Lord our God.**
R. It is right and just.

It is truly right and just, our duty and our salvation,
always and everywhere to give you thanks,
Lord, holy Father, almighty and eternal God,
through Christ our Lord.

For, though innocent, he suffered willingly for sinners
and accepted unjust condemnation to save the guilty.
His Death has washed away our sins,
and his Resurrection has purchased our justification.

And so, with all the Angels,
we praise you, as in joyful celebration we acclaim:

Holy, Holy, Holy Lord God of hosts . . .

Emphasize **truly**, **duty**, and **salvation**.

Pause briefly after **For** and again after **innocent**. Stress **innocent** and **willingly**. Raise the voice with **unjust condemnation** and pause briefly. Proclaim **the guilty** with humble self-awareness. Parallel **His Death** and **our sins**, though have more energy for the first part. Do the same for **his Resurrection** and **our justification**. Pause after both **Death** and **Resurrection**.

be divided between priest and sinner and shared in a banquet). In the Eucharistic Prayer, the priest enters the heavenly Temple, and unites our sinful life to the sacrifice of Christ, which reconciles us (the Trespass sacrifice—for the first time, given real power to remove sins). Then, priest and assembly together share in the Communion banquet of Christ's Body and Blood, in which we enjoy the union made possible by Christ's sacrifice on the Cross. The emphasis in the Preface on Christ as "innocent" and just makes clear that he was "unblemished" and thus worthy to make this kind of sacrifice. Until we share in the suffering and Death of Christ, we share his Resurrection only in hope and remain prone to sin and full of the desire to overlook our sinfulness, which is precisely why this feast comes every year!

Prayer over the People: The petition of this prayer is simply for the Lord to "look" on his family. The Psalms continually pray for the Lord to "look" upon his people (e.g., Psalm. 84:10; or to turn his face toward them, Psalm 4:6, *et passim*). The gaze of the Lord gives courage that he is watching to help in our need. The rest of the prayer explains why the Lord should look upon his family: because of all the Son did for us.

THURSDAY OF HOLY WEEK

The Chrism Mass

Collect

Pause after **O God**. Place emphasis on **anointed**, **Only Begotten Son**, and **Holy Spirit**. Pause after **Son**. Do not drop the voice with **Spirit** and pause only enough to take a breath since the thought continues on the next line. Proclaim **graciously grant** with slow gentleness. Pause after **that**. Place a downward emphasis on **sharers** and a rising emphasis on **consecration**. Put a parallel emphasis on **witness** and **world** and proclaim **Redemption** with greater energy.

O God, who anointed your Only Begotten Son with the Holy Spirit
and made him Christ and Lord,
graciously grant
that, being made sharers in his consecration,
we may bear witness to your Redemption in the world.
Through our Lord Jesus Christ, your Son,
who lives and reigns with you in the unity of the Holy Spirit,
one God, for ever and ever.

Prayer over the Offerings

Emphasize **power** and **sacrifice**; then pause briefly. Pray **mercifully** with grateful relief and keep **mercifully wipe away** as a unit. Parallel **old in us** and **increase in us**, pausing briefly after the latter. Parallel **grace of salvation** and **newness of life**.

May the power of this sacrifice, O Lord, we pray,
mercifully wipe away what is old in us
and increase in us grace of salvation and newness of life.
Through Christ our Lord.

Prayer after Communion

Pause after **you**, and proclaim **beseech** with humble confidence. The next line has a threefold emphasis: **that those** and **you renew** and **by your Sacraments**. Raise the voice with **renew**, making it the climax of the three. Linger on the phrase **pleasing fragrance**.

We beseech you, almighty God,
that those you renew by your Sacraments
may merit to become the pleasing fragrance of Christ.
Who lives and reigns for ever and ever.

Collect: Several times the Spirit acted upon Christ: in the Incarnation, at his baptism in the Jordan, in his Transfiguration, and, one could argue, with every act of power performed during his ministry. The anointing referenced in this prayer refers to the Resurrection in which the Spirit raised Christ from the dead, and the Father bestowed upon him the name above every other name: Lord (Philippians 2:11). This is when the Spirit thoroughly "spiritualized" the Body of Christ, making him a life-giving Spirit (1 Corinthians 15:45). In the Sacraments, we are given a "share" in the "spiritual body" (1 Corinthians 15:44) that belongs to Christ. We are anointed with Chrism oil in Baptism, Confirmation, and Holy Orders, but in every sacrament, the Spirit is given to bring us a deeper "share" in Christ's risen life. Each of these "consecrations" brings the "Redemption" of Christ into our lives in a different way. Insofar as we embrace that Redemption, we are charged to "bear witness" to the redeemed life of Christ that we experience in our mortal bodies.

Prayer over the Offerings: The Holy Spirit is sometimes described as the "power" of God. It is certainly the Spirit who makes Christ present and renders the liturgical sacrifice efficacious. In the Mass of Chrism, olive oil is an important symbol. The olive tree is a symbol of health and vigor. It is an old tree, with some specimens being more than 6,000 years old, and yet it still brings forth new life and health. When olive oil is blessed (oil of catechumens and the sick) or consecrated (sacred Chrism), it becomes the instrument for eternal life and health.

The space below is for your notes.

Refer to pages viii–x for an explanation of the pointing of the chants and to page xii for the Tones for the Presidential Prayers from *The Roman Missal*.

Pointed Text

Collect

A O God, who anointed your Only Begotten Son with the Holy Spirit
and made him Christ and **Lord**,
B graciously grant
that, being made sharers in his **con**secration,
C we may bear witness to your Redemption in the ***world***.
Through our Lord Jesus Christ, your Son,
who lives and reigns with you in the unity of the Holy Spirit,
one God, for ever and ever.

Prayer over the Offerings

A May the power of this sacrifice, O Lord, we **pray**,
B mercifully wipe away what is **old** in us
C and increase in us grace of salvation and newness of ***life***.
Through Christ our Lord.

Prayer after Communion

A We beseech you, almighty **God**,
B that those you renew **by** your Sacraments
C may merit to become the pleasing fragrance of ***Christ***.
Who lives and reigns for ever and ever.

The oil of catechumens and the sacred Chrism are both elements in the Sacraments of initiation, in which the "old man" is put off and the "new man" is put on (Colossians 3:9–10). The oil of the sick serves to "wipe away" sin and all that holds us to the "old self," so that we might be healed in mind and spirit. The "grace of salvation and newness of life" were given to us in Baptism, which is why this prayer asks for their "increase." Salvation and life are relational gifts into which one can grow ever deeper.

Prayer after Communion: The reference to "pleasing fragrance" refers to the aromatic balsam that is traditionally mixed with the oil to be consecrated for Chrism. Christ was a pleasing sacrifice to the Father in every way, fulfilling not only the blood sacrifices, but also the incense offerings of the Old Testament. The sacred Chrism is a quasi-sacrament of the Holy Spirit and, as such, communicates Christ to those who are anointed with it. Anyone or anything anointed with the sacred Chrism is permanently marked. This anointing makes the anointed a new creation in Christ, conformed to him and marked as his own. The working of the Spirit in all the Sacraments "renews," bringing refreshment and life, but the ultimate purpose of this renewal is to make our whole lives into a "pleasing" offering to God (Phiippians 4:18), just as Christ was. We are destined to become Christ. The "merit" comes not from our good works or good intentions, but from our submission to the renewal effected by the Spirit in the Sacraments.

Renewal of Priestly Promises

After the Homily the Bishop speaks with the priests in these or similar words.

Beloved sons,
on the anniversary of that day
when Christ our Lord conferred his priesthood
on his Apostles and on us,
are you resolved to renew,
in the presence of your Bishop and God's holy people,
the promises you once made?

The Priests, all together, respond: I am.

Strong emphasis on **resolved**. Stress **more united** and **more closely**. Pray **conformed** with reverence. Raise the voice with **denying yourselves** to bring out the seriousness of the call. Emphasize **sacred duties**. Speak the phrase **prompted by love of him** with tenderness. Proclaim **willingly and joyfully** distinctly and energetically.

(1.) Are you resolved to be more united with the Lord Jesus
and more closely conformed to him,
denying yourselves and confirming those promises
about sacred duties towards Christ's Church
which, prompted by love of him,
you willingly and joyfully pledged
on the day of your priestly ordination?

Priests: I am.

Emphasize **resolved**. Pronounce **faithful stewards** deliberately and with parallel emphasis to **mysteries of God**, which should be prayed with a hint of wonder, keeping the voice raised for the next line. Proclaim **sacred office of teaching** with reverence and firmness. Speak the next line as an important reminder. Draw out **zeal for souls**, praying it with restrained energy.

(2.) Are you resolved to be faithful stewards of the mysteries of God
in the Holy Eucharist and the other liturgical rites
and to discharge faithfully the sacred office of teaching,
following Christ the Head and Shepherd,
not seeking any gain,
but moved only by zeal for souls?

Priests: I am.

Then, turned towards the people, the Bishop continues:

This exhortation should be lighter and joyful. Be eager to ask for prayers for the Priests. The last two lines have a more serious tone.

(3.) As for you, dearest sons and daughters,
pray for your Priests,
that the Lord may pour out his gifts abundantly upon them,
and keep them faithful as ministers of Christ, the High Priest,
so that they may lead you to him,
who is the source of salvation.

Renewal of Priestly Promises: The Bishop addresses his Priests in a most intimate way: "Beloved sons." He is called to be teacher, father, brother, and friend to his Priests (*Sacerdotalis Coelibatum*, On Priestly Celibacy, #93). The Latin word used for "conferred" his priesthood is *communicavit*, which might be better translated "shared." This communicates the reality more clearly. There is only one Priest and one priesthood in the Church. Bishops and Priests are given a "share" in that one Priesthood of Christ. The verb "resolved" (*vultis*) brings out the Church's emphasis on the will, though without neglecting the role played by the affect. The "promises" were made before the Bishop and "God's holy people," which is a reference to 1 Peter 2:9. Priests are ordained to foster the holiness of God's own people.

(1.) Priestly ordination has already "united" and "conformed" the Priest to Christ. This renewal is intended to deepen that union and conformity. The way to accomplish this is specified, first of all, as the path of self-denial, which is the "example of humility" given to us by Christ. The Priest is called to examine himself and then, in some regard, to forget himself in service to his people. The second means of renewal is to "confirm" the promises made toward the Church. The best motive for making these promises is love for the bride of Christ—another area for examination and renewal. Lastly, the question presumes that the priestly promises were made "willingly and joyfully." Were they not made "willingly," there would be grounds to question the validity of the ordination. Joy

People: Christ, hear us. Christ, graciously hear us.

(4.) And pray also for me,
that I may be faithful to the apostolic office
entrusted to me in my lowliness
and that in your midst I may be made day by day
a living and more perfect image of Christ,
the Priest, the Good Shepherd,
the Teacher and the Servant of all.

People: Christ, hear us. Christ, graciously hear us.

May the Lord keep us all in his charity
and lead all of us,
shepherds and flock,
to eternal life.

All: Amen.

Avoid feigned humility or embarrassment with these words. Proclaim your need and your **lowliness** with simplicity. Proclaim **living** and **more perfect image** with desire for their realization. Speak each of the titles of Christ slowly, deliberately, and eagerly as though naming the true hopes of your heart.

Preface: The Priesthood of Christ and the Ministry of Priests.

Bring out the accent on **be** in **The Lord be with you**. Make a strong accent on **Lift**, and slow both notes of **hearts**. In the third dialogue, move to the word **thanks** before accenting, and hold that word slightly to give it emphasis. Broaden both notes of **Lord**, and hold **God**.

This long Preface may demand more breath control than most. In the first phrase, slow **Holy Spirit**, holding the last syllable briefly and taking a short breath.

is often said to be the surest sign of the presence of the Holy Spirit. One can hope that as the life of a Priest progresses, he will grow more and more attuned to the working of the Holy Spirit in his life, bringing about an ever growing joy. Whether true of the past or not, the renewal this day opens the door for the present and the future.

(2.) The Priest is not the master of the "mysteries of God." He is only their "steward." He is faithful to what has been given to him. A steward cares for the house and property of another in their absence. This is the attitude of the Church toward the liturgy. She tends the liturgy in the place of Christ to whom it all belongs. The "mysteries" refer to the transcendent reality that is Christ, present to his Church in the Spirit. In the various "liturgical rites," the Priest is the instrument of communion between the mystery that is Christ and the gathered assembly. The "sacred office of teaching" (*sacrum docendi munus*) is guided by the sacred office of ruling, that is, the kingly office (Christ the Head and Shepherd). The Priest continues the three charisms of Christ as Priest, prophet, and king. The motive for these duties is not what the Priest may profit in his ministry, but is wholly other-focused: "only by zeal for souls." Sometimes the Priest may be tempted to pit "zeal for souls" against being a "faithful steward," and either change the "mysteries" to fit his conception of what is good for his people, or neglect his people in presiding over the mysteries in a way that is disconnected from them.

Tie together, without pausing or breathing, **Begotten Son** and **High Priest**.

Hold briefly **-nant** of **covenant**. Hold **-cree** of **decree**, but do not pause; rather, continue in order to keep the sense of the full phrase.

Hold **Church** and pause to breathe there. Do not pause or breathe after **priesthood**, but continue the sense by going directly to **the people**. Hold **own**; pause and breathe. A slight hold on **-ness** of **kindness** is appropriate, but tie the word to **he also** without a break.

Broaden slightly, but without slowing greatly, **sacred ministry**. Do not break the line or breathe there, but rather continue with **through**. Slightly slow **laying on of hands** because it needs careful and clear articulation. Tie together **name** and **the** without a break. Hold -**tion** of **redemption** briefly and take a quick breath. In the next phrase, hold **-quet** of **banquet** and make a slight break with the voice, to indicate that this is the first of a set of three things mentioned. The second, which is the phrase **to lead** . . . needs the same handling at **charity**. The third, **to nourish . . .**, calls for a hold on **word**; but without a break or breath, continue with the ending, **and strengthen**, holding the last syllable **-ments** of **Sacraments** and pausing.

Tie together **you** and **and** without a break.

(3.) This exhortation lays out the liturgical relationship between the Priest and his people. Their prayers for him are intended to strengthen him in his mission to lead them to Christ. The words here are a strong reminder to both Priest and people that the Priest is not the source of salvation, only Christ is. The Priest is to lead others to the Savior. The people are not so much "his" as entrusted to him. The people have been purchased for God by the Blood of Christ. The Priest is "steward" not only of the liturgy, but of the people of God. The Priest is also named as a "minister" of the one who alone is "High Priest" of God's flock. The "abundant gifts" that are sought for the Priest are to keep him "faithful" in acting in the person of Christ.

(4.) Pope Saint Leo the Great often referred to his "lowliness" (*mea humilitate*). The scripture behind it is Mary's Magnificat: "For he has looked upon his handmaid's lowliness" (Luke 1:48). Living from the profound knowledge of one's "lowliness" evokes the blessing of God which Mary, in turn, received. The implication is that the Bishop, similarly, is called to safeguard the Body of Christ as Mary did in her womb and to bring forth Christ in the world. This is his "apostolic office." Whereas the priest is a "minister" of Christ, the High Priest, the Bishop, is a "living image of Christ the Priest." He is to be "in the midst" of the people—perhaps the expression of a preference for pastoral activity over administrative seclusion. The prayers of the people are sought that he may be truly a "living" and more perfect image of Christ." In addition to the sacred

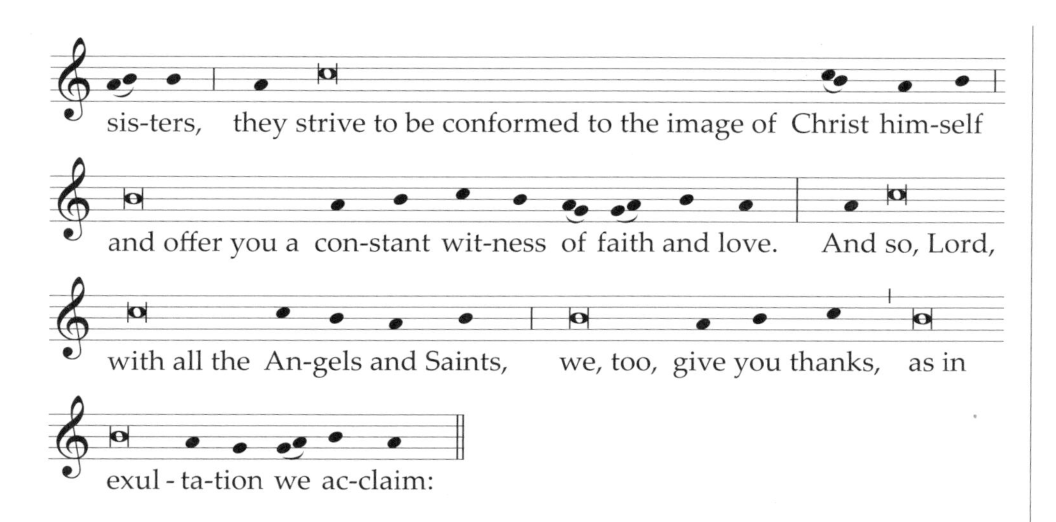

Hold **-ters** of **sisters**, taking a quick breath there. Hold **-self** of **himself** but, if possible, continue into the final phrase without a breath or a break. Broaden and slow **witness of faith and love**, holding the last word and taking a good breath after it.

In the concluding phrase, make a slight pause after **And so**. Respect the commas but try to keep this section together, without big breaks for breaths. Broaden the last phrase, especially on **thanks**. Slow **we ac-**, and put emphasis on **-claim**, so as to evoke the response of **Holy, Holy, Holy . . . .**

Holy, Holy, Holy Lord God of hosts . . .

Text without music:

V. **The Lord be with you.**
R. And with your spirit.

V. **Lift up your hearts.**
R. We lift them up to the Lord.

V. **Let us give thanks to the Lord our God.**
R. It is right and just.

It is truly right and just, our duty and our salvation,
always and everywhere to give you thanks,
Lord, holy Father, almighty and eternal God.

Emphasize **truly**, **duty**, and **salvation**.

For by the anointing of the Holy Spirit
you made your Only Begotten Son
High Priest of the new and eternal covenant,
and by your wondrous design were pleased to decree
that his one Priesthood should continue in the Church.

Pause after **For** and again briefly after **High Priest**. Emphasize **new and eternal covenant**. Proclaim **wondrous** with energy and keep the voice slightly raised for **decree**. Pause after **one Priesthood**.

offices of priest, prophet and king, there is added here the call to be the "Servant of all" (Mark 9:35). The Bishop is the "first" in the Diocese and therefore, according to the Gospel of Mark, he must be the "Servant of all."

Preface: The Priesthood of Christ and the Ministry of Priests

The key to Priesthood is the "anointing of the Holy Spirit." By this, Christ was made "High Priest," the Latin is *Pontifex*, which literally means "bridge builder." In Christ's Priesthood, he mediates and unites God and humanity. In his Ascension, Christ crossed the divide and began his work of intercession on our behalf (Hebrews). The shedding of his blood was the reality to which all the animal sacrifices of the past had pointed. In his sacrifice, he forged "the new and eternal covenant," that is, relationship or unbreakable bond between the divine and the human. The Priesthood, which "continues in the Church," makes present sacramentally this one and eternal act of priestly mediation by Christ.

The next paragraph mentions the baptismal priesthood, called "royal." This is given in Baptism, in which God makes a "people for himself." In Baptism, we are anointed with Chrism on the crown of the head: our whole person is marked by this priestly anointing, which makes us holy in our nature—fit for the Kingdom, hence the adjective "royal." In addition to this "royal priesthood," there is the ministerial Priesthood, given only to those Christ himself "chooses," albeit through the voice of the Bishop, who ordains. This "choosing" is

Pause briefly after **For**, and proclaim with knowledge the parallel structure **not only . . . but with . . . he also**. Pause briefly after **priesthood**. Keep the voice raised with **his own**. Pause after **brother's kindness** and briefly after **men**.

For Christ not only adorns with a royal priesthood
the people he has made his own,
but with a brother's kindness he also chooses men
to become sharers in his sacred ministry
through the laying on of hands.

A series of duties characterize this stanza. Each should be proclaimed slowly and deliberately. The first two lines go together, so pause only briefly after **name**. Thereafter, pause significantly at the end of each line. Proclaim the first duty with reverent awe; the second, with joy; the third, with loving concern; the fourth, with the eagerness of someone with good news to share; the fifth, with firmness of purpose.

They are to renew in his name
the sacrifice of human redemption,
to set before your children the paschal banquet,
to lead your holy people in charity,
to nourish them with the word
and strengthen them with the Sacraments.

Proclaim **As they give up their lives for you** with grateful wonder. Pause after **for you** in order to bring out the parallel with **and for the salvation of their brothers and sisters**. Proclaim **strive** with energy. **Conformed to the image of Christ himself** should be proclaimed slowly and majestically. Pick up the pace slightly with the last sentence and stress **constant witness**.

As they give up their lives for you
and for the salvation of their brothers and sisters,
they strive to be conformed to the image of Christ himself
and offer you a constant witness of faith and love.

And so, Lord, with all the Angels and Saints,
we, too, give you thanks, as in exultation we acclaim:

Holy, Holy, Holy Lord God of hosts . . .

done "with a brother's kindness." While Baptism makes us brothers to Christ, ordination associates the selected with him in a new way. It is "with a brother's kindness" that he bestows the anointing of the Spirit upon them, giving them a share in his priestly ministry on behalf of others.

All the baptized, as members of Christ's body, represent and witness Christ to the world. The ordained represent the Body as a whole, acting "in his name" for ministry that affects the Church as a whole. The "sacrifice of redemption" refers to the Eucharistic Prayer; the "paschal banquet" to the Priest's responsibility to provide Holy Communion (Matthew 24:45); "leading" the people in "charity" means that he must be the example of service and self-giving love, especially mindful of the poor; "nourishing" the people "with the word" refers to his responsibility to interpret the Scriptures in such a way as to draw the people deeper into the sacred mysteries; and, finally, "strengthening them with the Sacraments" refers to his duty to open up the Church's graces for God's holy people.

The Priest can accomplish these responsibilities efffectively if he empties himself to let Christ work through him. The people seek not the individual Priest, but the Christ whom his Priesthood makes present. This self-emptying is for personal union with God "for you" and "for the salvation" of others. The "image of Christ" is of the man so imbued with the Spirit that he became a life-giving spirit. The essential work of the Priest is to be transformed by the Spirit, who will accomplish the priestly ministry of Christ in and through him.

The Sacred Paschal Triduum

THURSDAY OF THE LORD'S SUPPER

At the Evening Mass

Collect

Slow down to enunciate clearly **most sacred Supper**.

Subordinate **when about to hand himself over to death** to the dominant idea of Jesus entrusting an ever-new sacrifice to the Church.

Make clear that it is the **Son** who **entrusted**.

Banquet of his love describes the **sacrifice**.

Take a clear pause after **charity** to distinguish the the benefits we draw from the mystery.

O God, who have called us to participate
in this most sacred Supper,
in which your Only Begotten Son,
when about to hand himself over to death,
entrusted to the Church a sacrifice new for all eternity,
the banquet of his love,
grant, we pray,
that we may draw from so great a mystery,
the fullness of charity and of life.
Through our Lord Jesus Christ, your Son,
who lives and reigns with you in the unity of the Holy Spirit,
one God, for ever and ever. *

Prayer over the Offerings

Stress **worthily**, which highlights the importance of the disposition we bring to liturgy and connects this "work of the people" to the **work of our redemption**.

Grant us, O Lord, we pray,
that we may participate worthily in these mysteries,
for whenever the memorial of this sacrifice is celebrated
the work of our redemption is accomplished.
Through Christ our Lord.

Prayer after Communion

In this sentence, the balances (**renewed/enjoy; Supper/banquet**) and contrasts (**present age/all eternity**) connect our worship with eternity.

Grant, almighty God,
that, just as we are renewed
by the Supper of your Son in this present age,
so we may enjoy his banquet for all eternity.
Who lives and reigns for ever and ever. **

* The Gloria is sung or recited.
The washing of the feet may follow the Homily. The Creed is not said. The Universal Prayer follows.

** The Transfer of the Blessed Sacrament follows the Prayer after Communion.

Collect: Mass is called "this most sacred Supper" because Jesus celebrated it as his final Passover supper with his closest disciples; and more, because during this Supper, Jesus bequeathed to his Church his everlasting love in the form of a banquet, and his ever-redemptive sacrifice in the form of the Eucharist. It is, therefore, a celebration pregnant with sacramental and sacrificial meaning. The phrase "when about to hand himself over to death" is meaningful. The verb is used often in the neo-Vulgate to describe the action of self-gift by Jesus and the actions surrounding him: he hands himself over to death; he is handed over to death; he hands himself over to the Father's will.

The petition comes from the fact that we are dealing with a mystery—in which our redemption is tied up. It is a mystery (Sacrament) with inexhaustible grace and salvific power. The Church prays that we might tap into such an ocean of grace, to share the fullness of the love that Jesus showed so vividly, and of the life that is available through the Sacrament.

Prayer over the Offerings: This prayer begins with the petition for the grace to participate "worthily" in the great Sacrament (mysteries) we are celebrating. The Latin original (*digne*) means "in a manner full of respect." The word is used because this Sacrament must not be celebrated casually. Rather, the prayer calls upon all to recognize the depth of what we are doing, and the need for God's help if we are to do these sacred actions in a manner befitting their importance.

The space below is for your notes.

Refer to pages viii–x for an explanation of the pointing of the chants and to page xii for the Tones for the Presidential Prayers from *The Roman Missal*.

Pointed Text

Collect

A O God, who have called us to participate
in this most sacred Supper,
in which your Only Begotten Son,
when about to hand himself over to death,
entrusted to the Church a sacrifice new for all eternity,
the banquet of his **love**,
B grant, we pray,
that we may draw from so **great** a mystery,
C the fullness of charity and of ***life***.
Through our Lord Jesus Christ, your Son,
who lives and reigns with you in the unity of the Holy Spirit,
one God, for ever and ever.

Prayer over the Offerings

A Grant us, O Lord, we **pray**,
B that we may participate worthily **in** these mysteries,
C for whenever the memorial of this sacrifice is celebrated
the work of our redemption is accom***plished***.
Through Christ our Lord.

Prayer after Communion

A Grant, almighty **God**,
B that, just as we are renewed
by the Supper of your Son in this **pre**sent age,
C so we may enjoy his banquet for all eter***ni***ty.
Who lives and reigns for ever and ever.

The second part of the prayer makes this point explicitly: we are engaged in the celebration of the memorial of the sacrifice of Jesus—which includes his words at the Last Supper, commemorated in a particular way this night, but which above all encompasses his Death on Calvary and his Resurrection (i.e., the entire Paschal Mystery). In liturgical language, memorial means that the very reality of the person or event is made present again. The reality here is the whole Paschal Mystery.

Prayer after Communion: Again, this prayer begins with the petition, calling God "almighty," since what is about to be asked is very great indeed. We have just celebrated the Holy Eucharist, commemorating and making present the very person of Jesus at the Last Supper, on the Cross, and at the Resurrection. Because it was Jesus's last meal with his disciples, Christian tradition has always called this the Last Supper. Because it brings us into contact with the richness of our salvation, through sacramental action, it is the most renewing thing the Church can do. Hence, mention is made of that renewal, which should transform our life.

As so often in the Prayer after Communion, the Church looks forward to the full fruition of what we have just finished doing. That is, the Church looks forward to being with the Holy Trinity for eternity, and sharing the richness of the vision of God, and the joy we shall know forever. It is this richness that leads the Church to speak of sharing Jesus's banquet in heaven, an image of joy and celebration.

Bring out the accent on **be** in **The Lord be with you**. In the next phrase, make a strong accent on **Lift**, and slow both notes of **hearts**. In the third dialogue, move to the word **thanks** before accenting, and hold that word slightly to give it emphasis. Broaden both notes of **Lord**, and hold **God**.

In the opening hymn of praise, articulate carefully **always** and **everywhere**. Hold **thanks** briefly, but without taking a breath, complete the phrase by continuing on with **Lord**, **holy Father** . . . .

In the very long sentence that begins the body of the text, the melodies on **-lasting sacrifice**, **saving Victim**, and **as his memorial** call for broadening and a hold (but not too long) at the ending syllable.

Sing **As we eat** with careful articulation and pausing, bringing out the contrast between the eating and drinking and their consequences.

Preface: The Sacrifice and the Sacrament of Christ:
The priesthood in Jesus's time was a hereditary position. The New Testament has reinterpreted this to show that Christ is indeed a true Priest, because he was called by God to be so, especially in being God's Only Begotten Son. We read this, particularly, in the letter to the Hebrews, chapters five to nine. Not only that, but his is an eternal Priesthood, since Christ exercises it in heaven. As Priest, the Preface states, Jesus instituted the "pattern" of a sacrifice that would be eternal (one could also have used the word "form"). That is, the "form" was to offer himself as a victim who could save—unlike the Aaronic priesthood that offered animals and flora, which were believed to "cover" the people's sins, but not remove them. Jesus's sacrifice takes away our sins.

And as Christ sat at the Last Supper with his disciples, an event so specially commemorated this night, he commanded them, and us, to make this same sacrifice/offering, doing so as a memorial. We have already seen in the comments on the Prayer over the Offerings the depth and wealth of meaning that is contained in that word "memorial"—which really is a command to "make present again, in sacramental form" precisely the offering that Jesus made for the salvation of the world. The result of our eating his sacrificed flesh, really present on our altars, renews us in grace, which is a unique kind of strength. Drinking his sacrificed blood, also really present, actually washes us clean (cf. the image in Revelation 7:14). Hence the joy, this night, as at every Holy Eucharist, in

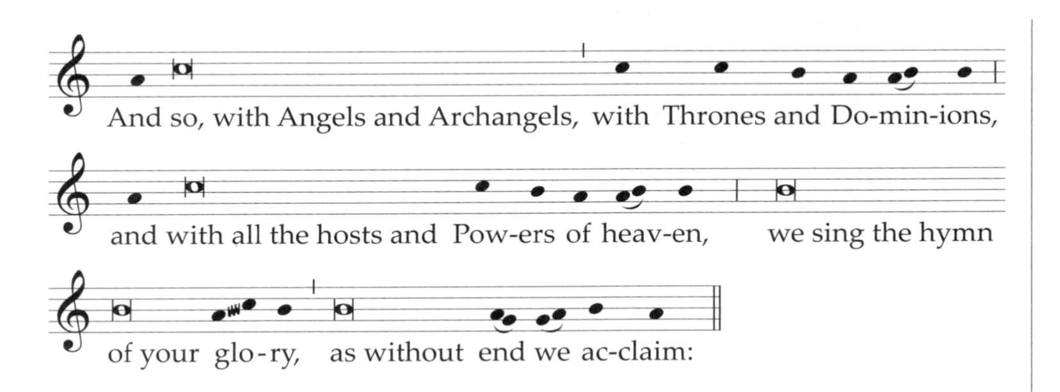

Make a slight pause after **And so**. Respect the commas but try to keep this section together, without big breaks for breaths. Broaden the last phrase, especially on **glory**. Slow **we ac-**, and put emphasis on **-claim**, so as to evoke the response **Holy, Holy, Holy . . . .**

Holy, Holy, Holy Lord God of hosts . . .

Text without music:

V. **The Lord be with you.**
R. And with your spirit.

V. **Lift up your hearts.**
R. We lift them up to the Lord.

V. **Let us give thanks to the Lord our God.**
R. It is right and just.

Emphasize **truly**, **duty**, and **salvation**.

It is truly right and just, our duty and our salvation,
always and everywhere to give you thanks,
Lord, holy Father, almighty and eternal God,
through Christ our Lord.

Pray the long first sentence slowly, with a pause at **sacrifice**.

For he is the true and eternal Priest,
who instituted the pattern of an everlasting sacrifice
and was the first to offer himself as the saving Victim,
commanding us to make this offering as his memorial.
As we eat his flesh that was sacrificed for us,
we are made strong,
and, as we drink his Blood that was poured out for us,
we are washed clean.

In the sentence beginning **As we eat**, by careful articulation and pausing, bring out the contrast between the eating and drinking and their consequences.

singing the glory of a God who has loved us so much.

(The Homily that follows reflects on the second Memorial Acclamation in light of tonight's reading from 1 Corinthians 11:23–26 and all that we commemorate in this liturgy. The Homily has been modified from the CD *Preparing Your Parish for the Revised Roman Missal: Homilies and Reproducibles for Faith Formation* © 2010, Liturgy Training Publications.)

"When We Eat This Bread . . ." Glory in Humble Service

Msgr. Joseph DeGrocco

At this Holy Thursday Evening Mass of the Lord's Supper, Church tradition asks us to commemorate the institution of the Eucharist, the institution of the Priesthood, and Jesus's command of love. In doing so, we can recognize that what binds all three of these together is their rootedness in Jesus's humble service, a humble service we are enjoined to live out today in our life. So tonight we commemorate the life-giving humble service of Jesus of Nazareth, Jesus the Christ, in all its fullness, and we pray to be so swept up in that life and service as it comes to us tonight that we are changed to be able to live that same life-giving service for one another, in union with him. Tonight we remember, particularly as we sing, "When we eat this Bread and drink this Cup, / we proclaim your Death, O Lord, / until you come again."

But our remembrance is not just remembrance as we might ordinarily think of it. No, tonight we are not mimicking the

Make a slight pause at **And so**.

And so, with Angels and Archangels,
with Thrones and Dominions,
and with all the hosts and Powers of heaven,
we sing the hymn of your glory,
as without end we acclaim: *

Holy, Holy, Holy Lord God of hosts . . .

Last Supper, nor does this liturgy ask us to pretend that we are actually at the Last Supper. Rather, our remembrance is in the Jewish sense of remembering. For our Jewish brothers and sisters, the Passover proclaimed in the First Reading for this Mass is an annual memorial of that great act of God that constituted the Israelites as his first people. But "memorial" means so much more than just mentally recalling. Even today, devout Jews believe that, in celebrating Passover, they are actually coming out of Egypt with their ancestors, being rescued by God now. The power of that past event is brought into the present and is made effective and active in the here and now. In that same way, we commemorate, we remember, the Paschal Mystery, the mystery of Jesus's life-giving Death and Resurrection—his Passover from the cross to new life. We do that at this Evening Mass of the Lord's Supper; we do that throughout the Three Days of the Sacred Triduum; we do that at every Eucharist. It is a commemoration that empowers us now, which saves us now, because the self-emptying, life-giving gift of Jesus's sacrifice is made present and powerfully given to us here and now. "When we eat this Bread and drink this Cup, / we proclaim your Death, O Lord, / until you come again."

That's why we can see the foot washing not only as an act of humble service, but also in its deeper, eucharistic meaning. Its greater significance is as an act of the self-emptying of Jesus, and as a sign of the way we must empty ourselves out of love for one another.

"I have given you a model to follow, so that as I have done for you, you should also do." Do what? Do the entire life that was symbolized by washing feet, the life that culminated in total abandonment, the total handing over to the Father on the cross. In fact, Jesus's Death on the cross only makes sense in terms of his whole life. His dying for us is simply the ultimate expression and logical conclusion of the way he lived for us. The self-emptying on the cross flowed from the self-emptying of his whole life, and it is this voluntary self-giving of Jesus to the Father that the Eucharist makes present to us. The Memorial Acclamation echoes the words of the Second Reading: "For as often as you eat this bread and drink the cup, you proclaim the death of the Lord until he comes" (1 Corinthians 11:27). We are called to proclaim that death not only here at Mass, but in the way we live the Eucharist through the self-gift, the self-emptying love we give to one another every day. So, to partake of the Eucharist must also mean partaking of Jesus's example of humble service and compassionate love, even to the point of death. It means walking the path that leads through death to eternal life.

Washing feet, service, and companionship with Jesus even all the way to the cross: these are expressions of a life caught up in the passing over which is celebrated in the Three Days of the Sacred Triduum—the Passover of the Lord Jesus. It is a Passover that is celebrated and lived out every time we celebrate the Eucharist.

FRIDAY OF THE PASSION OF THE LORD

The Celebration of the Passion of the Lord

Scripture often bids God to **Remember**. Do so here with reverence and gratitude. The request for sanctification is the dominant idea that should be stressed.

Prayer*

Remember your mercies, O Lord,
and with your eternal protection sanctify your servants,
for whom Christ your Son,
by the shedding of his Bzlood,
established the Paschal Mystery.
Who lives and reigns for ever and ever.
R. Amen.

Or:

Recalling Christ's sacrifice should be redolent of gratitude. By stressing **Passion** and **abolished**, signal that the latter flows from the former. Do not pause after **ancient sin**.

O God, who by the Passion of Christ your Son, our Lord,
abolished the death inherited from ancient sin
by every succeeding generation,
grant that just as, being conformed to him,
we have borne by the law of nature
the image of the man of earth,
so by the sanctification of grace
we may bear the image of the Man of heaven.
Through Christ our Lord.
R. Amen. **

* The liturgy begins in silence while the ministers go to the altar and lie prostrate.

** The Liturgy of the Word follows the prayer.

Prayer: This prayer is newly composed for the third edition of *The Roman Missal*. It begins with a citation from Psalm 25:6–7, begging God's "mercies." (In the liturgy prior to the Second Vatican Council, this verse was used as an Entrance antiphon for the Second Sunday of Lent as well as Ember Wednesday.) We have come to celebrate in a special way the Passion of the Lord. It is through that Passion that the "mercies" of the Lord have flowed upon us, the followers of Jesus, but we pray that these mercies will flow upon the whole world. (Indeed, the 10 Solemn intercessions we will pray at the end of the Liturgy of the Word invoke God's mercies on every person throughout the world.)

The Church prays also that God's protection will make us holy (sanctify). It was for this end that Christ shed his Blood. It was for this end that Christ established the whole of the Paschal Mystery—the celebration of which reaches a certain high point in today's liturgy. Embracing the Paschal Mystery sets us apart from the world, makes us one with Christ, who was set apart by the Father for the work of the world's redemption. That "setting apart" to be with Jesus is by definition what holiness is about. This is the core petition offered.

Pointed Text

Prayer

A Remember your mercies, O **Lord**,
B and with your eternal protection sancti**fy** your servants,
C for whom Christ your Son,
by the shedding of his Blood,
established the Paschal My***ster***y.
Who lives and reigns for ever and ever.
R. Amen.

Or:

A O God, who by the Passion of Christ your Son, our Lord,
abolished the death inherited from ancient sin
by every succeeding genera**tion**,
B grant that just as, being conformed to him,
we have borne by the law of nature
the image of the **man** of earth,
C so by the sanctification of grace
we may bear the image of the Man of hea***ven***.
Through Christ our Lord.
R. Amen.

The space below is for your notes.

Refer to pages viii–x for an explanation of the pointing of the chants and to page xii for the Tones for the Presidential Prayers from *The Roman Missal*.

Optional Prayer: This prayer has been transferred exactly from the liturgy celebrated before the publication of the new Missal. It begins by calling on God as the One who, by the "Passion of Christ," abolished the sin that we inherited from our first parents and which all generations of human beings are destined to inherit. We have come together today to observe in a special way the Death of God's Son. That Death occurred because of the earlier condemnation to death because of sin ("By the sweat of your face / shall you get bread to eat, / Until you return to the ground, / from which you were taken; / For you are dirt, / and to dirt you shall return" (Genesis 3:19). Thus, the Church, as it prays, is catechizing its members about the reason for a day such as Good Friday.

The petition explicitly parallels Christ and us. It mentions that we are "conformed" to/with him (i.e., made in the same form as he was). That is, all of us have the earthly image of human beings, just because it is a "law of nature." For us, though, as the earlier part of the prayer states, the form has been marred by sin. But the strong faith of the Church proclaims that, with Jesus's Death, life is not really ended. So we pray that we may be transformed to "bear the image of the Man of heaven." This transformation would take place by the holiness that God's grace alone confers.

First Part: The Liturgy of the Word

The Solemn Intercessions*

The music for the proclamation of the prayers by the Priest Celebrant follows precisely the pattern for the Solemn Tone of Prayer Cantillation, sometimes with the flexa doubled because the text is so long. Respect the commas carefully. Also, avoid the temptation to begin rushing these texts in the last few prayers. It is, indeed, a long part of the liturgical celebration, especially after the proclamation of the Passion Gospel from Saint John, but it is such an important part that every part must be treated with reverent solemnity.

I. For Holy Church

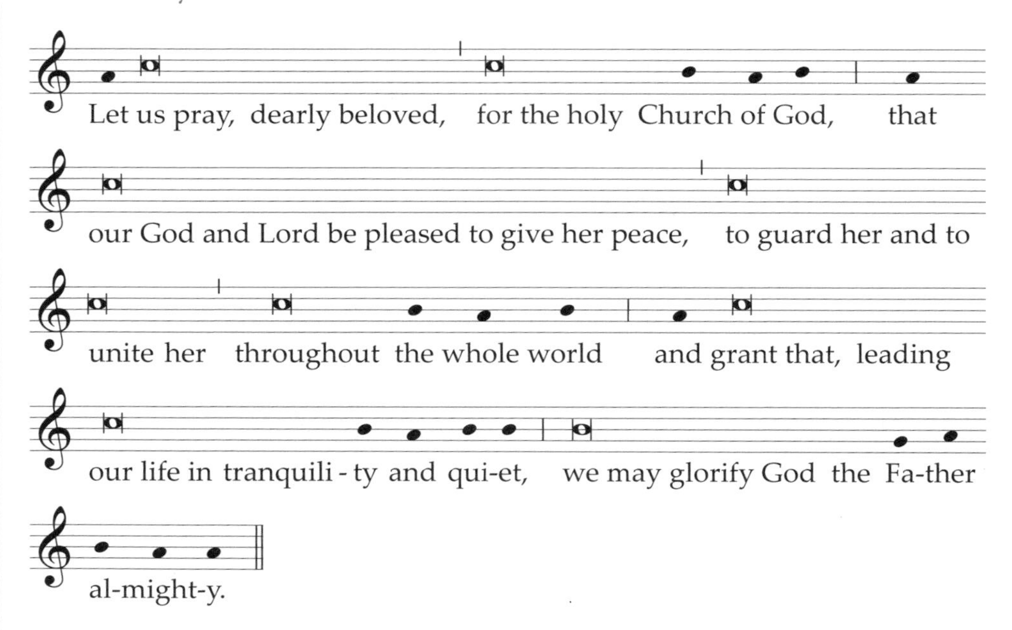

The prayer is sung in the simple tone or, if the invitations **Let us kneel—Let us stand** are used, in the solemn tone.

Let us pray, dearly beloved, for the holy Church of God,
that our God and Lord be pleased to give her peace,
to guard her and to unite her throughout the whole world
and grant that, leading our life in tranquility and quiet,
we may glorify God the Father almighty.

With each Prayer, the Deacon or cantor must speak the Invitation slowly so what we are asked to pray for is clearly articulated and heard.

Speak with love as you intercede for the **Church of God**. Note that the first petitions ask God to safeguard the Church and the last petition speaks of the Church's response.

* The Solemn Intercessions follow the Liturgy of the Word.

First Intercession: For Holy Church

This first of the great intercessory Prayers for this day's liturgy begins by speaking of Christ, even though the prayer is ostensibly for the Church. This is fitting, since the Father revealed his glory, his greatness, and his heavenly Being, in Christ, for the entire world (all the nations). Thus, the spotlight of glory is not on the Church, but on its Head, Christ.

The words of this prayer echo those of the risen Christ, who entered the room greeting the Apostles with the words: "Peace be with you. As the Father has sent me, so I send you" (John 20:21). It is the same peace for which we pray now.

The prayer goes on to beg God's watchful care "over the works of your mercy." The Latin original of this word (*misericordia*) was used by early Church Fathers, such as Saints Augustine and Ambrose, to mean the "charity" of God, the love which God has shown to humanity. That divine love was shown most powerfully in Christ, and therefore is shown in his Church also. One of God's great works of mercy is to call someone to be a member of his Son's body, a member of the Church. So to ask to watch over the works of his mercy certainly includes God's watching over the Church.

The conclusion of the petition likens the Church even more to Christ: as he was the means for God to reveal his glory to the whole world, so too the Church has "spread throughout the world"—surely a sign of God's mercy. Here we recall the glorified Christ, just before the Ascension, telling the disciples to spread the good news.

Prayer in silence. Then the Priest says:

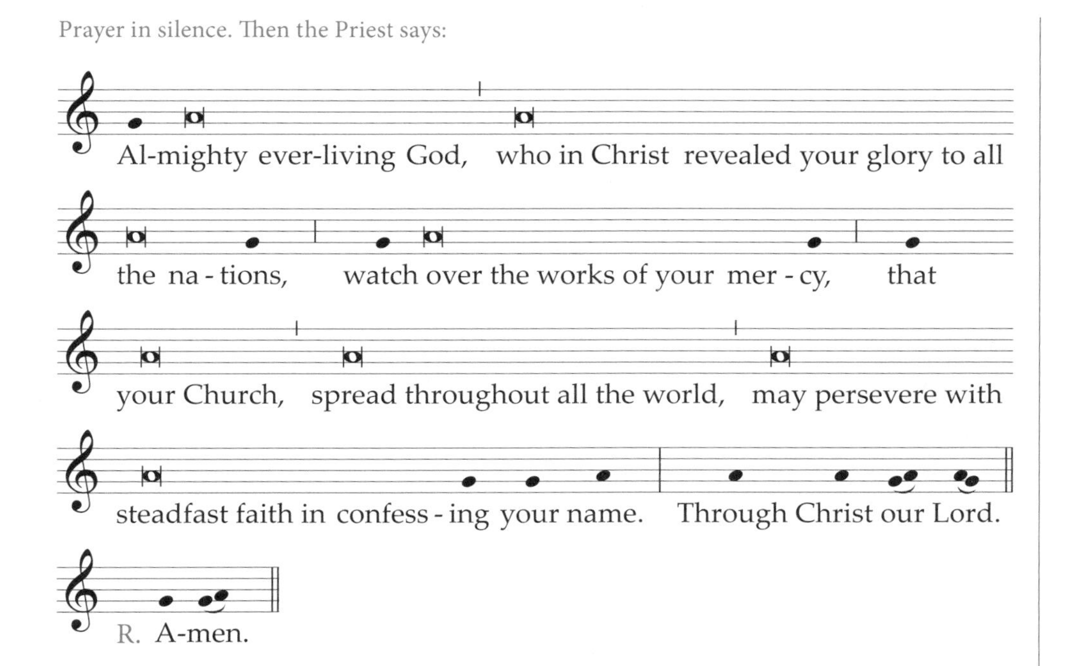

Almighty ever-living God,
who in Christ revealed your glory to all the nations,
watch over the works of your mercy,
that your Church, spread throughout all the world,
may persevere with steadfast faith in confessing your name.
Through Christ our Lord.
R. Amen.

This prayer first acknowledges God's **glory** then speaks his **works of . . . mercy**. Your voice should suggest both the majesty and the mercy by shifting from a faster pace and louder volume to a slower pace and softer tone.

"But you will receive power when the holy Spirit comes upon you, and you will be my witnesses in Jerusalem, throughout Judea and Samaria, and to the ends of the earth" (Acts 1:8).

We pray here, too, for perseverance in faith for all in the Church, i.e., all those baptized in the name of God (which is the same as saying, in the Person of God). By our election, we have confessed God's name, by being signed in the Trinity, and taking the name of Christ. The prayer begs the grace to continue such.

This intercession that the Church "may persevere with steadfast faith in confessing your name" is similar to the words of Saint Paul in adddressing the churches. To the Corinthians he stated: "Be on your guard, stand firm in the faith, be courageous, be strong" (1 Corinthinans 16:13). To the Philippians, he said: "Only, conduct yourselves in a way worthy of the gospel of Christ, so that, whether I come and see you or am absent, I may hear news of you, that you are standing firm in one spirit, with one mind struggling together for the faith of the gospel, not intimidated in any way by your opponents. . . . Yours is the same struggle as you saw in me and now hear about me"(Philippians 1:27–28, 30).

To the Thessalonians, he offered the following that their witness would remain strong: "May our Lord Jesus Christ who has loved us and given us everlasting encouragement and good hope through his grace, encourage your hearts and strengthen them in every good deed and word" (2 Thessalonians 2:16–17).

The music for the proclamation of the prayers by the Priest Celebrant follows precisely the pattern for the Solemn Tone of Prayer Cantillation, sometimes with the flexa doubled because the text is so long. Respect the commas carefully.

Proclaim **for our most Holy Father Pope N**. clearly and precisely.

Let us pray also for our most Holy Father Pope N.,
that our God and Lord,
who chose him for the Order of Bishops,
may keep him safe and unharmed for the Lord's holy Church,
to govern the holy People of God.

Prayer in silence. Then the Priest says:

Second Intercession: For the Pope

At the outset, this prayer identifies the choice of the Pope as God's decree, which is the basis of all reality. That God chooses the Pope is evident from Matthew 16:15–19. There, Jesus tells Peter that God gave him the words to say and, therefore, the Church will be built upon him. "He said to them, 'Who do you say that I am?' Simon Peter said in reply, 'You are the Messiah, the Son of the living God.' Jesus said to him in reply, 'Blessed are you, Simon son of Jonah. For flesh and blood has not revealed this to you, but my heavenly Father. And so I say to you, you are Peter, and upon this rock I will build my church, and the gates of the netherworld shall not prevail against it. I will give you the keys to the kingdom of heaven. Whatever you bind on earth shall be bound in heaven; and whatever you loose on earth shall be loosed in heaven."

The imagery of God's involvement continues: protect the Pope chosen for us—the latter phrase is ambiguous, but in the context, it surely refers to the fact that God was primarily doing the choosing. God's "kindness" is his love, in this case, for his chosen people, the Church. And therefore, we want that same kindness to extend in a special way to the Pope, protecting him from any evil.

Upon reaching the heart of the petition, we state explicitly that we, the Christian people, are governed by God our Creator. For this reason, we beg to grow in merit, because of the faith we place in God, our true leader—even though God wanted a Pope chosen ostensibly to lead his Church. The implication here is that we

Almighty ever-living God,
by whose decree all things are founded,
look with favor on our prayers
and in your kindness protect the Pope chosen for us,
that, under him, the Christian people,
governed by you their maker,
may grow in merit by reason of their faith.
Through Christ our Lord.
R. Amen.

III. For all orders and degrees of the faithful

Let us pray also for our Bishop N.,*
for all Bishops, Priests, and Deacons of the Church
and for the whole of the faithful people.

Proclaim clearly and precisely **for our Bishop N.**, **Bishops**, **Priests**, **Deacons**, **Church**, and **whole of the faithful people**.

Prayer in silence. Then the Priest says:

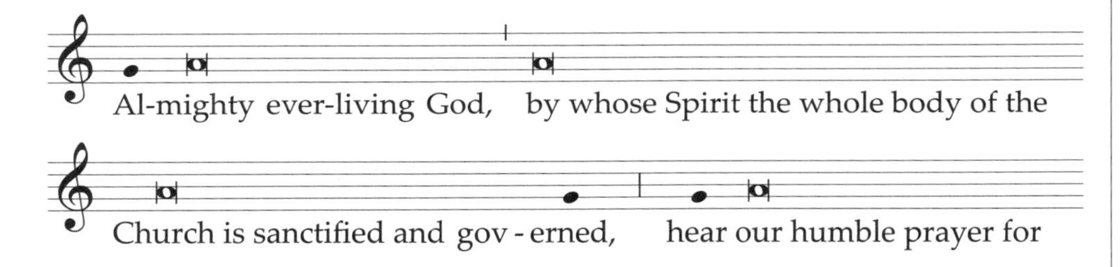

* Mention may be made here of the Coadjutor Bishop, or Auxiliary Bishops, as noted in the General Instruction of the Roman Missal, no. 149.

see God's authority working in the Pope, something which calls for faith, to see beneath the appearances of reality and the history of the Church.

It is a faith that hearkens to the disciples' commissioning. "Go, therefore, and make disciples of all nations, baptizing them in the name of the Father, and of the Son, and of the holy Spirit, teaching them to observe all that I have commanded you" (Matthew 28: 19–20).

Third Intercession: For all orders and degrees of the faithful
We have prayed for the Church, in general, and the Pope, in particular. This third intercession is intended to petition God for the rest of the clergy, including Bishops, Priests, and Deacons, and then for all the lay faithful. At the outset it is restated that the Church is made holy not by her efforts, and governed not by the obvious human leaders we have, but rather that God is behind any growth in holiness and is the One governing the entire body. In particular, the Holy Spirit is seen as the primary principle for holiness (sanctified), as well as the One moving hearts through wise governance.

The petition mentions the ministers specifically, since, through the Holy Spirit's movement, they lead the rest of the Church in the ways of holiness and animate the the Church to service. So the prayer for the ministers intends to state that by God's grace, all the rest can serve God faithfully—that is, with a spirit full of faith—if so animated by the ministers who lead

Almighty ever-living God,
by whose Spirit the whole body of the Church
is sanctified and governed,
hear our humble prayer for your ministers,
that, by the gift of your grace,
all may serve you faithfully.
Through Christ our Lord.
R. Amen.

IV. For catechumens

them. We pray that all may serve with faith, which means the leading ministers also are included in this petition, as well as the laity. The laity have roles of service, extending from simply praying for others on through serving as proclaimers of the Word of God, as extraordinary ministers of the Eucharist, in hospitality roles, and in various ministries of care for the sick, the dying, and the imprisoned and their families.

Fourth Intercession: For catechumens
Again the prayer is clear that God is the One who gives new offspring to the Church, since those who are coming to Baptism are responding to God's call and election. The petition requests an increase both of faith and of understanding. Particularly in the final weeks before Baptism, the Church has intensified its prayer for the catechumens' interior growth—the introduction to this prayer hopes for the grace of the catechumens opening "wide the ears of their inmost hearts" so as to receive the immense mercy/love that God wants to give them. The understanding prayed for here is certainly that of knowing the Church, its faith and Tradition, to which these candidates are coming. But surely it refers to a deeper reality also, that of understanding the mercy of God which expresses his person so deeply.

The intercession "that our God and Lord may open wide the ears of their inmost hearts" is most interesting. We usually do not think of our hearts as having

Let us pray also for (our) catechumens,
that our God and Lord
may open wide the ears of their inmost hearts
and unlock the gates of his mercy,
that, having received forgiveness of all their sins
through the waters of rebirth,
they, too, may be one with Christ Jesus our Lord.

The most important phrase in the petition is **for (our) catechumens**. Proclaim it clearly and concisely.

To avoid awkward imagery (**ears** on a **heart**) or odd juxtaposition (**too** / **one**) stress the following words, rather than the other options, in the lines in which they occur: **wide**, **unlock**, **forgiveness**, **waters**, **one**.

Prayer in silence. Then the Priest says:

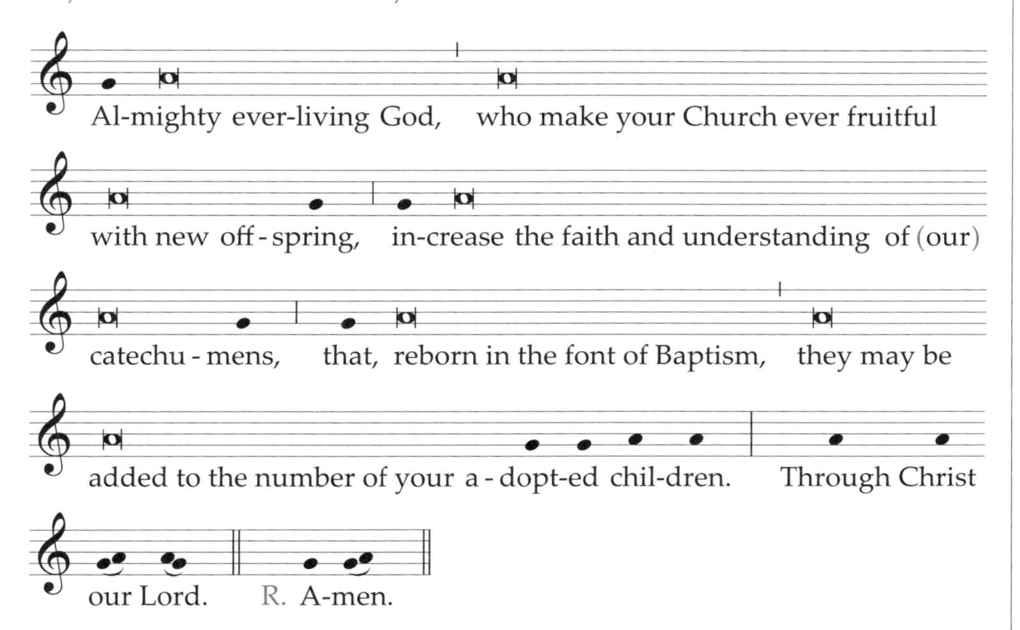

The music for the proclamation of the prayers by the Priest Celebrant follows precisely the pattern for the Solemn Tone of Prayer Cantillation, sometimes with the Flexa doubled because the text is so long. Respect the commas carefully.

Almighty ever-living God,
who make your Church ever fruitful with new offspring,
increase the faith and understanding of (our) catechumens,
that, reborn in the font of Baptism,
they may be added to the number of your adopted children.
Through Christ our Lord.
R. Amen.

ears. But is it not through our hearts that we listen to the word of God? And is it not through our hearts that we respond to God? These words of Samuel portray the heart as at the core of what we do: "If you wish with your whole heart to return to the Lord, put away your foreign gods and your Ashtaroth, devote yourselves to the Lord and worship him alone" (1 Samuel 7:3).

The second petition requests that, once reborn in the font of Baptism, the catechumens may become part of God's special family and people—among the number of God's adopted children. Such a petition to God makes clear the belief of the Church: these persons are God's children, and he is the One choosing and adopting them. Yes, they will be added to a parish register also; but the main thing is that they are in God's special family, from the moment of Baptism.

In many parishes, the Ephethetha Rite will be celebrated on Holy Saturday. During the rite, the Priest prays that the individual's ears may be opened to hear the word of God. The rite makes clear that it is through the help of God's grace that we are open to the words that we hear from scripture.

As with the other preparation rites, this rite incudes a Prayer of Blessing that tells how Christ has granted "rebirth in the Spirit." It asks, too, that the catechumens may be reborn as God's children.

At their Baptism, the catechumens will receive a candle from their godparents. The Priest Celebrant will tell them: "Walk always as children of the light" (RCIA, 230). That is, walk as God's children.

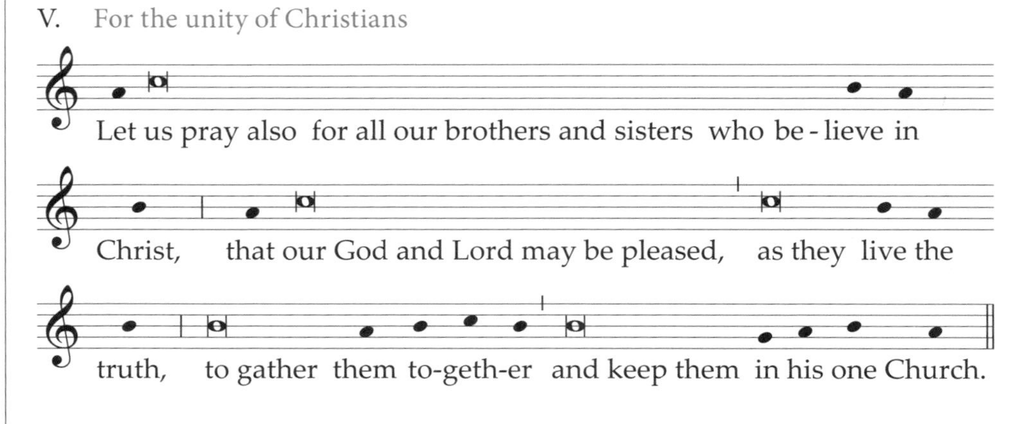

Lift out those for whom we pray: **our brothers and sisters who believe in Christ**.

Without losing track of the end point—**keep them in his one Church**—give strong emphasis to the acknowledgment that these brethren are living the truth.

Let us pray also for all our brothers and sisters who believe in Christ,
that our God and Lord may be pleased,
as they live the truth,
to gather them together and keep them in his one Church.

Prayer in silence. Then the Priest says:

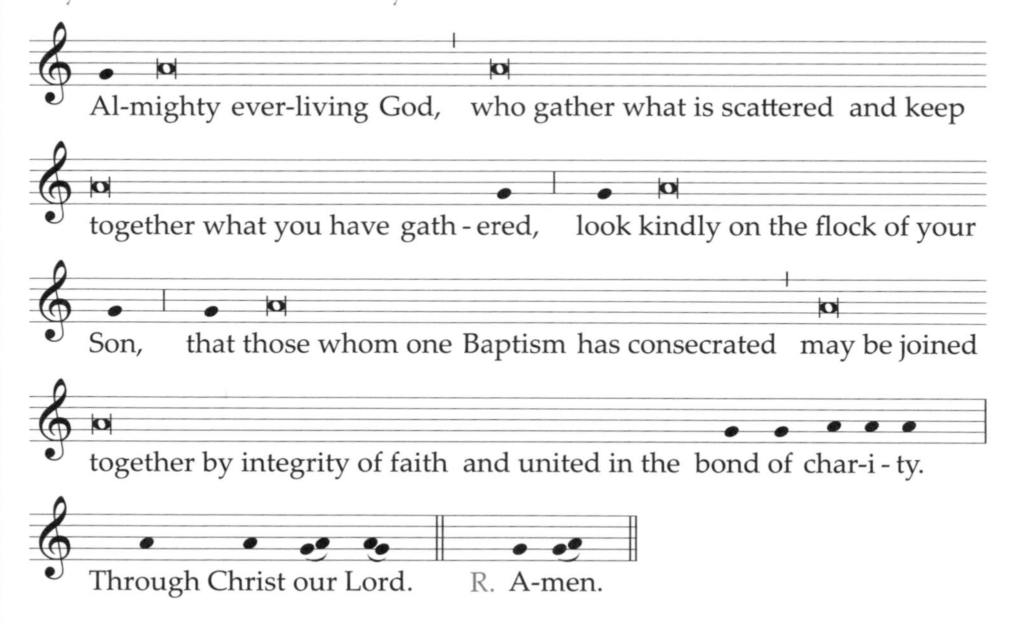

Fifth Intercession: For the unity of Christians

The image of God in the opening of this intercession is that of a shepherd: God gathers the scattered, and by his grace alone the flock can "keep together." The words "gathered and scattered" recall Isaiah 11:12, in which we hear of God gathering his dispersed Chosen People. "He shall raise a signal to the nations / and gather the outcasts of Israel; / The dispersed of Judah he shall assemble from the four corners of the earth."

Lumen Gentium, 6, describes the Church "as a sheepfold, the sole and necessary entrance to which is Christ (see John 10:1–10). It is also a flock, of which God foretold that he would himself be the shepherd (see Isaiah 40:11; Ezekiel 34:11 ff.), and whose sheep, although watched over by human shepherds, are nevertheless at all times brought to pasture by God himself . . . ."

God is asked to look kindly on all those who consider Jesus their Good Shepherd, because they believe in him and have consecrated that belief through the Sacrament of Baptism.

From the early days of the Church, members prayed for unity amidst their struggles. Saint Paul felt the need to counsel the Church of Philippi to stay gathered: "If there is any encouragement in Christ, any solace in love, any participating in the Spirit, any compassion and mercy, complete my joy by being of the same mind, with the same love, united in heart, thinking one thing" (Philippians 2:1).

Almighty ever-living God,
who gather what is scattered
and keep together what you have gathered,
look kindly on the flock of your Son,
that those whom one Baptism has consecrated
may be joined together by integrity of faith
and united in the bond of charity.
Through Christ our Lord.
R. Amen.

Speak the first two lines slowly to establish God's nature as unifier, then intercede for Christ's flock, stressing the words that speak of oneness and unity: **joined together**; **united**; **bond**.

VI. For the Jewish people

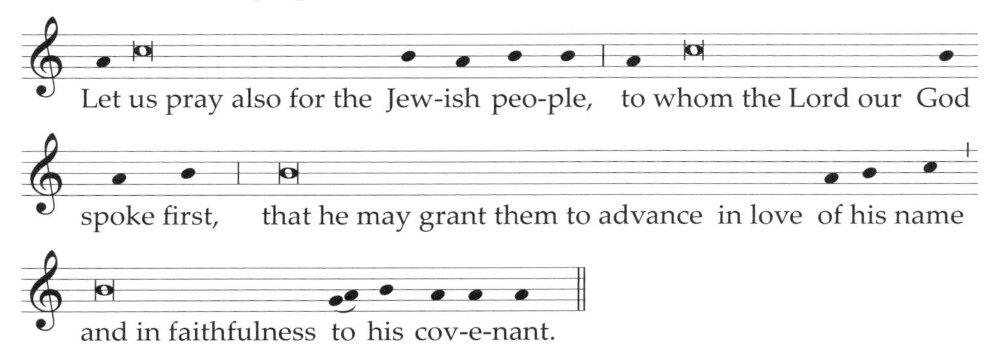

The music for the proclamation of the prayers by the Priest Celebrant follows precisely the pattern for the Solemn Tone of Prayer Cantillation, sometimes with the Flexa doubled because the text is so long.

Let us pray also for the Jewish people,
to whom the Lord our God spoke first,
that he may grant them to advance in love of his name
and in faithfulness to his covenant.

Pause briefly after **Jewish people**, then speak the balance of the prayer with tenderness and reverence for God's chosen people and their **covenant**.

But the sad fact is that the flock of Christ is divided now—whether through historical circumstance, theological dissension, or personal preference. The Introduction to *Unitatis Redintegratio* (Decree on Ecumenism) notes the movement "for the restoration of unity among all Christians" (1).

Today, the Church prays that we might be joined by "integrity of faith." The garment of faith has been torn by our divisions. It will take God's special grace to renew us in faith, so that every Christian's faith might reflect God's unfolding truth. Until that grace is given and received, we petition for the grace of charity to characterize our relations, so that we might manifest the life of Christ to each other, and thus come "to know the love of Christ which surpasses all knowledge" (Ephesians 3:19).

Sixth Intercession:
For the Jewish people

The opening of the prayer mentions God's promises, bestowed on Abraham and his descendants. This is important to state, because God has always been seen in Judaism as faithful to his promises. Thus, 1 Chronicles 16:15–16: "He remembers forever his covenant which he made binding for a thousand generations—which he entered into with Abraham. . . . " (Repeated in Psalm 105:8–9). The New Testament speaks of the same. In Romans 11:28–29, in referring to the Jews who have not converted to Christianity, Saint Paul states: "In respect to the gospel, they are enemies on your account; but in respect to election, they are

Prayer in silence. Then the Priest says:

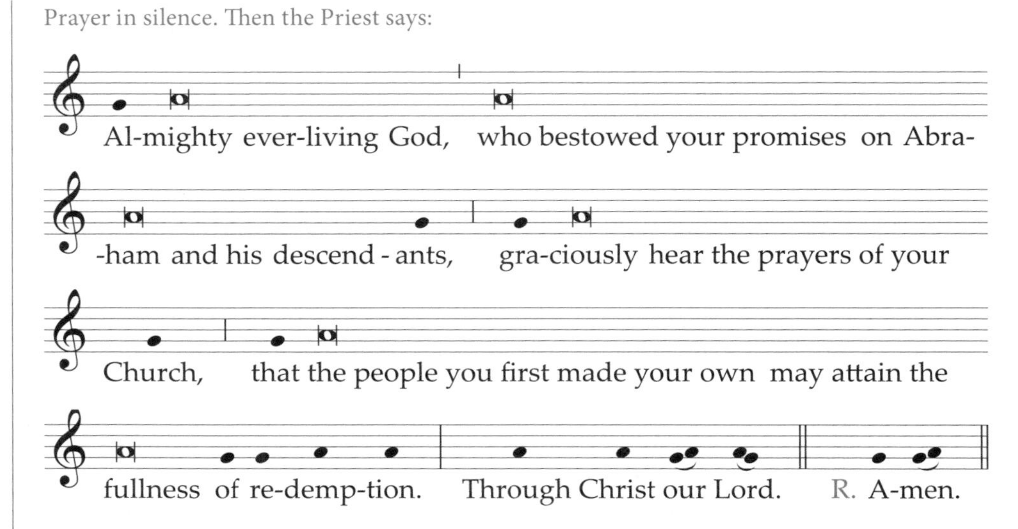

Speak of **Abraham** with affectionate familiarity. Remember you are praying that the descendants of Abraham, God's chosen people, will find **fullness of redemption**.

Almighty ever-living God,
who bestowed your promises on Abraham and his descendants,
graciously hear the prayers of your Church,
that the people you first made your own
may attain the fullness of redemption.
Through Christ our Lord.
R. Amen.

VII. For those who do not believe in Christ

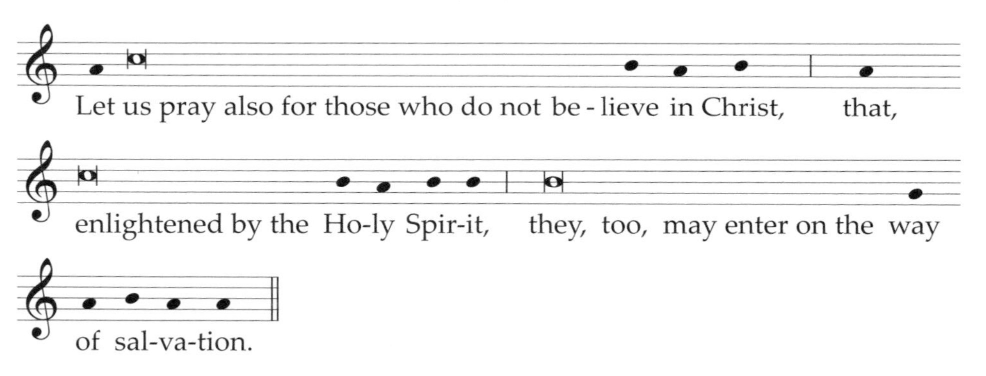

Proclaim clearly and precisely: **for those who do not believe in Christ**.

Let us pray also for those who do not believe in Christ,
that, enlightened by the Holy Spirit,
they, too, may enter on the way of salvation.

beloved because of the patriarchs. For the gifts and the call of God are irrevocable."

In the light of this great tradition, the Church lifts up its petition: that since God has made this people his own from far back in salvation history (Abraham, Isaac, Jacob, as well as Moses in the Exodus, Joshua coming into the Promised Land, etc.), he would bring them to the fullness of redemption. Some Jews might see the post-World War II return to Palestine as a culmination of their redemption. Christians cannot but see Jesus as that fullness. However, the prayer does not state that. Rather, following the Second Vatican Council's teaching (*Nostra Aetate* / On the Relationship of the Church to non-Christian Religions), it simply re-emphasizes God's special relationship with his people, while yet praying that they arrive at the fullness of redemption.

As *Nostra Aetate* (3) states, "The church of Christ acknowledges that in God's plan of salvation the beginnings of its faith and election are to be found in the patriarchs, Moses and the prophets. It professes that Christ's faithful who as people of faith are daughters and sons of Abraham are included in the same patriarch's call . . . ."

Seventh Intercession:
For those who do not believe in Christ
The first petition in this intercession begs that those who do not believe in Christ may find the truth, by the sincerity of their lives. This parallels a similar intercession in Eucharistic Prayer IV, which prays for "all who seek you with a sincere heart." That happy phrase echoes another phrase

Prayer in silence. Then the Priest says:

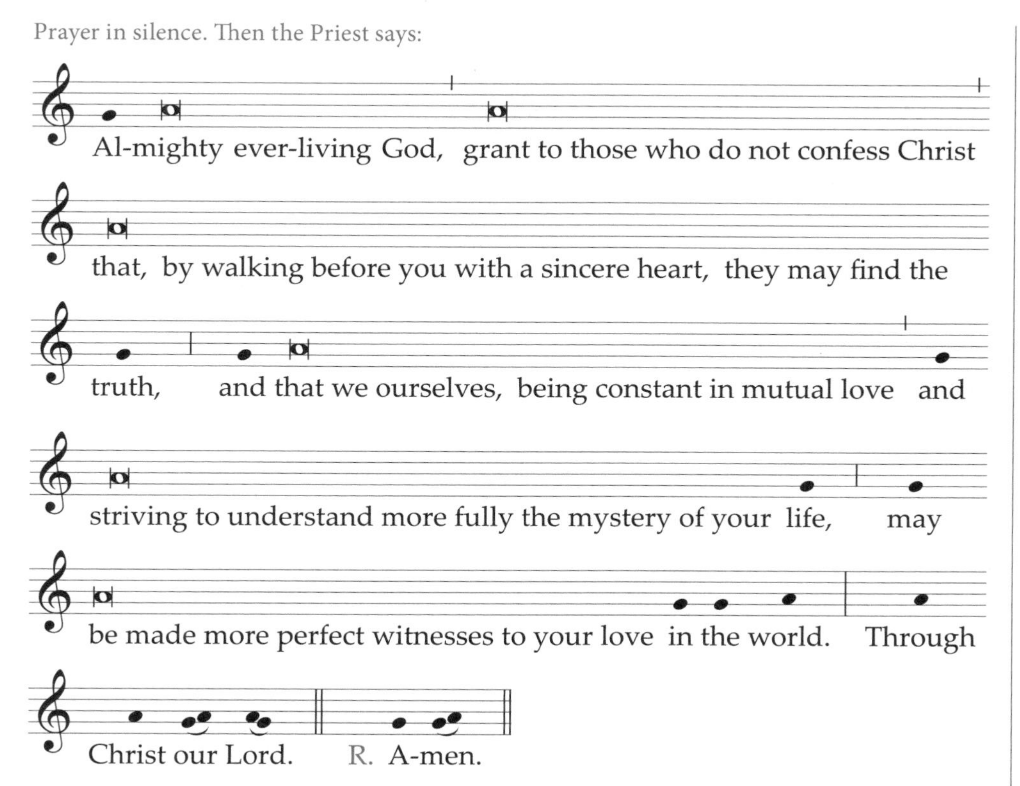

Almighty ever-living God,
grant to those who do not confess Christ
that, by walking before you with a sincere heart,
they may find the truth
and that we ourselves, being constant in mutual love
and striving to understand more fully the mystery of your life,
may be made more perfect witnesses to your love in the world.
Through Christ our Lord.
R. Amen.

Pray for **those who do not confess Christ** with compassionate respect. The prayer asks that they might walk **with a sincere heart**, and thus come to know **the truth**, which is Christ. Note we also pray for ourselves to become better **witnesses** to God's eternal love.

appearing in the same Eucharistic Prayer just after the Holy, Holy, Holy: "so that those who seek might find you." Saint Gregory of Nyssa said, "Finding God means seeking him unceasingly." The petition of the Church this day is for just such a finding of truth.

The second petition concerns the Church itself: that we be more perfect witnesses to God's love in the world. In the early Church, members were told that their actions influenced the regard that non-Christians held for the Church, as is seen in 1 Peter 2:11: "Maintain good conduct among the Gentiles, so that if they speak of you as evildoers they may observe your good works and glorify God on the day of salvation."

In the end, persons will not be converted to Christ so much by intellectual argument as by love; that is, by showing Christ to these persons through loving them as much as Christ himself loves them. On the way to this more perfect witness, we within the Church need to be bolstered by mutual love of one another—which will give us the grace and courage to go outside our circle to non-Christians. Involved also will be a coming to a greater understanding of the mystery of God's life, which is shared by non-Christians. In effect, we are praying that we might look at others just as God does, for he created them and loves them, even if they have not found the way to his Son, Jesus.

VIII. For those who do not believe in God

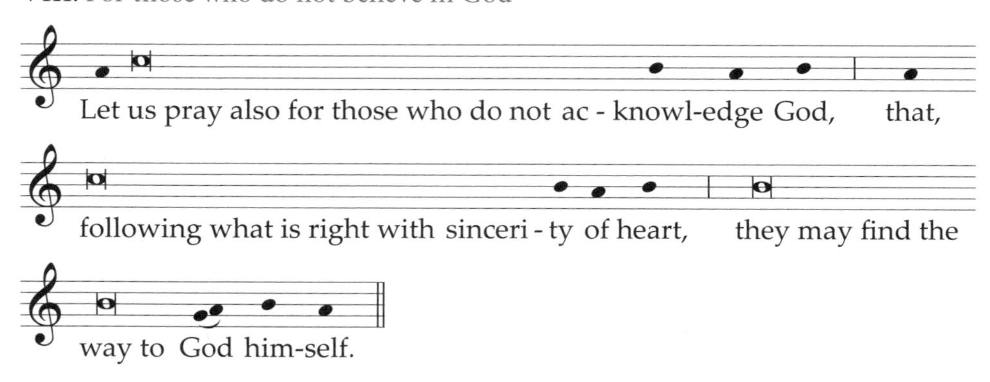

Each prayer widens the circle of kinship with humankind. Let your tone convey that this is not just the longing of our hearts, but of God's. Take a brief pause after **do not acknowledge God**.

Let us pray also for those who do not acknowledge God,
that, following what is right in sincerity of heart,
they may find the way to God himself.

Prayer in silence. Then the Priest says:

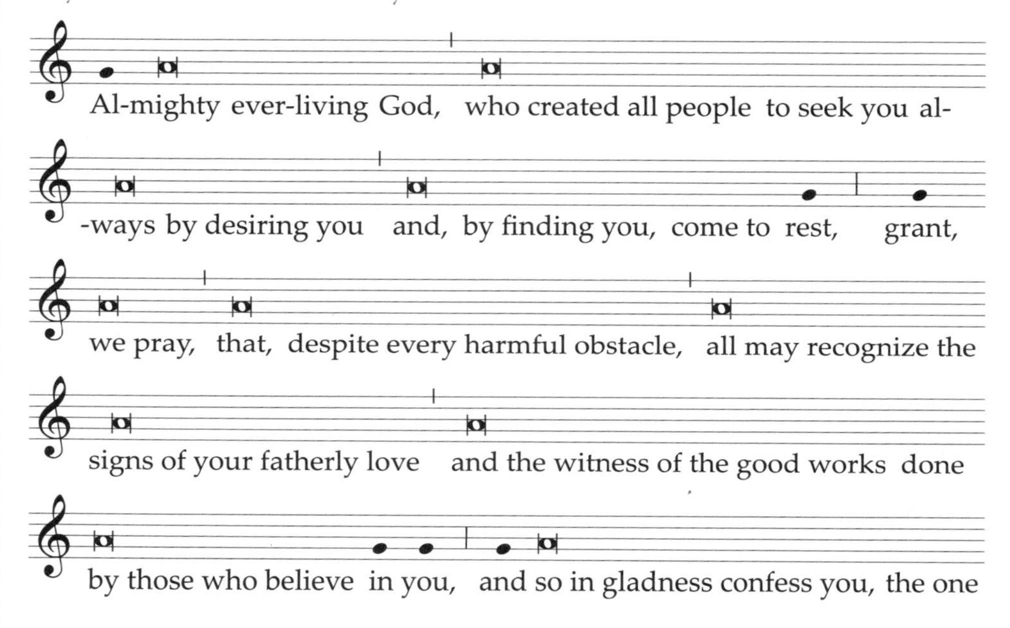

Eighth Intercession: For those who do not believe in God

This intercession breathes our Christian faith, even as it speaks of those without that faith.

The initial point the prayer makes is that God is the creator of all—not just of those who believe in him. Secondly, God created people with a desire in their hearts for the infinite, actually for God. The point of such desire, we believe, is that it will spur people to seek God—and, it is to be hoped, will indeed help them find God, bringing their hearts and souls to rest.

The petition begins by admitting the harmful obstacles to an atheist's finding faith. These obstacles vary — from deeply intellectual ones to historical ones to emotional reactions. But despite all of those, the Church prays for three things: (1) that everyone, through God's grace, may come to recognize God's fatherly love; (2) that atheists may be moved by the witness that believers give, especially, of their good works—seeing such good actions might lead to questions about the motivation for such, and thus back to the God who spurs us to charity; (3) the hope that the first two petitions will lead to conversion, to belief in God, and then to confession of that God in joy. Full conversion is implied, because the confession will be of the "one true God" and the Father of all humanity.

In the phrase, "and, by finding you, come to rest," we see the results of belief in God. The line recalls Psalm 4:8–9: "But you have given my heart more joy than they have when grain and wine abound. / In

Almighty ever-living God,
who created all people
to seek you always by desiring you
and, by finding you, come to rest,
grant, we pray,
that, despite every harmful obstacle,
all may recognize the signs of your fatherly love
and the witness of the good works
done by those who believe in you,
and so in gladness confess you,
the one true God and Father of our human race.
Through Christ our Lord.
R. Amen.

This prayer will be clearer if you imagine the words "may they" in front of **come to rest**.

For some, **every harmful obstacle** might include Christian community, so pray with compassion.

Signs of your fatherly love (grace at work in their lives) and **witness (of) those who believe in you** (Christian's love for one another) are distinct factors that we pray may lead to **gladness** and confession.

IX. For those in public office

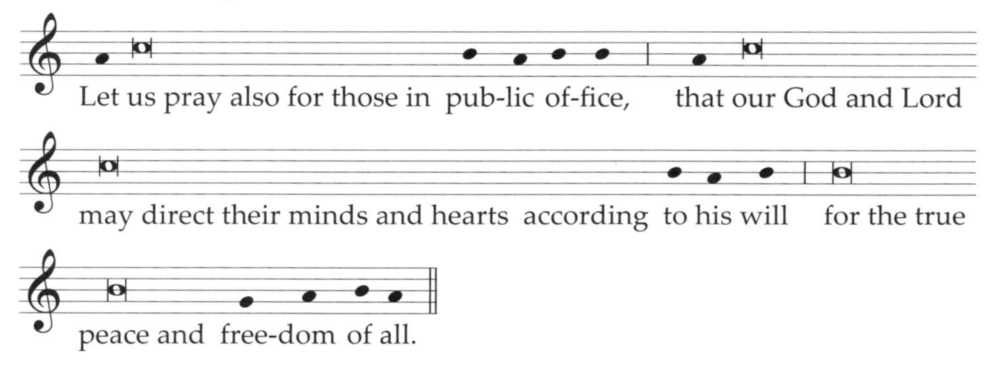

Let us pray also for those in public office,
that our God and Lord
may direct their minds and hearts according to his will
for the true peace and freedom of all.

Proclaim clearly and precisely: **For those in public office**.

peace, I shall both lie down and sleep, for you alone, Lord, make me secure."

We are reminded, too, of Saint Paul's hope in the first letter to the Corinthians that, "all may recognize the signs of your fatherly love and the witness of the good works done by those who believe in you, and so in gladness confess you, the one true God and Father of our human race." Paul urged that members of the Church realize the effect of what they do. Addressing the Corinthians, he states: "So whatever you eat or drink, or whatever you do, do everything for the glory of God. Avoid giving offense, whether to Jews, or Greeks or the church of God, just as I try to please everyone in every way, not seeking my own benefit but that of the many, that they may be saved" (1 Corinthians 10:31–33).

Ninth Intercession:
For those in Public Office

From the outset, the prayer asserts the authority of God in our private and public life. It is not government officials who have lordship over the human heart and the civil rights of peoples: it is God alone who has such. The petition for those in public office admits that these persons govern with authority over us. But the first phrase implies that this authority is partial and temporary, as contrasted with that of God, which is all-inclusive and eternal.

The Church asks God to look with favor on our secular leaders. And we pray that this divine favor will result in three things: (1) prosperity in the personal and civil order, that is, health and well-being; (2) peace that is deep and lasting, the kind

Prayer in silence. Then the Priest says:

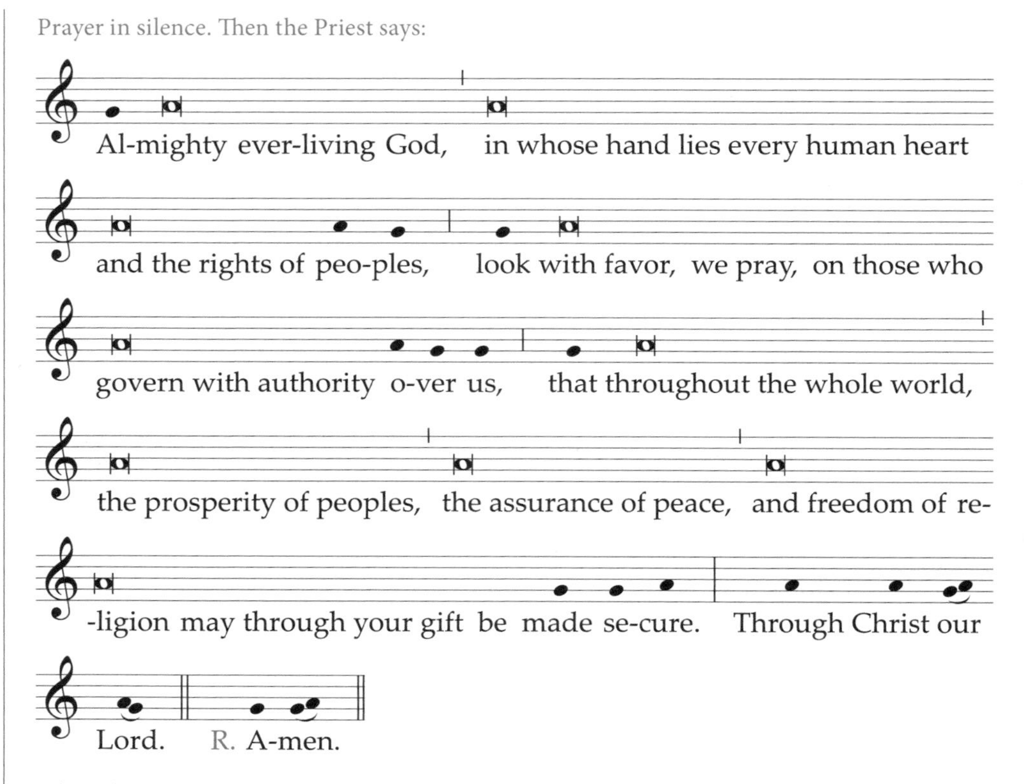

And the rights of peoples names the new intercession. Because God cares for our rights, we pray for those whose **authority** can grant or impinge on those rights. Especially **prosperity, peace, and freedom** are named.

Through your gift reminds us that wordly leaders are not the ultimate guarantors of our rights.

Almighty ever-living God,
in whose hand lies every human heart
and the rights of peoples,
look with favor, we pray,
on those who govern with authority over us,
that throughout the whole world,
the prosperity of peoples,
the assurance of peace,
and freedom of religion
may through your gift be made secure.
Through Christ our Lord.
R. Amen.

that gives assurance to people about their lives, so that there may be peace within their hearts; (3) freedom of religion, which history has shown can be threatened easily by those in public office if they lack the proper sense of their authority's limited extent in the face of God's rights and authority. The Church begs that these three will be made secure, certain, firm realities—thanks to the gift of God who can do all things.

From its first years, the Church has prayed for those who govern. "First of all, then, I ask that supplications, prayers, petitions, and thanksgivings be offered for everyone, kings and for all in authority, that we may lead a tranquil life in all devotion and dignity" (1 Timothy 2:1).

The requests that Pope Benedict XVI made in his address "Religious Freedom, the Path to Peace" on January 1, 2011, are similar to today's. The Pope pleaded for the "properity of peoples, the assurance of peace, and freedom of religion." He explained, "Religious freedom is an authentic weapon of peace, with an historical and prophetic mission. Peace brings to full fruition the deepest qualities and potentials of the human person, the qualities which can change the world and make it better. It gives hope for a future of justice and peace, even in the face of grave injustice and material and moral poverty."

X. For those in tribulation

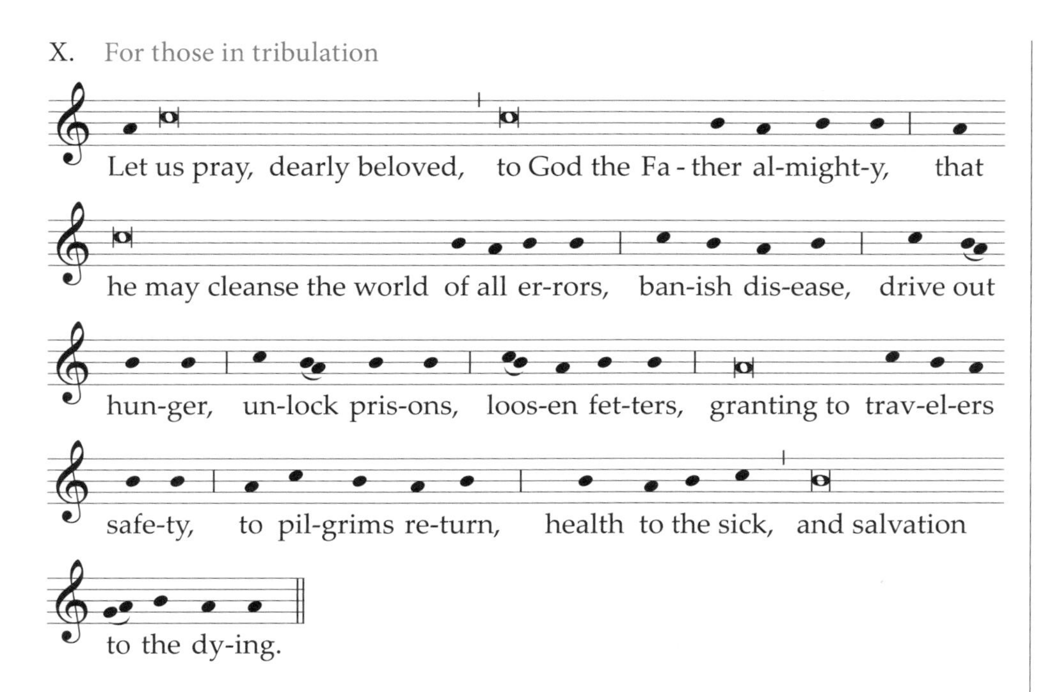

Let us pray, dearly beloved,
to God the Father almighty,
that he may cleanse the world of all errors,
banish disease, drive out hunger,
unlock prisons, loosen fetters,
granting to travelers safety, to pilgrims return,
health to the sick, and salvation to the dying.

Christ's sacrifice emboldens us to pray for what human eyes see as impossible. Proclaim these items as joyful poetry, arousing expectant hope and the resolve to cooperate with God to turn the impossible into reality.

Tenth Intercession: For those in tribulation

Three generic groups who need God's special help are mentioned in the body of this Intercession: people who are mourning—and God is called their comfort; people who toil—and God is called their strength; and all in any tribulation. For each of these groups, the Church prays that God will hear their difficulty, that their situation might be kept before God's eyes. The introduction to the prayer mentions nine such groups who may be suffering tribulation in different forms—those suffering illness and disease, hunger and imprisonment, those traveling or on pilgrimage, those sunk in the darkness of error, and above all, the dying.

The Church cares for all of these in its Sacraments and ministries and teaches that those in need are of prime concern. On the Cultural Diversity page on the United States Conference of Catholic Bishops' website, usccb.org, a Ministry of People on the Move and Pastoral Care of Migrants and Refugees are listed among the ministries.

Gaudium et spes teaches that it is our responsibility to seek to relieve the afflictions that people suffer. "To meet the requirements of justice and equity, every effort must be made, while respecting the rights of individuals and national characteristics, to put an end as soon as possible to the immense economic inequalities which exist . . ." (66).

Prayer in silence. Then the Priest says:

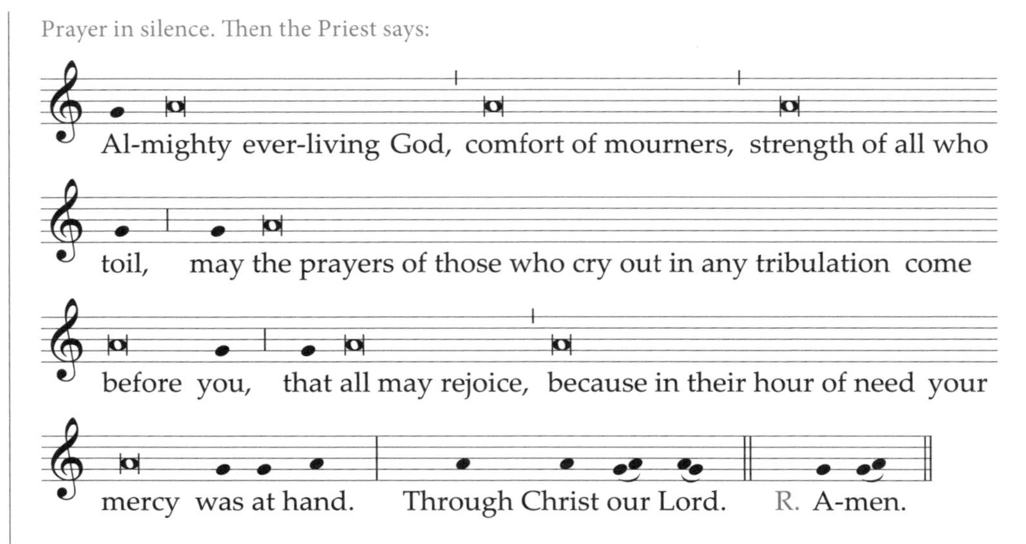

Identify God as **comfort** and **strength** and offer up the collective cry of all who suffer. Speak the reassuring words **in their hour of need your mercy was at hand** slowly and tenderly, as if offering that assurance to those who are grieving.

Almighty ever-living God,
comfort of mourners, strength of all who toil,
may the prayers of those who cry out in any tribulation
come before you,
that all may rejoice,
because in their hour of need
your mercy was at hand.
Through Christ our Lord.
R. Amen.

All those who are suffering are lifted up to the Lord in this intercession, that they might come to realize the mercy of the Lord, as the Psalmist came to know it: "Surely goodness and mercy shall follow me all the days of my life" (Psalm 23:6).

The "hour of need" referred to in the intercession is whenever one feels bereft. The Church petitions not just for the grace to bear tribulation, but for the gift to rejoice, simply because these people have come to experience God's merciful love in their lives.

The Church is to help people feel God's mercy. Catholic Social Teaching states the option for the poor and vulnerable. "A basic moral test is how our most vulnerable are faring. In a society marred by deepening divisions between rich and poor, our tradition recalls in the story of the Last Judgment (Matthew 25:31–46) and instructs us to put the needs of the poor and vulnerable first."

We carry on for Jesus, who in the synagogue at Nazareth opened the scroll and repeated the words from Isaiah: "The Spirit of the Lord is upon me, / because he has anointed me / to bring glad tidings to the poor. / He has sent me to proclaim liberty to captives / and recovery of sight to the blind, / to let the oppressed go free, / and to proclaim a year acceptable to the Lord" (Luke 4:18–19).

In this way we show the love of God. As Pope Benedict XVI states in *Deus Caritas Est*: "Seeing with the eyes of Christ, I can give to others much more than their outward necessities; I can give them the look of love which they crave" (18).

SECOND PART: THE ADORATION OF THE HOLY CROSS

After the Solemn Intercessions, the solemn Adoration of the Holy Cross takes place. Of the two forms of the showing of the Cross presented here, the more appropriate one, according to pastoral needs, should be chosen.

The Showing of the Holy Cross

First Form

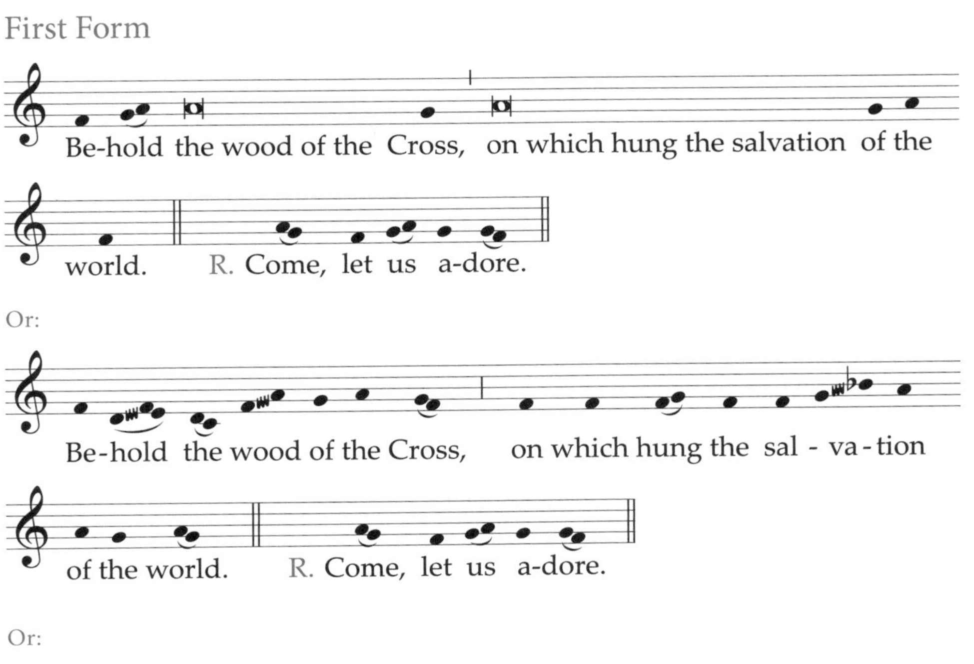

Although the **Cross** is held slightly during the first phrase, ideally it would be best to continue without a breath to the second phrase, beginning with **on which**. Slow **of the world**, to signal the people's response.

In the response, it would be appropriate to hold the two notes of **Come** and the two notes of **-dore**.

In the Second Form, because the melody is so elaborate, it will usually be necessary for the singer to take a breath after **Cross**, but that breath should be very short, so as to keep the sentence together. Of course, the plainchant quilismas on **-hold**, **wood**, and **va-** (of **salvation**) need broadening. The people's response is the same as in the First Form.

In the Third Form (the Latin), the principles elaborated for the Second Form are the same. One will need a very good breath before ***in quo***, so as to tie together, if at all possible, ***mundi*** and ***pependit***. (If not possible, steal a quick breath before ***pependit***.)

Behold the wood of the Cross,
on which hung the salvation of the world.
R. Come, let us adore.

The Adoration of the Holy Cross: We find the first evidence for this part of the Good Friday liturgy in the fourth century (Egeria, *Journal*, 37:1–3), in Jerusalem. In other churches—for example, North Africa—the liturgy on this day consisted only of the Liturgy of the Word, including the Gospel of the Passion. This may have been because the churches there had no relic of the Holy Cross—which Jerusalem had, and which Rome soon acquired. That fact expanded this day's liturgy to include the readings, prayers, and Adoration of the Holy Cross. (In time, a relic was not necessary, but only the image of the Crucifix.)

In the medieval period, especially in the lands north of the Alps, the dramatic elements of this day were increased. In this first rite, The Showing of the Holy Cross, the Priest Celebrant or other minister sings three times, "Behold the wood of the Cross . . . ," each time uncovering a part of the veiled Cross, with the people responding, "Come, let us adore" while kneeling. By the third time of this singing, the entire Cross is unveiled. We note that Jesus is not mentioned by name, but by attribution: ". . . on which hung the salvation of the world."

All in the church come forward to venerate the Cross with some gesture of reverence (traditionally, a kiss of the feet). This custom goes back to the fourth century. By the tenth-century *Pontificals*, we have explicit evidence of singing, with a mix of Greek and Latin, during this procession and veneration. This music is a moving act of reverence to Jesus, who at the moment of his profound humiliation still is God.

Then the Priest uncovers the right arm of the Cross and again, raising up the Cross, begins, Behold the wood of the Cross and everything takes place as above.

Finally, he uncovers the Cross entirely and, raising it up, he begins the invitation Behold the wood of the Cross a third time and everything takes place like the first time.

Second Form

The Priest or the Deacon accompanied by ministers, or another suitable minister, goes to the door of the church, where he receives the unveiled Cross, and the ministers take lighted candles; then the procession sets off through the church to the sanctuary. Near the door, in the middle of the church and before the entrance of the sanctuary, the one who carries the Cross elevates it, singing, Behold the wood of the Cross, to which all respond, Come, let us adore. After each response all kneel and for a brief moment adore in silence, as above.

THIRD PART: HOLY COMMUNION

Then the Priest, with hands joined, says aloud:

At the Savior's command
and formed by divine teaching,
we dare to say:

The Priest, with hands extended says, and all present continue:

Our Father, who art in heaven,
hallowed be thy name;
thy kingdom come,
thy will be done
on earth as it is in heaven.
Give us this day our daily bread,
and forgive us our trespasses,
as we forgive those who trespass against us;
and lead us not into temptation,
but deliver us from evil.

Communion Rite: There is no certainty as to why there is no consecratory Eucharistic Prayer on this day and that Holy Communion will consist only of the species of the Precious Body of the Lord, even for the Priest Celebrant. This unusual way of celebrating this day may go back to the earliest days of the Church, in which there was no Holy Mass on weekdays—Good Friday being no exception.

The Communion Rite begins with the most ancient of our Christian prayers, the Lord's Prayer, prayed by all. As always, when prayed at the beginning of the Communion part of Mass, it is particularly relevant to pray, "Give us this day our daily bread." The Lord's Prayer is followed by the usual embolism, a prayer that takes off from the final words, "Deliver us from evil."

In the medieval period, people began abstaining more and more from the reception of Holy Communion. So too on Good Friday. By the time of the Missal following the Council of Trent (1545–1563), only the Priest Celebrant was allowed to receive Holy Communion on this day. This practice lasted until the reforms of the liturgy in the twentieth century.

The Priest Celebrant proceeds to a personal prayer of preparation for Holy Communion ("May the receiving of your Body . . . ."). Then, in the usual manner as at Mass, he venerates the Sacrament, and shows it to the people, who respond, "Lord, I am not worthy . . . ."

The Priest Celebrant receives the Sacred species first. In the medieval period, he received it with unconsecrated wine, but that practice was abolished at the time

With hands extended, the Priest continues alone:

Deliver us, Lord, we pray, from every evil,
graciously grant peace in our days,
that, by the help of your mercy,
we may be always free from sin
and safe from all distress,
as we await the blessed hope
and the coming of our Savior, Jesus Christ.

He joins his hands.

The people conclude the prayer, acclaiming:

For the kingdom, the power and the glory are yours now and for ever.

Then the Priest, with hands joined, says quietly:

May the receiving of your Body and Blood,
Lord Jesus Christ,
not bring me to judgment and condemnation,
but through your loving mercy
be for me protection in mind and body
and a healing remedy.

The Priest then genuflects, takes a particle, and, holding it slightly raised over the ciborium, while facing the people, says aloud:

Behold the Lamb of God,
behold him who takes away the sins of the world.
Blessed are those called to the supper of the Lamb.

And together with the people he adds once:

Lord, I am not worthy
that you should enter under my roof,
but only say the word
and my soul shall be healed.

And facing the altar, he reverently consumes the Body of Christ, saying quietly: May the Body of Christ keep me safe for eternal life.

of the Council of Trent. The distribution of Holy Communion to the people then follows. If there is any remaining species, it is kept in a ciborium outside the main body of the church.

He then proceeds to distribute Communion to the faithful. During Communion, Psalm 22 (21) or another appropriate chant may be sung.

When the distribution of Communion has been completed, the ciborium is taken by the Deacon or another suitable minister to a place prepared outside the church or, if circumstances so require, it is placed in the tabernacle.

Then the Priest says: Let us pray, and, after a period of sacred silence, if circumstances so suggest, has been observed, he says the Prayer after Communion.

God has restored to life both **us** and **Christ**, so balance and stress both words. In the three subsequent lines, **preserve**, **partaking**, and **devoted** carry the meaning of the prayer.

Almighty ever-living God,
who have restored us to life
by the blessed Death and Resurrection of your Christ,
preserve in us the work of your mercy,
that, by partaking of this mystery,
we may have a life unceasingly devoted to you.
Through Christ our Lord.
R. Amen.

For the Dismissal the Deacon or, if there is no Deacon, the Priest himself, may say the invitation Bow down for the blessing.

Then the Priest, standing facing the people and extending his hands over them, says this Prayer over the People:

The poetically structured prayer acknowledges what has been done in this liturgy: **honored the Death of your Son**. Speak with awareness. The four lines after **resurrection** should be read as distinct petitions that express the deep longings of all the hearts present.

May abundant blessing, O Lord, we pray,
descend upon your people,
who have honored the Death of your Son
in the hope of their resurrection:
may pardon come,
comfort be given,
holy faith increase,
and everlasting redemption be made secure.
Through Christ our Lord.
R. Amen.

And all, after genuflecting to the Cross, depart in silence.

After the celebration, the altar is stripped, but the Cross remains on the altar with two or four candlesticks.

Vespers (Evening Prayer) is not celebrated by those who have been present at the solemn afternoon liturgical celebration.

Prayer after Communion: Significantly, this prayer calls God "ever-living," as it immediately notes that we have been restored to life through the Paschal Mystery of Christ. The original sin of Adam and Eve meant a condemnation to toil, suffering, and death, for each of their descendants. But Jesus has transformed that sad situation by his Death and Resurrection, the Paschal Mystery.

The Church petitions that God will keep us in the graces coming through that Paschal Mystery—the great sign of his mercy and love for humanity. It also presumes that, since God would allow his beloved Son to die a horrible death, God would show such love to sinners, those alienated from him. This is a tremendous work of mercy, which the Church wants to share always. Sharing in the Paschal Mystery of God's love, we petition that our lives will be so transformed that we will never stop our devotion to God, never stop loving God in return for his limitless love.

Prayer over the People: This prayer is a petitionary type of blessing for the people. The first two lines make this clear. We ask for this blessing because we have honored the death of God's beloved Son through our liturgical action today. That Death means salvation to all who would receive God's gift. And receiving such salvation, all undeserved, gives us hope that we too, like Jesus, will share in resurrection to life. Within the blessing, then, is a proclamation of the Church's faith and hope in the Resurrection. Good Friday at the end of its liturgy, then, is already anticipating Easter Sunday.

The space below is for your notes.

Refer to pages viii–x for an explanation of the pointing of the chants and to page xii for the Tones for the Presidential Prayers from *The Roman Missal*.

Pointed Text

A Almighty ever-living God,
who have restored us to life
by the blessed Death and Resurrection of your **Christ**,
B preserve in us the work of your mercy,
that, by partaking of ***this*** mystery,
C we may have a life unceasingly devoted to ***you***.
Through Christ our Lord.
R. Amen.

A May abundant blessing, O Lord, we pray,
descend upon your people,
who have honored the Death of your Son
in the hope of their resurrec**tion**:
B may pardon come,
comfort be given,
holy **faith** increase,
C and everlasting redemption be made se***cure***.
Through Christ our Lord.
R. Amen.

From the blessing requested, the Church hopes that four gifts of God's merciful grace will come upon us also. The first is pardon. We know Jesus has taken away sin by his great sacrifice on the Cross. By asking this, we acknowledge that our hearts are open to receive such a transforming gift. Next, the Church begs for comfort. This may mean on a simple physical level. It may also mean that God's people have been deeply moved in a spiritual sense, touched to the core of their being by what we have seen and heard of Jesus's sacrifice. God's grace and blessing would be our solace. Next, the Church begs for an increase of faith, so that Jesus's saving act may continue to work within us. And finally, this blessing begs that our eternal redemption be solidified, so that we may count on having God's blessing by sharing his mercy forever in heaven.

EASTER SUNDAY OF THE RESURRECTION OF THE LORD

THE EASTER VIGIL IN THE HOLY NIGHT

First Part:
The Solemn Beginning of the Vigil or Lucernarium

The Blessing of the Fire and Preparation of the Candle

The opening instruction should be proclaimed very solemnly, so that all will sense that it is a most sacred night. For the blessing, a server should hold the book so that the Priest Celebrant can see the text from the new fire. Slow the third line noticeably as the Sign of the Cross is made over the new fire, articulating each word carefully.

The Priest and faithful sign themselves while the Priest says: In the name of the Father, and of the Son, and of the Holy Spirit, and then he greets the assembled people in the usual way and briefly instructs them about the night vigil in these or similar words:

Dear brethren (brothers and sisters),
on this most sacred night,
in which our Lord Jesus Christ
passed over from death to life,
the Church calls upon her sons and daughters,
scattered throughout the world,
to come together to watch and pray.
If we keep the memorial
of the Lord's paschal solemnity in this way,
listening to his word and celebrating his mysteries,
then we shall have the sure hope
of sharing his triumph over death
and living with him in God.

Then the Priest blesses the fire, saying with hands extended:

Let us pray.

O God, who through your Son
bestowed upon the faithful the fire of your glory,
sanctify ✠ this new fire, we pray,
and grant that,
by these paschal celebrations,
we may be so inflamed with heavenly desires,
that with minds made pure
we may attain festivities of unending splendor.
Through Christ our Lord.
R. Amen.

The Blessing of the Fire and Preparation of the Candle

The liturgy usually expresses itself in sacramental terms, and in re-presenting the events of Sacred Scripture. Hence, in this opening instruction, the Priest Celebrant does not speak about this night as an occasion to think about or merely commemorate the Lord's Resurrection. Rather, this is the very night in which the Lord rose. That is what makes it "most sacred." Because the Church wants all its members to experience that Resurrection anew this night, it calls on them, everywhere, to gather, to "watch" (at the tomb) and to pray.

By keeping this Vigil, especially through listening to God's Word and celebrating the Sacraments (especially Baptism and Holy Eucharist), the Church is renewed in hope that it, too, will rise with Jesus and live with him forever in heaven.

God's glory in Sacred Scripture means his presence, life, and light. In praying that the new fire be blessed (sanctified), we are reminded that the fire is a kind of sign/sacrament of the divine glory. The petition asks that by this Vigil celebration, we might be inflamed interiorly with longing for heaven. Fire is a purifying agent, so it becomes a symbol of the grace the Church longs for, that of inner purification. Then we can hope to arrive at the object of our deepest longing, the everlasting Light of heaven. Thus, this earthly festive celebration is a foretaste and foreshadowing of the everlasting Feast of heaven.

The Easter Proclamation (Exsultet)

Longer Form of the Easter Proclamation

From the beginning, the voice should communicate exultation. When long lines of descending melody are sung, be careful not to run away with them, down the scale, for example, in **let the trumpet of sal-** (line two); **let all corners of the** (line five); **let this holy building** (line seven).

Soften the voice for the direct address to the people, **Therefore, dearest friends . . . .**

The Easter Proclamation (Exsultet)
(The words "exult," "be glad," and "rejoice" evidence that, even if proclaimed without singing, the hymn still should have an exultant tone. After the Preface begins, careful articulation needs to be given to the phrase "This is the night." In no way should the proclamation of the text ever be merely read. On the other hand, the voice needs to be varied; the highest pitch of exultation cannot be kept constant. Careful phrasing and pauses will make the recited proclamation of the hymn a wonderful experience for the listeners, even if this hymn should be sung, if at all possible.)

This Easter Proclamation, perhaps authored by Saint Ambrose but with citations from, and allusions to, the writings of other Fathers and the Scripture, begins with a prelude that is a paean of joy. (It is often called the Exsultet, from the first word of the Latin.) Once the prelude is finished, it launches into a kind of Eucharistic Prayer, beginning with the usual Preface dialogue between Priest Celebrant and people.

The prelude is addressed to four sets of listeners. The first is the hosts of heaven, the angelic choirs. (Whereas the Preface with the Eucharistic Prayer ends with an evocation of the hymns of the angelic choirs "Holy, Holy, Holy . . . ," the Exsultet begins with those choirs.)

Just after the Angels are told to sing, we hear that the "trumpet of salvation" is to sound. The "trumpet of salvation" is found in both the Old and New

Slow **perfect praises**.

Treat the Preface Dialogue and the first seven lines after it with recitative singing that is typical of the sung Prefaces. Bring out the accent on **be** in **The Lord be with you**. Make a strong accent on **Lift**, and slow both notes of **hearts**. In the third dialogue, move to the word **thanks** before accenting, and hold that word slightly to give it emphasis. Broaden both notes of **Lord**, and hold **God**.

Testaments. For example, after the salvation of Israel in the Exodus from Egypt, "on the morning of the third day, there were peals of thunder and lightning, and a heavy cloud over the mountain, and a very loud trumpet blast, so that all in the camp trembled" (Exodus 19:16 ff.). This was a wonderful prefiguring of another salvation to come on "the third day," that of the Resurrection of Jesus, here referred to as "our mighty King's triumph."

Jesus's victory over death is the assurance of our own, as Saint Paul says, referring to the trumpet sounding on the last day. ("Behold, I tell you a mystery. We shall not fall asleep, but we will all be changed, in an instant, in the blink of an eye, at the last trumpet. For the trumpet will sound, the dead will be raised incorruptible, and we shall be changed" [1 Corinthians 15: 51–52].)

In chapters eight, nine, and eleven in the book of Revelation, seven angels blow trumpets, announcing God's great deeds. ("Then the seventh angel blew his trumpet. . . . The twenty-four elders who sat on their thrones before God prostrated themselves and worshiped God and said: 'We give thanks to you, Lord God almighty, / . . . / For you have assumed your great power / and have established your reign'" [Revelation 11:15–17].)

The second addressee is the earth—the night of the Lord's Resurrection means that the darkness of the tomb has been conquered—and this, for all of the faithful. The glorious light of the risen Christ floods the entire earth. The third addressee is "Mother Church," whom the hymn por-

From **These then are the feasts**, each sentence brings out a new theological and spiritual dimension of the Easter celebration and the meaning of the Easter candle. Hence, each sentence needs to be clearly articulated, especially at the beginning **These** or **This**.

trays as arrayed with the light of Jesus's glory. The ecstatic singer hopes the power of the joyful voices of the faithful present will make "this holy building shake with joy." Coming to the people present here, and seeing them standing in the awe-producing holy light of the Easter candle, that is, in the glory of the risen Lord, the singer begs the prayer of all standing with lighted candles in their hands that he might sing well the candle's (again, that is the risen Christ's) praise. (The presumption is that the singer is a Deacon, which is why he says he has been numbered "among the Levites.")

The Preface-type dialogue, noted earlier, follows. ("The Lord be with you . . . Lift up . . . .")

The first part of the body of the hymn—which as indicated earlier is similar to a Eucharistic Prayer in some of its form—offers praise and acclamation to both the Father and the Son. This is done with "ardent love." The singing is called a "service": the Latin original *vocis ministerium*, a kind of ministry of the voice (the phrase already was used in the Verona Sacramentary, a very ancient Sacramentary of the Church), and it means that this is not just a question of singing something, but of truly serving God in the liturgy by the use of the singing voice.

The next section of the body of the hymn gives the motive for the acclamation and praise just mentioned. The motive, of course, is Jesus, who by his sacrificial Death ("pouring out . . . Blood") has paid the debt incurred by Adam and Eve, their original sin that has been passed down to all of

Articulate slowly and clearly **O truly necessary sin** and **O happy fault**.

Broaden noticeably **O truly blessed night**.

The repetitions at the end of this page and the top of the next need careful respect for the commas.

their descendants. And thus, Jesus has wiped the slate clean, so to speak, of that ancient and death-bringing sin.

There follows the anamnesis/memorial part of this Eucharistic Prayer. In the liturgy, memorial means making the reality present; it is a re-presenting of the person or original event. Eight events are brought forward in a poetic manner, usually utilizing the scriptural background.

First event: We bring together this night all the Passover celebrations, going back to the very first one in Egypt. At that celebration, the Israelites slayed a lamb and smeared its blood on their door posts, so that the Angel of death would "pass over" their houses and families, and only the Egyptians would suffer the consequences of that Angel's action (Exodus 12:1–30). But the hymn fuses that first ancient celebration with that of Jesus's Passover, his Paschal Death, and Resurrection. He is proclaimed as the one true Lamb, and his precious Blood now protects all who believe in him, safeguarding them from death. As Saint Paul says simply: "For our paschal lamb, Christ, has been sacrificed" (1 Corinthians 5:7).

Second event: The next event made present is the exodus of Israel from slavery in Egypt, and the miracle of their passing over/through the Red Sea dry-shod (Exodus 12:31–42; 14:10–31), along with the destruction of Pharoah and his army. The Fathers of the Church see this as prefiguring the sacrament of Baptism, when those who belong to Jesus pass through

the waters, to have their sins cleansed, death destroyed, and grace (a new Promised Land) given to them. All of that comes together at the Vigil celebration—already in the hymn with the Easter candle, and in a few moments, in the celebration or renewal of Baptism.

Third event: Next is recalled that God led his people out of Egypt and slavery "with a pillar of fire" at night (Exodus 13:21). This is recalled, especially at this moment, because there stands before us another "pillar of fire," the Easter candle, which sacramentalizes Jesus, the true "light of the world" (John 8:12). By his Paschal Mystery, the darkness of sin (not of nature) is banished, and human beings can live in a new kind of light. (cf. 1 Thessalonians 5:4–5: "But, you, brothers are not in darkness, . . . For all of you are children of the light and children of the day.) On this blessed night, that same reality occurs again, renewing our living in Christ, in the light (1 John 1:5: "God is light . . . in him there is no darkness.)"

Fourth event: Because Christians willingly follow Jesus the Light rather than the "world" (in the sense of a place still needing redemption to be effected), they are set apart from that world. The Church celebrates this in a special way, as Christ the Light stands before us in the Easter candle, the Lord, whose Resurrection we celebrate so joyfully this night. The "world" needs to know the redeeming act of Jesus, because it still is full of vices, as well as the darkness ("gloom") of sin. But Christians, thanks to their Baptism and following of Jesus, know

Take only a quick breath after **Morning Star**, so as to continue with **the one Morning Star . . . .**

Begin slowing with **has shed his peaceful light . . . .** Slow especially on **for ever and ever**, to cue the people to sing **Amen**. (For the best response from the people, it would be good for there to be catechesis on this before the Triduum.)

redemption. This is what joins them as members of Christ's Church and leads them out of sin and into grace.

Fifth event: Death is often seen in the liturgy as a prison of sorts (cf. many prayers in Masses and Offices for the Dead), and as the Apostles' Creed states, Christ went through the same reality—"he descended into hell; on the third day he rose again from the dead . . . ." But this night we celebrate Christ's rising from the dead, his victory over the forces of death, here called "the underworld."

At this point, the author is so overwhelmed by what God has done in crushing death that it is impossible to go on with the sixth event that this part of the Exsultet memorializes. The author breaks the list and bursts into more praise—somewhat in the same manner as at the beginning of the hymn. The text first addresses the fact that there would have been no value ("gain") to being born, if we were only destined for the "underworld." If Jesus had not redeemed us, we could hardly be so joyful this night.

Our celebrating the five events just noted leads the author to express admiration for what God has done, for the honor God bestows on us, the care with which God has surrounded and immersed us: God's saving acts leave the author in wonder and awe. The hymn goes on to sing of God's love, a divine love about which we are nearly speechless: "to ransom" us ("a slave"), God gave away not some ransom money, but his Only Begotten Son.

From the beginning, the voice should communicate exultation. When long lines of descending melody are sung, be careful not to run away with them, down the scale, for example, in **let the trumpet of sal-** (line two); **let all corners of the** (line five); **let this holy building** (line seven).

Treat the Preface Dialogue and the seven lines following, with recitative singing typical of the sung Prefaces. Bring out the accent on **be** in **The Lord be with you**. Make a strong accent on **Lift**, and slow both notes of **hearts**. In the third dialogue, move to the word **thanks** before accenting, and hold that word slightly for emphasis. Broaden both notes of **Lord** and hold **God**.

The next two lines state what has happened, and with a boldness that is not usual in pious poetry. The "sin of Adam" is described as "truly necessary," because it led to the extraordinary act of charity from God, which was the saving Death of Christ. This Death has completely obliterated the sentence of death that came from the sin of our first parents. The hymn calls that latter death a "happy fault"—a seeming contradiction. But it was necessary, because it led directly to our Redeemer, the Father's living sign of love.

Sixth event: At this point, the hymn returns to the "memorials." This is a most blessed night because it came to know the time, the very hour of Christ's rising from the dead. The night is here treated as if it were a person, one who had been waiting in the dark for the Resurrection (like the author of Psalm 130), and now can know the blessing of that great event.

Seventh event: This night will be "as bright as day." A prophetic proclamation of this is in Psalm 139:12: "Darknesss is not dark for you, / and night shines as the day. Darkness and light are one." Indeed, the Resurrection of Christ, symbolized powerfully in the light of this Easter candle before which we sing, has made the night "dazzling," almost blinding in its brightness. And thus, it is cause for all the Church to be filled with joy, with gladness. The hymn comments on the results of Jesus's act of redemption and Resurrection, in terms of this night's possessing the power to make us holy, to sanctify us. The results of this holiness are: ridding evil; washing away

From **These then are the feasts**, each sentence brings out a new theological and spiritual dimension of the Easter celebration and the meaning of the Easter candle. Hence, each sentence needs to be clearly articulated, especially at the beginning **These** or **This**.

any sins and faults in us, thus restoring innocence to sinners; and joy to those who weep at the thought of the results of sin and death.

Once again, at this point, the author of the hymn breaks the order of the memorials. The next section of the hymn, with its parallel to a Eucharistic Prayer, is the offering. We should recall that, at Mass, we explicitly recognize that all our material gifts have come from God, are gifts of God's grace; and then we offer them back to him, transformed by the power of the Holy Spirit and the words of Jesus into the offering of Jesus himself. So also here, we recognize that this is a night of grace—of God's special gift—and the Easter candle is the great gift in point at this moment. So when the Church solemnly offers that candle to the Father, it is just as in the Eucharistic Prayers an offering of Jesus to the Father. The candle is a material element—made by bees and "the work of your servants' hands," indeed, by the hands of those so devoted to the Father, they are considered to be in his service (*ministerium*). Using terms from the Psalms as well as the liturgy, this offering is likened to our evening sacrifice of praise ("Let my prayer be incense before you; / my uplifted hands an evening sacrifice [Psalm 141:2]; "For them, we offer you this sacrifice of praise" [Eucharistic Prayer I]). Since the candle represents Christ, this gift is one of noble excellence, to be surpassed only by the gift of the Church during the Eucharistic Prayer this night.

And again, the author feels the need to burst into praise, as the hymn continues

Articulate slowly and clearly **O truly necessary sin** and **O happy fault**.

to contemplate the glory of Christ risen, in the candle. Since the beginning of the hymn, we have been praising this pillar of fire which, foreshadowed by that pillar of fire in the desert for the people exiting Egypt, is glowing this night simply for God's honor. Many other candles can (and have been) lighted from this Easter candle, and yet its flame remains undiminished. Everyone in the congregation is holding a small candle, which has been lighted from the Easter candle, symbolizing that all have been enlightened from Christ the light. (References to light in Scripture are: "The true light, which enlightens everyone was coming into the world" [John 1:9]; also, "For it is impossible in the case of those who have once been enlightened and tasted the heavenly gift and shared in the holy Spirit and tasted the good word of God . . ." [Hebrews 6:4].) Another comment about the work of bees is inserted: the candle never dims because it continues to be fed by the melting wax around the wick. And thus, a "torch so precious" is sustained.

Eighth event: This praise-filled digression leads to the eighth and final memorial: this night is so blessed because heaven and earth are wed in the risen Lord, symbolized still by the Easter candle in our midst. The divine and human were present in Jesus, from the moment of his conception in Mary's womb (Luke 1:32–33). But now, thanks to the Paschal Mystery, that extraordinary communion is extended to and made possible for his followers. This can be considered a culminating blessing.

Broaden noticeably **O truly blessed night**.

Concluding: In the final section of the hymn—still following the analogy of the Eucharistic Prayers—the Intercessions are found. Actually, these are still mixed with the offering that just preceded them. The section begins with terms very like those in the Eucharistic Prayers: "Therefore, O Lord, we pray you . . . ." And, as the entire text of the hymn has done, the prayers are centered on the candle itself. Made holy by God's blessing and Christ's Resurrection, the Church prays that the candle's light will never grow dim. Thus, it will overcome the darkness of this night, and any other night which needs Christ the light.

The text returns to one line of offering: that God might receive the Church's offering of this candle as a "pleasing fragrance." These words are used repeatedly in the books of Exodus, Leviticus, and Numbers, to express the Israelites' hope for how God would receive their sacrifices. The latter part of the line regards the candle as so wonderful and powerful that the Church prays that its light may mingle with the lights of heaven. The basic Scripture in the background is God's creation of the luminaries of the sky, both for day and for night (Genesis 1:14–18; cf. also, "Who made the great lights, / God's love endures forever; The sun to rule the day / . . . / The moon and stars to rule the night / God's love endures forever" [Psalm 136:7–9]). In the New Testament, the letter of James speaks of God as the "Father of lights" (James 1:17). This image may well be in the back of the author's mind also.

The last petition is that this Easter candle's flame will be found burning by

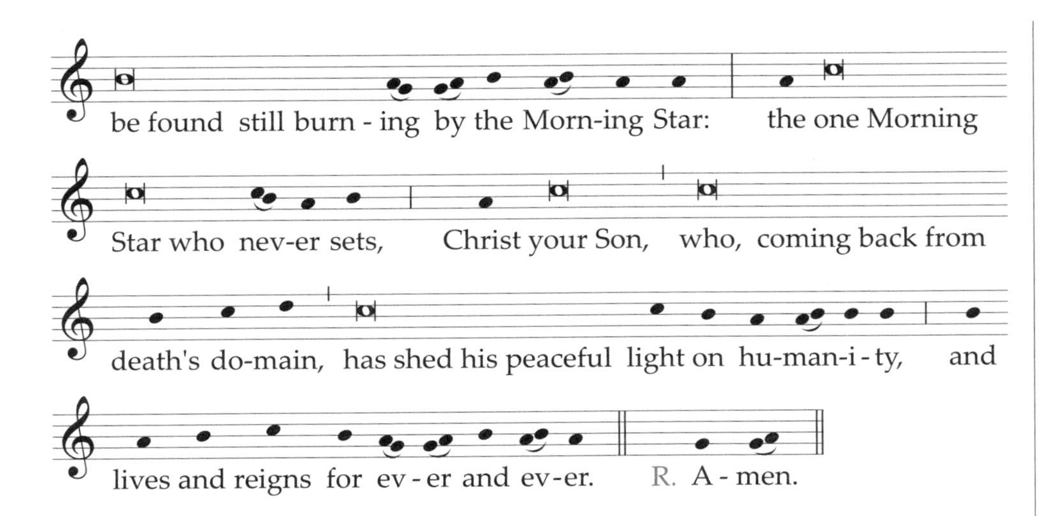

Take only a quick breath after **Morning Star**, so as to continue with **the one Morning Star . . . .**

Begin slowing with **has shed his peaceful light . . .** but do so especially on **for ever and ever**, to cue the people for the response **Amen**.

Christ, the Morning Star, when he comes. (Revelation 22:16—"I, Jesus, sent my angel to give you testimony for the churches, I am the root and offspring of David, the bright morning star.") As Christ has risen from the dead, he, the Morning Star, "never sets" (will not die again). The light he has brought to humanity is depicted as "peaceful," because it is he who has made our peace with God; indeed, he is our peace and reconciliation, as light of the world. ("For he is our peace, . . . abolishing the law with its commandments and legal claims, that he might create in himself one new person in place of the two, thus establishing peace . . . . He came and preached peace to you who were far off and peace to those who were near . . . " [Ephesians 2:14–17]). The author of the hymn may also have in mind the text from the letter to the Hebrews: "May the God of peace, who brought up from the dead the great shepherd of the sheep by the blood of the eternal covenant, Jesus our Lord . . ." (Hebrews 13:20).

The hymn concludes with the usual ending for almost all of the prayers at Mass, and all sing "Amen" as the response.

Second Part:
The Liturgy of the Word

Listen and **meditate** describe the tone you must set with this prayer. Let your unrushed and thoughtful demeanor invite all to open ears and hearts to God's word.

Dear brethren (brothers and sisters),
now that we have begun our solemn Vigil,
let us listen with quiet hearts to the Word of God.
Let us meditate on how God in times past saved his people
and in these, the last days, has sent us his Son as our Redeemer.
Let us pray that our God may complete this paschal work
of salvation
by the fullness of redemption.

Prayers after the Readings

After the first reading (On creation: Gn 1: 1–2: 2 or 1: 1, 26–31a) and the Psalm (104 [103] or 33 [32]).

Let us pray.

Speak joyfully of the wonder of God's creation, taking no pauses between **works** and **beginning**. After **beginning**, slow your delivery and speak very deliberately of the surpassing wonder of Christ's self-sacrifice.

Almighty ever-living God,
who are wonderful in the ordering of all your works,
may those you have redeemed understand
that there exists nothing more marvelous
than the world's creation in the beginning
except that, at the end of the ages,
Christ our Passover has been sacrificed.
Who lives and reigns for ever and ever.
R. Amen.

Or, On the creation of man:

The joy with which you speak of creation and redemption contrasts with concern over the **enticements of sin**. Positive tone returns when you mention **eternal joys**.

O God, who wonderfully created human nature
and still more wonderfully redeemed it,
grant us, we pray,
to set our minds against the enticements of sin,
that we may merit to attain eternal joys.
Through Christ our Lord.
R. Amen.

Prayer after the First Reading: The Reading has just described the creation of things both inanimate and living. It is significant, then, that God is titled "ever-living." The phrase in apposition to this is a comment on the ordering of the six days of creation—creation is wonderful because God is so. As the petition begins, it jumps to the reality of redemption, which is celebrated in a special way this night. Yes, those redeemed need to marvel at the world's creation and the wonderful work that God did in creating it. But they need to marvel even more at the fact that Christ our Passover has been sacrificed—a phrase lifted directly from Saint Paul (cf. 1 Corinthians 5:7). We celebrate this with joy.

Hinted at is the Church's belief that the Paschal Death and Resurrection of Christ have made us a new creation—again the terminology is that of Saint Paul (cf. 2 Corinthians 5:17)—and that the order of the old creation has passed away. That is why Saint Paul saw the coming and the sacrifice of Christ as "the end of the ages" (1 Corinthians 10:11). Calling Christ "our Passover" means that we can celebrate with our Jewish brothers and sisters at Passover their liberation from the slavery of Egypt—except that we celebrate, in Christ, our liberation from sin and death.

When the short form of the First Reading is proclaimed, the next Collect is prayed. At the center of the short form of the Genesis story is the creation of man. Thus this prayer begins by identifying the "wonderful" part of God's creation as his calling human beings into existence, whereas in the longer reading, the entire

The space below is for your notes.

Refer to pages viii–x for an explanation of the pointing of the chants and to page xii for the Tones for the Presidential Prayers from *The Roman Missal*.

Pointed Text

Let us pray.

A Almighty ever-living God,
who are wonderful in the ordering of all your **works**,
B may those you have redeemed understand
that there exists nothing more marvelous
than the world's creation in the beginning
except that, at the end **of** the ages,
C Christ our Passover has been sac***ri***ficed.
Who lives and reigns for ever and ever.
R. Amen.

Or, On the creation of man:

A O God, who wonderfully created human nature
and still more wonderfully redeemed **it**,
B grant us, we pray,
to set our minds against the en**tice**ments of sin,
C that we may merit to attain eternal ***joys***.
Through Christ our Lord.
R. Amen.

six days of creation are seen as resulting in a wonderful order. The description of God states the even greater work of God in redeeming fallen human nature.

The petition, made against the backdrop of creation, prays for the grace to set ourselves firmly against any enticements to turn away from God's gifts. By turning away from sin, we hope to merit everlasting joy in heaven. Thus, the joy of Easter here will usher in joy that will last forever.

Prayer after the Second Reading: In both the long and short forms of the Second Reading, God's promise to Abraham that he would be the father of many nations (Genesis 22:15–18) appears; so reference is made to this promise in the Collect. The long appositional phrase describes God as "supreme Father of the faithful." As we have just listened to the story about Abraham's fatherhood, the prayer provides us with a perspective on the scriptural passage by calling attention to God's much greater fatherhood. The Church passes beyond the Hebrew Testament from the outset, speaking of God as Father of the "faithful," and of the increase in God's children through the grace of adoption to so many. This Collect anticipates the Baptisms that will be celebrated in parishes, stating that through the Paschal Mystery we celebrate in a special way this night, we are extending the promise made to Abraham as the father of nations.

The short petition that follows highlights the grace that God gives when he

The three lines from **who increase** to **the whole world** comprise a single thought, so no pauses, but also no rushing.

Since as you once swore connects to the pervious clause about Abraham, not the one that follows, there is no need for a pause after **father** or **nations**.

After the second reading (On Abraham's sacrifice: Gn 22: 1–18 or 1–2, 9a, 10–13, 15–18) and the Psalm (16 [15]).

Let us pray.

O God, supreme Father of the faithful,
who increase the children of your promise
by pouring out the grace of adoption
throughout the whole world
and who through the Paschal Mystery
make your servant Abraham father of nations,
as once you swore,
grant, we pray,
that your peoples may enter worthily
into the grace to which you call them.
Through Christ our Lord.
R. Amen.

After the third reading (On the passage through the Red Sea: Ex 14: 15–15: 1) and its canticle (Ex 15).

Let us pray.

Observe the comma after **single people**, then speak the two lines that follow as a single thought. **Now you bring** connects what follows with **what you once bestowed**; be sure to suggest that parallel.

O God, whose ancient wonders
remain undimmed in splendor even in our day,
for what you once bestowed on a single people,
freeing them from Pharaoh's persecution
by the power of your right hand,
now you bring about as the salvation of the nations
through the waters of rebirth,
grant, we pray, that the whole world
may become children of Abraham
and inherit the dignity of Israel's birthright.
Through Christ our Lord.
R. Amen.

Or:

The comma after **former times** must not break the connection between the **who by the light** clause and the

O God, who by the light of the New Testament
have unlocked the meaning
of wonders worked in former times,

calls people to belong to him, by the grace of adoption, in Baptism. The Church prays that all who are so called may enter their new state worthily, that is, may surrender totally to God, just as Abraham did when he was willing to sacrifice his son, Isaac.

Prayer after the Third Reading: One of the great wonders in the history of salvation, to which the first lines of this Collect refer, was the salvation and exodus of the people of Israel from a much stronger force, that of Pharoah and the Egyptians. The prayer attributes the liberation of Israel to the "power of (God's) right hand," which is always a symbol for strength and honor (cf., for example, Psalms 16:11; 20:7; 44:3; 108:6, to name just a few; but also others could be cited, such as Isaiah 41:10 and 48:13).

In the light of the great wonders of the Exodus, the Prayer contrasts the new wonders coming from the waters of baptismal rebirth, a new kind of "exodus from slavery" (to sin and death), with the bringing salvation not just to one people but to all the nations of the world. That is why the Collect ends with a petition that the promise made to Abraham be fulfilled and that all those reborn in Baptism share in the special blessings God gave to him, and thus share in the very birthright of Israel itself, to be God's Chosen People.

Optional Prayer, after the Third Reading: The second Collect for the Third Reading mirrors the imagery of the first. We have just heard in the reading about God's wonderful deed of liberating Israel

After the second reading (On Abraham's sacrifice: Gn 22: 1–18 or 1–2, 9a, 10–13, 15–18) and the Psalm (16 [15]).

Let us pray.

A O God, supreme Father of the faithful,
who increase the children of your promise
by pouring out the grace of adoption
throughout the whole world
and who through the Paschal Mystery
make your servant Abraham father of nations,
as once you **swore**,

B grant, we pray,
that your peoples may **en**ter worthily

C into the grace to which you call ***them***.
Through Christ our Lord.

R. Amen.

After the third reading (On the passage through the Red Sea: Ex 14: 15–15: 1) and its canticle (Ex 15).

Let us pray.

A O God, whose ancient wonders
remain undimmed in splendor even in our day,
for what you once bestowed on a single people,
freeing them from Pharaoh's persecution
by the power of your right hand
now you bring about as the salvation of the nations
through the waters of re**birth**,

B grant, we pray, that the whole world
may become chil**dren** of Abraham

C and inherit the dignity of Israel's birth***right***.
Through Christ our Lord.

R. Amen.

Or:

A O God, who by the light of the New Testament
have unlocked the meaning
of wonders worked in former times,

The space below is for your notes.

Refer to pages viii–x for an explanation of the pointing of the chants and to page xii for the Tones for the Presidential Prayers from *The Roman Missal*.

from the much stronger political and military force of Egypt. Thus, a people enslaved received a new lease on life. From the outset of the prayer, the Church recognizes that God has unlocked much deeper meaning to that first liberation, thanks to the New Testament interpretation of it (cf. one interpretation is from Saint Paul in 1 Corinthians 10:1–4). Thus, the passing through the Red Sea prefigures the passing through the saving waters of Baptism (sacred font). And the people of Israel prefigures the Christian people who, particularly on this night, are liberated anew from spiritual slavery.

The petition begs for all nations to share in Israel's unique privilege of being God's Chosen People, by means of faith, rather than physical lineage. This will happen through the gift of the Holy Spirit, which all receive in the Sacraments of Christian Initiation. It is the Spirit who gives new birth, new enlivening, and indeed, eternal life. Saint John highlights this in his Gospel account of the dialogue with Nicodemus: "I solemnly assure you, no one can see the reign of God without being begotten of water and the Spirit" (John 3:3). Faith is our response to the gift of the Spirit; salvation is the upshot of that gift.

Prayer after the Fourth Reading: The reading just proclaimed comes near the end of the second of the books of Isaiah, often referred to as the "Book of Consolation." In sharp contrast to the first part of the prophet's writing, often filled with condemnation for sinful Israel, this part speaks more of restoration and

next two lines in which **Sea** and **font** and **nation** and **Christian people** are balanced.

so that the Red Sea prefigures the sacred font
and the nation delivered from slavery
foreshadows the Christian people,
grant, we pray, that all nations,
obtaining the privilege of Israel by merit of faith,
may be reborn by partaking of your Spirit.
Through Christ our Lord.
R. Amen.

After the fourth reading (On the new Jerusalem: Is 54: 5–14) and the Psalm (30 [29]).

Let us pray.

For the honor of your name is a frequent motive ascribed to God in the Old Testament. **Surpass** and **increase** are critical in this prayer that acknowledges God's promise of growth and sees it fulfilled through the Church.

Almighty ever-living God,
surpass, for the honor of your name,
what you pledged to the Patriarchs by reason of their faith,
and through sacred adoption increase the children of
your promise,
so that what the Saints of old never doubted would come to pass
your Church may now see in great part fulfilled.
Through Christ our Lord.
R. Amen.

After the fifth reading (On salvation freely offered to all: Is 55: 1–11) and the canticle (Is 12).

Let us pray.

Speak **graciously increase the longing of your people** slowly and deliberately to emphasize the necessity of responding to God's initiative. In the word **progress**, the accent falls on the second syllable.

Almighty ever-living God,
sole hope of the world,
who by the preaching of your Prophets
unveiled the mysteries of this present age,
graciously increase the longing of your people,
for only at the prompting of your grace
do the faithful progress in any kind of virtue.
Through Christ our Lord.
R. Amen.

After the sixth reading (On the fountain of wisdom: Bar 3: 9–15, 31–4: 4) and the Psalm (19 [18]).

Use the words **constantly** and **call** to highlight God's initiative in sending our grace to all the **nations**.

Let us pray.

O God, who constantly increase your Church
by your call to the nations,

salvation. A vision of a better future thus opens up for Israel. In this light, the Collect begs God to surpass the promises previously made to Israel, especially to the patriarchs, who believed that God would save and love even more the Chosen People. This prayer says that a better future for Israel comes through adoption as God's new people. Members of the Church, conscious of those entering it through Christian Initiation this evening, see its members as the new children of God's promise.

The petition prays that all the faith shown and lived by the holy ones of old, whether during the Old Testament or the New Testament period, might come to fulfillment in the Church today. This celebration of Easter is a special celebration of faith. It needs to be seen and celebrated in the light of all those people of faith who came before us.

Prayer after the Fifth Reading: The reading just proclaimed from the book of Isaiah has a message of consolation similar to that of the Fourth Reading. God uses the voice of the prophet to call his people to himself, to promise them satisfaction for their deepest longings and hopes. In the process, the prophet promises that people will be summoned to join in the promises to Israel. In this light, the Collect speaks of God as the sole hope of the world—the answer human beings seek. It says bluntly that the prophets, such as Isaiah, whom we have just heard, were unveiling mysteries not just for their time but for ours. Their

so that the Red Sea prefigures the sacred font
and the nation delivered from slavery
foreshadows the Christian peo**ple**,
B grant, we pray, that all nations,
obtaining the privilege of Israel by me**rit** of faith,
C may be reborn by partaking of your Spi***rit***.
Through Christ our Lord.
R. Amen.

After the fourth reading (On the new Jerusalem: Is 54: 5-14) and the Psalm (30 [29]).

Let us pray.

A Almighty ever-living **God**,
B surpass, for the honor of your name,
what you pledged to the Patriarchs by reason of their faith,
and through sacred adoption increase the children **of**
your promise,
C so that what the Saints of old never doubted would come to pass
your Church may now see in great part ful***filled***.
Through Christ our Lord.
R. Amen.

After the fifth reading (On salvation freely offered to all: Is 55: 1-11) and the canticle (Is 12).

Let us pray.

A Almighty ever-living God,
sole hope of the world,
who by the preaching of your Prophets
unveiled the mysteries of this present **age**,
B graciously increase the longing **of** your people,
C for only at the prompting of your grace
do the faithful progress in any kind of vir***tue***.
Through Christ our Lord.
R. Amen.

After the sixth reading (On the fountain of wisdom: Bar 3: 9–15, 31–4: 4) and the Psalm (19 [18]).

Let us pray.

A O God, who constantly increase your Church
by your call to the na**tions**,

The space below is for your notes.

Refer to pages viii–x for an explanation of the pointing of the chants and to page xii for the Tones for the Presidential Prayers from *The Roman Missal*.

prophecies foretell the promises being fulfilled on this Easter Vigil.

The petition asks that God might increase the longing in people's hearts—it is particularly strong in the catechumens and has brought them to this joyful night. If God enters into the hearts of both those to be baptized in a few moments and those living Baptism for many years, then by being faithful to God's call and grace, all of us will progress in virtue. And thus, all will know the profoundly spiritual satisfaction once promised through the prophets.

Prayer after the Sixth Reading: The Sixth Reading tells of God's gift of wisdom manifest in his work of creation, manifest in the truth of the Law given to Israel and its descendants, manifest in lives dedicated to living according to God's way. (and we know, manifest in Jesus, who is the Wisdom of God Incarnate; cf. 1 Corinthians 1:24). The Collect begins with a kind of overview as to what is happening this night: catechumens are entering the Church through baptismal initiation; that is, God increases the Church by making a call to all peoples to come to him. Those with faith can see that the wisdom given of old by God has enduring value and contains sure promise of God's favor.

The petition looks to the catechumens who are to be washed clean by the waters of Baptism—that is, clean from sin and blindness of heart that darken the soul and make it impossible to receive and follow God's wisdom. The Church begs that all who have received Baptism might rest in the certainty of God's constant protection (this is the spirit of Psalm 90). But the

graciously grant
to those you wash clean in the waters of Baptism
the assurance of your unfailing protection.
Through Christ our Lord.
R. Amen.

After the seventh reading (On a new heart and new spirit: Ez 36: 16–28) and the Psalm (42–43 [41–42]).

Each address to God expresses some aspect of God's nature and/or our relationship to him. Don't waste those salutations.

Take special care with the lines following the semicolon carefully balancing **down/up**, **old/new**, and **restored/came into being**.

Let us pray.
O God of unchanging power and eternal light,
look with favor on the wondrous mystery of the whole Church
and serenely accomplish the work of human salvation,
which you planned from all eternity;
may the whole world know and see
that what was cast down is raised up,
what had become old is made new,
and all things are restored to integrity through Christ,
just as by him they came into being.
Who lives and reigns for ever and ever.
R. Amen.

Or:

Note the mention of how **both Testaments** prepare us to **celebrate the Paschal Mystery**. This prayer nicely contrasts the **gifts . . . (of) this night** with those **to come**.

O God, who by the pages of both Testaments
instruct and prepare us to celebrate the Paschal Mystery,
grant that we may comprehend your mercy,
so that the gifts we receive from you this night
may confirm our hope of the gifts to come.
Through Christ our Lord.
R. Amen.

After the last reading from the Old Testament with its Responsorial Psalm and its prayer, the altar candles are lit, and the Priest intones the Gloria in excelsis Deo. When the hymn is concluded, the Priest says the Collect in the usual way.

A slow and joy-filled delivery of **radiant with the glory of the Lord's Resurrection**, which is the source of our renewal in mind and body, is warranted.

Let us pray.
O God, who make this most sacred night radiant
with the glory of the Lord's Resurrection,
stir up in your Church a spirit of adoption,
so that, renewed in body and mind,
we may render you undivided service.
Through our Lord Jesus Christ, your Son,
who lives and reigns with you in the unity of the Holy Spirit,
one God, for ever and ever.

image means more deeply that God, in his wisdom, will always dwell in the depths of the souls of members of the Church, until we hear the ultimate call of God to dwell forever "in the shelter of his wings."

Prayer after the Seventh Reading: The prophet Ezekiel excoriates the Israelites for their unfaithfulness to God, especially in falling victim to the idolatry of their neighbors. And yet, God promises this will be transformed, and Israel will receive a new heart and spirit out of the goodness of God, thanks to the cleansing God will provide. In this Collect, God is seen to be of unchanging power and eternal light.

We petition that God look with favor on the Church and accomplish the work of salvation he began with Israel. In effect, we pray for new wonders in our time, so that peoples will come to know that, as Mary sang in her Canticle, "he has lifted up the lowly" (Luke 1:52). And we pray that the old may be made new—this is a common vision for Saint Paul, thus: ". . . put on the new man, one who grows in knowledge as he is formed anew in the image of his creator" (Colossians 3:10; but see also Ephesians 2:15). The next to last line is again Pauline: ". . . the plan he was pleased to decree in Christ . . . to restore all things in heaven and on earth under Christ's leadership . . ." (Ephesians 1:10). And the final phrase ties this restoration to the first creation.

Optional Prayer after the Seventh Reading: A kind of summary of salvation history opens this Collect, as it states that

B graciously grant
to those you wash clean in the wa**ters** of Baptism
C the assurance of your unfailing protec***tion***.
Through Christ our Lord.
R. Amen.

After the seventh reading (On a new heart and new spirit: Ez 36: 16–28) and the Psalm (42–43 [41–42]).

Let us pray.
A O God of unchanging power and eternal **light**,
B look with favor on the wondrous mystery of the whole Church
and serenely accomplish the work of human salvation,
which you planned from **all** eternity;
C may the whole world know and see
that what was cast down is raised up,
what had become old is made new,
and all things are restored to integrity through Christ,
just as by him they came into be***ing***.
Who lives and reigns for ever and ever.
R. Amen.

Or:

A O God, who by the pages of both Testaments
instruct and prepare us to celebrate the Paschal Mys**ter**y,
B grant that we may compre**hend** your mercy,
C so that the gifts we receive from you this night
may confirm our hope of the gifts to ***come***.
Through Christ our Lord.
R. Amen.

After the last reading from the Old Testament with its Responsorial Psalm and its prayer, the altar candles are lit, and the Priest intones the Gloria in excelsis Deo. When the hymn is concluded, the Priest says the Collect in the usual way.

Let us pray.
A O God, who make this most sacred night radiant
with the glory of the Lord's Resurrec**tion**,
B stir up in your Church a spirit **of** adoption,
C so that, renewed in body and mind,
we may render you undivided ser***vice***.
Through our Lord Jesus Christ, your Son,
who lives and reigns with you in the unity of the Holy Spirit,
one God, for ever and ever.

The space below is for your notes.

Refer to pages viii–x for an explanation of the pointing of the chants and to page xii for the Tones for the Presidential Prayers from *The Roman Missal*.

both the Old and New Testaments instruct and prepare us to celebrate a night like this Easter Vigil, in which the Paschal Mystery takes front and center as the focus of our faith and our joy. Since this comes at the end of the Old Testament readings and just before the two New Testament readings, the Church is praying with deep joy at the gifts given to us through the Word of God in all its varied forms.

The petition asks the grace to comprehend this a marvelous gift of God's Word. The Hebrew word for "mercy" means God's love, his profound gift of himself in love—which is what happens sacramentally when the Word is proclaimed. Concluding is a prayer that the gifts we receive tonight, including the Word and the Sacrament(s) of initiation, may strengthen our hope for the everlasting gifts that are to come in heaven.

Collect: The petition asks that God "stir up" the spirit of adoption that has made us his own. We are seeking help to avoid taking for granted our being chosen to be God's Church. Such a spiritual awakening as to who we are will lead us to renewal. When we take our adoption seriously, we will return to God the love that he has lavished on us. The prayer requests the grace to stay aware of our true roots. This will render our service to God undivided in our heart, at the core of our being.

In the Introduction to the Baptismal Liturgy, look at the elect or gesture toward them when exhorting to the people **these our brothers and sisters**. The Blessing is extremely important and should be proclaimed most solemnly. If the Easter candle is lowered into the font, be sure this is done where a majority of people can see the action. It will be necessary to catechize the people and practice with them, if one expects them to acclaim musically **Springs of water** at the Candle ritual. Take the same serious approach to the Blessing of Water when there is no one in the congregation to be baptized: make it solemn and noble.

The usual Preface tone is used throughout for the invocations and the Blessings. Simply respect the sense of the text, with holds and pauses at the end of sentences and many phrases. In general, the singing is recitative, as the texts are so long. It would be well to define clearly the different events or uses of water mentioned in the Blessings by the way one articulates the phrases and pauses at the end of them.

THIRD PART:
BAPTISMAL LITURGY

If there are candidates to be baptized:

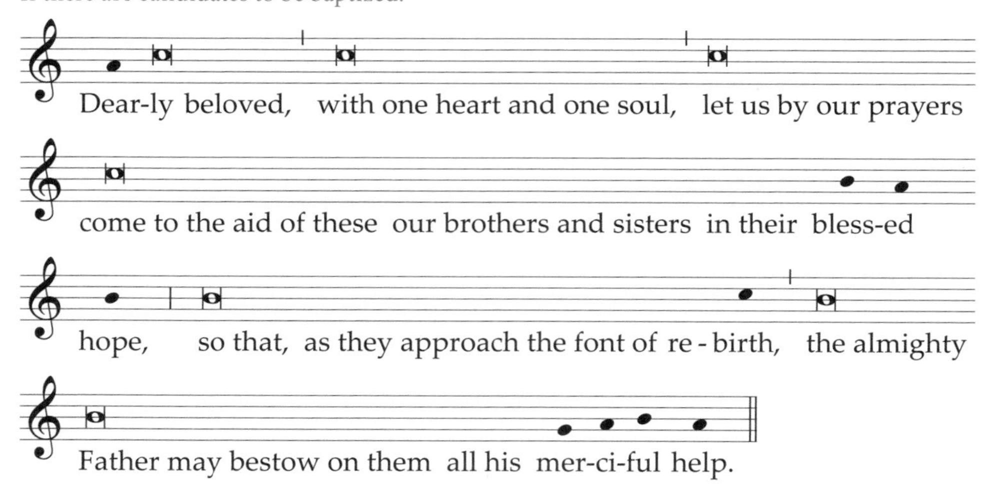

Dearly beloved,
with one heart and one soul, let us by our prayers
come to the aid of these our brothers and sisters in their blessed hope,
so that, as they approach the font of rebirth,
the almighty Father may bestow on them
all his merciful help.

If the font is to be blessed, but no one is to be baptized:

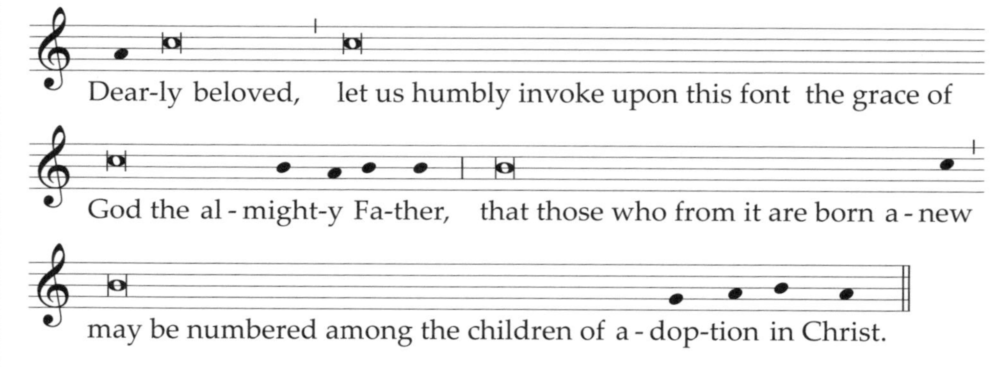

Part III: Baptismal Liturgy (if there are candidates to be baptized.)

The Priest Celebrant calls on the faithful to have "one heart and soul," that is, to be the unified body of Christ we have been called to be—and into which the newly baptized will be inserted. He exhorts the Church to prayer—to help the catechumens take this final step, that will bring their hopes (of salvation) to fruition. The Church prays that, as the catechumens approach the font, they will have the Father's help to complete this step, a help equal to God's redeeming love. The merciful help indicates the salvation offered by Christ's redemption on the Cross. In Romans 11:32, Paul states, "For God delivered all to disobedience, that he might have mercy upon all."

Repeatedly, Paul describes God's gift of salvation as coming from his mercy. "But God who is rich in mercy, because of the great love he had for us, even when we were dead in our transgressions, brought us to life with Christ (by grace you have been saved) . . ." (Ephesians 2:4–5).

Blessing of the font, but no one is to be baptized: The Church's petition at the beginning of this blessing is made "humbly," especially in the light of God's immense power that will be exercised during Baptisms at this font. As the water of this font is poured, the numbers of adopted children will grow. "For those who are led by the Spirit of God are children of God. For you did not receive a spirit of slavery to fall back into fear, but you received a spirit of adoption, through which we cry, 'Abba, Father!' " (Romans 8:15).

Dearly beloved,
let us humbly invoke upon this font
the grace of God the almighty Father,
that those who from it are born anew
may be numbered among the children of adoption in Christ.

The theme of **adoption** is strong tonight. There is tenderness in the invocation of God's grace upon the womb-like font that will produce newborn **children of adoption**.

If there are candidates to be baptized, the Priest, with hands extended, says the following prayer:

Almighty ever-living God,
be present by the mysteries of your great love
and send forth the spirit of adoption
to create the new peoples
brought to birth for you in the font of Baptism,
so that what is to be carried out by our humble service
may be brought to fulfillment by your mighty power.
Through Christ our Lord.
R. Amen.

The font is identified as a place of **adoption** and new **birth**, both of which call for a tender tone. Carefully balance **carried out** and **humble service** with **brought to fulfillment** and **mighty power**.

Blessing of Baptismal Water

The Priest then blesses the baptismal water, saying the following prayer with hands extended:

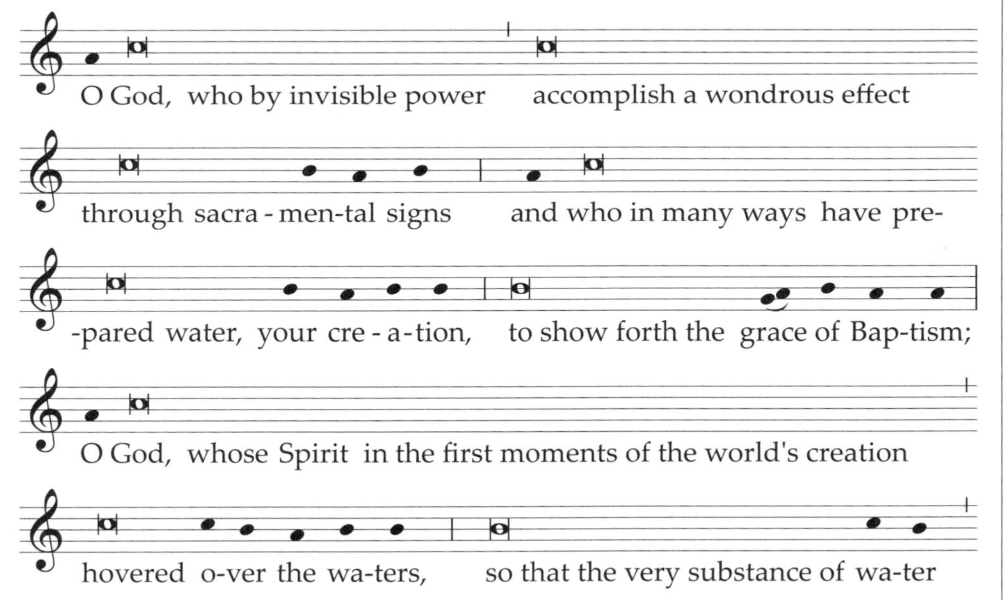

Blessing of Baptismal Water
The grace of God is invoked in the blessing upon the font, so that soon the grace of God may emanate from this font. This will be the place of new birth for those God has called to be his children in Christ.

1. From the outset, this blessing highlights sacramentality, that is, the way in which God's invisible power works its marvels through visible things. All of this the Church sees, especially tonight, as certain signs (that are sacramental) display one thing exteriorly and materially, while having another meaning interiorly or spiritually. The case in point here is natural water. As we heard in the readings, God created water, one of the first elements of natural creation (Genesis 1:9–10). But the creation of that natural reality was to ready a natural element to carry a supernatural grace, that of Baptism. As the *Catechism of the Catholic Church,* 1147, states, "God speaks to man through visible creation. The material cosmos is so presented to man's intelligence that he can read there traces of its Creator."

2. The first day of creation is evoked (Genesis 1:1–2), and the blessing emphasizes the vision that, even at the beginning, water should be seen in the light of its use this night for the Sacrament of Baptism. What at the beginning was intended to be life-giving on the natural level (cf. Genesis 1:20) is now to be seen as life-giving on the supernatural and eternal level.

3. The next event evoked in the Blessing is the flood in Noah's time (Genesis 6:13—8:22). Although the flood wrought universal havoc and destruction, because of the sinfulness of earth's inhabitants, so also it proved, by God's providence, to be salvation for a few upright persons (Genesis 7:13). In this way, this event was sacramental, a natural sign pointing to the later spiritual reality contained in Christian initiation and its blessed water, the destruction of sin and death, and the giving of new life by regeneration.

4. The Blessing then recounts the Exodus (Exodus 14:15–31). In this event, by means of passing through the Red Sea out of the slavery they had known in Egypt, God's Chosen People were saved from destruction by their enemies. This event foreshadowed and prefigured what will happen in a few moments with this blessed water: God's new people, those baptized at the font this night, are saved from even more pernicious enemies—the devil and his minions.

5. The next part of the Blessing brings us to Jesus, the Chosen One from among the Chosen People. He submitted to baptism at the Jordan (Mark 1:9–11 and parallels; John 1:29–34). His was a baptism not just with water but also with the Holy Spirit (John 1:34). In this rite, Jesus was designated as God's Son, Beloved, the Chosen One. And in this way, he prefigured those baptized this night who will then become God's chosen ones. The *Catechism of the Catholic Church*, 1224, states that Jesus's

And, if appropriate, lowering the paschal candle into the water either once or three times, he continues:

submission to the baptism in the Jordan was "a manifestation of his self-emptying."

Jesus, at his Death on the Cross for the salvation of the world, had water (as well as blood) issue from his side. In 1 John 5:6–7, this is attested: "This is the one who came through water and blood, Jesus Christ, not by water alone, but by water and blood. The Spirit is the one that testifies and the Spirit is truth. So there are three that testify, the Spirit, the water, and the blood, and the three are of one accord."

The pouring forth of both water and blood was interpreted by many Fathers of the Church as prefiguring the saving waters of Baptism (as well as the Holy Eucharist). Because of its importance in God's plan for salvation to reach the world, Jesus commissioned his disciples to go throughout that world and baptize, in the name of the Trinity: "Go, therefore, and make disciples of all nations, baptizing them in the name of the Father, and of the Son, and of the holy Spirit, teaching them to observe all that I have commanded you. And behold, I am with you always, until the end of the age" (Matthew 28:19–20).

In the light of all this saving richness of grace, present in sacramental form here this night, the Church blesses the water to be used in the celebration of the Sacrament of Baptism in a few moments. It prays for God simply to look upon his people and open up the (blessed) waters of Baptism for the salvation of the candidates here this night.

and, holding the candle in the water, he continues:

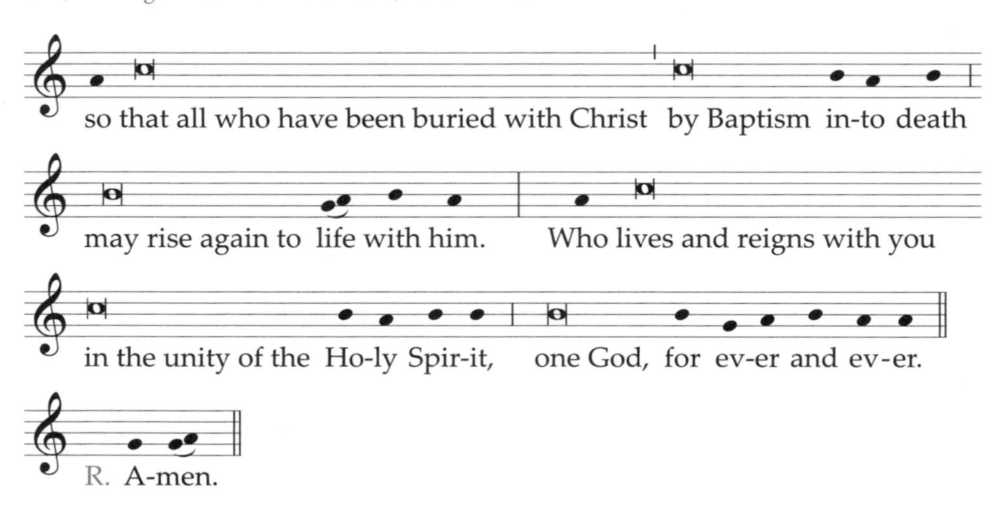

Then the candle is lifted out of the water, as the people acclaim:

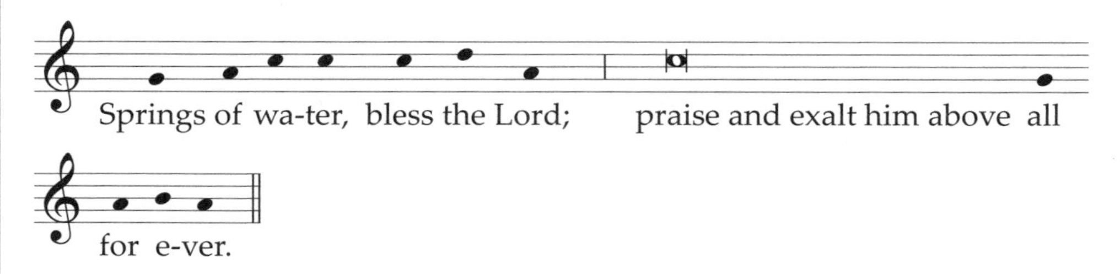

Five long, relative clauses precede the request that **God . . . look . . . up on the face of your Church**. The content of all five clauses must be held aloft simultaneously, like a juggler tossing five bowling pins at once, before speaker and listeners can arrive at their destination. The voice must suggest that the main thought remains unfinished as each clause is spoken. Articulate each **O God** as if stacking ideas one atop the next, creating a cumulative until arriving at the verb, **look**, that binds all together.

Text without music:

The Priest then blesses the baptismal water, saying the following prayer with hands extended:

O God, who by invisible power
accomplish a wondrous effect
through sacramental signs
and who in many ways have prepared water, your creation,
to show forth the grace of Baptism;

6. Jesus received the anointing of the Holy Spirit in a special way in his baptism. In the culminating part of this Blessing, the Church prays that the Holy Spirit may come into this water, thanks to the grace of Jesus present here also. The result will be that human nature, in those to be baptized, will be cleansed of original sin and all other sin (squalor of the life of old—of the "old man"; cf. Saint Paul, Romans 6:6; Ephesians 4:22; Colossians 3:9). "For if we have grown into union with him through a death like his, we shall be also be united with him in the resurrection. We know that our old self was crucified with him, so that our sinful body might be done away with, that we might no longer be in slavery to sin. For a dead person has been absolved from sin" (Romans 6:6–7).

7. The Easter candle was proclaimed earlier as a kind of sacrament of the risen Christ earlier in the liturgy. To lower it into the font is a vivid sign of Jesus risen coming to transform this water. Jesus transforms the water through the power of the Holy Spirit, whose presence he brings, when he comes in his risen state (cf. John 20:23; Acts 2:32–33). In the second part of the ritual with the candle, the Church prays for all to be baptized: as Christ, symbolized by the candle, remains buried in the water, so may those who go with him (sacramentally) to death and burial, rise to new and eternal life with him, at which point the candle is lifted out of the water.

The people's acclamation at this point, ("Springs of water, bless the Lord; praise and exalt him forever") calling on the

O God, whose Spirit
in the first moments of the world's creation
hovered over the waters,
so that the very substance of water
would even then take to itself the power to sanctify;

Hovered over the waters evokes Genesis, and **power to sanctify** names one of water's sacramental significations. Give both proper stress.

O God, who by the outpouring of the flood
foreshadowed regeneration,
so that from the mystery of one and the same element of water
would come an end to vice and a beginning of virtue;

The word **flood** sets the context; unless we hear it, the meaning of **end** and **beginning** (which need careful balancing) won't be clear.

O God, who caused the children of Abraham
to pass dry-shod through the Red Sea,
so that the chosen people,
set free from slavery to Pharaoh,
would prefigure the people of the baptized;

Don't rush and lose the allusion to the Exodus. Much knowledge of scripture is packed in these prayers.

O God, whose Son,
baptized by John in the waters of the Jordan,
was anointed with the Holy Spirit,
and, as he hung upon the Cross,
gave forth water from his side along with blood,
and after his Resurrection, commanded his disciples:
"Go forth, teach all nations, baptizing them
in the name of the Father and of the Son and of the Holy Spirit,"
look now, we pray, upon the face of your Church
and graciously unseal for her the fountain of Baptism.

Three major moments are enumerated here: Jesus's baptism; Death on the Cross, and the issue of blood and water from his side; the Great Commission.

This long relative clause contains subordinate clauses. Drop your voice for the subordinate clauses, then increase your energy on the predicates that follow: **was anointed**, **gave forth water**, and **commanded his disciples**.

May this water receive by the Holy Spirit
the grace of your Only Begotten Son,
so that human nature, created in your image
and washed clean through the Sacrament of Baptism
from all the squalor of the life of old,
may be found worthy to rise to the life of newborn children
through water and the Holy Spirit.

Make it clear that it is **human nature** that is **created**, **washed clean** and that we pray will be **found worthy to rise**.

waters to praise the Lord, comes from the Canticle of the Three Young Men who had been saved by God from the evil of persecution (Daniel 3:77). These men, who had been thrown in a furnace, were rescued by an angel who "drove the fiery flames out of the furnace and made the inside of the furnace as though a dew-laden breeze were blowing through it" (Daniel 3:49–50). While still in the furnace, the men sing a long hymn of praises to God. After extolling the heavens, fire and heat, cold and chill, more than halfway through the hymn, they sing, "You springs, bless the Lord; praise and exalt him above all forever." We, too, have been rescued from death, so our words join theirs.

Before the immense power of God to set apart and thus "make holy" natural things that he created, the Church is humble as it petitions that divine power to work in this water to bless it this night. What God created in the natural order thus will have a new power in the supernatural order. The water to be blessed will be sprinkled over the faithful present at this Vigil, and thus will remind them of the water poured over them (or, into which they were immersed) at their Baptism.

The Church prays for renewal of that original grace, so that we might live constantly in the faith that has been sacramentalized in us through water and the Holy Spirit, when we were first baptized. Saint Paul continually prayed for the members of the early Church, and asked for their prayers in return. He implored them to be steadfast in the faith, because their citizenship was elsewhere. "But our

Note the Trinitarian formula utilized in this portion of the prayer.

Stress and balance the Pauline theology of being **buried with Christ** and rising to new **life with him**.

And, if appropriate, lowering the paschal candle into the water either once or three times, he continues:

May the power of the Holy Spirit,
O Lord, we pray,
come down through your Son
into the fullness of this font,

and, holding the candle in the water, he continues:

so that all who have been buried with Christ
by Baptism into death
may rise again to life with him.
Who lives and reigns with you in the unity of the Holy Spirit,
one God, for ever and ever.
R. Amen.

Then the candle is lifted out of the water, as the people acclaim:

Springs of water, bless the Lord;
praise and exalt him above all for ever.

The Blessing of Water

If no one present is to be baptized and the font is not to be blessed, the Priest introduces the faithful to the blessing of water, saying:

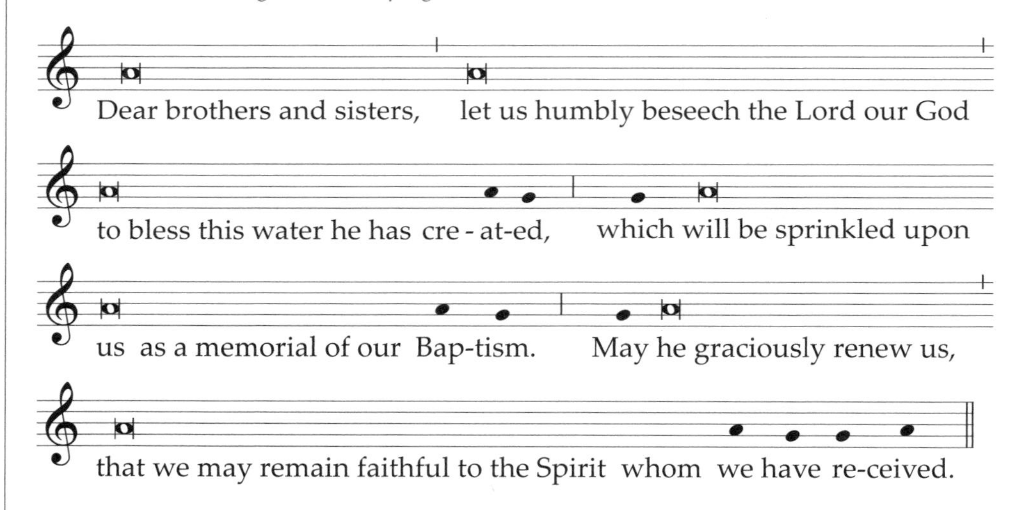

citizenship is in heaven, and from it we also await a savior, the Lord Jesus Christ. He will change our lowly body to conform with his glorified body by the power that enables him also to bring all things into subjection to himself" (Philippians 3:20–21).

The Prayer of Blessing: The Church asks at the beginning of the blessing that God be present to us. God's presence is salvific, because God's love (mercy) has already been given to us in a most powerful way when we were baptized. Our keeping vigil this night is a sign of our longing for the divine presence, above all, the presence of Jesus in his Resurrection. The Liturgy of the Word has helped us recall the wonders of creation and that each part of creation pleased God. As Genesis 1:31 states, "God looked at everything he had made, and he found it very good." Creation was blessed and told to propagate: "Let the waters teem with an abundance of living creatures, and on the earth let birds fly beneath the dome of the sky. . . . And God blessed them saying, ' Be fertile, multiply, and fill the water of the seas; and let the birds multiply on the earth," (Genesis 1:20, 22). "Then God said, 'Let us create man in our image, after our likeness. . . . God blessed them, saying to them, 'Be fertile and multiply; fill the earth and subdue it," (Genesis 1:26, 28). From the Epistle (Romans 6:3–11),

And after a brief pause in silence, he proclaims the following prayer with hands extended:

we heard of the new way of living for which Christ has redeemed us: "Consequently, you too must think of yourselves as being dead to sin and living for God in Christ Jesus." In the Gospel (Matthew 28:1–10), we are told not only of the empty tomb but that the women "went away quickly from the tomb" to anounce that Jesus was raised from the dead.

In the light of those wonderful works of God, the Church asks that the water be blessed. It lists both the natural blessings and the supernatural blessings that are connected with water: (1) it makes the earth fruitful (Genesis 2:10; 9:11); (2) it refreshes and cleanses human bodies; (3) it was the means God used, in merciful love, to free his people Israel from slavery in Egypt, and then which gave them strength in the desert (Exodus 14:15–31; 17:1–7); (4) it was used symbolically by the prophets to proclaim the coming of a new covenant between God and his people (Isaiah 55:1–3; Jeremiah 31:12, 31ff.; Ezekiel 34:25–6); (5) it was used by Christ, baptized in the Jordan, as a sign for making holy those who shared such a ritual; and (6) in the Church, it is used to renew the nature tainted by original sin and other sin in a washing that brings about new birth.

As the blessing makes explicit the many uses of water, we again hear about salvation history. This is a vigil in which, again and again, we tell of God's mercy and the blessings provided to us. We rejoice with the Israelites. After crossing the sea on dry land, the Israelites praised the Lord, not only for this event, but for the

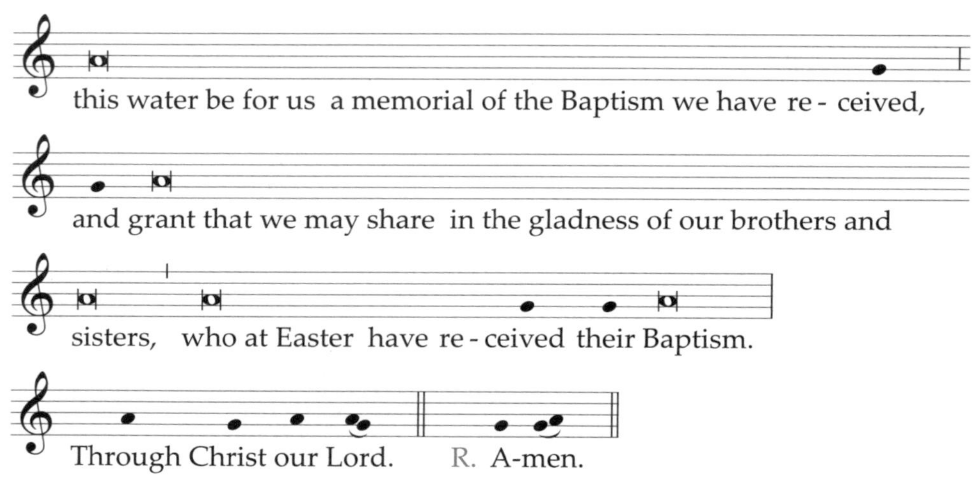

Here we ask God to **bless** the water, mindful that the blessing makes present our Baptism. These lines move briskly with joyful energy.

Text without music:

Dear brothers and sisters,
let us humbly beseech the Lord our God
to bless this water he has created,
which will be sprinkled upon us
as a memorial of our Baptism.
May he graciously renew us,
that we may remain faithful to the Spirit
whom we have received.

And after a brief pause in silence, he proclaims the following prayer, with hands extended:

The prayer begins with a reference to those keeping vigil at this very liturgy. For them you use the image of water to review salvation history, first calling to mind the two main works of God's mercy: **creation** and **redemption**. Name the exodus experience with respect and awe and allude to the prophets with great dignity.

Lord our God,
in your mercy be present to your people
who keep vigil on this most sacred night,
and, for us who recall the wondrous work of our creation
and the still greater work of our redemption,
graciously bless this water.
For you created water to make the fields fruitful
and to refresh and cleanse our bodies.
You also made water the instrument of your mercy:
for through water you freed your people from slavery
and quenched their thirst in the desert;
through water the Prophets proclaimed the new covenant
you were to enter upon with the human race;

mercy he shows and for where he is leading them: "In mercy you led the people you redeemed; / in your strength you guided them to your holy dwelling" (Exodus 15:13). God not only has redeemed us but is guiding us to him.

As those to whom God has made a covenant are guided, they are cared for, invited for refreshment: "All you who are thirsty, / come to the water! / . . . / Come to me heedfully, / listen, that you may have life. / I will renew with you the everlasting covenant, / the benefits assured to David. / . . . / So shall you summon a nation you knew not, / and nations that knew you not shall run to you, / Because of the LORD, the Holy One of Israel, who has glorified you" (Isaiah 55:1–5).

The protection and blessing for those with whom he has made a covenant are continual. In Ezekiel, God's people are referred to as sheep, with whom he will make a covenant and whom he guards and refreshes: "I will save my sheep, so that they may no longer be despoiled . . . . I will appoint one shepherd over them, my servant David; he shall pasture them and be their shepherd. . . . I will make a covenant of peace with them . . . . I will place them about my hill, sending rain in due season, rain that shall be a blessing to them" (Ezekiel 34:22–26).

With all this sacramental meaning inherent in water, the Church blesses water anew this night, so that it might be a renewal of the reality of Baptism (and not just a memory of it) in its members. Such a renewal will lead to a deep awareness of the many catechumens throughout the

and last of all,
through water, which Christ made holy in the Jordan,
you have renewed our corrupted nature
in the bath of regeneration.
Therefore, may this water be for us
a memorial of the Baptism we have received,
and grant that we may share
in the gladness of our brothers and sisters,
who at Easter have received their Baptism.
Through Christ our Lord.
R. Amen.

Link Christ's baptism and our **regeneration** with solemn gratitude. The prayer ends in joyful solidarity with the newly baptized.

Church who are becoming members of the body of Christ through Baptism this night. Those who are receiving the Sacraments of initiation tonight are filled with joy; at the end of the Blessing, the Church prays that all of us might share such joy. May we rejoice with them, understanding the importance of this night.

We ask God to accept the people's prayers along with the sacrificial offerings. Carefully balance what was begun with the **healing of eternity**.

Prayer over the Offerings

Accept, we ask, O Lord,
the prayers of your people
with the sacrificial offerings,
that what has begun in the paschal mysteries
may, by the working of your power,
bring us to the healing of eternity.
Through Christ our Lord.

This prayer reminds us that partaking of the Eucharist does not necessarily make us one. Make an earnest prayer for that unity for which Jesus longed.

Prayer after Communion

Pour out on us, O Lord, the Spirit of your love,
and in your kindness make those you have nourished
by this paschal Sacrament
one in mind and heart.
Through Christ our Lord.

Prayer over the Offerings: In this prayer, the Church offers to God prayers and material offerings. The material elements brought up to the altar in the Preparation Rite are intended to be symbols of the offering of our hearts. By accompanying this offering with prayers, we try to express clearly that this is a spiritual gift, not merely an external exercise. This is quite in accord with the words of the psalmist, who was speaking for God in saying that Israel's external sacrifices were not what God wanted: "Offer praise as your sacrifice to God; / fulfill your vows to the Most High" (Psalm 50:14). Through such an offering of ourselves, we join Jesus in his offering to the Father, through the Paschal Mystery, that we have celebrated movingly in the past three days. The offering we make with Jesus is to sustain us on our earthly journey, to keep us in touch with God, by the exercise of our faith and the gift of our love. The Church prays that, by God's power (grace), what we do here ritually will ultimately bring us to eternity, where all ills will be healed, all sorrow turned into joy.

Prayer after Communion: The prayer begins immediately with the petition that God may pour out upon us the Spirit of divine love. This was the vision of the Psalmist also (Psalm 104:30), and it is used more than once in the liturgy as antiphon and responsory: "Lord, send out your Spirit, and renew the face of the earth."

We have just received Jesus in the Sacrament of Holy Communion, which is the nourishment God promised his people, a manna that brings us into profound union with the Lord, the living Bread come

Pointed Text

Prayer over the Offerings

A Accept, we ask, O Lord,
the prayers of your people
with the sacrificial of**fer**ings,
B that what has begun in the paschal mysteries
may, by the working **of** your power,
C bring us to the healing of eter***ni***ty.
Through Christ our Lord.

Prayer after Communion

B Pour out on us, O Lord, the Spirit **of** your love,
C and in your kindness make those you have nourished
by this paschal Sacrament
one in mind and ***heart***.
Through Christ our Lord.

The space below is for your notes.

Refer to pages viii–x for an explanation of the pointing of the chants and to page xii for the Tones for the Presidential Prayers from *The Roman Missal*.

down from heaven (John 6:51). God's care for his people was already manifested in the desert by the first manna provided for them (cf. Exodus 16 et passim). Now, in Jesus, the Living Bread, we have the most profound sign of God's loving kindness.

And so we ask the Spirit to sustain us in that union with Jesus that has resulted from our sharing in the Sacrament. Our union with Jesus also has led to union with one another. We cannot be united with the Head without being united with the Body as well. Therefore, the prayer concludes with a plea that God will extend his loving kindness again, and make the theory of our unity into a vibrant reality.

Solemn Blessing

The verbs here are **bless** and **defend**.

Assault of sin is a striking and unexpected image. Don't waste it.

May almighty God bless you
through today's Easter Solemnity
and, in his compassion,
defend you from every assault of sin.
R. Amen.

Prize of immortality is another novel expression that merits attention.

And may he, who restores you to eternal life
in the Resurrection of his Only Begotten,
endow you with the prize of immortality.
R. Amen.

Joyfulness dominates this third part of the blessing. Note all the exuberant words: **celebrate**, **gladness**, **exulting**, **joy**.

Now that the days of the Lord's Passion have drawn to a close,
may you who celebrate the gladness of the Paschal Feast
come with Christ's help, and exulting in spirit,
to those feasts that are celebrated in eternal joy.
R. Amen.

And may the blessing of almighty God,
the Father, and the Son, ✠ and the Holy Spirit,
come down on you and remain with you for ever.
R. Amen.

To dismiss the people the Deacon or, if there is no Deacon, the Priest himself sings or says:

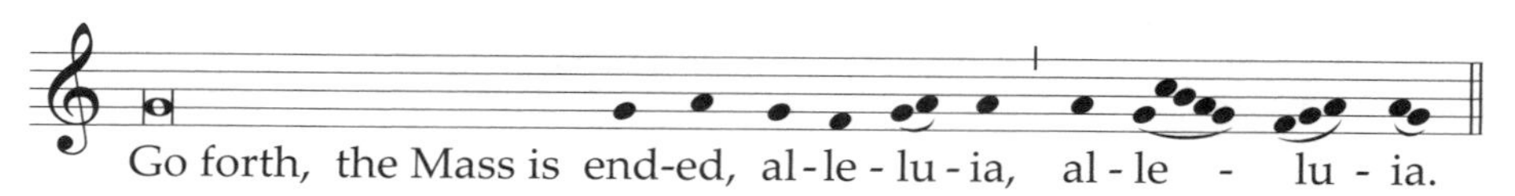

A slight pause before the singing of the alleluias is appropriate. Make the latter as joyful as possible, with a smile in the voice.

Or:

All reply:

Thanks be to God, al-le-lu-ia, al-le - lu - ia.

Solemn Blessing: Though the Missal offers many variations of Solemn Blessings, their use, left to the discretion of the Priest, often remains more the exception than the rule. Available throughout the liturgical year, Solemn Blessings most often dignify the liturgies of the more significant moments in our communal life. However, the typical invitation formula, "Bow your heads and pray for God's blessing," poses a challenge for the assembly who somehow must know when to respond to the Priest's invocations. A clear lift of the voice and a slowing tempo at the end of each petition will signal the assembly to speak their "Amen."

Today's blessing acknowledges that the spiritual battle rages despite Christ's Easter victory. Sin continues its "assault," but we battle on with Christ at our side and with Resurrection grace empowering us. The second petition reminds us that though we've been restored to life, assurance of the "prize of immortality" rests on God's mercy and on our fidelity to Christ. The third invocation also reinforces the notion that, while we are privileged to celebrate this great feast, it will only be with Christ's continued help and the guidance of his Holy Spirit that we will experience the joy of the eternal banquet.

Solemn Blessing

B May almighty God bless you
through today's Eas**ter** Solemnity
C and, in his compassion,
defend you from every assault of ***sin***.
R. Amen.

B And may he, who restores you to eternal life
in the Resurrection of his On**ly** Begotten,
C endow you with the prize of immortal***i***ty.
R. Amen.

A Now that the days of the Lord's Passion have drawn to a **close**,
B may you who celebrate the gladness of the Paschal Feast
come with Christ's help, and exult**ing** in spirit,
C to those feasts that are celebrated in eternal ***joy***.
R. Amen.

A And may the blessing of almighty **God**,
B the Father, and the Son, + and the **Ho**ly Spirit,
C come down on you and remain with you for e***ver***.
R. Amen.

The space below is for your notes.

Refer to pages viii–x for an explanation of the pointing of the chants and to page xii for the Tones for the Presidential Prayers from *The Roman Missal*.

At the Mass during the Day

Collect

The words **conquered** and **unlocked** are key to the meaning of this solemnity. Note that renewal comes through God's **Spirit** and the request is that we **rise up in the light of life**.

O God, who on this day,
through your Only Begotten Son,
have conquered death
and unlocked for us the path to eternity,
grant, we pray, that we who keep
the solemnity of the Lord's Resurrection
may, through the renewal brought by your Spirit,
rise up in the light of life.
Through our Lord Jesus Christ, your Son,
who lives and reigns with you in the unity of the Holy Spirit,
one God, for ever and ever.

Prayer over the Offerings

Do not let your tone contradict the words **Exultant** and **gladness** that open this prayer.

Exultant with paschal gladness, O Lord,
we offer the sacrifice
by which your Church
is wondrously reborn and nourished.
Through Christ our Lord.

Prayer after Communion

This prayer summarizes what has occurred—**renewed by the paschal mysteries**—and our desired consequence—**the glory of the resurrection**. The motif, again, is joy.

Look upon your Church, O God,
with unfailing love and favor,
so that, renewed by the paschal mysteries,
she may come to the glory of the resurrection.
Through Christ our Lord.

Collect: Because so much of the Easter Vigil imagery is tied up with Christ's "unlocking" the gates that would imprison us in hell, the same is used here, but this time with the idea of unlocking the gates of heaven. They had been closed by the sin of Adam and Eve. With their expulsion from paradise, Angels were stationed at the door to paradise to prohibit entrance (Genesis 3:23–24).

Since we are keeping the Solemnity of Jesus's Resurrection, we beg a share of the same Resurrection for ourselves—this, because we are followers of Jesus, and long for the fulfillment of his promise: "Whoever follows me will not walk in darkness, but will have the light of life" (John 8:12). The Collect uses that terminology. We pray that this share in the Resurrection might happen through renewal brought about by God's Holy Spirit. The Prayer after Communion at the Easter Vigil said much the same thing: our rising to new and everlasting life is assured only by the grace of the Holy Spirit, the "giver of life" (Nicene-Constantinople Creed).

Prayer over the Offerings: The opening words are strongly reminiscent of the Exsultet. The repetition in the first line would be tedious except that Easter is the greatest feast of the year. Hence, it is plausible that the Church should be "exultant" with paschal "gladness."

With the gifts soon to be offered in the Eucharistic Prayer, the text states, "we offer the sacrifice." This prayer heralds the reality that takes place from the bringing of the gifts as signs of the gift of our hearts, through the Prayer of Offering.

Pointed Text

Collect

A O God, who on this day,
through your Only Begotten Son,
have conquered death
and unlocked for us the path to eter**ni**ty,
B grant, we pray, that we who keep
the solemnity of the Lord's **Res**urrection
C may, through the renewal brought by your Spirit,
rise up in the light of ***life***.
Through our Lord Jesus Christ, your Son,
who lives and reigns with you in the unity of the Holy Spirit,
one God, for ever and ever.

Prayer over the Offerings

B Exultant with paschal glad**ness**, O Lord,
C we offer the sacrifice
by which your Church
is wondrously reborn and nour***ished***.
Through Christ our Lord.

Prayer after Communion

A Look upon your Church, O God,
with unfailing love and fa**vor**,
B so that, renewed by the **pas**chal mysteries,
C she may come to the glory of the resurrec***tion***.
Through Christ our Lord.

The space below is for your notes.

Refer to pages viii–x for an explanation of the pointing of the chants and to page xii for the Tones for the Presidential Prayers from *The Roman Missal*.

We are reborn through the sacrifice, because our sacrifice is united to that of Jesus, and through the Paschal Mystery, he brings us new life (reborn). It is almost too marvelous to describe that God would grant such a grace of mercy and compassion. That is why the text uses "wondrously" in describing our rebirth. By God's even greater love, we are invited to share in a Holy Communion of the sacrifice now become Sacrament. Thus, as the prayer says, we are not only reborn but also nourished spiritually by what we are doing.

Prayer after Communion: We have just received Holy Communion, and the Church rests serene in the light of such love coming to us from God. Christ himself has come to us in sacramental form, thus showing how much God loves us. He gives us Jesus as a sign of that divine love. We pray that God may continue to show his love and favor in the Church, to sustain it on its journey toward heaven. The Psalmist of old sang, "The promises of the LORD I will sing forever" (Psalm 89:2). So the Church longs that those promises, the signs of God's undying love for us his people, will be there always.

The Church prays that, in the light of the renewal that has occurred in the reception of Communion, what is begun in the liturgy will be completed in life. We pray that by celebrating in Sacrament the Resurrection of Jesus, and being renewed by God's unfailing love, we may arrive at the resurrection of our persons, that is, the "glory" which this solemnity foretells.

SECOND SUNDAY OF EASTER

(or of Divine Mercy)

Collect

Linger over **everlasting mercy** and proclaim it with gentleness. Place a parallel emphasis on **very recurrence** and **paschal feast**. Start strong with **kindle the faith** and pause briefly. Draw out the word **own**. Pause briefly after **we pray** and speak **grace** with a measure of joy. Pause briefly after **grasp**. The next three lines have a parallel rhythm, but with increasing intensity: **washed**, **Spirit**, **Blood**. They proclaim marvelous mysteries.

God of everlasting mercy,
who in the very recurrence of the paschal feast
kindle the faith of the people you have made your own,
increase, we pray, the grace you have bestowed,
that all may grasp and rightly understand
in what font they have been washed,
by whose Spirit they have been reborn,
by whose Blood they have been redeemed.
Through our Lord Jesus Christ, your Son,
who lives and reigns with you in the unity of the Holy Spirit,
one God, for ever and ever.

Prayer over the Offerings

Pause briefly after **Accept** and keep **O Lord**, **we pray** together. Be mindful of the accent for **ob-LA-tions**. Pause after **that** and proclaim **renewed** with energy. Emphasize **confession** and **Baptism**. Pause briefly after **attain** to draw out **unending**.

Accept, O Lord, we pray,
the oblations of your people
(and of those you have brought to new birth),
that, renewed by confession of your name and by Baptism,
they may attain unending happiness.
Through Christ our Lord. *

Prayer after Communion

Pause briefly after **Grant** and then proceed slowly. Pause briefly after **reception** and then proclaim **paschal Sacrament** with reverent clarity. Draw out the word **continuing** and pause briefly after **minds** and raise the voice with **minds** and end warmly with **hearts**.

Grant, we pray, almighty God,
that our reception of this paschal Sacrament
may have a continuing effect
in our minds and hearts.
Through Christ our Lord. **

* Use Preface I of Easter in the Order of Mass. Commentary, and proclamation and chant tips, for the Preface can be found at *www.StudyThePresidentialTexts.com/Prefaces* and in *The Order of Mass: A Roman Missal Study Edition and Workbook*, pages 48–49. If Eucharistic Prayer I is used, the proper form of the Communicantes is prayed from the Order of Mass. It is found in *The Order of Mass: A Roman Missal Study Edition and Workbook*, page 129.

** You may use the Solemn Blessings for Easter Time in the Order of Mass, page 169 in *The Order of Mass: A Roman Missal Study Edition and Workbook*.

Collect: The risen Christ still bears the wounds of his Passion, which is why his mercy is "everlasting." Christ "kindled" the faith of Thomas ("my Lord and my God") on this day by revealing his (glorious) wounds; in the Eucharist, he kindles today the faith of those who look to him. The Latin behind "the people you have made your own" is *sacratae tibi plebis*, literally, of the people consecrated or made sacred to you. Being consecrated to God means simply that he takes us for himself and to himself. "Grace" was bestowed on Easter, especially in the Sacraments of initiation conferred that day. The rest of Easter Time and beyond is the opportunity to deepen that initial grace. The octave Sunday, also called "Mystagogy Sunday," is where the grace bestowed initially may be more fully grasped and rightly understood, implying that we can misunderstand God's grace. The most essential elements to be grasped and understood include that the "font" is the womb of the Church, that the "Spirit" is the divinity of Christ, and the "Blood" is the God-man, whose mercy is "everlasting."

Prayer over the Offerings: In this prayer, the Church shows solicitude to those newly baptized by making it clear that they are now privileged to bring their sacrifices to the altar to be united to Christ. They belong to God's people. There are two requirements for membership in God's people: faith and Baptism. Faith is not passive consent but active engagement in the mystery. To believe with one's whole person means being willing to take ownership of this new identity to others. The word "oblations," though somewhat uncom-

Pointed Text

Collect

A God of everlasting mercy,
who in the very recurrence of the paschal feast
kindle the faith of the people you have made your **own**,
B increase, we pray, the grace you **have** bestowed,
C that all may grasp and rightly understand
in what font they have been washed,
by whose Spirit they have been reborn,
by whose Blood they have been re***deemed***.
Through our Lord Jesus Christ, your Son,
who lives and reigns with you in the unity of the Holy Spirit,
one God, for ever and ever.

Prayer over the Offerings

B Accept, O Lord, we pray,
the oblations **of** your people
(and of those you have brought **to** new birth),
C that, renewed by confession of your name and by Baptism,
they may attain unending hap***pi***ness.
Through Christ our Lord.

Prayer after Communion

B Grant, we pray, al**might**y God,
C that our reception of this paschal Sacrament
may have a continuing effect
in our minds and ***hearts***.
Through Christ our Lord.

The space below is for your notes.

Refer to pages viii–x for an explanation of the pointing of the chants and to page xii for the Tones for the Presidential Prayers from *The Roman Missal.*

mon, brings a certain dynamism. It refers to the action that follows from the people "bringing" their sacrifices to the altar. Literally, it is what happens "on account of bringing forward." We are charged only to bring something forward and surrender it to God through the hands of the Priest, who joins it to Christ in the Eucharistic Prayer. The main verb of the prayer is "accept" (*suscipe*), and the final petition is dependent on this verb. The Lord is asked to accept the oblations so that "unending happiness" may be attained.

Prayer after Communion: The Latin word behind "reception" (*perceptio*) has more the sense of "to grasp, take in, or comprehend in an intuitive way." It does not mean that the communicant has encompassed the mystery, but has received the entire mystery, which encompasses the communicant. This somewhat loose connection with intuiting is the reason the prayer mentions "minds and hearts" (the Latin only has *mentibus*, "minds," but the sense is it includes the whole rational/spiritual dimension of the person). The Sacrament is qualified as "paschal" not simply to emphasize Easter Time, but also to connect us to the action of Christ, who passed from suffering and Death to new life. This is the "continuing effect" that is sought by reception of the Sacrament: to bring our interior life through suffering and death to self into life for others. Receiving Communion brings us into the presence of Christ, where we are confronted with infinite self-gift, which calls and challenges us to "continue" our journey into the new life of Christ.

THIRD SUNDAY OF EASTER

Collect

Proclaim **exult for ever** with energy and keep the voice raised after **O God** because the thought continues with the next line. Give equal energy to **youthfulness of spirit**. Pause after **so that**. Three verbal groupings follow: **rejoicing now**, **restored glory**, and **our adoption**. Raise the voice with assurance for **confident**. Emphasize **rejoicing** and pause briefly after it.

May your people exult for ever, O God,
in renewed youthfulness of spirit,
so that, rejoicing now in the restored glory of our adoption,
we may look forward in confident hope
to the rejoicing of the day of resurrection.
Through our Lord Jesus Christ, your Son,
who lives and reigns with you in the unity of the Holy Spirit,
one God, for ever and ever.

Prayer over the Offerings

Pause briefly after **Receive** and keep **O Lord, we pray** together. Proclaim **exultant** with energy. Pause after **and**. Proclaim **such great gladness** with deliberate emphasis on each word. Place parallel emphasis on **gifts** and **fruit**. Draw out **perpetual**.

Receive, O Lord, we pray,
these offerings of your exultant Church,
and, as you have given her cause for such great gladness,
grant also that the gifts we bring
may bear fruit in perpetual happiness.
Through Christ our Lord. *

Prayer after Communion

Place emphasis on **kindness** and **people**. Speak **grant** with some energy. Pause ever so briefly after **those** and after **renew**. Emphasize **pleased**. Proclaim **eternal mysteries** with reverence. Draw out the phrase **incorruptible glory**.

Look with kindness upon your people, O Lord,
and grant, we pray,
that those you were pleased to renew by eternal mysteries
may attain in their flesh
the incorruptible glory of the resurrection.
Through Christ our Lord. **

* Select from Prefaces I–V of Easter in the Order of Mass. Commentary, and proclamation and chant tips, for the Preface can be found at *www.StudyThePresidentialTexts.com/Prefaces* and in *The Order of Mass: A Roman Missal Study Edition and Workbook*, pages 48–57.

** You may use the Solemn Blessings for Easter Time in the Order of Mass, page 169 in *The Order of Mass: A Roman Missal Study Edition and Workbook*.

Collect: The word "spirit" in the phrase "youthfulness of spirit" is not *spiritus* but *animae*. "Youthfulness," therefore, refers to the human spirit in the sense of attitude and emotion. Faith in the Resurrection renews us intellectually and emotionally. There is a new way of perceiving oneself and the world. The phrase "restored glory of our adoption" implies that before the fall, humanity enjoyed the privilege of being adopted sons and daughters of God. More importantly, it is an allusion to the Son of God, in whose image we are created and now, in the light of the Resurrection, re-created. The translation of the last two lines differs slightly from the original Latin. The Latin states that God's people look forward not to the rejoicing of the day of Resurrection, but to the day itself in the hope of certain rejoicing. The hope is for that day to be a day of rejoicing, but what we look forward to is the reality (the person) that is the cause for rejoicing. Rejoicing is the consequence of meeting Christ who is the "day" of Resurrection.

Prayer over the Offerings: The Church is "exultant" because, in the Resurrection, she has been set free from her slavery to sin to leap (exult) in the freedom of virtue. Recall the exulting of creation in Psalm 114. In this prayer, each member of the Church brings a gift (*munus*) to the altar. The "cause" that prompts us to do this ultimately comes from the life and energy flowing from Christ's Resurrection. This prayer contrasts the "great gladness" (*tanti gaudii*) of the Church—a result of each person receiving the gift of the Holy

Pointed Text

Collect

A May your people exult for ever, O God,
in renewed youthfulness of spi**<u>rit</u>**,
B so that, rejoicing now in the restored glory of **our** adoption,
C we may look forward in confident hope
to the rejoicing of the day of resurrec***tion***.
Through our Lord Jesus Christ, your Son,
who lives and reigns with you in the unity of the Holy Spirit,
one God, for ever and ever.

Prayer over the Offerings

A Receive, O Lord, we pray,
these offerings of your exultant **<u>Church</u>**,
B and, as you have given her cause for **such** great gladness,
C grant also that the gifts we bring
may bear fruit in perpetual hap***pi***ness.
Through Christ our Lord.

Prayer after Communion

A Look with kindness upon your people, O **<u>Lord</u>**,
B and grant, we pray,
that those you were pleased to renew by e**ter**nal mysteries
C may attain in their flesh
the incorruptible glory of the resurrec***tion***.
Through Christ our Lord.

The space below is for your notes.

Refer to pages viii–x for an explanation of the pointing of the chants and to page xii for the Tones for the Presidential Prayers from *The Roman Missal*.

Spirit—with the "perpetual happiness" (*perpetuae laetitiae*) that comes when all the redeemed are assembled in communal celebration. In the Eucharist, we have a foretaste of this process when the sacrifice of each one becomes united ("bears fruit") in the one sacrifice of Christ. We each receive the Body of Christ singly, but are thereby united to each other in the one body of Christ, the Church. We may bring a gift of suffering and challenge, but the blessing of Christ can redeem it to become joy and strength.

Prayer after Communion: The "look" of the Lord could strike fear in the hearts of creatures (cf. Exodus 14:24) or could strengthen those same hearts by the kindly light of his face (cf. Psalm 42:3). The impression can be of a child after some performance looking to Father for approval. A look, a smile, a nod, and the joy of approval wells up. The "mysteries" are called "eternal." The divine reality to which this sacramental expression points is eternal. Christ and the Paschal Mystery are forever. This power of "forever" "renews" and sustains us. The Holy Spirit is that power. The Resurrection of Christ is different from the "resurrection" of Lazarus because it is "incorruptible." This Risen One will never fall back into death or corruption. The proclamation of "flesh" *(carnis)* being glorified is a powerful statement of the power of God to raise up the lowliest of creatures. "Flesh" is used by Saint Paul to refer to that which is utter weakness, sin, and corruption. And yet, the power of the Resurrection is able to transform it into something gloriously transcendent.

FOURTH SUNDAY OF EASTER

Pause briefly after **Almighty**. Proclaim **lead us** with a note of hopeful longing. Pause briefly after **share** to pronounce **joys of heaven** with enthusiasm. Speak **humble flock** without pretense of any kind and do not pause until after **may reach**. Proclaim **brave shepherd** with a strong but reverent voice.

Collect

Almighty ever-living God,
lead us to a share in the joys of heaven,
so that the humble flock may reach
where the brave Shepherd has gone before.
Who lives and reigns with you in the unity of the Holy Spirit,
one God, for ever and ever.

Pause after **Grant** and keep **we pray, O Lord** together. Place mild stress on **always** and hang on the word **delight**. Pause after **renewal** and stress **constantly**. Finish strong with **unending joy**.

Prayer over the Offerings

Grant, we pray, O Lord,
that we may always find delight in these paschal mysteries,
so that the renewal constantly at work within us
may be the cause of our unending joy.
Through Christ our Lord. *

Pronounce **Look** with some solemnity. Pause briefly after **to settle** and proclaim **eternal pastures** with energy. Speak **sheep you have redeemed** with heartfelt gratitude and keep the voice raised with **redeemed** for the line that follows. Give reverent emphasis to **Precious Blood**.

Prayer after Communion

Look upon your flock, kind Shepherd,
and be pleased to settle in eternal pastures
the sheep you have redeemed
by the Precious Blood of your Son.
Who lives and reigns for ever and ever. **

* Select from Prefaces I–V of Easter in the Order of Mass. Commentary, and proclamation and chant tips, for the Preface can be found at *www.StudyThePresidentialTexts.com/Prefaces* and in *The Order of Mass: A Roman Missal Study Edition and Workbook*, pages 48–57.

** You may use the Solemn Blessings for Easter Time in the Order of Mass, page 169 in *The Order of Mass: A Roman Missal Study Edition and Workbook*.

Collect: The Latin word for "share" is *societatem*, which more literally means society or association. The Church on earth is sometimes referred to as a *societas*. The prayer is asking not simply to be led to a "share" of heavenly joys but to the assembly of heavenly joys. Heaven is taking one's appropriate place within the redeemed and glorified body of Christ. The biblical (and Catholic) view of heaven is always communal. The Latin behind the next two lines is a bit awkward in English, but may have a rather inspiring message of hope. More literally the prayer states: ". . . the humility of the flock . . . the bravery (fortitude) of the Shepherd . . . ." Jesus came to redeem the whole of the person. Even our "lowliness" the Lord desires to lead, by his strength, into transcendence. The "humility" of the Virgin Mary is called "blessed" in the light of the resurrection, and she states that the Lord "has raised up the lowly." The "brave Shepherd" is not content with what this world deems fitting. He created us for his kingdom and desires to transform our vices into virtues.

Prayer over the Offerings: The Latin behind this prayer asks that we may find delight "through" these paschal mysteries. In this prayer, the Church is saying that we should be drawn through the Sacraments toward the reality they express: Jesus Christ. The Sacraments are a means and will pass away with the coming of the kingdom. The word for "renewal" is *reparationis*, which can mean more literally making ready again. Adam and Eve were placed in the garden to prepare them for something much greater. After the fall, Christ came to

Pointed Text

Collect

A Almighty ever-living **God**,
B lead us to a share in the **joys** of heaven,
C so that the humble flock may reach
where the brave Shepherd has gone be***fore***.
Who lives and reigns with you in the unity of the Holy Spirit,
one God, for ever and ever.

Prayer over the Offerings

A Grant, we pray, O **Lord**,
B that we may always find delight in these **pas**chal mysteries,
C so that the renewal constantly at work within us
may be the cause of our unending ***joy***.
Through Christ our Lord.

Prayer after Communion

A Look upon your flock, kind Shep**herd**,
B and be pleased to settle in e**ter**nal pastures
C the sheep you have redeemed
by the Precious Blood of your ***Son***.
Who lives and reigns for ever and ever.

The space below is for your notes.

Refer to pages viii–x for an explanation of the pointing of the chants and to page xii for the Tones for the Presidential Prayers from *The Roman Missal*.

restart this preparation process. When Christians are baptized into his body, this process of renewal begins an interior transformation that "constantly" works "within us." The "work" belongs to the Holy Spirit who comes to dwell within the believers. The Greek for liturgy includes the word "work." It is the participation of the "people" of God in the "work" of God. The "renewal" that is "at work within us" is fostered by the liturgy, where we are drawn more deeply through the Sacraments into Christ himself, our "unending joy."

Prayer after Communion: The word translated as "Look upon" (*intende*) literally means to stretch toward. The sense is of the Shepherd (the Latin is *Pastor bone*: Good Shepherd) bending down from on high to protect and be near his sheep. The translation leaves out a word that modifies "Look upon," namely, *placatus*, which means having made peace or having been reconciled. This is an important modifier because of the mention of "redeemed by the Precious Blood." We, "who once were far off have been brought near by the blood of Christ" (Ephesians 2:13). The Blood of Christ has made our peace with God the Father (Ephesians 2:14), and we have just received it in Holy Communion. The "kind Shepherd" (here, it is God the Father) is asked to look "peaceably," precisely because the prayer mentions redemption by Christ's Blood. The pastoral image of "settling" the flock in "eternal pastures" means a "location" where all that is necessary for a full and abundant life is present. The "pastures" do not dry up in heaven. They are watered by the Spirit of God.

FIFTH SUNDAY OF EASTER

Collect

Pause briefly after **Almighty**. Give parallel stress to **constantly accomplish**. Proclaim **Paschal Mystery** with a certain energy. Emphasize **pleased**, **new**, and **Baptism**. Pause briefly after **may** and **care**. Keep the voice raised with **much fruit**. Proclaim **joys** with reverent but eager anticipation.

Almighty ever-living God,
constantly accomplish the Paschal Mystery within us,
that those you were pleased to make new in Holy Baptism
may, under your protective care, bear much fruit
and come to the joys of life eternal.
Through our Lord Jesus Christ, your Son,
who lives and reigns with you in the unity of the Holy Spirit,
one God, for ever and ever.

Prayer over the Offerings

Pause briefly after **O God**. Parallel **wonderful exchange** (proclaimed with solemnity) and **effected in this sacrifice**. Pause briefly after **partakers**. Proclaim **one supreme Godhead** with deliberate pacing and majesty. Pause briefly after **that** and keep the voice raised for **truth**. Pause briefly after **ours**. Emphasize **worthy** and then more subtly **way of life**.

O God, who by the wonderful exchange effected in this sacrifice
have made us partakers of the one supreme Godhead,
grant, we pray,
that, as we have come to know your truth,
we may make it ours by a worthy way of life.
Through Christ our Lord. *

Prayer after Communion

Proclaim **Graciously** with reverent longing. Pause briefly after **people**. Pronounce **those you have imbued** as one phrase and with a sense of confidence. Proclaim **heavenly mysteries** with grateful joy. Parallel **former ways** and **newness of life**.

Graciously be present to your people, we pray, O Lord,
and lead those you have imbued with heavenly mysteries
to pass from former ways to newness of life.
Through Christ our Lord. **

* Select from Prefaces I–V of Easter in the Order of Mass. Commentary, and proclamation and chant tips, for the Preface can be found at *www.StudyThePresidentialTexts.com/Prefaces* and in *The Order of Mass: A Roman Missal Study Edition and Workbook*, pages 48–57.

** You may use the Solemn Blessings for Easter Time in the Order of Mass, page 169 in *The Order of Mass: A Roman Missal Study Edition and Workbook*.

Collect: This is a new Collect for this Sunday. (It used to be identical to the Twenty-third Sunday in Ordinary Time.) The "Paschal Mystery" (*paschale sacramentum*) refers to the Sacrament of Baptism, the "Paschal" Sacrament, par excellence. The "Mystery" of Christ's Death and Resurrection, into which Baptism incorporates the believer, is "accomplished" in us when we participate in the Sacraments. The challenge is for us to let the "Mystery within us" affect us. The seeds of our renewal were planted with "Holy Baptism" and the life of grace we live can bring those seeds to perfection ("accomplish" them). The result of the Lord's accomplishing his Mystery within us is twofold. On the earth, it enables us to "bear much fruit," though we need God's "protective care." The second result is coming to the "joys of life eternal." This is distinct from bearing much fruit, which is for the Church and the world. Despite all that we may accomplish (the "fruit" we bear with God's grace), the kingdom remains a gift that we cannot deserve or earn (Luke 17:10).

Prayer over the Offerings: The phrase "wonderful exchange" (*veneranda commercia*) could be translated more literally as the "exchange about to be venerated." The "exchange" refers to the Incarnation, where we gave the Son our lowliness (our flesh) and he gave us his divinity. But it also refers to the bread and wine (symbolic of our sacrificial offerings) that we give to God in the Eucharist, and the Body and Blood of Christ, which he returns to us. When this second sacramental exchange is effected on the altar, our response is one of

Pointed Text

Collect

A Almighty ever-living **God**,
B constantly accomplish the Paschal Myster**y** within us,
C that those you were pleased to make new in Holy Baptism
may, under your protective care, bear much fruit
and come to the joys of life eter***nal***.
Through our Lord Jesus Christ, your Son,
who lives and reigns with you in the unity of the Holy Spirit,
one God, for ever and ever.

Prayer over the Offerings

A O God, who by the wonderful exchange effected in this sacrifice
have made us partakers of the one supreme God**head**,
B grant, we pray,
that, as we have come to **know** your truth,
C we may make it ours by a worthy way of ***life***.
Through Christ our Lord.

Prayer after Communion

A Graciously be present to your people, we pray, O **Lord**,
B and lead those you have imbued with heav**en**ly mysteries
C to pass from former ways to newness of ***life***.
Through Christ our Lord.

The space below is for your notes.

Refer to pages viii–x for an explanation of the pointing of the chants and to page xii for the Tones for the Presidential Prayers from *The Roman Missal*.

veneration. We worship the Real Presence and are overwhelmed to be given a share in that presence. In Christ, our humanity has been taken up into the "one supreme Godhead" and in receiving Holy Communion, we too are given a share in that glory. The petition of the prayer has a wonderful "Roman" practicality. May we not only "come to know your truth" (*cognovimus* implies a personal knowing), but more importantly may that knowledge of the truth be lived out in our lives as a truth that we embrace as ours.

Prayer after Communion: The petition of this prayer for the Lord to "be present" does not mean that he is absent. The petition is that he be present "graciously." The Latin could also be translated as "Graciously draw near." The Lord is always present. The prayer seeks to draw out a particular kind of presence. The assembly has just received the Real Presence of Christ in Holy Communion and now asks for that presence to be effective in bestowing grace upon God's people. The "Heavenly mysteries" refer to the whole pattern of Christ's life. In the Sacraments, we are "imbued" with his mystery. The reality of Christ enters within us sacramentally and the life we live becomes more and more Christ's life (Galatians. 2:20). He "leads" us away from the old life of sin and death, from the nature of the world. The verb "to pass" (*transire*) is important because it brings out the real transition that occurs in going from the old of this world to the "newness" of Christ. We must die to the old. None of it may accompany us to the new life.

SIXTH SUNDAY OF EASTER

Pause briefly after **Grant**. Pause briefly after **celebrate**. Proclaim **heartfelt devotion** with energy and sincerity, pausing briefly. Pause after **that**. There is a parallel rhythm to what follows. Keep the voice raised with **remembrance**.

Collect

Grant, almighty God,
that we may celebrate with heartfelt devotion these days of joy,
which we keep in honor of the risen Lord,
and that what we relive in remembrance
we may always hold to in what we do.
Through our Lord Jesus Christ, your Son,
who lives and reigns with you in the unity of the Holy Spirit,
one God, for ever and ever.

Slow down with **rise up** and raise the voice accordingly. Proclaim **sacrificial offerings** with reverence. Pause after **so that**. Proclaim **purified** and **graciousness** with equal energy. Pause briefly after **conformed** and after **mysteries** and proclaim **mighty love** with energy and wonder.

Prayer over the Offerings

May our prayers rise up to you, O Lord,
together with the sacrificial offerings,
so that, purified by your graciousness,
we may be conformed to the mysteries of your mighty love.
Through Christ our Lord. *

Pause briefly after **Almighty**. Pause after **eternal life**. Give parallel emphasis to **eternal life** and **Resurrection of Christ**. Pause after **we pray**, and again after **our hearts**. Keep the voice rasised with **Sacrament**. Emphasize the parallel rhythm of **fruits of this paschal Sacrament** and **strength of this saving food**.

Prayer after Communion

Almighty ever-living God,
who restore us to eternal life in the Resurrection of Christ,
increase in us, we pray, the fruits of this paschal Sacrament
and pour into our hearts the strength of this saving food.
Through Christ our Lord. **

* Select from Prefaces I–V of Easter in the Order of Mass. Commentary, and proclamation and chant tips, for the Preface can be found at *www.StudyThePresidentialTexts.com/Prefaces* and in *The Order of Mass: A Roman Missal Study Edition and Workbook*, pages 48–57.

** You may use the Solemn Blessings for Easter Time in the Order of Mass, page 169 in *The Order of Mass: A Roman Missal Study Edition and Workbook.*

Collect: The phrase "heartfelt devotion" (*affectu sedulo*) is a key indicator of what it means to celebrate in Easter Time. Our devotion in the Sacraments must always be heartfelt. Easter "joy" (*laetitiae*) does not mean we pretend everything is beautiful. The Christian should never feel compelled to pretend. If our heart is troubled, then that is the "devotion" we bring to the Eucharist. Joy, however, remains, because it is not an emotion but a gift of the Holy Spirit. Though I have a troubled heart, I can still have a joyful heart because my faith teaches me that the victory of the "risen Lord" will also be my victory. The current experience may be difficult, but the hope of triumph is already present. It is essential to offer in the Eucharist whatever affections of the heart are with us at the moment, because the Lord can only transform what we offer. Every year that we "relive in remembrance" the mysteries of Christ with sincerity, the reality of Christ takes deeper root in our souls. This reality must always find expression "in what we do."

Prayer over the Offerings: In the Eucharistic Prayer, the Priest offers up the prayer and raises the gifts, all part of the action of uniting the "sacrificial offerings" of the people to Christ who is seated at the right hand of the Father. This is the mediatory role of the Priest as he steps between heaven and earth to offer prayer and sacrifice. Uniting our offerings to the Blood of Christ, we are "purified" (Hebrews 9:11–22). The "graciousness" that effects the purification is the Holy Spirit, the gift of God, who purifies and transforms from within.

Pointed Text

Collect

A Grant, almighty **God**,
B that we may celebrate with heartfelt devotion these days of joy,
which we keep in honor of the **ri**sen Lord,
C and that what we relive in remembrance
we may always hold to in what we ***do***.
Through our Lord Jesus Christ, your Son,
who lives and reigns with you in the unity of the Holy Spirit,
one God, for ever and ever.

Prayer over the Offerings

A May our prayers rise up to you, O Lord,
together with the sacrificial of**fer**ings,
B so that, purified **by** your graciousness,
C we may be conformed to the mysteries of your mighty ***love***.
Through Christ our Lord.

Prayer after Communion

A Almighty ever-living God,
who restore us to eternal life in the Resurrection of **Christ**,
B increase in us, we pray, the fruits of this **pas**chal Sacrament
C and pour into our hearts the strength of this saving ***food***.
Through Christ our Lord.

The space below is for your notes.

Refer to pages viii–x for an explanation of the pointing of the chants and to page xii for the Tones for the Presidential Prayers from *The Roman Missal*.

This working of the Holy Spirit "conforms" us to the "mysteries" that are Christ. In this twofold process, we are purified from sin and conformed to Christ. Our work in this process is simply to ask, raise our prayers in humble supplication, and receive all that the Lord desires to give. The "mighty love" (*magnae pietatis*) refers to the proper love and devotion that exists between a parent and child. We seek to be conformed to such a love both as child of God, and as parent to others whom we may beget in the faith by our witness to Christ.

Prayer after Communion: Our restoration to eternal life begins with the "paschal Sacrament," that is, Baptism. This restoration does not happen in this world, but rather "in the Resurrection of Christ," which transcends this world. In this world, we taste only the Sacrament of eternal life, the Sacrament of Resurrection. In our death, the Sacrament will give way to fullness. In the meantime, we remain with the Sacraments and pray that their "fruits" will increase in us. Saint Paul provides a list of "fruits" of the Spirit (Galatians 5:22–23). These are the essential virtues for life in the kingdom. The Sacraments we receive on earth prepare us for the life we will live forever in the kingdom of heaven. The "saving food" of the Eucharist provides us with the "strength" (*fortitudinem*) not to be discouraged by the hardships (and failures) of this life. This strength is poured "into our hearts." The Psalms are constantly praying for strength of heart, also called "courage." This is precisely where the Lord touches us. He gives us courage not to give up, but to remain faithful even in the midst of trials.

THE ASCENSION OF THE LORD

Solemnity

Where the Solemnity of the Ascension is not to be observed as a Holyday of Obligation, it is assigned to the Seventh Sunday of Easter as its proper day.

At the Vigil Mass

This Mass is used on the evening of the day before the Solemnity, either before or after First Vespers (Evening Prayer I) of the Ascension.

Collect

Pause after **O God**. Raise the voice and proclaim with energetic joy **ascended to the heavens**. Keep the voice raised and pause only briefly with **heavens**. Pause after **we pray** and do not pause after **that**. The next line is tricky. Pause after **worthy**. We are not **worthy for him**, but rather **worthy for him to live with us**. Pause briefly after **with us**. Pronounce **always on earth** together. The last line has a three beat rhythm: **and we with him in heaven**. Proclaim this slowly and lovingly.

O God, whose Son today ascended to the heavens
as the Apostles looked on,
grant, we pray, that, in accordance with his promise,
we may be worthy for him to live with us always on earth,
and we with him in heaven.
Who lives and reigns with you in the unity of the Holy Spirit,
one God, for ever and ever.

Prayer over the Offerings

Pause after **O God**, and briefly after **Son**. Be slow and deliberate on **Only Begotten Son**. Pray **High Priest** with solemnity. Do not separate the next four phrases with much of a pause and pray each distinctly: **is seated**, **ever-living**, **at your right hand**, **to intercede for us**. Emphasize **with confidence** and proclaim **throne of grace** with reverent humility. Pray the last line with joyful gratitude.

O God, whose Only Begotten Son, our High Priest,
is seated ever-living at your right hand to intercede for us,
grant that we may approach with confidence the throne of grace
and there obtain your mercy.
Through Christ our Lord. *

Prayer after Communion

The rhythm of the first line places emphasis on **gifts**, **received**, and **altar**. Proclaim **kindle** with fiery energy and **longing** with sincere affection. Speak **cause us to press forward** with determination and authority. Pause after **forward**.

May the gifts we have received from your altar, Lord,
kindle in our hearts a longing for the heavenly homeland
and cause us to press forward, following in the Savior's footsteps,
to the place where for our sake he entered before us.
Who lives and reigns for ever and ever. **

* Use either Preface I or II of the Ascension in the Order of Mass. Commentary, and proclamation and chant tips, for the Preface can be found at *www.StudyThePresidentialTexts.com/Prefaces* and in *The Order of Mass: A Roman Missal Study Edition and Workbook*, pages 58–61. If Eucharistic Prayer I is used, the proper form of the Communicantes is prayed from the Order of Mass. It is found in *The Order of Mass: A Roman Missal Study Edition and Workbook*, page 129.

** You may use the Solemn Blessings for the Ascension of the Lord in the Order of Mass, page 170 in *The Order of Mass: A Roman Missal Study Edition and Workbook*.

Collect: The "heavens" to which the Son ascended are more a metaphysical than a physical reality. He "ascended" into the fullness that is God, who fills all places. The word "today" (*hodie*) is an important liturgical term. In the liturgy, the events of Christ's life become present to the Church. Christ has ascended into eternity and is present to us in an eternal "today" (Hebrews 3:7–15; 4:4–11). In the liturgy, the Church becomes present to Christ's "today." The reference to the "Apostles looking on" marks them as eyewitnesses to this mystery. The faith of the Church is built on the foundation of the Apostles' testimony (Ephesians 2:20). The last two lines make clear that the Ascension is not an ending but a beginning. By "his promise," we are made "worthy" to be with him both in this life and in the next. The only thing that would drive him away would be our rejection of him in sin. His presence with us on earth is what helps to prepare us to be present with him forever in heaven.

Prayer over the Offerings: This prayer clearly proclaims the connection between the Solemnity of the Ascension and the priesthood. In his Ascension, Christ enters the tabernacle, which is the "throne of grace" upon which the Father sits. He ascends with the Blood he shed upon the Cross for us. At the heavenly mercy seat, he makes continual intercession for us. He does not offer multiple sacrifices because he has a life that does not pass away. He is "ever-living" and therefore, ever-interceding with his blood from the one sacrifice of

The space below is for your notes.

Refer to pages viii–x for an explanation of the pointing of the chants and to page xii for the Tones for the Presidential Prayers from *The Roman Missal.*

Pointed Text

Collect

A O God, whose Son today ascended to the heavens
as the Apostles looked **on**,
B grant, we pray, that, in accordance **with** his promise,
C we may be worthy for him to live with us always on earth,
and we with him in hea***ven***.
Who lives and reigns with you in the unity of the Holy Spirit,
one God, for ever and ever.

Prayer over the Offerings

A O God, whose Only Begotten Son, our High Priest,
is seated ever-living at your right hand to intercede for **us**,
B grant that we may approach with confidence the **throne** of grace
C and there obtain your mer***cy***.
Through Christ our Lord.

Prayer after Communion

A May the gifts we have received from your altar, **Lord**,
B kindle in our hearts a longing for the heavenly homeland
and cause us to press forward, following in the **Sa**vior's footsteps,
C to the place where for our sake he entered before ***us***.
Who lives and reigns for ever and ever.

the Cross. In the Eucharistic Prayer, the Priest Celebrant enters the holy of holies, where he unites our offerings to the one and eternal offering of Christ. In approaching the altar for the Eucharistic Prayer, the Priest approachies the point of entry to the "throne of grace." The Priest wears special clothing—first of all, as a reminder of the holy place he enters. The altar is the centerpiece of every church—it is the point of connection with the heavenly mercy seat.

Prayer after Communion: The "gifts received from the altar" are the result of Christ's intercession at the right hand of the Father. The Church joins them to Christ's upward movement to the Father. These gifts are a foretaste of eternal life. This is how they can "kindle . . . a longing." They are a taste of mercy and love, which is why they light a fire in our hearts. Only love would make another "press forward" to endure suffering and death, which is what comes to those who "follow in the Savior's footsteps." They are the footsteps of his Passion. Only his Passion makes us worthy to follow his Ascension to heaven. The prayer gives an additional title for Christ, which is not translated here: *praecursor*. Christ is Savior in the sense that he opened the way for us to follow. Only he as human and divine could open the way. Holy Communion stirs up the love and the courage to go through trials, because it fills us with the "longing" for union that follows such trials.

THE ASCENSION OF THE LORD

At the Mass during the Day

Collect

Pause briefly after **us** and **joys**. Emphasize **Gladden** and **holy joys**. Pause briefly after **rejoice** and be crisp with **devout**. Pause briefly after **Christ** and **Son**, and proclaim **our exaltation** with awestruck enthusiasm. Raise the voice for **in glory** and give a parallel stress to **in hope**.

Gladden us with holy joys, almighty God,
and make us rejoice with devout thanksgiving,
for the Ascension of Christ your Son
is our exaltation,
and, where the Head has gone before in glory,
the Body is called to follow in hope.
Through our Lord Jesus Christ, your Son,
who lives and reigns with you in the unity of the Holy Spirit,
one God, for ever and ever.

Or:

Pause briefly after **we pray**. Pause briefly after **we** and **Son**. Keep the voice raised with **to the heavens**. Pause briefly before and after **in spirit**, proclaiming it gently. Emphasize **already**.

Grant, we pray, almighty God,
that we, who believe that your Only Begotten Son, our Redeemer,
ascended this day to the heavens,
may in spirit dwell already in heavenly realms.
Who lives and reigns with you in the unity of the Holy Spirit,
one God, for ever and ever. *

Prayer over the Offerings

Pause ever so briefly after **now**. Proclaim **wondrous Ascension** with awestruck joy. Proclaim **most holy exchange** with measured reverence. Raise the voice with **rise up**. Emphasize **heavenly**.

We offer sacrifice now in supplication, O Lord,
to honor the wondrous Ascension of your Son:
grant, we pray,
that through this most holy exchange
we, too, may rise up to the heavenly realms.
Through Christ our Lord.

* Use either Preface I or II of the Ascension in the Order of Mass. Commentary, and proclamation and chant tips, for the Preface can be found at *www.StudyThePresidentialTexts.com/Prefaces* and in *The Order of Mass: A Roman Missal Study Edition and Workbook*, pages 58–61. If Eucharistic Prayer I is used, the proper form of the Communicates is prayed from the Order of Mass. It is found in *The Order of Mass: A Roman Missal Study Edition and Workbook*, pages 129.

Collect: The "holy joys" (*sanctis gaudiis*) refer to the personal, or interior, exultation experienced by beleivers who have felt the touch of the Lord. The verb "to rejoice" refers to the experience of bringing such personal "joy" into the community of believers, where it is shared and magnified by the asembly. The primary place for this is the Eucharist, where we offer "devout thanksgiving." The adjective "devout" (*pia*) refers to the devotion between parent and child. We give thanks to the Father with filial devotion, rejoicing in the community for the joys bestowed. Christ's Ascension is like a vanguard who goes first, so that the rest may follow. The imagery of Head and Body strengthens our faith and hope. Certainly, the Body will not be separated from its Head. Our hope, then, remains well founded and strong as long as we remain in his Body, the Church. Our Head is already "in glory" and our hope for that glory keeps us rooted in faith.

Optional Collect: Christ ascended to heaven as both the "Only Begotten Son" of God and "our Redeemer." These titles emphasize his divinity and humanity. He is the Son from all eternity who returns to the bosom of the Father. He is also the Lamb who was slain in order to redeem fallen humanity. The prayer states that he ascended "this day" (*hodierna die*), accentuating that the reality of Christ in glory is eternally present; his action is always "today" in the Church. The main petition of the prayer is that through faith, we ("who

The space below is for your notes.

Refer to pages viii–x for an explanation of the pointing of the chants and to page xii for the Tones for the Presidential Prayers from *The Roman Missal.*

Pointed Text

Collect

A Gladden us with holy joys, almighty **God**,
B and make us rejoice with devout thanksgiving,
for the Ascension of Christ your Son
is our **ex**altation,
C and, where the Head has gone before in glory,
the Body is called to follow in ***hope***.
Through our Lord Jesus Christ, your Son,
who lives and reigns with you in the unity of the Holy Spirit,
one God, for ever and ever.

Or:

A Grant, we pray, almighty **God**,
B that we, who believe that your Only Begotten Son, our Redeemer,
ascended this day **to** the heavens,
C may in spirit dwell already in heavenly ***realms***.
Who lives and reigns with you in the unity of the Holy Spirit,
one God, for ever and ever.

Prayer over the Offerings

A We offer sacrifice now in supplication, O Lord,
to honor the wondrous Ascension of your **Son**:
B grant, we pray,
that through this most ho**ly** exchange
C we, too, may rise up to the heavenly ***realms***.
Through Christ our Lord.

believe") may dwell already with Christ "in spirit" (*mente*). The act of faith involves the whole person and is an invitation to the Holy Spirit to indwell our hearts. By the presence of the Spirit in our hearts, the "heavenly realms" have begun to dwell in us. The prayer asks that we may be present to these "heavenly realms." In other words, we live on earth the life of Christ in heaven. We need not wait to be physically present to be interiorly present.

Prayer over the Offerings: At first glance, it is strange that we honor Christ's Ascension by "supplication." Reflecting further, however, sacrificial supplication is the perfect way to honor this feast. One of the main reasons for Christ's ascending to the Father is to intercede for us and leave us the banquet of his Body and Blood. In this light, the most fitting honor we can give on this day is to seek his intercession and partake of his gift of Holy Communion. The word for "wondrous" (*venerabili*) includes the idea of something that should be venerated. In the phrase "most holy exchange" (*commerciis sacrosanctis*), we give the Son our lowliness, and he bestows on us his glory. Because of this "exchange," the prayer is able to ask that we may follow Christ in his movement to the Father. This movement involves a surrender of attachement to self and earthly things. We will rise beyond the things of this world. Any "attachments" to this world will prevent us from being able to rise.

Prayer after Communion

Pause briefly after **Almighty**. Pause after **earth**, speaking it humbly. Proclaim **divine mysteries** with reverent energy. Place emphasis on **Christian** to distinguish the kind of hope. Pause after **hope**. Give stress to **nature**, **united**, and **you**. Speak each word slowly and distinctly.

Almighty ever-living God,
who allow those on earth to celebrate divine mysteries,
grant, we pray,
that Christian hope may draw us onward
to where our nature is united with you.
Through Christ our Lord.

** You may use the Solemn Blessings for the Ascension of the Lord in the Order of Mass, page 170 in *The Order of Mass: A Roman Missal Study Edition and Workbook.*

Prayer after Communion: The word for "those on earth" (*in terra constitutos*) means those "established" on the earth. The implication is that we belong to the earth, but are "allowed" "to celebrate divine mysteries." The Latin has more literally "to touch divine mysteries." This is a great privilege for us. It is not that God is reluctant to bring us close to his mysteries; rather, the issue is whether we can receive such gifts to our salvation or to our condemnation (1 Corinthians 11:27–29). The petition of the prayer mentions "Christian hope" and its power to "draw us onward." Hope is the virtue that keeps us walking forward even when the lights in the tunnel have been extinguished. We go forward because someone we trust or love has told us that there is daylight at the other end of the tunnel. In this prayer, "hope" is rooted in the Ascension, which gives us courage to endure the hardships of this life and to remain faithful. The motivation behind this Christian hope is for "our nature" (*substantia*) to be "united" with God. "Nature" refers to the deepest part of our humanity. This is no shallow union based on appearance or emotion. God desires us in our substance.

Prayer after Communion

A Almighty ever-living God,
who allow those on earth to celebrate divine mys**ter**ies,
B grant, we pray,
that Christian hope may **draw** us onward
C to where our nature is united with ***you***.
Through Christ our Lord.

The space below is for your notes.

Refer to pages viii–x for an explanation of the pointing of the chants and to page xii for the Tones for the Presidential Prayers from *The Roman Missal*.

SEVENTH SUNDAY OF EASTER

Collect

Proclaim the first line with humble confidence. Pause after **we**. Pause only briefly after **race**. Raise the voice with **as he promised** and keep it raised for **until the end of the world**. Proclaim **abiding presence** with joyful love.

Graciously hear our supplications, O Lord,
so that we, who believe that the Savior of the human race
is with you in your glory,
may experience, as he promised,
until the end of the world,
his abiding presence among us.
Who lives and reigns with you in the unity of the Holy Spirit,
one God, for ever and ever.

Prayer over the Offerings

Pause after **O Lord**, but hardly at all after **faithful**. Proclaim **sacrificial offerings** with reverent solemnity. Give parallel emphasis to **acts of devotedness** and **glory of heaven**.

Accept, O Lord, the prayers of your faithful
with the sacrificial offerings,
that through these acts of devotedness
we may pass over to the glory of heaven.
Through Christ our Lord. *

Prayer after Communion

Pause briefly after **Hear us**. Proclaim **grant us confidence** with the certainty of faith. Proclaim **sacred mysteries** with reverence. Proclaim **there will be accomplished** with serene confidence. Pause briefly after **accomplished**. Place emphasis on **whole Church**. Pause after **pass** and pronounce **Christ her Head** distinctly and nobly.

Hear us, O God our Savior,
and grant us confidence,
that through these sacred mysteries
there will be accomplished in the body of the whole Church
what has already come to pass in Christ her Head.
Who lives and reigns for ever and ever. **

* Use either Preface I–V or Easter Time or Prefaces I–II of the Ascension in the Order of Mass. Commentary, and proclamation and chant tips, for the Preface can be found at *www.StudyThePresidentialTexts.com/Prefaces* and in *The Order of Mass: A Roman Missal Study Edition and Workbook*, pages 48–57.

** You may use the Solemn Blessings for the Easter Time in the Order of Mass, page 169 in *The Order of Mass: A Roman Missal Study Edition and Workbook.*

Collect: The "supplications" that God's people make to him are variations on the dominant petition of this prayer: that they may "experience" the Savior's "abiding presence" with them. The mention of Christ as "Savior of the human race" calls to mind the universal invitation to salvation in Christ. We who long to experience his presence on earth must have such an encounter before we can convincingly offer this salvation to others. There is a connection between faith in Christ's presence with the Father in "glory" (the Latin has "majesty") and faith in his presence among us. The first is an act of faith in Christ's divinity, which alone would make his "abiding presence among us" possible. Any encounter that leads us deeper into conversion and the mystery of salvation is an experience of the abiding presence of the Savior. This is an experience that draws us deeper into Truth or Goodness or Beauty or Unity. His abiding presence is found therein.

Prayer over the Offerings: The Latin brings out well the parallel between "prayers of the faithful" and "sacrifical offerings." A literal rendering of the Latin would have: "the prayers of the faithful with the offerings of the sacrifices." Prayers is parallel to offerings, and faithful is parallel to sacrifices. The faithful are ultimately the sacrifices to be offered in the Eucharist. The best way to influence another is to become holy. The "acts of devotedness" (*piae devotionis officia*) refer to our duty as baptized members of Christ to offer prayer

Pointed Text

Collect

A Graciously hear our supplications, O **Lord**,
B so that we, who believe that the Savior of the human race
is with you **in** your glory,
C may experience, as he promised,
until the end of the world,
his abiding presence among ***us***.
Who lives and reigns with you in the unity of the Holy Spirit,
one God, for ever and ever.

Prayer over the Offerings

A Accept, O Lord, the prayers of your faithful
with the sacrificial of**fer**ings,
B that through these acts **of** devotedness
C we may pass over to the glory of hea***ven***.
Through Christ our Lord.

Prayer after Communion

A Hear us, O God our Savior,
and grant us con**fi**dence,
B that through these sacred mysteries
there will be accomplished in the body of **the** whole Church
C what has already come to pass in Christ her ***Head***.
Who lives and reigns for ever and ever.

The space below is for your notes.

Refer to pages viii–x for an explanation of the pointing of the chants and to page xii for the Tones for the Presidential Prayers from *The Roman Missal*.

and sacrifice. "Devotedness" means our filial responsibility to the Father to care for one another. In Baptism, we become sons and daughters of the Father, and siblings to Christ and one another. This prayer proclaims that when we offer and receive the Sacraments with filial devotion, the grace and truth of Christ enable us to "pass over" from this world "to the glory of heaven." "Glory" is the experience of transcendent Beauty that raises us ever nearer to God.

Prayer after Communion: Through his Passion and Resurrection, Christ accomplished in his person redemption and salvation. It is the gift of the Holy Spirit that opens these riches to the Church. This prayer comes just before the Solemnity of Pentecost and is asking for the gift of the Spirit to be fruitful in the Church. The "sacred mysteries" refer primarily to the Sacrament of the Eucharist but also to the whole of the Paschal Mystery accomplished in Christ. The liturgy is the means through which the grace of Christ is bestowed on the Church. In the liturgy, the fullness of Christ's redemption and salvation is made present sacramentally by the work of the Holy Spirit. The faithful receive this grace, for example, in Holy Communion. The real work then begins of letting these sacred mysteries transform us. The prayer prays for the "whole Church." We do well not to judge who belongs to the Church. We are exhorted to pray for every member.

PENTECOST SUNDAY

Solemnity

At the Vigil Mass

Extended form

Dear brethren (brothers and sisters),
we have now begun our Pentecost Vigil,
after the example of the Apostles and disciples,
who with Mary, the Mother of Jesus, persevered in prayer,
awaiting the Spirit promised by the Lord;
like them, let us, too, listen with quiet hearts to the Word of God.
Let us meditate on how many great deeds
God in times past did for his people
and let us pray that the Holy Spirit,
whom the Father sent as the first fruits for those who believe,
may bring to perfection his work in the world.

Do not pause long after **Pentecost Vigil**, because this thought is completed by the following line. Keep the voice raised with **Vigil** and also with **disciples**. Observe the commas in the line **who with Mary . . . .** Proclaim **listen with quiet hearts** together and then pause briefly. Give parallel emphasis to **how many** and **great deeds**.

Pause briefly after **perfection**. Emphasize **his work**.

Prayers after the Readings

After the first reading (On Babel: Gn 11: 1–9) and the Psalm (33 [32]: 10–11, 12–13, 14–15; R. v. 12b).

Let us pray.

Grant, we pray, almighty God,
that your Church may always remain that holy people,
formed as one by the unity of Father, Son and Holy Spirit,
which manifests to the world
the Sacrament of your holiness and unity
and leads it to the perfection of your charity.
Through Christ our Lord.
R. Amen.

Pause briefly after **we pray** and again briefly after **Church**. Pause briefly after **one**. Stress **unity** and give equal emphasis to each person of the Trinity. Proclaim distinctly and slowly **Sacrament**, **holiness**, and **unity**. Pause briefly after **leads it**. Proclaim **perfection of your charity** with hopeful longing.

After the second reading (On God's Descent on Mount Sinai: Ex 19: 3–8, 16–20b) and the canticle (Dn 3: 52, 53, 54, 55, 56; R. v. 52b) or the Psalm (19 [18]: 8, 9, 10, 11; R. Jn 6: 68c).

Address: Mary and the Apostles are the model for this Vigil. They are envisioned as gathered together listening to the Word of God (the Old Testament), seeking to discern its interpretation in light of Christ's Death and Resurrection. We achieve this kind of discernment by listening to the Word "with quiet hearts." There is, then, a necessary preparation for this kind of Vigil listening. In John's account of the Gospel, Jesus says, "Do not let your hearts be troubled. You have faith in God; have faith also in me" (John 14:1). In addition, the prayer states that the disciples "persevered in prayer" as they awaited the Spirit. Two ways to "quiet" the heart are persevering prayer and the faith-filled surrender of anxieties. We are instructed to listen for God's "many great deeds" accomplished "for his people." This is to strengthen our faith in God's care for us and thereby to "quiet" our hearts further. A specific prayer intention is also provided in this address: to pray that the Holy Spirit perfect "his work in the world." The "work" of the Spirit is the Body of Christ. The Church still groans as she awaits the fullness of redemption (Romans 8:23). This Vigil is an important occasion to express those groans in prayer for the coming of the Spirit.

Prayer after the First Reading: The Church manifests the unity of the Trinity to the world most perfectly when she gathers to celebrate the Eucharist with one mind and one heart. This "unity" of the Trinity is the Holy Spirit, who also bonds the members of Christ's Body together. It was the Pentecost event that reversed the divisions

The space below is for your notes.

Refer to pages viii–x for an explanation of the pointing of the chants and to page xii for the Tones for the Presidential Prayers from *The Roman Missal.*

Pointed Text

Dear brethren (brothers and sisters),
we have now begun our Pentecost Vigil,
after the example of the Apostles and disciples,
who with Mary, the Mother of Jesus, persevered in prayer,
awaiting the Spirit promised by the Lord;
like them, let us, too, listen with quiet hearts to the Word of God.
Let us meditate on how many great deeds
God in times past did for his people
and let us pray that the Holy Spirit,
whom the Father sent as the first fruits for those who believe,
may bring to perfection his work in the world.

Prayers after the Readings

After the first reading (On Babel: Gn 11: 1–9) and the Psalm (33 [32]: 10–11, 12–13, 14–15; R. v. 12b).

Let us pray.

A Grant, we pray, almighty **God**,
B that your Church may always remain that holy people,
formed as one by the unity of Father, Son and **Ho**ly Spirit,
C which manifests to the world
the Sacrament of your holiness and unity
and leads it to the perfection of your char***i***ty.
Through Christ our Lord.
R. Amen.

After the second reading (On God's Descent on Mount Sinai: Ex 19: 3–8, 16–20b) and the canticle (Dn 3: 52, 53, 54, 55, 56; R. v. 52b) or the Psalm (19 [18]: 8, 9, 10, 11; R. Jn 6: 68c).

of the tower of Babel. Those divisions were ultimately not about language, but the lack of holiness (the confusion of languages was simply the manifestation of other divisions). Unity is closely bound in this prayer to holiness. The initial petition is that the Church always remain a "holy people," which is then explained as being "formed as one by the unity . . . ." The Greek word "diabolic" means to throw apart, divide. Its opposite is the "symbolic," which throws together. The liturgy uses the symbolic to form a unity of God's people, leading them deeper into holiness. The Church is called to be a Sacrament of "holiness and unity" to the world. The divisions within Christianity are a diabolical threat to this mission of the Church. Where this mission is realized, the "world" is inspired, by the Church's witness, to perform acts of charity.

Prayer after the Second Reading: The "fire and lightning" on Mount Sinai are understood here as foreshadowings of the "fire of the Spirit," which does not set the external world aflame, but instead acts as a purifying fire for the interior of humanity. Another prefigurement of the Holy Spirit was the "ancient Law," fulfilled in the "eternal commandment" of divine love. The Law was unable to take away sin. It simply pointed out where sin was occurring (Romans 5:20). With the gift of the Spirit, the victory over sin and death achieved by Christ (including forgiveness of sins) is "poured out" on the Apostles and on the whole Church. The adjective "wondrously" is the translation of the Latin *ineffabiliter*,

Let us pray.

Pause after **O God**. Proclaim **fire** and **lightning** with energy.

Stress **this day** and pause briefly. Contrast **new** and **fire of the Spirit**.

Again, by way of contrast, gently stress **we**.

Proclaim **wondrously** with energy.

Stress **new** and **every**.

Keep the voice raised with **rejoicing** and proclaim **eternal commandment** with reverence.

O God, who in fire and lightning
gave the ancient Law to Moses on Mount Sinai
and on this day manifested the new covenant
in the fire of the Spirit,
grant, we pray,
that we may always be aflame with that same Spirit
whom you wondrously poured out on your Apostles,
and that the new Israel,
gathered from every people,
may receive with rejoicing
the eternal commandment of your love.
Through Christ our Lord.
R. Amen.

After the third reading (On the dry bones and God's spirit: Ez 37: 1–14) and the Psalm (107 [106]: 2–3, 4–5, 6–7, 8–9; R. v. 1 or Alleluia).

Let us pray.

Keep the voice raised with **fallen**. There is a parallel rhythm between this line and the next. Pause after **we pray** and do not pause after **peoples**. Pause briefly after **renewed**.

Lord, God of power,
who restore what has fallen
and preserve what you have restored,
increase, we pray, the peoples
to be renewed by the sanctification of your name,
that all who are washed clean by holy Baptism
may always be directed by your prompting.
Through Christ our Lord.
R. Amen.

Or:

Pause briefly after **O God**, and again after **rebirth**.

Keep the voice raised with **flesh**.

Proclaim **incorruptible glory** slowly and with majesty.

O God, who have brought us to rebirth by the word of life,
pour out upon us your Holy Spirit,
that, walking in oneness of faith,
we may attain in our flesh
the incorruptible glory of the resurrection.
Through Christ our Lord.
R. Amen.

which literally means "ineffably." The point is that communication of the whole Paschal Mystery of Christ to the Church through the "pouring out" of the Spirit is beyong words to tell. To be continually "aflame" with the Spirit means to hold the law of love always active in one's heart (as well as to be ever more deeply purified from sin). This new commandmant is to be "received with rejoicing" (*laetanter*), that is, a joy that is shared with others. The law of love is similarly to be shared.

Prayer after the Third Reading: Given the scripture that precedes this prayer, the Lord's title as "God of power" refers to the power of resurrection. In the Resurrection of Jesus, God not only "restores what has fallen," but he makes the restoration permanent and glorious. The phrase "sanctification of your name" is similar to the second petition of the Our Father: "hallowed be your name." This is a prayer for God to manifest his holiness in the world. In this Collect, we ask for the manifestation of God's holiness to take place within the various peoples of the world. Since the prayer hints that such a renewal would be followed by Baptism, the implication is that this "holiness" of God would lead to the stirrings of faith that must precede Baptism. The presence of this holiness also seems to be required in order to be "directed by [God's] prompting." Just as the prophet Ezekiel was attuned to the prompting of God, so all of God's people, filled with the Spirit in Baptism, may hear and heed God's prophetic prompting in their lives. One of the gifts of Baptism is

Let us pray.

A O God, who in fire and lightning
gave the ancient Law to Moses on Mount Sinai
and on this day manifested the new covenant
in the fire of the Spir**it**,

B grant, we pray,
that we may always be aflame with that same Spirit
whom you wondrously poured out on **your** Apostles,

C and that the new Israel,
gathered from every people,
may receive with rejoicing
the eternal commandment of your ***love***.
Through Christ our Lord.

R. Amen.

After the third reading (On the dry bones and God's spirit: Ez 37: 1–14) and the Psalm (107 [106]: 2–3, 4–5, 6–7, 8–9; R. v. 1 or Alleluia).

Let us pray.

A Lord, God of power,
who restore what has fallen
and preserve what you have re**stored**,

B increase, we pray, the peoples
to be renewed by the sanctification **of** your name,

C that all who are washed clean by holy Baptism
may always be directed by your prompt***ing***.
Through Christ our Lord.

R. Amen.

Or:

A O God, who have brought us to rebirth by the word of **life**,

B pour out upon us your **Ho**ly Spirit,

C that, walking in oneness of faith,
we may attain in our flesh
the incorruptible glory of the resurrec***tion***.
Through Christ our Lord.

R. Amen.

The space below is for your notes.

Refer to pages viii–x for an explanation of the pointing of the chants and to page xii for the Tones for the Presidential Prayers from *The Roman Missal.*

prophecy, meaning the duty to witness one's faith to the world and the power of God in one's life.

Optional prayer after the Third Reading: The last two lines of this prayer are nearly identical to the Prayer after Communion for the Third Sunday of Easter.

The "word of life" refers to the Gospel of Jesus Christ. In the reading from Ezekiel, the "word of the Lord" prefigures the Gospel, especially in its power to raise the dead, though Ezekiel's "resurrection" is resuscitation. The "rebirth" of the New Testament flows from the Death and Resurrection of Christ, which is completed in us through the "pouring out" of the Holy Spirit. The gift of the Spirit always works to bind and unite those who receive it into one Body. The Spirit accomplishes this in one way by kindling the gift of faith. Believers are not simply to sit on their faith, but to "walk" in it. This means that we must exercise our faith (put it into practice) and grow deeper in it. Our faith must not remain a child's faith, but must mature as we mature. Only with Christ and the New Testament is the Spirit poured, for the first time, within God's people. This enables the interior transformation of the person. Only when the heart is purified may the "flesh" attain to the glory of the resurrection. This is a glory that does not fade, but is eternal.

Second optional prayer after the Third Reading: (This prayer is identical [in translation] to the Collect for the Third Sunday of Easter.)

Or:

The whole prayer should be prayed with an air of exuberance. Proclaim **exult for ever** together and with joyful energy. Draw out **renewed** slightly and be strong with **youthfulness of spirit**. Pause briefly after **so that** and after **now**. Pause briefly after **look forward**. Proclaim **confident hope** with raised voice.

May your people exult for ever, O God,
in renewed youthfulness of spirit,
so that, rejoicing now in the restored glory of our adoption,
we may look forward in confident hope
to the rejoicing of the day of resurrection.
Through Christ our Lord.
R. Amen.

After the fourth reading (On the outpouring of the Spirit: Joel 3: 1–5) and the Psalm (104 [103]: 1–2a, 24, 35c, 27–28, 29bc–30; R. v. 30 or Alleluia).

Let us pray.

Keep the voice raised with **promise** and pause only briefly. Pause after **we pray**. Emphasize **witnesses**.

Proclaim **Gospel of our Lord Jesus Christ** with evangelical authority and reverence.

Fulfill for us your gracious promise,
O Lord, we pray, so that by his coming
the Holy Spirit may make us witnesses before the world
to the Gospel of our Lord Jesus Christ.
Who lives and reigns for ever and ever.
R. Amen. *

* The extended vigil may be combined with Evening Prayer or Mass. If done during Mass, a reader proclaims the reading from the book of Romans and Mass continues as usual. The remaining prayers are found in the spread for the simple form of the Vigil Mass, pages 164–168 in *Essential Presidential Prayers and Texts*. The Preface is found in the spread for the Mass during the Day, pages 176–177 in *Essential Presidential Prayers and Texts*. You may use the Solemn Blessing for the Holy Spirit in the Order of Mass, page 170 in *The Order of Mass: A Roman Missal Study Edition and Workbook*. The double alleluia dismissal is used.

The phrase "youthfulness of spirit" (*animae iuventute*) refers to the interior attitude and emotion of the human being. It could also be translated youthfulness of soul or mind. The Latin includes three other important words left out here: *Spiritu Sancto tuo*. The full translation would be: "in youthfulness of soul renewed by your Holy Spirit." The Holy Spirit raised Jesus from the dead, filling his whole person with the power of life that never fades or grows weary (Isaiah 40:31). This prayer proclaims that, already now, believers can experience a measure of this youthful renewal in their soul or mind. This does not mean that one's thinking or feeling becomes immature as in youth, but strong, flexible and vibrant as in youth. The Holy Spirit works this renewal, and we get a glimpse of his work in the risen Christ, who is our "restored glory." Christ is the "day" of resurrection. We look forward in confident hope to rejoicing in Christ and, though the Holy Spirit, having a share in his glory. The Latin word for "rejoicing" (*laetatur*) implies that our celebration of "restored glory" is accomplished most fittingly in Christ's Body, the Church, because it is a shared joy.

Prayer after the Fourth Reading: The "gracious promise" of the Lord was to send the Holy Spirit upon the Church after the Resurrection of Christ. The promise holds for every believer in every time, which is why it can be fulfilled now "for us." The word translated as "gracious" (*propitiatus*) includes a sacrificial meaning. The fulfillment of this promise, which is the gift of the Holy Spirit, cleanses us from sin. It

Or:

A May your people exult for ever, O God,
in renewed youthfulness of spir**it**,
B so that, rejoicing now in the restored glory of **our** adoption,
C we may look forward in confident hope
to the rejoicing of the day of resurrec***tion***.
Through Christ our Lord.
R. Amen.

After the fourth reading (On the outpouring of the Spirit: Joel 3: 1-5) and the Psalm (104 [103]: 1-2a, 24, 35c, 27-28, 29bc-30; R. v. 30 or Alleluia).

Let us pray.

A Fulfill for us your gracious promise,
B O Lord, we **pray**, so that by his coming
the Holy Spirit may make us witnesses be**fore** the world
C to the Gospel of our Lord Jesus ***Christ***.
Who lives and reigns for ever and ever.
R. Amen.

The space below is for your notes.

Refer to pages viii–x for an explanation of the pointing of the chants and to page xii for the Tones for the Presidential Prayers from *The Roman Missal.*

removes all obstacles that hinder believers from giving witness to Jesus. To become "witnesses before the world" means that we stand up for our faith before both lax Christians and non-Christians. It is nowhere implied that we are to be provocative toward others, but neither are we to hide our identity as believers. The "Gospel" is good news, and the work of the Holy Spirit is to kindle the flame of belief in this good news so strongly that we are eager to share it. Consider the kinds of "news" that we eagerly share with others in various forms. Consider, too, what kind of Gospel news could provoke the same zeal. In this Vigil, we are to pray perseveringly for the outpouring of the Holy Spirit who will fill us with zeal for the Gospel.

PENTECOST SUNDAY

Solemnity

At the Vigil Mass

Simple form

Collect

Pause briefly after **Almighty**.

Encompassed (pronounced in -kəm -pəst) is given stress equal to **sign** and **fifty**. Proclaim each slowly and distinctly. Pause after **grant that**. Proclaim **heavenly grace** with gentleness and gratitude. Proclaim each word of **one great confession** slowly and deliberately.

Almighty ever-living God,
who willed the Paschal Mystery
to be encompassed as a sign in fifty days,
grant that from out of the scattered nations
the confusion of many tongues
may be gathered by heavenly grace
into one great confession of your name.
Through our Lord Jesus Christ, your Son,
who lives and reigns with you in the unity of the Holy Spirit,
one God, for ever and ever.

Or:

Pause briefly after **we pray**. Proclaim **splendor** richly. Keep the voice raised with **glory** and pause only briefly. Pause after **and that**. Proclaim **bright** lightly and vibrantly. Pause briefly after **your light** and briefly after **hearts**. Stress **born again**.

Grant, we pray, almighty God,
that the splendor of your glory
may shine forth upon us
and that, by the bright rays of the Holy Spirit,
the light of your light may confirm the hearts
of those born again by your grace.
Through our Lord Jesus Christ, your Son,
who lives and reigns with you in the unity of the Holy Spirit,
one God, for ever and ever.

Prayer over the Offerings

Emphasize **blessing of your Spirit**. Pause briefly after **through them** and again briefly after **imbued**. Emphasize **such love** and keep the voice raised. Give parallel emphasis to **truth of your saving mystery** and **shine forth for the whole world.**

Pour out upon these gifts the blessing of your Spirit,
we pray, O Lord,
so that through them your Church may be imbued with such love
that the truth of your saving mystery
may shine forth for the whole world.
Through Christ our Lord. *

* The Preface is found in the spread for the Mass during the day. See pages 176–177 in this book.

Collect: Easter Time sheds light on the whole mystery of Christ as the Church ponders Christ's life anew from the perspective of the Resurrection. The 50 days are symbolic in a number of ways: 40 (a common length for great events) + 10 (a number of completeness); 7 (a perfect number; days in a week) × 7 + 1 (the extra day goes beyond the weekly cycle of this world's time and symbolizes eternity); 50 was the number of days from the exodus from Egypt to the covenant on Sinai; and 50 was the number of days between the Jewish feast of Passover and the Feast of Booths. The idea is not that "fifty days" can encompass the Paschal Mystery, but that fifty days is a "sign" (the Latin is "mystery") of the Paschal Mystery. The main petition of this prayer is for the reversal of Babel, where humanity's pride caused rebellion against God, which led to division and chaos. The healing of this division comes about through "heavenly grace" that leads all into union and into "confession" of the "name" of God. To confess God's name is to surrender to his power over us.

Optional Collect: The "splendor" of God's glory refers to the various charisms or gifts of the Spirit. The splendor of these gifts adorns the Church for ministry in the world (1 Corinthians 12–14). The "bright rays of the Holy Spirit" refers to the light of Truth that enlightens the hearts and minds of believers. The "light of your light" (*lux tuae lucis*) is a Trinitarian formula. Normally, the Latin *Lux* is used exclusively for the divine ("God is light . . ." [1 John 1:5]). In the Creed, Christ is named "light from light" (*lux de luce*). In this prayer, the Holy Spirit is named

The space below is for your notes.

Refer to pages viii–x for an explanation of the pointing of the chants and to page xii for the Tones for the Presidential Prayers from *The Roman Missal.*

Pointed Text

Collect

A Almighty ever-living God,
who willed the Paschal Mystery
to be encompassed as a sign in fifty **days**,
B grant that from out of the scattered nations
the confusion of **ma**ny tongues
C may be gathered by heavenly grace
into one great confession of your ***name***.
Through our Lord Jesus Christ, your Son,
who lives and reigns with you in the unity of the Holy Spirit,
one God, for ever and ever.

Or:

A Grant, we pray, almighty **God**,
B that the splendor of your glory
may shine **forth** upon us
C and that, by the bright rays of the Holy Spirit,
the light of your light may confirm the hearts
of those born again by your ***grace***.
Through our Lord Jesus Christ, your Son,
who lives and reigns with you in the unity of the Holy Spirit,
one God, for ever and ever.

Prayer over the Offerings

A Pour out upon these gifts the blessing of your Spirit,
we pray, O **Lord**,
B so that through them your Church may be imbued **with** such love
C that the truth of your saving mystery
may shine forth for the whole ***world***.
Through Christ our Lord.

as the "light" of God's light. He is the light which goes forth from the face (Christ) of God. This light that is the Holy Spirit (as opposed to the gifts of the Spirit mentioned earlier in the prayer) acts to confirm or strengthen hearts that have been washed in the Blood of Christ and "born again" by God's grace. Only the strength of the Spirit can keep us faithful to the grace we have received through faith and in Baptism.

Prayer over the Offerings: The "blessing" of the Spirit is described as a gift of "love." According to the Gospel of John, the work of the Spirit is to make Christ present (John 14:26; 16:13–15). In this sense, the love with which the Spirit imbues the Church is the very love that Christ showed in giving his life for us. The redeeming love of Christ is the "saving mystery" that the Spirit reveals in the consecrated gifts of the Eucharist. The Spirit blesses the sacrificial gifts, and when the Church receives those same gifts in Communion, she is strengthened to witness to the love of Christ for the "whole world." There is an excellent connection made here between love and truth. The "truth of your saving mystery" is the "love" that Christ showed in shedding his Blood on the Cross for us. The depth of our love is the extent to which we give ourselves away in sacrifice and in forgetfulness of self. This is what the Spirit and the Son do completely. The Church's hope is that the more we sincerely receive the gift of Eucharistic love, the more we will show this love to the rest of the world.

Pause briefly after **aflame**. Place emphasis on **always** and **same**. Proclaim **wondrously** with energy and awe.

Prayer after Communion

May these gifts we have consumed
benefit us, O Lord,
that we may always be aflame with the same Spirit,
whom you wondrously poured out on your Apostles.
Through Christ our Lord. *

* You may use the Solemn Blessings for the Holy Spirit in the Order of Mass, page 170 in *The Order of Mass: A Roman Missal Study Edition and Workbook*. The double alleluia dismissal is used.

Prayer after Communion: As with other Prayers after Communion, this prayer notes the difference between consuming the sacred gifts and benefitting from them. The first is a physical act; the second is a spiritual one. Holy Communion is both physical and spiritual. We consume the physical accidents of bread and wine and receive, by God's grace, the spiritual reality of Christ's risen and glorified Body and Blood. If we "benefit" from the sacred meal, our hearts will "be aflame" with the presence of the Holy Spirit. In the Apostles, the Spirit worked to cast out fear. He strengthened and encouraged their hearts in the face of dangers (for example, when Peter wished to flee the persecutions in Rome). He also gave them words to proclaim their experience of faith in Jesus. Since we are given the "same Spirit," we can expect similar "benefits" in us. The "flame" of the Spirit gives us a further indication of his benefits. They are warm, communal, and loving. The opposite is to be cold, isolated, and self-centered. Whenever we find ourselves becoming more isolated or fearful, it is almost always a bad sign. The perfect love of the Spirit drives out all fear.

Prayer after Communion

A May these gifts we have consumed
benefit us, O **Lord**,
B that we may always be aflame with **the** same Spirit,
C whom you wondrously poured out on your Apos***tles***.
Through Christ our Lord.

The space below is for your notes.

Refer to pages viii–x for an explanation of the pointing of the chants and to page xii for the Tones for the Presidential Prayers from *The Roman Missal*.

PENTECOST SUNDAY

At the Mass during the Day

Collect

Pause after **O God**. Proclaim **mystery** with reverence and **great feast** with energy. Pause briefly after **Church** and again after **we pray**. Keep the voice raised for **Spirit**. Pause after **and** but not after **work**, though speak slowly.
Pause briefly after **once more**.

O God, who by the mystery of today's great feast
sanctify your whole Church in every people and nation,
pour out, we pray, the gifts of the Holy Spirit
across the face of the earth
and, with the divine grace that was at work
when the Gospel was first proclaimed,
fill now once more the hearts of believers.
Through our Lord Jesus Christ, your Son,
who lives and reigns with you in the unity of the Holy Spirit,
one God, for ever and ever.

Prayer over the Offerings

Pause briefly after **Grant**.

Emphasize **more abundantly** and proclaim **hidden mystery** with reverent delight.
Proclaim **graciously** with gentle longing.

Grant, we pray, O Lord,
that, as promised by your Son,
the Holy Spirit may reveal to us more abundantly
the hidden mystery of this sacrifice
and graciously lead us into all truth.
Through Christ our Lord. *

Prayer after Communion

Pause after **O God**. Emphasize **heavenly gifts**. Pause briefly after **we pray** and again briefly after **Spirit**. Keep the voice raised with **upon her** and do not pause long. Pause very briefly after **gain her** in order to emphasize **abundance** and **eternal**.

O God, who bestow heavenly gifts upon your Church,
safeguard, we pray, the grace you have given,
that the gift of the Holy Spirit poured out upon her
may retain all its force
and that this spiritual food
may gain her abundance of eternal redemption.
Through Christ our Lord. **

* If Eucharistic Prayer I is used, the proper form of the Communicantes is prayed from the Order of Mass. It is found in *The Order of Mass: A Roman Missal Study Edition and Workbook*, page 129.

** You may use the Solemn Blessing for the Holy Spirit in the Order of Mass, page 170 in *The Order of Mass: A Roman Missal Study Edition and Workbook*. The double alleluia dismissal is used.

Collect: The "mystery" of Pentecost is how the Holy Spirit binds in holiness people of diverse cultures, ethnicities, political ideologies, etc. The Church is not bound by any prejudice. All find sanctity in her waters. Indeed, the main work of the Spirit is to sanctify and to unite. In the Spirit, communion is always possible. "In Christian realities there are no distinctions which separate, all is communion; the very distinctions are often a source of communion. It is sin alone that creates distinctions which separate" (F.X. Durwell, *Holy Spirit of God*, pp. 237–238, footnote 15). This is an important point of theology. Where communion is broken, the Spirit has been neglected. The zeal of the infant Church was a gift of the Holy Spirit. The Spirit is as active today as at the time of the Apostles, and the more we cooperate with grace to overcome sin, the more the gifts of the Spirit will shine forth in the life of the Church. The "hearts of believers" is fertile ground for the graces of the Spirit.

Prayer over the Offerings: This prayer recalls the promise that Jesus made in John 16:13–15 regarding the "Spirit of truth." The indwelling of the Spirit continually purifies believers of sin. As the darkness of sin is dispelled, the light of truth is revealed. Because of our limitations, this process is usually gradual. The "hidden mystery" of Christ's sacrifice will remain a mystery in the time and space of this world. With each new experience, however, we see the one mystery in new light.

The space below is for your notes.

Refer to pages viii–x for an explanation of the pointing of the chants and to page xii for the Tones for the Presidential Prayers from *The Roman Missal.*

Pointed Text

Collect

A O God, who by the mystery of today's great feast
sanctify your whole Church in every people and na**tion**,
B pour out, we pray, the gifts of the Holy Spirit
across the face of the earth
and, with the divine grace that was at work
when the Gospel was **first** proclaimed,
C fill now once more the hearts of belie***vers***.
Through our Lord Jesus Christ, your Son,
who lives and reigns with you in the unity of the Holy Spirit,
one God, for ever and ever.

Prayer over the Offerings

A Grant, we pray, O **Lord**,
B that, as promised **by** your Son,
C the Holy Spirit may reveal to us more abundantly
the hidden mystery of this sacrifice
and graciously lead us into all ***truth***.
Through Christ our Lord.

Prayer after Communion

A O God, who bestow heavenly gifts upon your **Church**,
B safeguard, we pray, the grace **you** have given,
C that the gift of the Holy Spirit poured out upon her
may retain all its force
and that this spiritual food
may gain her abundance of eternal redemp***tion***.
Through Christ our Lord.

The Latin word behind "lead into" is *reseret*, more commonly translated as "open" in the sense of unlocking and opening a door. Christ is sometimes called the door or the gate, and the Spirit is the key to unlock the door. Christ is the "truth" that the Spirit unlocks for us. The adverb "graciously" carries sacrificial resonance, implying that the Spirit unlocks the truth for us by cleansing us through the sacrificial offering of Christ's Blood.

Prayer after Communion: Our true home is with Christ in heaven. This is why the Lord bestows "heavenly gifts" upon us. The "grace" that God has given refers, first, to the Holy Communion the Church has just shared. This bread, too, is from heaven and must be "safeguarded" from all sin. Protected from sin, the great gift (*munus*) of the Spirit will "retain all its force." It is not that sin diminishes the Spirit, but rather that it enfeebles our receptivity to the Spirit. The *munus* of the Spirit refers to the entire mission or office of the Spirit in the Church and not to any single charism. The Spirit's full indwelling safeguards the Church and keeps her sound in the faith of Christ. The phrase "poured out upon her" would be more accurately translated "poured into her" and thereby connotes the indwelling action of the Spirit more fully. Holy Communion is named as "spiritual food." Through the Eucharistic Prayer, the bread and wine have been so thoroughly taken over by the Spirit, that they communicate the fullness of Christ—precisely the mission of the Spirit.

Bring out the accent on **be** in **The Lord be with you.** In the response, accent **spirit**, by slightly holding both syllables. In the next phrase, make a strong accent on **Lift**, and slow both notes of **hearts**. In the third dialogue, move to the word **thanks** before accenting, and hold that word slightly to give it emphasis. Broaden both notes of **Lord** and hold **God**.

At the end of the first phrase of the body, hold **-tion** of **completion** and take a good breath there, because the next two lines go together. Tie together without holding **Spirit today** and **on those**. Hold **-dren** of **children** at the end of the phrase, but without breathing continue with **by uniting**. Slow slightly and broaden the last three words, enunciating each syllable carefully. In the next phrase, hold slightly **-it** of **Spirit** but then continue without a break to **as the**. The same handling goes with **birth**, and continue without a break to **opened**. Hold **God** at the end of the phrase and take a breath there. Hold **earth** in the next phrase but do not breathe there, going on to **in profession**. Slow and broaden the ending of the phrase.

Preface: The Mystery of Pentecost

The Paschal Mystery will be brought "to completion" when all of God's children by adoption have reached union with Christ. This is what Saint Paul means when he writes, "When everything is subjected to him, then the Son himself will [also] be subjected to the one . . . so that God may be all in all" (1 Corinthians 15:28). It is certainly the goal of every family to attain perfect harmony. The family of God is no different. The whole of the Paschal Mystery finds fulfillment in such a communion, and the Holy Spirit is the means to that communion. The Preface states, "you bestowed the Holy Spirit today" (*hodie*). The "today" of Christianity is rich in meaning. In the liturgy, the events of the Paschal Mystery become present to the Church. The Father bestowed the Spirit on the Apostles at Pentecost and he continues to do so for us "today" (Hebrews 3:7–15; 4:4–11). In the liturgy, the Church becomes present to God's "today," which is as much a person or place as it is a time. The Father bestowed the Spirit first on the person of Christ. The Body of Christ is the eternal "today" where the Spirit is poured forth, and this is what makes the human race members of Christ's Body and "adopted children" of God. Our union with Christ first begins in the Sacrament of Baptism and is deepened with each successive Sacrament. It is brought to completion with the death of the believer when the individual is emptied of all that is earthly. Only then does it become possible to receive the fullness of the Spirit, wherein the believer is glorified and finds complete union with Christ in the

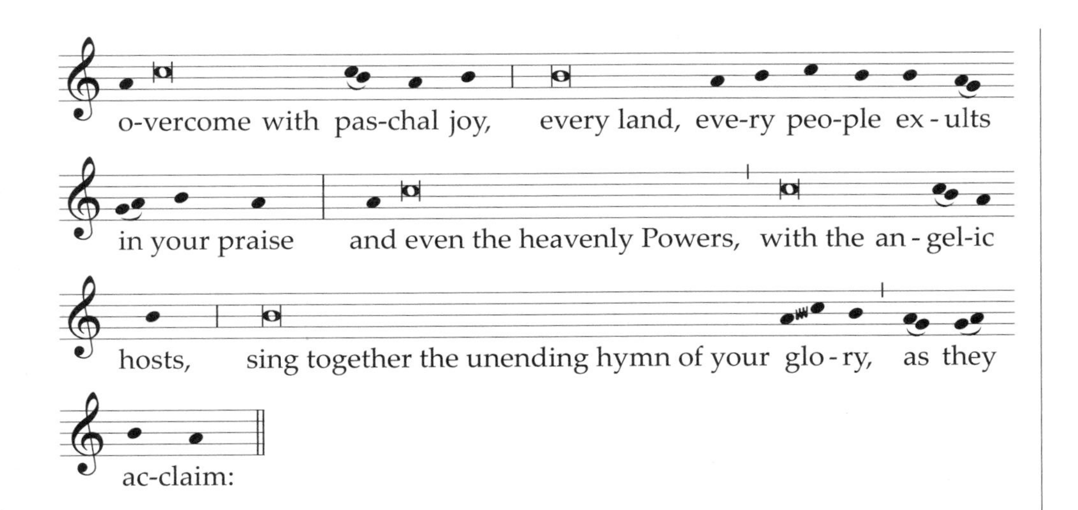

Holy, Holy, Holy Lord God of hosts . . .

Text without music:

V. **The Lord be with you.**
R. And with your spirit.

V. **Lift up your hearts.**
R. We lift them up to the Lord.

V. **Let us give thanks to the Lord our God.**
R. It is right and just.

It is truly right and just, our duty and our salvation,
always and everywhere to give you thanks,
Lord, holy Father, almighty and eternal God.

For, bringing your Paschal Mystery to completion,
you bestowed the Holy Spirit today
on those you made your adopted children
by uniting them to your Only Begotten Son.
This same Spirit, as the Church came to birth,
opened to all peoples the knowledge of God
and brought together the many languages of the earth
in profession of the one faith.

Pause after **For** and speak the remainder of the line with measured rhythm. Place some emphasis on **today** and keep the voice raised for **children**. Pause after **peoples**.

Proclaim **knowledge of God** with reverence. Speak **many languages** slowly and deliberately. Place emphasis on **one**.

Spirit. Another working of the Spirit is to introduce "knowledge of God" (*scientiam deitatis*) into the hearts of "all peoples." This gift of "knowledge" is simultaneous with the birth of the Church. When the Spirit raised Christ from the dead and formed his Body into the Church, knowledge of God was given to humanity in a way that we could hear and understand it, that is, in the person of Christ, who can be heard, seen, and touched (1 John 1:1). The last work of the Spirit mentioned by the Preface is to unite all peoples through the profession of one faith. The Spirit does not destroy diversity in fostering communion. It is precisely our differences, when seen in the light of faith, which enable communion.

Therefore, overcome with paschal joy,
every land, every people exults in your praise
and even the heavenly Powers, with the angelic hosts,
sing together the unending hymn of your glory,
as they acclaim:

Holy, Holy, Holy Lord God of hosts . . .

Ordinary Time

SECOND SUNDAY IN ORDINARY TIME

Collect

Pause briefly after **Almighty**. Stress **all** and pause briefly after **heaven**. Proclaim **mercifully** with tender gentleness and **pleading** with a hint of yearning. Proclaim **your peace** with sincere longing and **our times** with a hint of urgency.

Almighty ever-living God,
who govern all things,
both in heaven and on earth,
mercifully hear the pleading of your people
and bestow your peace on our times.
Through our Lord Jesus Christ, your Son,
who lives and reigns with you in the unity of the Holy Spirit,
one God, for ever and ever.

Prayer over the Offerings

Pause briefly after **Grant us**. Speak **worthily** with a desire to please. Give some stress to **whenever** and proclaim **work of our redemption** with dignity and solemnity.

Grant us, O Lord, we pray,
that we may participate worthily in these mysteries,
for whenever the memorial of this sacrifice is celebrated
the work of our redemption is accomplished.
Through Christ our Lord. *

Prayer after Communion

Pause briefly after **O Lord** and even less briefly after **nourished**. Proclaim **one heavenly Bread** with measured deliberation. Stress **one** and proceed slowly with **mind and heart**.

Pour on us, O Lord, the Spirit of your love,
and in your kindness
make those you have nourished
by this one heavenly Bread
one in mind and heart.
Through Christ our Lord.

* Select from Prefaces I–VIII of the Sundays in Ordinary Time in the Order of Mass. Commentary, and proclamation and chant tips, for the Preface can be found at *www.StudyThePresidentialTexts.com/Prefaces* and in *The Order of Mass: A Roman Missal Study Edition and Workbook*, pages 62–77.

Collect: God is almighty (i.e., one who governs all things). We have a hard time imagining absolute power, because we see power from the perspective of weakness, which is why power corrupts us. We wield power out of fear of mortality. God, however, fears nothing. The power that a parent has over an infant might come close to how it is for God. A father or mother has nothing to fear from their child, who trusts them utterly. Parents wield that kind of power with gentleness, love, and solicitude. It is similar for God toward all things both in heaven and on earth. He governs from absolute power, which never has need, let alone need to defend himself. God's governance is not extraordinary, at least in the sense of doing deeds he would not ordinarily do. The daily miracles of a sunrise and majesty of the mountains are reflections of his governance. The peace of God is reconciliation with him. No other peace will endure unless it flows from this peace of communion with God.

Prayer over the Offerings: The word behind participate (*frequentare*) means to be present to another in the way that a student, for example, is present to his or her academic classes. The mysteries refer immediately to this celebration of the Eucharist, but more importantly to the reality behind every liturgy of the Church, which is Christ. Think of memorial in the sense of a grand monument, which in this case is the ritual imitation of Christ's Death and Resurrection—the addition of "this sacrifice" makes this clear. This memorial is

Pointed Text

Collect

A Almighty ever-living God,
who govern all things,
both in heaven and on **earth**,
B mercifully hear the pleading **of** your people
C and bestow your peace on our ***times***.
Through our Lord Jesus Christ, your Son,
who lives and reigns with you in the unity of the Holy Spirit,
one God, for ever and ever.

Prayer over the Offerings

A Grant us, O Lord, we **pray**,
B that we may participate worthily **in** these mysteries,
C for whenever the memorial of this sacrifice is celebrated
the work of our redemption is accom***plished***.
Through Christ our Lord.

Prayer after Communion

A Pour on us, O Lord, the Spirit of your **love**,
B and in your kindness
make those you have nourished
by this one hea**ven**ly Bread
C one in mind and ***heart***.
Through Christ our Lord.

The space below is for your notes.

Refer to pages viii–x for an explanation of the pointing of the chants and to page xii for the Tones for the Presidential Prayers from *The Roman Missal*.

Christ's self-offering. When we engage this monument, the Holy Spirit goes to work. The work of redemption is a divine action. The human action in this work involves opening our mind and heart to be receptive of God's action. When we memorialize Christ, the Spirit works, and redemption is accomplished. Redemption is any experience of being brought closer to God. The freedom of redemption is always freedom for God.

Prayer after Communion: The word *infunde* could be translated "pour on" or "pour into." In the context of the new reality flowing from the New Testament, the Spirit acts internally. He is sent to indwell his chosen people. He is the Spirit of your love (*tuae caritatis*), referring to the divine love (*agape* in Greek). This is a love characterized by self-gift. In this sense, the prayer could have asked for the Spirit of your Son, because Jesus embodied God's self-gift in his sacrifice on the cross. This love is contrasted with a different word further on for those who have received Holy Communion. The Latin text is slightly different than its translation here. More literally, it states: "make those . . . harmonious with one filial devotion (*una pietate*)." The divine love toward us is *caritas*, and our love toward the divine, the love of adopted children toward our heavenly Father, is *pietas*. The beauty of the prayer is that our *pietas* is brought to perfection by having divine *caritas* poured into us.

THIRD SUNDAY IN ORDINARY TIME

Collect

Pause briefly after **Almighty**. Raise the voice to emphasize **according**. Stress **name** and keep the voice raised at **Son**. Pause briefly after **abound** in order to emphasize **good works**.

Almighty ever-living God,
direct our actions according to your good pleasure,
that in the name of your beloved Son
we may abound in good works.
Through our Lord Jesus Christ, your Son,
who lives and reigns with you in the unity of the Holy Spirit,
one God, for ever and ever.

Prayer over the Offerings

Proclaim **accept our offerings** with gentle confidence and **sanctifying** with gratitude. Emphasize the last line on **salvation**.

Accept our offerings, O Lord, we pray,
and in sanctifying them
grant that they may profit us for salvation.
Through Christ our Lord. *

Prayer after Communion

Pause briefly after **we pray** and pray **receiving** with acceptance and **grace** with tenderness. Emphasize **you bring** and **new life**. Pause after **always**, placing some stress on it. Proclaim **glory** with energy.

Grant, we pray, almighty God,
that, receiving the grace
by which you bring us to new life,
we may always glory in your gift.
Through Christ our Lord.

* Select from Prefaces I–VIII of the Sundays in Ordinary Time in the Order of Mass. Commentary, and proclamation and chant tips, for the Preface can be found at *www.StudyThePresidentialTexts.com/Prefaces* and in *The Order of Mass: A Roman Missal Study Edition and Workbook*, pages 62–77.

Collect: The Latin behind "your good pleasure" (*beneplacito tuo*) more literally means "what pleases you well." God is well pleased by right behavior, by a well-ordered affect, by just decisions, by appropriate responses. If we believe that God created humanity, it follows that God knows best what will bring us fulfillment. To fulfill our nature is to act pleasingly to him. Blessed Pope John Paul II often said that Christ reveals man to himself. Christ was the first of our race to fulfill our nature as God created it to be fulfilled. In doing so, he acted in accord with God's "good pleasure" and was called the "beloved Son." This is why the prayer asks that our actions be done in his name. Christ is the model for our acting. To follow in his footsteps is for us to become beloved sons and daughters of God. Our "good works" are only accomplished in the light of Christ's work of self-gift and sacrificial love.

Prayer over the Offerings: The word *munera*, "offerings," denotes so much more than bread and wine, which are symbolic of the greater reality to which *munus* refers. It can include "mission" in the sense of assignment or vocation from God; it can mean the "duty" or "office" of both responsibility and privilege; it can refer to the "gifts" or "talents" that we have received from God. It is from this rich assortment of "offerings" that we bring gifts to God, in the form of bread and wine, and present them to him in the Eucharist. The word for

Pointed Text

Collect

A Almighty ever-living **God**,
B direct our actions according to **your** good pleasure,
C that in the name of your beloved Son
we may abound in good ***works***.
Through our Lord Jesus Christ, your Son,
who lives and reigns with you in the unity of the Holy Spirit,
one God, for ever and ever.

Prayer over the Offerings

A Accept our offerings, O Lord, we **pray**,
B and in sanctify**ing** them
C grant that they may profit us for salva***tion***.
Through Christ our Lord.

Prayer after Communion

A Grant, we pray, almighty **God**,
B that, receiving the grace
by which you bring us **to** new life,
C we may always glory in your ***gift***.
Through Christ our Lord.

The space below is for your notes.

Refer to pages viii–x for an explanation of the pointing of the chants and to page xii for the Tones for the Presidential Prayers from *The Roman Missal.*

"accept" (*suscipe*) paints the picture of God taking our offerings and supporting us, strengthening us by taking them to himself to bless them, "sanctify them." The "sanctifying" action of the Lord on our "offerings" turns them from a human strength or struggle into something which "profits us for salvation." Until we offer our assets to the Lord for his blessing, they will bear no fruit beyond this life. Christians must long to bear fruit that will endure.

Prayer after Communion: This prayer touches upon the key activity for humanity: to receive. God created us for the purpose of receiving his self-gift of love, but often we are unwilling to receive the gift. The "grace" offered to us is specified as a grace which "brings to new life" (*vivificationis*). Christ came so that we might have life and have it more abundantly. The prayer (in its Latin form) presumes that we have received this grace. Within the context of the Eucharist, that grace of new vigor would be received in Holy Communion. With this prayer, the Church asks that we may eagerly seek after the consequences of accepting this self-gift of God, which is to "glory in his gift." The word for "gift" (*munere*) is the same word, in singular form, used in the Prayer over the Offerings. Those "offerings" were accepted by God, sanctified, united as one in Christ and returned as Holy Communion. Our "glory" is that God takes what we give him and raises it to union with him.

FOURTH SUNDAY IN ORDINARY TIME

Collect

Pause briefly after **Grant us**. Stress **honor you** and pause briefly, giving added stress to **all**. Pause briefly after **everyone**. Proclaim **truth of heart** with measured deliberateness.

Grant us, Lord our God,
that we may honor you with all our mind,
and love everyone in truth of heart.
Through our Lord Jesus Christ, your Son,
who lives and reigns with you in the unity of the Holy Spirit,
one God, for ever and ever.

Prayer over the Offerings

Pause briefly after **O Lord**. Emphasize **offerings**. Speak **be pleased** with gentle pleading and proclaim **transform them** with hopeful energy. Be deliberate and measured with the last line.

O Lord, we bring to your altar
these offerings of our service:
be pleased to receive them, we pray,
and transform them
into the Sacrament of our redemption.
Through Christ our Lord. *

Prayer after Communion

Stress **nourished** and **redeeming**, being tender with the first and energetic with the second. Pause very briefly after **help**. Emphasize **eternal**. Pause briefly after **faith**. Stress **ever**.

Nourished by these redeeming gifts,
we pray, O Lord,
that through this help to eternal salvation
true faith may ever increase.
Through Christ our Lord.

* Select from Prefaces I–VIII of the Sundays in Ordinary Time in the Order of Mass. Commentary, and proclamation and chant tips, for the Preface can be found at *www.StudyThePresidentialTexts.com/Prefaces* and in *The Order of Mass: A Roman Missal Study Edition and Workbook*, pages 62–77.

Collect: In *A Man for All Seasons*, Saint Thomas More says that God made the animals for innocence and plants for simplicity, but "man he made to serve him wittily, in the tangle of his mind." Tragically, we can get lost in the mind or try to escape our thoughts, but we are expected to use the gift of rational thought and self-awareness to our fullest potential. God delights in our musings, simple and profound, poetry and prose, scientific and artistic. Christ is named the *Logos* in John's Gospel account, the "Word" that is eternally begotten from the mind of the Father. The *Logos* is the rational principle of creation, and humanity honors God by using reason to explore, understand, and celebrate the world and the heavens. The prayer calls us to love others "in truth of heart" (*rationabili affectu*). The mind and heart should be guided by reason (the *Logos*). Our mind must be rooted in a rich affective life, and affections must be ordered by a steady logic.

Prayer over the Offerings: The altar in the church is qualified here as belonging to God, "*your* altar." In Eucharistic Prayer I, we pray that the gifts may be carried "to your altar on high." The altar in church is a symbol of the "altar on high." Ultimately, that altar on high is the Body of Christ. He is altar, priest, and victim. He belongs to God, "your altar." He lives now "on high." The gifts brought to every altar are being brought to Christ. The prayer asks Christ to receive our gifts and "transform them" into himself, the "Sacrament of our redemp-

Pointed Text

Collect

A Grant us, Lord our **God**,
B that we may honor you with **all** our mind,
C and love everyone in truth of ***heart***.
Through our Lord Jesus Christ, your Son,
who lives and reigns with you in the unity of the Holy Spirit,
one God, for ever and ever.

Prayer over the Offerings

A O Lord, we bring to your altar
these offerings of our ser**vice**:
B be pleased to receive **them**, we pray,
C and transform them
into the Sacrament of our redemp***tion***.
Through Christ our Lord.

Prayer after Communion

B Nourished by these redeeming gifts,
we **pray**, O Lord,
C that through this help to eternal salvation
true faith may ever in***crease***.
Through Christ our Lord.

The space below is for your notes.

Refer to pages viii–x for an explanation of the pointing of the chants and to page xii for the Tones for the Presidential Prayers from *The Roman Missal*.

tion." These "offerings" are the fruits of "our service." This may be understood in more than one way. Primarly, the "service" refers to the service of the Eucharist in which the Eucharistic Prayer is offered. In a secondary way, "service" could be understood as the self-gift of the faithful. When the faithful place the labors of their "service" on the offerings, ritually speaking, the priestly "service" of offering the Eucharistic Prayer will bless and enrich their labors.

Prayer after Communion: The word translated here as "gifts" is singular in the Latin (*munere*), and is the same word that was used in the Prayer over the Offerings, though it was plural there (*munera*). This illustrates how the Lord takes the many gifts we offer and unites them into the one gift of Communion in the Body and Blood of his Son. Through the Eucharistic Prayer, those many gifts have become one redeeming gift. They are perfected by being raised to the perfection that is Jesus Christ. This is what makes them "redeeming" and a "help to eternal salvation." They place us in communion with Christ, our eternal salvation. Holy Communion is understood as a means for deepening Christian faith. It is called "true" faith to mark it specifically as faith in the mystery of Christ, who is the truth. To receive the Eucharist worthily is to be nourished, strengthened in the Christ, whom we receive sacramentally. We grow in trust by exercising the muscle that is our faith.

FIFTH SUNDAY IN ORDINARY TIME

Collect

Pause briefly after **O Lord**, expressing solicitude in the voice with **Keep your family safe**. Stress **unfailing**. Pause briefly after **that** and after **hope**. Give parallel emphasis to **solely** and **heavenly**. Pause briefly after **always**, emphasizing it.

Keep your family safe, O Lord, with unfailing care,
that, relying solely on the hope of heavenly grace,
they may be defended always by your protection.
Through our Lord Jesus Christ, your Son,
who lives and reigns with you in the unity of the Holy Spirit,
one God, for ever and ever.

Prayer over the Offerings

Emphasize **created** and give parallel emphasis to **sustain** and **frailty**, proclaiming the latter with humility.

Keep the voice raised with **now**. Stress both **Sacrament** and **eternal**.

O Lord our God,
who once established these created things
to sustain us in our frailty,
grant, we pray,
that they may become for us now
the Sacrament of eternal life.
Through Christ our Lord. *

Prayer after Communion

Pause briefly after **O God** and **willed**. Give parallel emphasis to **one Bread** and **one Chalice**. Pause briefly after **we pray**. Stress **so** and keep the voice raised somewhat with **live**. Give an equal emphasis to this third occurrence of **one** as to the previous two. Proclaim **joyfully** and **salvation** with parallel energy.

O God, who have willed that we be partakers
in the one Bread and the one Chalice,
grant us, we pray, so to live
that, made one in Christ,
we may joyfully bear fruit
for the salvation of the world.
Through Christ our Lord.

* Select from Prefaces I–VIII of the Sundays in Ordinary Time in the Order of Mass. Commentary, and proclamation and chant tips, for the Preface can be found at *www.StudyThePresidentialTexts.com/Prefaces* and in *The Order of Mass: A Roman Missal Study Edition and Workbook*, pages 62–77.

Collect: The Christian family is God's family, and the word translated as "care" (*pietate*) refers to the devotion between a parent and child. God will never grow weary caring for us, nor should we ever grow weary of "relying" on him. "Relying" (*innititur*) includes the meaning of striving. We achieve nothing lasting on our own, that is, without grace. What disposes us most wonderfully to grace, however, is our striving, but only a striving that relies entirely on the hope for grace. I should not look toward other Christians' accomplishments, but rather toward their strivings and, more importantly, toward their surrender in hope of "heavenly grace." My health may lead through no effort of mine to a pleasant dispostion, while another's unpleasant demeanor may be his best effort at overcoming poor health. The prayer ends by reminding us that, despite our best striving, we will need to be "defended" by God's "protection." "Sin is a demon lurking at the door" (Genesis 4:7), but we can "master it" with God's protection.

Prayer over the Offerings: This is a beautiful prayer about the relationship between nature and grace. Wheat and grapes were "established" in the order of nature as sustenance for the "frailty" of mortal humanity. In the Eucharist, the grace of the Holy Spirit raises the order of nature to a supernatural level. Bread and wine are nourishment on an earthly level. In the Eucharist, they become nourishment on a spiritual level. All "created things" find their perfection by being in-spirited, by being penetrated and raised by the Holy Spirit to the

Pointed Text

Collect

A Keep your family safe, O Lord, with unfailing **care**,
B that, relying solely on the hope of hea**ven**ly grace,
C they may be defended always by your protec***tion***.
Through our Lord Jesus Christ, your Son,
who lives and reigns with you in the unity of the Holy Spirit,
one God, for ever and ever.

Prayer over the Offerings

A O Lord our God,
who once established these created things
to sustain us in our frail**ty**,
B grant, we pray,
that they may become **for** us now
C the Sacrament of eternal ***life***.
Through Christ our Lord.

Prayer after Communion

A O God, who have willed that we be partakers
in the one Bread and the one Cha**lice**,
B grant us, we pray, so to live
that, made **one** in Christ,
C we may joyfully bear fruit
for the salvation of the ***world***.
Through Christ our Lord.

The space below is for your notes.

Refer to pages viii–x for an explanation of the pointing of the chants and to page xii for the Tones for the Presidential Prayers from *The Roman Missal*.

level of the risen and glorified life of Christ. From the perspective of heaven, then, bread and wine were always meant to be spiritual food; water was always meant to convey the death of sin and life of grace; oil was always meant to become a sacrament of the Holy Spirit that sets us apart as holy. All creation becomes revelatory of eternity. The Latin has a word play between "frailty" and "eternal life": *fragilitatis* and *aeternitatis* (frailty and eternity).

Prayer after Communion: The use of the word "willed" is significant on two levels. First, it highlights the great importance that the Church attaches to the will. It is the will, the place of commitment, that permanently impacts us. Secondly, the use of "willed" in relation to God communicates revelation. God has "willed" his people to eat his Body and drink his Blood. The threefold repetition of "one" is highly indicative of the importance the Church places on unity in the Church. The "one Bread" and "one Chalice" are given to us precisely to make us "one in Christ." The goal is less individual communion with Christ as communion with Christ that effects communion with the whole Church. When the Church lives this profound union with Christ and others, the natural consequence is a "joyful" witness to the world that not only affects people, but leads them to salvation. The Christian failure to fulfill Jesus's command of unity in his Body severely handicaps our bearing salvific fruit in the world.

SIXTH SUNDAY IN ORDINARY TIME

Collect

Pause briefly after **O God** and again briefly after **teach us**. Do not pause significantly after **abide**. Stress **so fashioned**. Emphasize on **dwelling** and pause briefly after it. Proclaim **pleasing** with gentle delight.

O God, who teach us that you abide
in hearts that are just and true,
grant that we may be so fashioned by your grace
as to become a dwelling pleasing to you.
Through our Lord Jesus Christ, your Son,
who lives and reigns with you in the unity of the Holy Spirit,
one God, for ever and ever.

Prayer over the Offerings

Pause briefly after **oblation**, which is pronounced ob-LA-tion. Give equal emphasis to **cleanse** and **renew**, and the same for **source** and **eternal**.

May this oblation, O Lord, we pray,
cleanse and renew us
and may it become for those who do your will
the source of eternal reward.
Through Christ our Lord. *

Prayer after Communion

Proclaim **heavenly delights** with joyful awe. **That** is dependent on **we pray**. Think of it as the reason we pray is so that . . . and try to proclaim it with that in mind. Stress **always** and **that food**, pausing briefly after **food**. Emphasize **truly**.

Having fed upon these heavenly delights,
we pray, O Lord,
that we may always long
for that food by which we truly live.
Through Christ our Lord.

* Select from Prefaces I–VIII of the Sundays in Ordinary Time in the Order of Mass. Commentary, and proclamation and chant tips, for the Preface can be found at *www.StudyThePresidentialTexts.com/Prefaces* and in *The Order of Mass: A Roman Missal Study Edition and Workbook*, pages 62–77.

Collect: The Latin word for "teach" (*asseris*) is difficult to translate in this prayer. It means to sow or plant. The idea is that God has so planted himself in our hearts as to be rooted there, to "abide" or remain there. This is no temporary action. He comes to stay—at least, for as long as he is welcome. The place where he comes to stay is our "hearts" (*pectoribus*). While rationality is often associated with the mind, the heart, as the seat of affections, is often associated with our will. The heart in a body is often compared to the altar in a church. It is the place of prayer and sacrifice. Scripture speaks of the Lord strengthening the heart. It is also the place where the evil one can insinuate temptations (John 13:2). The petition of the prayer asks that we may be "so fashioned" (*exsistere*, literally to stand out or exist) "by your grace" as to become the dwelling place of God alone. Literally, we long to exist by means of God's grace (i.e., the Holy Spirit) filling up our heart entirely.

Prayer over the Offerings: First, the "oblation" of the faithful "cleanses." This is a process of removing what does not belong, which would include our earthly attachments. The things that need to be removed are the things that should be offered in the oblation of the Mass, in which we surrender them into the hands of the priest who sacrifices them to God. The second action of the "oblation" is "renewal." Having been cleansed, we are disposed for the renewing action of the Holy Spirit. Like Christ, we are stripped of earthly things to

Pointed Text

Collect

B O God, who teach us that you abide
in hearts that are **just** and true,
C grant that we may be so fashioned by your grace
as to become a dwelling pleasing to ***you***.
Through our Lord Jesus Christ, your Son,
who lives and reigns with you in the unity of the Holy Spirit,
one God, for ever and ever.

Prayer over the Offerings

A May this oblation, O Lord, we **pray**,
B cleanse **and** renew us
C and may it become for those who do your will
the source of eternal re***ward***.
Through Christ our Lord.

Prayer after Communion

B Having fed upon these heavenly delights,
we **pray**, O Lord,
C that we may always long
for that food by which we truly ***live***.
Through Christ our Lord.

The space below is for your notes.

Refer to pages viii–x for an explanation of the pointing of the chants and to page xii for the Tones for the Presidential Prayers from *The Roman Missal.*

be clothed in the glory of heavenly things. This is what it means to "do God's will." We follow in the footsteps of Christ by "removing" all that is of the earth and these things, when surrendered to God, are transformed by the Spirit to become helps on our way to renewed life in God. The Latin word for "reward" has an English cognate: remuneration. God will never be outdone. What we surrender on the altar will become an "eternal" remuneration.

Prayer after Communion: The word "delights" communicates the sense of Communion as a delicious treat that whets our appetite for the banquet yet to come in heaven, where we will be transformed so as to receive the fullness of the heavenly banquet, of which these "delights" are the Sacrament. The goal of the Eucharist is the transubstantiation of the bread and wine so that we may be transformed into lifegiving spirits. The verb translated as "to long" is *appetamus* from which English takes the word "appetite." It could be translated "so that we may always hunger," though the word "long" communicates that this appetite is spiritual. The phrase "that food" is somewhat ambiguous. The Latin is *eadem*, which means "the same" in reference to the "heavenly delights." This is the mystery of the now and not yet. The heavenly delights are the Real Presence of Christ, satisfying us (now), and yet, they are also a Sacrament that leads us to long for more of the same (not yet).

SEVENTH SUNDAY IN ORDINARY TIME

Collect

Pause briefly after **we pray**. Proclaim **always pondering** with measured emphasis and raise the voice with **spiritual**. Pause briefly after **carry out** and again briefly after **that**.

Grant, we pray, almighty God,
that, always pondering spiritual things,
we may carry out in both word and deed
that which is pleasing to you.
Through our Lord Jesus Christ, your Son,
who lives and reigns with you in the unity of the Holy Spirit,
one God, for ever and ever.

Prayer over the Offerings

Pause briefly after **observance** and **offer**.

Place parallel emphasis on **honor** and **majesty**.

As we celebrate your mysteries, O Lord,
with the observance that is your due,
we humbly ask you,
that what we offer to the honor of your majesty
may profit us for salvation.
Through Christ our Lord. *

Prayer after Communion

Pause briefly after **we pray**. Express **experience** and **effects** with parallel emphasis and a certain desire. Stress **pledged** and pause briefly after **us**.

Grant, we pray, almighty God,
that we may experience the effects of the salvation
which is pledged to us by these mysteries.
Through Christ our Lord.

* Select from Prefaces I–VIII of the Sundays in Ordinary Time in the Order of Mass. Commentary, and proclamation and chant tips, for the Preface can be found at *www.StudyThePresidentialTexts.com/Prefaces* and in *The Order of Mass: A Roman Missal Study Edition and Workbook*, pages 62–77.

Collect: This prayer reminds us that to be pleasing to God, we must be more than mere talk. It is not enough to cry "Lord, Lord." The verb to carry out (*exsequentes*) stresses that our words and actions cannot be for certain times. We must act with integrity, in private and in public, until the conclusion of our life. There is some advice offered for how we may be strengthened to accomplish such a large task. It is by "always pondering spiritual things." The idea is that we should strive to see and do everything from the perspective of heaven, of "spiritual things." The Latin word is *rationabilia*, which calls to mind the Logos of John's Gospel, the incarnate Word, who is fully permeated by the divine Spirit and is the ordering principle behind all created things. In all that we do, no matter how mundane, with the help of God's grace, we can perceive the plan of God behind it. Coming to perceive God's plan in creation is the grace we need to be pleasing to him "in both word and deed."

Prayer over the Offerings: The word translated as "celebrate" (*exsequentes*) more literally means "to pursue to the end." The "mysteries" are the saving events of the life of Christ from his conception to his Second Coming that are made sacramentally present in the liturgy. The Christian strives to make these events our own. The "observance" that is the Father's due is the perfect self-offering of Christ, whom the Church offers on the altar. "Observance" refers to the liturgical services of the Church. The initial content of

Pointed Text

Collect

A Grant, we pray, almighty **God**,
B that, always pondering spir**it**ual things,
C we may carry out in both word and deed
that which is pleasing to ***you***.
Through our Lord Jesus Christ, your Son,
who lives and reigns with you in the unity of the Holy Spirit,
one God, for ever and ever.

Prayer over the Offerings

A As we celebrate your mysteries, O Lord,
with the observance that is your **due**,
B we **hum**bly ask you,
C that what we offer to the honor of your majesty
may profit us for salva***tion***.
Through Christ our Lord.

Prayer after Communion

A Grant, we pray, almighty **God**,
B that we may experience the effects of **the** salvation
C which is pledged to us by these mys***ter***ies.
Through Christ our Lord.

The space below is for your notes.

Refer to pages viii–x for an explanation of the pointing of the chants and to page xii for the Tones for the Presidential Prayers from *The Roman Missal*.

"what we offer" is whatever Priest and people lay on the altar from the substance of their lives. When we honestly offer some part of ourselves, it gives "honor" to God, though this honor is brought to perfection only when our offerings are united to the sacrifice of Christ in the Eucharist. If we open our hearts to Christ in this way, then he will become part of us as we receive Communion, or better, we will become part of him.

Prayer after Communion: The "effects" of our salvation are tantalizing thoughts to ponder. We have the Resurrection appearances of Christ to whet our appetite. In some ways, though, it is perhaps better to ponder not so much the "effects" of salvation as salvation itself. Salvation is to be in right relationship with God. From such right relationship flow many things. Being right with God is to be filled with perfect love, which means that all fear would be driven out. No more fear of death or injury. No more fear of not being loved, of not being good enough, of not being talented enough. It is good to pray for such things, but in this life, and specifically in Holy Communion (and in every gift of the Holy Spirit), we receive only a "pledge" of the fullness yet to come. This limitation is because we have not yet experienced the transformation of resurrection which would make us capable of receiving fully what we have already received in Sacrament.

EIGHTH SUNDAY IN ORDINARY TIME

Collect

Pause briefly after **Grant us**. Parallel emphasis on **course** and **directed**. Proclaim **peaceful rule** with stated tranquility. Keep the voice raised with **rejoice** and speak it with some energy. Proclaim **untroubled** with strong faith.

Grant us, O Lord, we pray,
that the course of our world
may be directed by your peaceful rule
and that your Church may rejoice,
untroubled in her devotion.
Through our Lord Jesus Christ, your Son,
who lives and reigns with you in the unity of the Holy Spirit,
one God, for ever and ever.

Prayer over the Offerings

Pause briefly after **O God** and very briefly after **gifts**. Pronounce ob-LA-tions (not o-BLA-tions). Pause briefly after **oblations** but not after **signs**, which is part of the phrase: **signs of our desire**. Proclaim **we ask of your mercy** with gentle and humble graciousness. Pause briefly after **grant** and after **help us**. Parallel **source of merit** and **merit's reward**.

O God, who provide gifts to be offered to your name
and count our oblations as signs
of our desire to serve you with devotion,
we ask of your mercy
that what you grant as the source of merit
may also help us to attain merit's reward.
Through Christ our Lord. *

Prayer after Communion

Stress **nourished** and **saving**. Proclaim **beseech your mercy** with knowledge of our need. Keep the voice raised with **Sacrament**. Parallel **feed us in the present age** and **partakers of life eternal**.

Nourished by your saving gifts,
we beseech your mercy, Lord,
that by this same Sacrament
with which you feed us in the present age,
you may make us partakers of life eternal.
Through Christ our Lord.

* Select from Prefaces I–VIII of the Sundays in Ordinary Time in the Order of Mass. Commentary, and proclamation and chant tips, for the Preface can be found at *www.StudyThePresidentialTexts.com/Prefaces* and in *The Order of Mass: A Roman Missal Study Edition and Workbook*, pages 62–77.

Collect: The translation of this prayer leaves out a phrase that would add a certain clarity and emphasis to its meaning. The Latin prays that the world be directed by God's rule, which is peaceful to us. That little phrase brings out the sacrificial character of this prayer. God rules the world with justice, and our sinfulness calls for justice in the same way that society calls for justice after a crime. In the sacrifice of God's Son on the cross, the path to peace from our sinfulness has been opened, and God's "rule" to us can be peaceful. It is important to note that the "peaceful rule" of this prayer is less concerned with the lack of conflict than with reconciliation of humanity to God. This enables the Church to be "untroubled in devotion." She stands confident that the sacrifice of Christ has firmly established this peace and she has only to be a living example of it to the world to fulfill her mission. The Church's "devotion" is precisely her fidelity to representing Christ's peace to the world.

Prayer over the Offerings: The "gifts" that the Lord provides in the Eucharist are the bread and wine. These gifts become "our oblations" when we make them ours by transforming them into "signs of our desire." The most important thing that we bring to the Eucharist is desire. Here we find direction to serve the one we love. Being in love brings a desire to do everything for the other with a personal touch. This is what "devotion" means. It is the fruit of love that seeks some personal expression of that love. For example, in the

Pointed Text

Collect

A Grant us, O Lord, we **pray**,
B that the course of our world
may be directed by your peaceful rule
and that your Church **may** rejoice,
C untroubled in her devo***tion***.
Through our Lord Jesus Christ, your Son,
who lives and reigns with you in the unity of the Holy Spirit,
one God, for ever and ever.

Prayer over the Offerings

A O God, who provide gifts to be offered to your name
and count our oblations as signs
of our desire to serve you with devo**tion**,
B we ask of your mercy
that what you grant as the **source** of merit
C may also help us to attain merit's re***ward***.
Through Christ our Lord.

Prayer after Communion

A Nourished by your saving gifts,
we beseech your mercy, **Lord**,
B that by this same Sacrament
with which you feed us in the **pre**sent age,
C you may make us partakers of life eter***nal***.
Through Christ our Lord.

The space below is for your notes.

Refer to pages viii–x for an explanation of the pointing of the chants and to page xii for the Tones for the Presidential Prayers from *The Roman Missal*.

Eucharist, we (quietly) personalize the gifts by placing on them our struggles. When we do this, the gifts become oblations. The "source of merit" for us is the glorified person of Christ, who sends upon us his Holy Spirit. This "source" is manifested in the graces that come throughout the day. Such graces (merit) attain their proper reward in the perfection of the Spirit. To see such a reward is to catch a glimpse of humanity redeemed.

Prayer after Communion: The Latin for "gifts" is *munere*, which is singular. The many gifts that we offer in the Eucharist are returned to us in Holy Communion as one gift, all united in Christ. The word for "nourished" (*satiati*) could also be translated as satisfied or satiated. No person or thing can satisfy our heart, because we have been created to be companions of the absolute. Holy Communion is intended to strengthen us to live a life of faith and witness "in the present age." The Word proclaimed earlier from the ambo is received sacramentally in Communion. It helps us to untangle our hearts, where desires are pulled in countless directions. In the Eucharist, we perceive our true nourishment and the other thirsts as so many variations on this thirst for God. As we let the Sacrament work to heal and nurture us, we are being prepared from the inside out for the kind of life awaiting us in heaven. In heaven, we will drink from the stream of Life itself, which is the Holy Spirit.

NINTH SUNDAY IN ORDINARY TIME

Collect

Pause briefly after **O God**. Stress **never fails**. Pause briefly after **from us**, and again after **grant all**. Try to bring out the parallels between **keep from us** and **grant all** and between **that might harm us** and **that works for our good**.

O God, whose providence never fails in its design,
keep from us, we humbly beseech you,
all that might harm us
and grant all that works for our good.
Through our Lord Jesus Christ, your Son,
who lives and reigns with you in the unity of the Holy Spirit,
one God, for ever and ever.

Prayer over the Offerings

Pause briefly after **compassion**, which should be proclaimed with humility. Proclaim **eagerly** and **sacred** with energy and pause briefly after **offerings**. Draw out the word **purifying**. Stress **cleansed** and **very mysteries**.

Trusting in your compassion, O Lord,
we come eagerly with our offerings to your sacred altar,
that, through the purifying action of your grace,
we may be cleansed by the very mysteries we serve.
Through Christ our Lord. *

Prayer after Communion

Pause briefly after **Spirit** and equally briefly after **feed**.
Pause after **professing you** (but not after **that**). Catch the rhythm between **not just** and **but also**. Keep the voice raised on **truth**. Pause briefly after **enter** to stress **Kingdom of Heaven**.

Govern by your Spirit, we pray, O Lord,
those you feed with the Body and Blood of your Son,
that, professing you not just in word or in speech,
but also in works and in truth,
we may merit to enter the Kingdom of Heaven.
Through Christ our Lord.

* Select from Prefaces I–VIII of the Sundays in Ordinary Time in the Order of Mass. Commentary, and proclamation and chant tips, for the Preface can be found at *www.StudyThePresidentialTexts.com/Prefaces* and in *The Order of Mass: A Roman Missal Study Edition and Workbook*, pages 62–77.

Collect: God's "providence" is to be Emmanuel to the human race. He is always with us in whatever events that may come our way. Sometimes we question where God was when evil things have happened. In the moment, we can be so caught up in our emotion that we are unable to perceive anything or anyone else. God is certainly present and with his power to save, but there are two further factors to consider. First is whether we called upon the Lord, who never imposes himself upon the unwilling. God has a passion for our freedom and will never compromise that (and oftentimes there are multiple human wills involved). Second, we are often quick to fault God for failing to do a good thing for us, but in reality it is difficult for humans to see clearly what is truly "harmful" for us and what works most "for our good." The sickness of a parent might be the occasion for reconciliation in the family, for growth in selfless love, or for accepting our powerlessness and surrendering to the almighty.

Prayer over the Offerings: The word translated as "compassion" is *pietate*, which refers to the type of devotion owed between a parent and child. As the Priest prepares to enter heaven symbolically in the Eucharistic Prayer, he calls upon the Fatherly love that God has for his Son, and for us in his Son. The Eucharistic Prayer is the dialogue between the Father and the Son in which the Church inserts herself. This is why it is most fitting to invoke *pietas* in the Prayer over the Offerings. The word for "we serve" is *famulamur*, which

Pointed Text

Collect

A O God, whose providence never fails in its de**sign**,
B keep from us, we humbly beseech you,
all **that** might harm us
C and grant all that works for our ***good***.
Through our Lord Jesus Christ, your Son,
who lives and reigns with you in the unity of the Holy Spirit,
one God, for ever and ever.

Prayer over the Offerings

A Trusting in your compassion, O **Lord**,
B we come eagerly with our offerings to your **sa**cred altar,
C that, through the purifying action of your grace,
we may be cleansed by the very mysteries we ***serve***.
Through Christ our Lord.

Prayer after Communion

A Govern by your Spirit, we pray, O Lord,
those you feed with the Body and Blood of your **Son**,
B that, professing you not just in word or in speech,
but also in works **and** in truth,
C we may merit to enter the Kingdom of Hea***ven***.
Through Christ our Lord.

The space below is for your notes.

Refer to pages viii–x for an explanation of the pointing of the chants and to page xii for the Tones for the Presidential Prayers from *The Roman Missal*.

calls to mind the service of a household servant. The "sacred altar" is symbolic of the most sacred altar in heaven, the risen Body of Christ. Having invoked *pietas*, the Priest "comes eagerly with our offerings" to unite them to Christ. The reason for our eagerness is our desire to "be cleansed" by the "purifying action" of grace. This is the Holy Spirit who will be called upon in the epiclesis of the Prayer to take away all that is not of Jesus.

Prayer after Communion: In raising Christ from the dead, the Holy Spirit completely permeated the Body of Christ so that he "became a lifegiving spirit" (1 Corinthians 15:45). When the faithful receive Christ in the Sacrament of his Body and Blood, they receive this spiritualized Body, and the Spirit who governs Christ knocks at the door of each one's heart to govern there, too. We are to live by the Spirit and not by the flesh (Romans 8:2–17). If we cooperate with him, then he will lead us from glory to glory. The Spirit will push us to live what we profess. The word translated as "speech" is *lingua*, which can also mean tongue. There is a contrast between "word" and "works," and "speech" and "truth." In Latin, the play with "tongue" may call to mind that sometimes we can speak with a forked tongue. Allowing ourselves to be governed by the Spirit is equal to allowing ourselves to be governed by Christ, the King. If Christ is our King, then we have already entered his Kingdom.

TENTH SUNDAY IN ORDINARY TIME

Collect

Pause briefly after **O God** and briefly after **we**. Proclaim **call on you** with a pleading confidence. Pause briefly after **prompting**. Keep the voice raised with **right**. Give a parallel rhythm to **at your prompting** and **by your guidance**.

O God, from whom all good things come,
grant that we, who call on you in our need,
may at your prompting discern what is right,
and by your guidance do it.
Through our Lord Jesus Christ, your Son,
who lives and reigns with you in the unity of the Holy Spirit,
one God, for ever and ever.

Prayer over the Offerings

Pause briefly after **service**. Place emphasis on **acceptable** and pronounce **ob-LA-tion**.
Speak more slowly the phrases **to grow** and **in charity**.

Look kindly upon our service, O Lord, we pray,
that what we offer
may be an acceptable oblation to you
and lead us to grow in charity.
Through Christ our Lord. *

Prayer after Communion

Proclaim **healing work** with soothing gentleness.
Pause briefly after **we pray** and briefly after **lead us**. Speak **to what is right** slowly, with emphasis on **right**.

May your healing work, O Lord,
free us, we pray, from doing evil
and lead us to what is right.
Through Christ our Lord.

* Select from Prefaces I–VIII of the Sundays in Ordinary Time in the Order of Mass. Commentary, and proclamation and chant tips, for the Preface can be found at *www.StudyThePresidentialTexts.com/Prefaces* and in *The Order of Mass: A Roman Missal Study Edition and Workbook*, pages 62–77.

Collect: There is the order of creation and of grace, and God is the source for both. It is in this twofold sense that the prayer says "all good things come" from him. To be a good Christian, it is imperative to be aware of "our need." Being a Christian, by definition, means to let Christ accomplish what we cannot. When the prayer asks to "discern what is right," this refers, in part at least, to discerning the needs of ourselves and others so that we will know what to ask from God. Such knowledge is given to us by the light of the Holy Spirit: "at your prompting." One of the gifts of the Spirit is knowledge, and this includes foremost, knowledge of self, which leads to calling on God for help. Precisely because of our weaknesses, we need the Lord to be present with us from beginning to end, not only at the prompting of a good deed, but in the guiding of it to the end. The Christian must always be ready to turn inspiration into action, but never to do without the guidance of God.

Prayer over the Offerings: The "look" of the Lord is enough to make an oblation "acceptable." The look of a loved one can impact us for good or ill, to encourage or to discourage. No word need be spoken, because the face communicates an enormous amount of information to those acquainted with the person. The face of the Lord is Christ. In some way, the prayer is asking God to shine Christ upon our service and its oblation, and since the goal is to transform the oblation into Christ, this seems most fitting. "Our service" refers to

Pointed Text

Collect

A O God, from whom all good things **come**,
B grant that we, who call on you **in** our need,
C may at your prompting discern what is right,
and by your guidance do ***it***.
Through our Lord Jesus Christ, your Son,
who lives and reigns with you in the unity of the Holy Spirit,
one God, for ever and ever.

Prayer over the Offerings

A Look kindly upon our service, O Lord, we **pray**,
B that what we offer
may be an acceptable obla**tion** to you
C and lead us to grow in char***i***ty.
Through Christ our Lord.

Prayer after Communion

A May your healing work, O **Lord**,
B free us, we pray, from **do**ing evil
C and lead us to what is ***right***.
Through Christ our Lord.

The space below is for your notes.

Refer to pages viii–x for an explanation of the pointing of the chants and to page xii for the Tones for the Presidential Prayers from *The Roman Missal*.

the offering of the Eucharistic Prayer—the main "service" of the Mass. Every human being not corrupted by pride longs to be accepted by someone in this world. The Church, too, longs for her gift to be acceptable. The reason is so that the "acceptable oblation" can lead us deeper into "charity." This is no reference to almsgiving but to divine love itself. If our Eucharistic offering is accepted by God, then the fruits of that offering lead us deeper into God.

Prayer after Communion: Communion is often called a spiritual remedy. In the prayer, this "healing work" of the Lord is the means for two consequences: freeing from evil and leading to right. The word translated as "free . . . from," *expediat*, literally means to free one's foot from (e.g., a snare or trap). The word translated as "evil" is *perversitatibus* and may be translated as perversities, but it calls to mind feet wandering off the right path. The focus is on freeing "us" who do these things. The prayer acknowledges corruption within the human heart. The word *clementer* (translated here as "we pray") means with clemency, graciously, mercifully. Because we can do nothing to earn God's healing power, we invoke his clemency, to intervene. With the last line, there is a nice play between "free us . . . from wandering off the path" and "lead us to what is right." There is still a solid contrast between "evil" and "right," as well. The prayer ends with Christ leading God's people into what is right.

ELEVENTH SUNDAY IN ORDINARY TIME

Collect

Pause briefly after **O God**. Proclaim **strength** slowly but with great force.

Emphasize **without you** and pause briefly.

Emphasize **always** and **following**. Pause briefly after **please you** and give parallel stress to **our resolve** and **our deeds**.

O God, strength of those who hope in you,
graciously hear our pleas,
and, since without you mortal frailty can do nothing,
grant us always the help of your grace,
that in following your commands
we may please you by our resolve and our deeds.
Through our Lord Jesus Christ, your Son,
who lives and reigns with you in the unity of the Holy Spirit,
one God, for ever and ever.

Prayer over the Offerings

Pause briefly after **O God**. Stress **twofold needs**.

Keep the voice raised with **food**.

Proclaim **sustenance** with gentle conviction. Emphasize **body or in spirit**.

O God, who in the offerings presented here
provide for the twofold needs of human nature,
nourishing us with food
and renewing us with your Sacrament,
grant, we pray,
that the sustenance they provide
may not fail us in body or in spirit.
Through Christ our Lord. *

Prayer after Communion

Emphasize **Holy**. Stress **union** and **you**. Place a similar emphasis on **in your Church** as on **in you**.

As this reception of your Holy Communion, O Lord,
foreshadows the union of the faithful in you,
so may it bring about unity in your Church.
Through Christ our Lord.

* Select from Prefaces I–VIII of the Sundays in Ordinary Time in the Order of Mass. Commentary, and proclamation and chant tips, for the Preface can be found at *www.StudyThePresidentialTexts.com/Prefaces* and in *The Order of Mass: A Roman Missal Study Edition and Workbook*, pages 62–77.

Collect: The virtue of hope requires some assurance to be persevering until the end. We desire some sign of the master's approval that our work in his absence is pleasing. Strength is named as the virtue that will keep hope bright, but it is not any strength, but the strength of God. This is then contrasted with "mortal frailty," which will always need "help." God's grace is specifically invoked in two areas: "our resolve" (*voluntate*) and "our deeds" (*actione*). "Resolve" refers to firm decisions of the will, the ones that set us securely on a path. The "will" is an important area of Church teaching. We do not move God by our thoughts, but by acts of the will and by the way we live "our deeds." The understanding, then, is that, first, we receive grace, which can lead to a firm resolve to change our behavior, and then to the changed behavior itself. The beauty of the prayer (and this process) is the combination of grace and mortal frailty, which leads to the "following" of God's "commands."

Prayer over the Offerings: Jesus possessed two natures, one human, one divine. We possess only a human nature, but that nature has a twofold aspect. We are both physical and spiritual, and each aspect has needs or hungers. The Eucharist addresses this twofold need. The accidents of bread and wine nourish the body, and the substance of Christ's Body and Blood renews our spirit. The Lord has not rejected the body in favor of the spirit. To the contrary, he sustains the first eagerly, but with the express purpose of bringing it under

Pointed Text

Collect

A O God, strength of those who hope in you,
graciously hear our **pleas**,
B and, since without you mortal frailty can do nothing,
grant us always the help **of** your grace,
C that in following your commands
we may please you by our resolve and our ***deeds***.
Through our Lord Jesus Christ, your Son,
who lives and reigns with you in the unity of the Holy Spirit,
one God, for ever and ever.

Prayer over the Offerings

A O God, who in the offerings presented here
provide for the twofold needs of human na**ture**,
B nourishing us with food
and renewing us **with** your Sacrament,
C grant, we pray,
that the sustenance they provide
may not fail us in body or in spir***it***.
Through Christ our Lord.

Prayer after Communion

B As this reception of your Holy Communion, O Lord,
foreshadows the union of the faith**ful** in you,
C so may it bring about unity in your ***Church***.
Through Christ our Lord.

The space below is for your notes.

Refer to pages viii–x for an explanation of the pointing of the chants and to page xii for the Tones for the Presidential Prayers from *The Roman Missal*.

submission to the latter. This kind of submission enabled Jesus to lay down his life freely unto death. In the garden of Gethsemani, his flesh drew back in anticipation, but he subdued it and willingly underwent his Passion. When we receive this offering in faith, it does not fade with time. It becomes like a perpetual spring that wells up from within us, in accordance both with our faith and with the strength of our spirit to drink it in.

Prayer after Communion: The prayer expresses the paradox in Communion of "who receives whom?" On the one hand, we receive Christ into us by "reception" of Holy Communion, but this action foreshadows the fact that we are being received into Christ. Our "union" with Christ is still incomplete in this world. Until we are able to suffer the coming of the Spirit as completely as Jesus, our union will remain partial. Every excess in this life demonstrates tragically our incompleteness and desire for union. If all the members of the Church, however, are striving to enter Christ, then unity among the members will follow. We can never seek union with Christ secondarily to union with another. It will not work. God alone can satisfy the deep longings of the human heart. God must always come first. The petition for unity in the Church recognizes the necessity of solidarity in this life. We must acknowledge the solitude that we bear and support one another in dealing with it appropriately.

TWELFTH SUNDAY IN ORDINARY TIME

Collect

Proclaim **revere and love** slowly and deliberately. Keep the voice raised with **guidance**. Pause briefly after **firm**. Proclaim **firm** and **foundation** with strength.

Grant, O Lord,
that we may always revere and love your holy name,
for you never deprive of your guidance
those you set firm on the foundation of your love.
Through our Lord Jesus Christ, your Son,
who lives and reigns with you in the unity of the Holy Spirit,
one God, for ever and ever.

Prayer over the Offerings

Pause briefly after **O Lord**.
Pause after **grant that**.
Pause briefly after **offering**. Proclaim **heart pleasing to you** with joyful hope.

Receive, O Lord, the sacrifice of conciliation and praise
and grant that, cleansed by its action,
we may make offering of a heart pleasing to you.
Through Christ our Lord. *

Prayer after Communion

Proclaim **renewed and nourished** with energy and gratitude. Pause briefly after **Body** and **Blood** and proclaim each with reverence. Strong emphasis on **constant devotion**. Proclaim **sure pledge** with confidence and **redemption** with quiet strength.

Renewed and nourished
by the Sacred Body and Precious Blood of your Son,
we ask of your mercy, O Lord,
that what we celebrate with constant devotion
may be our sure pledge of redemption.
Through Christ our Lord.

* Select from Prefaces I–VIII of the Sundays in Ordinary Time in the Order of Mass. Commentary, and proclamation and chant tips, for the Preface can be found at *www.StudyThePresidentialTexts.com/Prefaces* and in *The Order of Mass: A Roman Missal Study Edition and Workbook*, pages 62–77.

Collect: Four important words need to be explained in this prayer. The Latin for "revere" is *timor*, meaning fear or dread. It implies being overwhelmed by one greater than ourselves. Alongside reverence, the prayer asks "equally" (*pariter* is not translated) for "love." *Amor* refers to an instinctual desire for union with another. The combination of *timor* and *amor* connotes a fascination with the God who is Beauty, Goodness, Truth, and Power beyond imagination. Reverence keeps us humble, while love draws us on. The end of the prayer asks that we be set firm on the "foundation of your love," *dilectio*, which means esteem or regard. It is a deep love that we give because of who the other has become to us. Thus, the Father calls Jesus his "beloved Son." God sets us on the foundation of the "love," which he has for his own Son. Lastly, the "guidance" which God provides is the indwelling of the Holy Spirit in those who have been "set firm" in Christ through Baptism.

Prayer over the Offerings: The "sacrifice" that we offer is Christ, who reconciled the world to God in himself. The prayer asks the Father to receive the Death and Resurrection of his Son, which "cleansed" us. Through Baptism, we are washed in his sacrifice, which brings us back to right relationship with God, and leads to praise. In the Eucharist, the cleansing power of the cross is made present to us ritually, and we are given the opportunity to "receive the sacrifice" as well. The prayer asks the Father to "receive" it, but its power for us is

Pointed Text

Collect

A Grant, O Lord,
that we may always revere and love your holy **name**,
B for you never deprive **of** your guidance
C those you set firm on the foundation of your ***love***.
Through our Lord Jesus Christ, your Son,
who lives and reigns with you in the unity of the Holy Spirit,
one God, for ever and ever.

Prayer over the Offerings

A Receive, O Lord, the sacrifice of conciliation and **praise**
B and grant that, cleansed **by** its action,
C we may make offering of a heart pleasing to ***you***.
Through Christ our Lord.

Prayer after Communion

A Renewed and nourished
by the Sacred Body and Precious Blood of your **Son**,
B we ask of your mer**cy**, O Lord,
C that what we celebrate with constant devotion
may be our sure pledge of redemp***tion***.
Through Christ our Lord.

The space below is for your notes.

Refer to pages viii–x for an explanation of the pointing of the chants and to page xii for the Tones for the Presidential Prayers from *The Roman Missal*.

effective only when we, too, "receive" it. Being cleansed by Jesus means being given a share in his suffering and Death. Psalm 51:19 says "God, do not spurn a broken, humbled heart." The heart that is "pleasing" to God has united itself to the sacrifice of Christ. In practice this means giving ourselves in love for others without reserve. The broken heart is alive and full of affection. It is capable of loving and being loved.

Prayer after Communion: The word translated as "nourished" (*alimonia*) implies the healthy kind of growth that would enable one to reach old age. The "nourishment" of Christ's Body and Blood leads us deeper to "maturity, to the measure of the full stature of Christ" (Ephesians 4:13). This heavenly food promotes our growth in Christ. Just as a child is regularly nurtured, the Christian must return to the Eucharist "with constant devotion." Our hearts must be continually renewed because the world saps the growth we gain spiritually from the Sacraments. The mystery of Christ, however, is greater than the world. That mystery is given to us in Holy Communion as a "sure pledge" of the redemption that has already been achieved in Christ. As we receive the redeemed humanity of Christ in Communion, his redemption grows in us and becomes our redemption. What we enact in mystery begins to live in us in reality. The Death of Christ grows in us until we die in him and then are raised in him.

THIRTEENTH SUNDAY IN ORDINARY TIME

Brief pause after **O God**. Give parallel emphasis to **grace of adoption** and **children of light**. Proclaim with an insistent pleading **may not be wrapped** and **always be seen to stand**. Parallel the rhythm of **in the darkness of error** and **in the bright light of truth**, though proclaim the first with dread and the second with joy.

Collect

O God, who through the grace of adoption
chose us to be children of light,
grant, we pray,
that we may not be wrapped in the darkness of error
but always be seen to stand in the bright light of truth.
Through our Lord Jesus Christ, your Son,
who lives and reigns with you in the unity of the Holy Spirit,
one God, for ever and ever.

Brief pause after **O God**. Proclaim **graciously** with dignity and **effects** with energy. Parallel **deeds** and **worthy**. Proclaim **sacred gifts** with reverence.

Prayer over the Offerings

O God, who graciously accomplish
the effects of your mysteries,
grant, we pray,
that the deeds by which we serve you
may be worthy of these sacred gifts.
Through Christ our Lord. *

Proclaim **offered** and **received** slowly and emphatically. Brief pause after **life**. Brief pause after **so that**. Pray **bound** with a measure of enthusiasm and **lasting charity** with firm conviction. Brief pause after **fruit**.

Prayer after Communion

May this divine sacrifice we have offered and received
fill us with life, O Lord, we pray,
so that, bound to you in lasting charity,
we may bear fruit that lasts for ever.
Through Christ our Lord.

* Select from Prefaces I–VIII of the Sundays in Ordinary Time in the Order of Mass. Commentary, and proclamation and chant tips, for the Preface can be found at *www.StudyThePresidentialTexts.com/Prefaces* and in *The Order of Mass: A Roman Missal Study Edition and Workbook*, pages 62–77.

Collect: The verb translated as "chose" (*voluisti*) also means "willed." The fact that God has chosen us to be "children of light" is a matter of divine will. The word for "light" (*lux, lucis*) refers to God ("God is light . . ." [1 John 1:5]). From all eternity, God has willed us to be his children by adoption, and in his Son and through his Holy Spirit ("grace") he has "chosen us." The phrase "grace of adoption" is reversed in the Latin: "adoption of grace," which communicates that this adoption is different from others. It is adoption in grace, which is to say, in the Holy Spirit, meaning that this adoption changes our nature. It raises us from "the darkness of error." We are given renewed vision to see the foolishness of our former desires. When we are "wrapped" in sin, even knowledge of error does not keep us from it. The adoption of "grace" is not only an intellectual enlightenment, in which we see our errors, but are helpless to change them. Grace also sets our whole person in truth, that is, in Christ.

Prayer over the Offerings: What are the "effects" of God's mysteries? The primary "work" of God is the Paschal Mystery. The goal of this work, which is here called its "effects," is to bring humanity into union with God through Christ. The "effects" of these mysteries, then, is the transformation of humanity into Christ. God's work in Christ has been accomplished. What remains is his work of bringing us into the same risen glory and interior union. Our work is to make our "deeds" fittingly serve God by being more Christ-like, that is, by

Pointed Text

Collect

A O God, who through the grace of adoption
chose us to be children of **light**,
B grant, we pray,
that we may not be wrapped in the dark**ness** of error
C but always be seen to stand in the bright light of ***truth***.
Through our Lord Jesus Christ, your Son,
who lives and reigns with you in the unity of the Holy Spirit,
one God, for ever and ever.

Prayer over the Offerings

A O God, who graciously accomplish
the effects of your mys**ter**ies,
B grant, we pray,
that the deeds by **which** we serve you
C may be worthy of these sacred ***gifts***.
Through Christ our Lord.

Prayer after Communion

A May this divine sacrifice we have offered and received
fill us with life, O Lord, we **pray**,
B so that, bound to you in **last**ing charity,
C we may bear fruit that lasts for e***ver***.
Through Christ our Lord.

The space below is for your notes.

Refer to pages viii–x for an explanation of the pointing of the chants and to page xii for the Tones for the Presidential Prayers from *The Roman Missal.*

becoming ever more other-centered. The prayer implies that our "deeds" of service are to become the "sacred gifts" offered on the altar. This is how our deeds become fitting: they must be placed upon the "sacred gifts" to be offered in the Eucharist. In doing this, we let go of any attachment to them, and we surrender to the Lord's purifying action. Our goal is to imitate the holiness we celebrate in the liturgy.

Prayer after Communion: The word translated as "sacrifice" (*hostia*) can also refer to the one who is sacrificed. By adding the adjective "divine," the prayer is clear that the reference is to Jesus. In the Eucharist, we offer and receive Christ, our victim, priest, and altar. Through the sacrifice of Christ, we are filled with the Holy Spirit, the Lord and giver of life. When Jesus was broken upon the Cross, he breathed his life-giving Spirit upon the Church, and all that was good in him was opened up to the Church. The word "charity" calls to mind the love of total self-gift that is at the heart of the Trinity, which Christ revealed on the Cross, and which the Holy Spirit communicates to the Church. In the Eucharistic sacrifice, we become "bound" to God in this kind of self-gift. The phrase translated as "lasts for ever" is *semper maneat*, which comes from the farewell discourse of John, in which Jesus says that we cannot bear fruit unless we remain in him (John 15:4). To be "bound in charity" is to remain in him.

FOURTEENTH SUNDAY IN ORDINARY TIME

Collect

Pause briefly after **O God**. Proclaim **abasement of your Son** in the knowledge of the line that follows. Stress **holy**. Emphasize **rescued** and **sin**, keeping the voice raised with **sin**. Stress **eternal**.

O God, who in the abasement of your Son
have raised up a fallen world,
fill your faithful with holy joy,
for on those you have rescued from slavery to sin
you bestow eternal gladness.
Through our Lord Jesus Christ, your Son,
who lives and reigns with you in the unity of the Holy Spirit,
one God, for ever and ever.

Prayer over the Offerings

Pause briefly after **oblation** (pronounced ob-LA-tion). Proclaim **purify** with a note of confident pleading. Pause briefly after **day by day**. Stress **closer**.

May this oblation dedicated to your name
purify us, O Lord,
and day by day bring our conduct
closer to the life of heaven.
Through Christ our Lord. *

Prayer after Communion

Pause briefly after **Grant**. Proclaim **such great gifts** slowly and deliberately. Proclaim **prize of salvation** with reverent awe and elation. Proclaim the last line with evident gratitude.

Grant, we pray, O Lord,
that, having been replenished by such great gifts,
we may gain the prize of salvation
and never cease to praise you.
Through Christ our Lord.

* Select from Prefaces I–VIII of the Sundays in Ordinary Time in the Order of Mass. Commentary, and proclamation and chant tips, for the Preface can be found at *www.StudyThePresidentialTexts.com/Prefaces* and in *The Order of Mass: A Roman Missal Study Edition and Workbook*, pages 62–77.

Collect: Humility is truth. The word translated as "abasement" is *humilitas* (humility). In the "abasement" of Jesus, humanity finds itself precisely where it should be in relation to God and the world. Jesus did not want for the necessities of life (food, clothing, and shelter), yet he also lived the virtue of poverty, that is, all that he had he shared with others. Christ shared his life to the point of suffering and Death. The "truth" of our humanity lies in this revelation that for us to be "raised up," we must live a similar poverty. Emptied of the world, we can be filled with "holy joy" (*sanctam laetitiam*), which implies a spiritual gladness that comes from sharing what we have and who we are with others. "Slavery to sin" is when we chain ourselves to the things of this world, seeing them as our posssession and right, with little concern for others. The verb behind "bestow" is *perfrui* in Latin. This verb is used when we "enjoy" something or someone for its own sake (e.g., the eternal gladness of heaven).

Prayer over the Offerings: "Name" is a euphemism for God (cf. John 17:6, "I revealed your name . . ."). The "oblation" is being offered, or "dedicated," to God. In the end, we are offering Christ to God on our behalf. It is Christ, in the power of his Holy Spirit, who acts to "purify us." This is an interior purification; therefore, it is the work of the Spirit of Christ. The Latin of the last two lines differs in some regard from the translation. A more literal translation would be, "and day by day may it (the oblation) bear us on to the action of the heav-

Pointed Text

Collect

A O God, who in the abasement of your Son
have raised up a fallen **world**,
B fill your faithful with **ho**ly joy,
C for on those you have rescued from slavery to sin
you bestow eternal glad***ness***.
Through our Lord Jesus Christ, your Son,
who lives and reigns with you in the unity of the Holy Spirit,
one God, for ever and ever.

Prayer over the Offerings

B May this oblation dedicated to your name
purify **us**, O Lord,
C and day by day bring our conduct
closer to the life of hea***ven***.
Through Christ our Lord.

Prayer after Communion

A Grant, we pray, O **Lord**,
B that, having been replenished by **such** great gifts,
C we may gain the prize of salvation
and never cease to praise ***you***.
Through Christ our Lord.

The space below is for your notes.

Refer to pages viii–x for an explanation of the pointing of the chants and to page xii for the Tones for the Presidential Prayers from *The Roman Missal.*

enly life." The key word is "action," which the Church also uses to designate the Eucharistic "action" (*actio or actio sacrifica*). Our liturgical Eucharist is a Sacrament of the heavenly one. In this prayer, the Church asks that the action in the liturgy may carry us to the heavenly action to which it points. The translation captures this sense of our participation in the earthly liturgy bringing us closer to the heavenly one.

Prayer after Communion: Whenever we return to the Eucharist, we are filled again ("replenished") by the mystery of Christ communicated through the consecrated offerings: "such great gifts." Though filled with the Real Presence, it is possible for these gifts to fail in purpose. If we refuse the grace given, God leaves us in our stubbornness of heart. This is why the prayer beseeches that we may, in fact, gain what the Sacrament offers: the prize of salvation. More literally, this phrase may be translated as "salutary or salvific gifts." The "great gifts" (*muneribus*) become, when we open our hearts and minds to them, "saving gifts" (*salutaria dona*). Such graciousness stirs hearts to praise and if we receive worthily God's gifts, we have reason for eternal praise because we are granted eternal life. As Saint Augustine taught, our praise of God is not singing words of praise but living a life that fulfills God's plan in us. To live a Christian life to the full is to give God the best praise of all.

FIFTEENTH SUNDAY IN ORDINARY TIME

Collect

Pause briefly after **O God**. Stress **light of your truth**. Keep the voice raised with **astray**.
Do not pause significantly after **profess**.
Pause after **grace** and proclaim the parallel between **to reject whatever is contrary** and **to strive after all**.

O God, who show the light of your truth
to those who go astray,
so that they may return to the right path,
give all who for the faith they profess
are accounted Christians
the grace to reject whatever is contrary to the name of Christ
and to strive after all that does it honor.
Through our Lord Jesus Christ, your Son,
who lives and reigns with you in the unity of the Holy Spirit,
one God, for ever and ever.

Prayer over the Offerings

Pray the first line with humble pleading.

Pause after **grant that**. Proclaim **ever greater holiness** slowly and deliberately.

Look upon the offerings of the Church, O Lord,
as she makes her prayer to you,
and grant that, when consumed by those who believe,
they may bring ever greater holiness.
Through Christ our Lord. *

Prayer after Communion

Pause after **gifts**.

Parallel **participation** and **saving effects**. Proclaim **saving effects upon us** slowly. Pause briefly after **us**.

Having consumed these gifts, we pray, O Lord,
that, by our participation in this mystery,
its saving effects upon us may grow.
Through Christ our Lord.

* Select from Prefaces I–VIII of the Sundays in Ordinary Time in the Order of Mass. Commentary, and proclamation and chant tips, for the Preface can be found at *www.StudyThePresidentialTexts.com/Prefaces* and in *The Order of Mass: A Roman Missal Study Edition and Workbook*, pages 62–77.

Collect: The "light" of God's truth is *lumen*, which refers to the revelation or illumination of God. This is the light or glory that is reflected from Christ, who is Truth. Anyone or anything could be an instrument of *lumen* for God to bring another back to the faith. The Latin for "right path" is *via*. In the Acts of the Apostles, Christianity was called "the way," referring to the way of life, which is Christ, that the Christian follows. The rest of the prayer revolves around the "name." First, there is the name Christian and second, the name of Christ. This is about identity and integrity. We receive the name of Christian in Baptism. It is already defined for us. Christianity is not a way of life, but a life to be lived, and that life is Christ's. The content of our Christian life is already given. It is the Beatitudes, the evangelical counsels (poverty, chastity, and obedience), and to pray with and for the Church. In the end, it is to reject the world and to accept death. This is the "grace," the gift of Christianity.

Prayer over the Offerings: The prayer asks the Lord to "look upon" or consider the offerings placed on the altar. The idea is that the merciful gaze of the Lord can make them worthy. When each of the faithful surrender their gifts in the Eucharist, they become the Church's gifts, the prayer that the Church makes to God. Just prior to entering the Eucharistic Prayer, we ask God to look so that our offering may not be in vain. Notice the feminine pronouns in reference to the Church who is our mother and the bride of

Pointed Text

Collect

A O God, who show the light of your truth
to those who go astray,
so that they may return to the right **path**,
B give all who for the faith they profess
are accounted Christians
the grace to reject whatever is contrary to the **name** of Christ
C and to strive after all that does it ho***nor***.
Through our Lord Jesus Christ, your Son,
who lives and reigns with you in the unity of the Holy Spirit,
one God, for ever and ever.

Prayer over the Offerings

A Look upon the offerings of the Church, O Lord,
as she makes her prayer to **you**,
B and grant that, when consumed by those **who** believe,
C they may bring ever greater ho***li***ness.
Through Christ our Lord.

Prayer after Communion

A Having consumed these gifts, we pray, O **Lord**,
B that, by our participation **in** this mystery,
C its saving effects upon us may ***grow***.
Through Christ our Lord.

The space below is for your notes.

Refer to pages viii–x for an explanation of the pointing of the chants and to page xii for the Tones for the Presidential Prayers from *The Roman Missal*.

Christ. The main possession of the Church is her prayer. This prayer goes on to remind us of the necessity of faith for those who would benefit from this sacred action. The grace offered in any of the Sacraments is dependent on our faith to make that grace effective in us. As our faith deepens, the benefit we receive from the Sacrament will also grow. The combination of faith and the Sacrament will bring "ever greater holiness."

Prayer after Communion: As faithful believers, we are charged not only to "consume" the Body and Blood of the Lord, but to "participate" in his mystery. The more frequently that we share in Eucharist (the Latin for participation is actually *frequentatione*, which could be translated as "frequenting"), the more we are able to open ourselves to the life and power it makes present. God invites us to the liturgy over and over again so that we might grow out of sin and into holiness. This is an acknowledgment of our weakness. The "saving effects" (*nostrae salutis effectus*) of the Eucharist have to do with the mysteries of Christ becoming our mysteries. What Christ achieved in his person has passed over into the Sacraments, and when we receive the Sacraments, his accomplishments and grace pass to us. Christ forgave sins, and we can receive forgiveness of minor sins by receiving Communion worthily. Christ effected reconciliation, and we can experience the same reconciliation.

SIXTEENTH SUNDAY IN ORDINARY TIME

Collect

Strike a note of humble plea with **Show favor**. Proclaim **mercifully** with gentleness and **gifts of your grace** with reverent joy. Stress **fervent** and pause briefly. Proclaim **hope**, **faith and charity** slowly and deliberately. Stress **ever**. Pause briefly after **watchful**.

Show favor, O Lord, to your servants
and mercifully increase the gifts of your grace,
that, made fervent in hope, faith and charity,
they may be ever watchful in keeping your commands.
Through our Lord Jesus Christ, your Son,
who lives and reigns with you in the unity of the Holy Spirit,
one God, for ever and ever.

Prayer over the Offerings

Pause briefly after **O God**. Proclaim **one perfect sacrifice** with deliberate emphasis. Pause briefly after **completion**. Emphasis on **this sacrifice**. Proclaim **make it holy** with expectant confidence and pause briefly after **holy**. Emphasize **each has offered**. Proclaim **honor of your majesty** with reverence. Stress **all**.

O God, who in the one perfect sacrifice
brought to completion varied offerings of the law,
accept, we pray, this sacrifice from your faithful servants
and make it holy, as you blessed the gifts of Abel,
so that what each has offered to the honor of your majesty
may benefit the salvation of all.
Through Christ our Lord. *

Prayer after Communion

Proclaim **Graciously** with humble gentleness. Pause briefly after **people**. Stress **heavenly**. Place a parallel emphasis on **former ways** and **newness of life**.

Graciously be present to your people, we pray, O Lord,
and lead those you have imbued with heavenly mysteries
to pass from former ways to newness of life.
Through Christ our Lord.

* Select from Prefaces I–VIII of the Sundays in Ordinary Time in the Order of Mass. Commentary, and proclamation and chant tips, for the Preface can be found at *www.StudyThePresidentialTexts.com/Prefaces* and in *The Order of Mass: A Roman Missal Study Edition and Workbook*, pages 62–77.

Collect: "Show favor" (*Propitiare*) is a sacrificial term. This "favor" is sought after an apology and making amends. God has shown his favor in raising Christ Jesus from the dead. Because of this, all who approach God following in the footsteps of Christ can be assured of the same favor. The prayer boldly requests help in walking in the footsteps of Christ. The Holy Spirit is God's "grace," and the prayer seeks the "gifts" of that grace, specifically the theological virtues of "hope, faith and charity." No one could receive the "favor" of resurrection without these gifts. Placing hope ahead of faith, the prayer emphasizes the eschatological tenor of this prayer. Faith provides the content and reason to hope, but hope enables us to persevere. The Latin of the last line brings out this eschatological focus with the words persevere and vigil (*perseverent and vigili*). The way we keep God's commands (above all, the command to charity) is through vigilant perseverance, awaiting the resurrection.

Prayer over the Offerings: The verb "brought to completion" affirms the revelation of the Old Testament as authentically pointing to the Truth that was to come. In reading and studying the Old Testament, Christians can come to a fuller understanding of the New Testament revelation of Christ. Even though the Church believes that all sacrifices have been fulfilled in the "one perfect sacrifice" of Christ, she still uses the language of sacrifice for the Eucharist. We join ourselves to Christ's offering on the Cross. The prayer requests

Pointed Text

Collect

A Show favor, O Lord, to your servants
and mercifully increase the gifts of your **grace**,
B that, made fervent in hope, **faith** and charity,
C they may be ever watchful in keeping your com***mands***.
Through our Lord Jesus Christ, your Son,
who lives and reigns with you in the unity of the Holy Spirit,
one God, for ever and ever.

Prayer over the Offerings

A O God, who in the one perfect sacrifice
brought to completion varied offerings of the **law**,
B accept, we pray, this sacrifice from your faithful servants
and make it holy, as you blessed the **gifts** of Abel,
C so that what each has offered to the honor of your majesty
may benefit the salvation of ***all***.
Through Christ our Lord.

Prayer after Communion

A Graciously be present to your people, we pray, O **Lord**,
B and lead those you have imbued with hea***ven***ly mysteries
C to pass from former ways to newness of **life**.
Through Christ our Lord.

The space below is for your notes.

Refer to pages viii–x for an explanation of the pointing of the chants and to page xii for the Tones for the Presidential Prayers from *The Roman Missal*.

the Lord to "accept" and "make holy" the Eucharistic offerings "as you blessed" (the Latin has "with the same blessing") "the gifts of Abel." This is from the Roman Canon, which calls Abel "your servant Abel the just." As God was pleased to accept Abel's sacrifice, we ask him to accept and bless ours in his servant Christ. We offer something in the Mass for the benefit of all. The best way to inspire another's holiness is to grow in holiness oneself.

Prayer after Communion: Having just received Holy Communion, the Lord is certainly present to his people sacramentally. The prayer is not requesting God to be somewhere that he already is, but rather requesting that his presence be "gracious." The Latin is *propitius*, meaning beneficial. Receiving Communion requires faith (which is a grace) and an interior receptivity to the working of the Spirit. We have been "imbued with heavenly mysteries" in various ways in the course of Mass. This grace works to strengthen our hearts to trust more and love more. The stronger we become in these virtues, the more readily we will follow God's lead to make changes in our lives. Saint Paul writes of putting off the old man ("former ways") and putting on the new. The "old man" is the fallen Adam; the "new man" is the second Adam, risen and glorious. We "pass" from the first to the second through the suffering of the Cross, in which we put to death all attachments to the world.

SEVENTEENTH SUNDAY IN ORDINARY TIME

Pause briefly after **O God**. Stress **protector** and **hope**. Do not overstress **nothing** but give equal weight to **firm foundation** and **holy**. Proclaim **abundance** with energy, and pause briefly. Speak **mercy** with gentleness. Pause briefly after **grant that** and proclaim **ruler and guide** slowly and confidently. Speak **good things that pass** as one phrase with a steady inflection. Give parallel stress to **even now** and **ever endure**.

Collect

O God, protector of those who hope in you,
without whom nothing has firm foundation, nothing is holy,
bestow in abundance your mercy upon us
and grant that, with you as our ruler and guide,
we may use the good things that pass
in such a way as to hold fast even now
to those that ever endure.
Through our Lord Jesus Christ, your Son,
who lives and reigns with you in the unity of the Holy Spirit,
one God, for ever and ever.

Pause ever so briefly on either side of **O Lord, we pray**. No significant pause after **offerings**. Stress **powerful working** and **grace**. Proclaim **most sacred mysteries** with reverent awe and pause briefly. Keep the voice raised with **life**. Stress **eternal**.

Prayer over the Offerings

Accept, O Lord, we pray, the offerings
which we bring from the abundance of your gifts,
that through the powerful working of your grace
these most sacred mysteries may sanctify our present way of life
and lead us to eternal gladness.
Through Christ our Lord. *

The first two lines of this prayer should be proclaimed slowly and with evident awe and wonder. Pause briefly after **we pray** and stress **this gift**. Proclaim **love beyond all telling** with humble gratitude.

Prayer after Communion

We have consumed, O Lord, this divine Sacrament,
the perpetual memorial of the Passion of your Son;
grant, we pray, that this gift,
which he himself gave us with love beyond all telling,
may profit us for salvation.
Through Christ our Lord.

* Select from Prefaces I–VIII of the Sundays in Ordinary Time in the Order of Mass. Commentary, and proclamation and chant tips, for the Preface can be found at *www.StudyThePresidentialTexts.com/Prefaces* and in *The Order of Mass: A Roman Missal Study Edition and Workbook*, pages 62–77.

Collect: We must be careful how we understand God as "protector." God protects the "firm foundation" on which we walk in faith toward heaven. God protects our "holiness" by bestowing his mercy "in abundance" upon us when we sin. God is "ruler" in the sense of one who leads us into "right" ways, safe for reaching heaven, though not necessarily safe for avoiding turmoil in this life. God is "guide" in the sense that he is always with us, especially in turmoil. With this clearer understanding of God's action in the world, we can grasp the petition that we use the things of this world, even the "good things," always with a view to their helping us to set our hearts more firmly on heavenly realities. With our eyes fixed firmly on the goal, we will be less distracted by the baubles of this world or by its suffering. We experience good things in this life that will endure, especially the friendships established in honesty and integrity, and we do well to value them into eternity.

Prayer over the Offerings: God has given us from his "abundance" life, ability, and countless helps. We can offer in thanksgiving the gifts we have developed and used well, or we can offer from our weakness the gifts still in need of maturing or even that have been perverted through our sinfulness. The "powerful working" of God's grace can receive and transform them. The phrase "our present way of life" is a translation of the Latin *praesentis vitae nos conversatione*. The key word is the last one, which can mean way of life, but refers to

Pointed Text

Collect

A O God, protector of those who hope in you,
without whom nothing has firm foundation, nothing is ho**ly**,
B bestow in abundance your mercy upon us
and grant that, with you as our rul**er** and guide,
C we may use the good things that pass
in such a way as to hold fast even now
to those that ever en***dure***.
Through our Lord Jesus Christ, your Son,
who lives and reigns with you in the unity of the Holy Spirit,
one God, for ever and ever.

Prayer over the Offerings

A Accept, O Lord, we pray, the offerings
which we bring from the abundance of your **gifts**,
B that through the powerful working **of** your grace
C these most sacred mysteries may sanctify our present way of life
and lead us to eternal glad***ness***.
Through Christ our Lord.

Prayer after Communion

A We have consumed, O Lord, this divine Sacrament,
the perpetual memorial of the Passion of your **Son**;
B grant, we pray, that this gift,
which he himself gave us with love be**yond** all telling,
C may profit us for salva***tion***.
Through Christ our Lord.

The space below is for your notes.

Refer to pages viii–x for an explanation of the pointing of the chants and to page xii for the Tones for the Presidential Prayers from *The Roman Missal*.

an ongoing conversion of morals. The prayer asks that the mysteries sanctify us through a "conversion of morals" in our present life. It refers to our way of being and living in the world. Sanctification can never affect us only superficially. By the nature of the Holy Spirit, sanctification will always be an interior, holistic process. Only such a thorough conversion can prepare us for the gladness (*gaudia*, interior or personal joys) that is eternal.

Prayer after Communion: In the Gospel accounts, the risen Christ appears bearing the marks of his Crucifixion, though his wounds no longer bring suffering for himself, but healing for others. In the same way, the "divine Sacrament," which makes present the glorified Body and Blood of Christ, is also "the perpetual memorial" of his Passion. The Eucharist is a living monument, which points to the suffering, Death and Resurrection of Christ. The faithful take this "memorial" within them, and all that is of Christ is opened up to them. The word "love" (*caritas* in Latin) refers to the divine love that impels those imbued by it to give themselves to others without attachments or pretensions. Such divine love is beyond expression in words, because Christ fulfilled his words of love by dying on the Cross. The Church does the same by dying to sin. The "gift" of this ineffable charity cannot coexist beside sin. If accepted humbly, however, the gift roots out sin and leads us deeper to salvation.

EIGHTEENTH SUNDAY IN ORDINARY TIME

Collect

Proclaim **unceasing kindness** with energy, drawing out **unceasing**. Stress **glory**. Pause briefly after **in you**. Give a parallel rhythm to the next two lines, pausing briefly after **safe** and **restored**.

Draw near to your servants, O Lord,
and answer their prayers with unceasing kindness,
that, for those who glory in you as their Creator and guide,
you may restore what you have created
and keep safe what you have restored.
Through our Lord Jesus Christ, your Son,
who lives and reigns with you in the unity of the Holy Spirit,
one God, for ever and ever.

Prayer over the Offerings

Proclaim **Graciously** with gentleness and **sanctify** with hope. Pause briefly after **gifts**. Pronounce ob-LA-tion, and stress **spiritual sacrifice**. Pause briefly after **of us** and proclaim **eternal offering** slowly.

Graciously sanctify these gifts, O Lord, we pray,
and, accepting the oblation of this spiritual sacrifice,
make of us an eternal offering to you.
Through Christ our Lord. *

Prayer after Communion

Stress **constant protection**. Place emphasis on **heavenly**. Go slowly and compassionately with **never-failing care**. Pause briefly after **worthy** and proclaim it with dignity. Stress **eternal**.

Accompany with constant protection, O Lord,
those you renew with these heavenly gifts
and, in your never-failing care for them,
make them worthy of eternal redemption.
Through Christ our Lord.

* Select from Prefaces I–VIII of the Sundays in Ordinary Time in the Order of Mass. Commentary, and proclamation and chant tips, for the Preface can be found at *www.StudyThePresidentialTexts.com/Prefaces* and in *The Order of Mass: A Roman Missal Study Edition and Workbook*, pages 62–77.

Collect: The word "servants" (*famulis*) refers here to household servants, who were often considered to be part of the family. While the Lord is always present to us, the prayer seeks a more intense presence. The request of the Lord to "answer prayers" implies that we have been offering prayers. The Lord will not act upon us without our permission. The Church calls for a period of silence between the "Let us pray" and the Collect, so that the assembly may call to mind the prayers and petitions they bring to the start of this Mass. To glory in another is to be enriched or ennobled by them. Those who glory in God as Creator and guide have been blessed by a light to know their creaturely status. The fallenness of all creation leaves it a dangerous place. The Death and Resurrection of Christ has made new or "restored" this creation fully in himself and by anticipation in the rest. The work of the Spirit sustains this new life, protecting it until it can be brought to fulfillment with Christ in heaven.

Prayer over the Offerings: The word "graciously" (*propitius*) is sacrificial here, asking the grace of God to draw near in response to the sacrifice about to be offered. The verb "sanctify" refers to the primary action of the Holy Spirit, who consecrates, ennobles with gifts, and sets apart from the profane to designate for God. The oblation of the Eucharist is called a "spiritual" sacrifice because it is sanctified by the Holy Spirit. In the same way that Christ's humanity has been completely imbued with the Spirit in his Resurrection,

Pointed Text

Collect

A Draw near to your servants, O Lord,
and answer their prayers with unceasing kind**ness**,
B that, for those who glory in you as their Crea**tor** and guide,
C you may restore what you have created
and keep safe what you have re***stored***.
Through our Lord Jesus Christ, your Son,
who lives and reigns with you in the unity of the Holy Spirit,
one God, for ever and ever.

Prayer over the Offerings

A Graciously sanctify these gifts, O Lord, we **pray**,
B and, accepting the oblation of this spir**it**ual sacrifice,
C make of us an eternal offering to ***you***.
Through Christ our Lord.

Prayer after Communion

A Accompany with constant protection, O **Lord**,
B those you renew with these heavenly gifts
and, in your never-failing **care** for them,
C make them worthy of eternal redemp***tion***.
Through Christ our Lord.

The space below is for your notes.

Refer to pages viii–x for an explanation of the pointing of the chants and to page xii for the Tones for the Presidential Prayers from *The Roman Missal.*

so too, the oblation of the Church is so thoroughly suffused by the Spirit that it is transformed into Christ. When the sacrifice becomes "spiritual" in this way, it becomes acceptable to the Father. The divine nature of Christ is self-gift in love. This is why Christ will never cease to offer himself in love to the Father, to his Bride, the Church, and to the world. As the Church is transformed into Christ, she, too, begins to offer herself unceasingly to others.

Prayer after Communion: The prayer for the Lord's company might equally be a prayer for our spiritual and mental accompaniment with him. The offerings of bread and wine have been transformed into "heavenly gifts" (*munere*). The "renewal" they effect is preparation for heavenly life. They fill us with the life of the risen Christ much as does a seed that is planted. In our death, this seed will spring up to a new life, provided that we have tended it. The prayer beseeches that the Lord protect this "renewal" through constant companionship. The protection is for the seed that has been planted within us for the next world. The Lord safeguards the grace of faith, hope, and love within us, provided we invoke his protection. The word translated here as "care" (*fovere*), means to cherish tenderly. While never infringing upon our free will, the Lord reaches out with tender care in Holy Communion to foster and protect the renewal he offers, making us "worthy of eternal redemption."

NINETEENTH SUNDAY IN ORDINARY TIME

Collect

Pause briefly after **Almighty**.
Pause after **whom** but only briefly after **Spirit**.
Proclaim **we dare** with reverence but no drama. Keep the voice raised with **hearts**. Pause briefly after **adoption** and after **merit**.
Proclaim **inheritance** with energy and **you have promised** with certain hope.

Almighty ever-living God,
whom, taught by the Holy Spirit,
we dare to call our Father,
bring, we pray, to perfection in our hearts
the spirit of adoption as your sons and daughters,
that we may merit to enter into the inheritance
which you have promised.
Through our Lord Jesus Christ, your Son,
who lives and reigns with you in the unity of the Holy Spirit,
one God, for ever and ever.

Prayer over the Offerings

Pause briefly after **O Lord**. Proclaim **in your mercy** with tenderness and pause briefly after it. Stress **you**. Proclaim **by your power** with strength and pause briefly after it. Stress **transform**, pausing only briefly. Proclaim **mystery of our salvation** with reverence.

Be pleased, O Lord, to accept the offerings of your Church,
for in your mercy you have given them to be offered
and by your power you transform them
into the mystery of our salvation.
Through Christ our Lord. *

Prayer after Communion

Think of **communion in your Sacrament** as the communion received or experienced in your Sacrament. In this light, stress **communion**. Pause briefly after **consumed**. Pause briefly after **confirm us** and proclaim **light of your truth** with peaceful joy.

May the communion in your Sacrament
that we have consumed, save us, O Lord,
and confirm us in the light of your truth.
Through Christ our Lord.

* Select from Prefaces I–VIII of the Sundays in Ordinary Time in the Order of Mass. Commentary, and proclamation and chant tips, for the Preface can be found at *www.StudyThePresidentialTexts.com/Prefaces* and in *The Order of Mass: A Roman Missal Study Edition and Workbook*, pages 62–77.

Collect: In the scripture passages from Romans 8:15 and Galatians 4:6, a direct connection is made between receiving the "spirit of adoption" and calling God "Abba, Father." Even though we have become adopted children through the gift of Baptism, there is still trepidation—rightly so—to call the "Almighty and ever-living God" our Father. Every child both respects and reveres his father, though when their wills clash, the respect may be present partly out of fear of the father who is greater than the child in every way. When the prayer asks that the "spirit of adoption" be brought "to perfection in our hearts," it is praying for a maturity that does not obey simply because God is "bigger than" we are, but because as our Father, he knows what is best for us. We do well to hold our Father with equal parts of tender affection and reverent awe. A similar maturity will understand the "promised inheritance" as a desire to make us worthy ("able") to share his inheritance.

Prayer over the Offerings: The plea to accept the Eucharistic offerings in these Prayers over the Offerings, is always, in the end, a prayer to accept the ones offering. In this case, we are charged to identify ourselves with the offerings on the altar. In God's "mercy," he has made us an acceptable offering through our Baptism and reception of the Holy Spirit. In Baptism, God has given us the name of his Son. It is this name, and all of our failures to live that name, that we offer on the altar. Regardless of how we have failed, the Lord's power to

Pointed Text

Collect

A Almighty ever-living God,
whom, taught by the Holy Spirit,
we dare to call our Fa**ther**,
B bring, we pray, to perfection in our hearts
the spirit of adoption as your **sons** and daughters,
C that we may merit to enter into the inheritance
which you have pro***mised***.
Through our Lord Jesus Christ, your Son,
who lives and reigns with you in the unity of the Holy Spirit,
one God, for ever and ever.

Prayer over the Offerings

A Be pleased, O Lord, to accept the offerings of your **Church**,
B for in your mercy you have given them **to** be offered
C and by your power you transform them
into the mystery of our salva***tion***.
Through Christ our Lord.

Prayer after Communion

B May the communion in your Sacrament
that we have consumed, save **us**, O Lord,
C and confirm us in the light of your ***truth***.
Through Christ our Lord.

The space below is for your notes.

Refer to pages viii–x for an explanation of the pointing of the chants and to page xii for the Tones for the Presidential Prayers from *The Roman Missal.*

transform us is greater. If we have committed a conscious, free and serious sin, then we can receive the Sacrament of Penance before making a Eucharistic offering, but after receiving Penance, we can lay even our mortal sin of the past on God's altar to be transformed into grace. The paradox is that God demands that we surrender our weaknesses and failures to him and he gives them back to us as part of the "mystery of our salvation."

Prayer after Communion: The word "Sacrament" is plural in the Latin, which implies that it refers to all the mysteries of Christ summed up in the Eucharist. The faithful are united with Christ and with one another by participation in those sacred mysteries. This communion does not belong to this world. In entering that communion, we step outside of this worldly existence, gaining a step into heaven. The prayer states that we consume the Sacrament, but closer to the truth is that the union with Christ consumes us, making us part of him. The word "light" is *lux* in Latin, which usually refers to God ("God is light . . ." [1 John 1:5]). We could rephrase this line, then, to ask God to "confirm us in divine truth." The word "confirm" means to be rooted. Communion with Christ roots us in truth. If we are thus firmly rooted in Christ, then we need not fear the challenges to religious truth that will come. We can listen with patience and try to see what, if any, ray of truth they are grasping.

TWENTIETH SUNDAY IN ORDINARY TIME

Collect

Pause briefly after **O God**. Speak **love you** warmly and **good things** joyfully.
Pause briefly after **we pray**. Proclaim **warmth of your love** with a full heart. Proclaim **all things** and **above all things** with a parallel rhythm.
Pause after **surpass**. Proclaim **every human desire** slowly and reverently.

O God, who have prepared for those who love you
good things which no eye can see,
fill our hearts, we pray, with the warmth of your love,
so that, loving you in all things and above all things,
we may attain your promises,
which surpass every human desire.
Through our Lord Jesus Christ, your Son,
who lives and reigns with you in the unity of the Holy Spirit,
one God, for ever and ever.

Prayer over the Offerings

Pronounce **ob-LA-tion**.
Pause briefly after **about**. Proclaim **glorious** with some exhilaration.
Pause briefly after **offering** (but not after **that**). Place emphasis on **very self**.

Receive our oblation, O Lord,
by which is brought about a glorious exchange,
that, by offering what you have given,
we may merit to receive your very self.
Through Christ our Lord. *

Prayer after Communion

The phrase **partakers of Christ** should flow together. Proclaim the second line with humility. The last two lines have a parallel rhythm. Place emphasis on **image on earth** and **coheirs in heaven**.

Made partakers of Christ through these Sacraments,
we humbly implore your mercy, Lord,
that, conformed to his image on earth,
we may merit also to be his coheirs in heaven.
Who lives and reigns for ever and ever.

* Select from Prefaces I–VIII of the Sundays in Ordinary Time in the Order of Mass. Commentary, and proclamation and chant tips, for the Preface can be found at *www.StudyThePresidentialTexts.com/Prefaces* and in *The Order of Mass: A Roman Missal Study Edition and Workbook*, pages 62–77.

Collect: The word "love" appears three times in this prayer. The first occurrence (*diligentibus*), referring to the mature love of those prepared for heaven, is the end result of the next two occurrences. The petition asks the Lord to "fill our hearts" with the "warmth of your love" (*tui amoris affectum*). *Amor* is an instinctual type of love that flows from one's nature. It is moved by a desire to love one similar to ourselves. With the qualifier "warmth," we seek not a love that reaches out with no discrimination other than likeness of nature, but an "affectionate" love that responds to moral qualities and actions. We ask God to give us his love, which is given for who we are (*amor*), but also his love that is stirred by qualities and behaviors (*amoris affectum*). This is called *dilectio* in Latin, and it is this kind of love that moves us to "love" (*diligentes*) God "in all things and above all things." Loving in this way, we are ready to receive gifts that are beyond any desire experienced in this life.

Prayer over the Offerings: We ask God to receive our oblation and then we ask to be worthy to receive the Lord in return. This is the "glorious exchange." We offer ourselves to God and he offers himself to us. Though not an equal exchange, the nearer we can approach to making a total offering of ourselves, the nearer we come to what God gives us. The example for this exchange is the Son who received our human nature from the Virgin Mary, then, in the resurrection of his humanity, his human nature received divinity. There is a

Pointed Text

Collect

A O God, who have prepared for those who love you
good things which no eye can **see**,
B fill our hearts, we pray, with the warmth **of** your love,
C so that, loving you in all things and above all things,
we may attain your promises,
which surpass every human de***sire***.
Through our Lord Jesus Christ, your Son,
who lives and reigns with you in the unity of the Holy Spirit,
one God, for ever and ever.

Prayer over the Offerings

A Receive our oblation, O Lord,
by which is brought about a glorious ex**change**,
B that, by offering what **you** have given,
C we may merit to receive your very ***self***.
Through Christ our Lord.

Prayer after Communion

A Made partakers of Christ through these Sa**cra**ments,
B we humbly implore your **mer**cy, Lord,
C that, conformed to his image on earth,
we may merit also to be his coheirs in hea***ven***.
Who lives and reigns for ever and ever.

The space below is for your notes.

Refer to pages viii–x for an explanation of the pointing of the chants and to page xii for the Tones for the Presidential Prayers from *The Roman Missal*.

slight difference in Latin between the verbs for "receive." The first, referring to the Lord's receiving, is *suscipe*, and paints the picture of the Lord's placing his hands under the gifts and drawing them up to him. The second refers to our receiving from the Lord and is *accipe*. It paints the picture of receiving a gift from the hands of another handing it down toward us. Such a posture of reception is the primary way of being in relation to God.

Prayer after Communion: When "Sacraments" (*sacramenta*) is given in the plural, it is often better to understand it in the sense of "mysteries." The prayer intends the sacred mysteries of Christ communicated in each Sacrament. Especially in Holy Communion, we share in these mysteries, which means that the effects of the events of Christ's life are made present within us. Thus presented with the interior image of Christ, we are given the chance to be conformed to that image, provided we desire and embrace it. This means embracing the renunciation of self and an attachment to this world. If we carry the Death of Christ in us on earth, Christ will bring us to be "coheirs" with him in heaven. Humanity was created in the "image" of God (Genesis 1:26–27), but damaged that image through sin. On the earth, Christ was God's image without the corruption of sin. This refers to his interior integrity. The gift of Communion works within to lead us to the interior integrity necessary for eternal life.

TWENTY-FIRST SUNDAY IN ORDINARY TIME

Collect

Pause after **O God**.
Pause briefly after **unite** and place emphasis on **single purpose**. Pause briefly after **people**. Have a parallel rhythm for the next two phrases.
Place parallel emphasis on **uncertainties** and **fixed**. Stress **that place**.
Proclaim **true gladness** with a sense of joyful relief.

O God, who cause the minds of the faithful
to unite in a single purpose,
grant your people to love what you command
and to desire what you promise,
that, amid the uncertainties of this world,
our hearts may be fixed on that place
where true gladness is found.
Through our Lord Jesus Christ, your Son,
who lives and reigns with you in the unity of the Holy Spirit,
one God, for ever and ever.

Prayer over the Offerings

Pause after **O Lord** and briefly after **yourself**, keeping the voice raised with **adoption**. Pause after **sacrifice**. Place parallel emphasis on **one** and **once**. Proclaim **graciously** with warm gentleness. Proclaim **unity and peace** slowly and deliberately.

O Lord, who gained for yourself a people by adoption
through the one sacrifice offered once for all,
bestow graciously on us, we pray,
the gifts of unity and peace in your Church.
Through Christ our Lord. *

Prayer after Communion

Pause briefly after **within us**.
Proclaim **healing work** with heartfelt gentleness. Place similar emphasis on **perfect** and **sustain**. Pause briefly after **perfect**. Pause briefly after **all things**. Proclaim **please you** peacefully.

Complete within us, O Lord, we pray,
the healing work of your mercy
and graciously perfect and sustain us,
so that in all things we may please you.
Through Christ our Lord.

* Select from Prefaces I–VIII of the Sundays in Ordinary Time in the Order of Mass. Commentary, and proclamation and chant tips, for the Preface can be found at *www.StudyThePresidentialTexts.com/Prefaces* and in *The Order of Mass: A Roman Missal Study Edition and Workbook*, pages 62–77.

Collect: The expression "in a single purpose" (*unius voluntatis*) is more literally, "in one will." What is united in this single "will" are the minds "of the faithful." Knowing this can help us to understand that God is not out to brainwash us by forcing our minds into one way of thinking. The "faithful" are those who regularly pray in the Our Father, "thy will be done." Daily, they pray to surrender their wills to God's will. This prayer says that God does not leave them hanging but reveals his will (his "commands") and unites the faithful around it, not grudgingly, but willingly (they "desire" his promises). The "uncertainties" of this world could be natural disasters (tornadoes, earthquakes, droughts, floods, etc.) or personal tragedies (disease, accidents, conflicts, loss, etc.). Amid all these and more, the commands, the promises, and the love of the Lord do not change. If we root ourselves in those realities, then we will find peace in this life and eternal gladness in the next.

Prayer over the Offerings: This prayer brings out the great desire in God to gain our love and to give himself in love sacrificially. From eternity, God acted in time, and the value of that action is eternal. Its value is not bound by time and reaches all those who lived and died before Christ. This is why the Church professes in the Apostles' Creed that Christ descended into hell (literally to the place of the dead). He was bringing the effects of his once-for-all sacrifice to those who had died and who were willing to accept it. For those born

The space below is for your notes.

Refer to pages viii–x for an explanation of the pointing of the chants and to page xii for the Tones for the Presidential Prayers from *The Roman Missal.*

Pointed Text

Collect

A O God, who cause the minds of the faithful
to unite in a single pur**pose**,
B grant your people to love what you command
and to desire **what** you promise,
C that, amid the uncertainties of this world,
our hearts may be fixed on that place
where true gladness is ***found***.
Through our Lord Jesus Christ, your Son,
who lives and reigns with you in the unity of the Holy Spirit,
one God, for ever and ever.

Prayer over the Offerings

A O Lord, who gained for yourself a people by adoption
through the one sacrifice offered once for **all**,
B bestow graciously on **us**, we pray,
C the gifts of unity and peace in your ***Church***.
Through Christ our Lord.

Prayer after Communion

A Complete within us, O Lord, we pray,
the healing work of your mer**cy**
B and graciously perfect **and** sustain us,
C so that in all things we may please ***you***.
Through Christ our Lord.

after Christ, he similarly bestows the effects of his sacrifice through the preaching of the Gospel and the celebration of the Sacraments. In such moments, we are invited to become God's own "people by adoption." The prayer offers two fruits of accepting this invitation: the gifts of "unity and peace." God's peace is a deep-down kind that is not disturbed by worldly anxieties. Unity is not the surrender of identity, but it is the will to be united in the gift of self—varied as that self may be.

Prayer after Communion: Every Christian must be fully aware of the need for healing. Sin has created divisions within, between our flesh and our spirit. The work of Christ is to bring "complete healing." Sometimes this may require us metaphorically "to cut off" some part of our lives: certain friends, habits, and patterns of behavior. Full healing will almost always be painful, but it is an incredible work of "mercy" to be rid of sinful habits. Because such healing is often painful and we are always at risk of falling back to sin, the prayer asks the Lord to "perfect and sustain" us and to do so "graciously," that is, lovingly in the power of the Spirit. The word translated as "sustain" (*foveri*) could also mean to nurture or foster, implying that, once healed, the process of strengthening our eternal health goes on. To sustain such conversion of life is to become subservient to the Spirit, who not only heals but invigorates and raises ever higher.

TWENTY-SECOND SUNDAY IN ORDINARY TIME

Collect

Pause briefly after **might**. Stress **every good gift**. Pause briefly after **so that**. Parallel the rhythm to **what is good** and **what you have nurtured**.

God of might, giver of every good gift,
put into our hearts the love of your name,
so that, by deepening our sense of reverence,
you may nurture in us what is good
and, by your watchful care,
keep safe what you have nurtured.
Through our Lord Jesus Christ, your Son,
who lives and reigns with you in the unity of the Holy Spirit,
one God, for ever and ever.

Prayer over the Offerings

Proclaim **sacred offering** with reverence. Stress **always** and pause briefly after it. Proclaim **blessing of salvation** with gratitude. Give a parallel rhythm to **celebrates in mystery** and **accomplish in power**.

May this sacred offering, O Lord,
confer on us always the blessing of salvation,
that what it celebrates in mystery
it may accomplish in power.
Through Christ our Lord. *

Prayer after Communion

Give parallel emphasis to **this bread** and **heavenly table**. Proclaim **food of charity** with delight. Give a similar stress to **confirm** and **stir**. Pause briefly after **us** and stress **you**.

Renewed by this bread from the heavenly table,
we beseech you, Lord,
that, being the food of charity,
it may confirm our hearts
and stir us to serve you in our neighbor.
Through Christ our Lord.

* Select from Prefaces I–VIII of the Sundays in Ordinary Time in the Order of Mass. Commentary, and proclamation and chant tips, for the Preface can be found at *www.StudyThePresidentialTexts.com/Prefaces* and in *The Order of Mass: A Roman Missal Study Edition and Workbook*, pages 62–77.

Collect: The word "might" (*virtutum*), used here of God, describes his strength for enabling and supporting what is good. This is further expanded in the phrase that names him "giver of every good gift" (the Latin has "of what is best": *optimum*). The request to put a love (*amorem*) of the divine name in our hearts seems to flow from the previous phrase in which God gives what is best. By so giving, he evokes such a love (*amor* implies a love that desires union with what attracts and is similar to itself). This love is able to deepen "our sense of reverence" (*religionis augmento*) because of its awareness that the gifts within us come from God. When there is only reverence for the good that comes our way, we grow in virtue ("what is good" in us). Such virtue in fallen humanity is always prone to being lost, so the prayer asks for the Lord's "watchful care" (*vigilanti studio*—vigilant zeal) in safeguarding the virtue that he sows into our hearts, cultivates, and nourishes to full bloom.

Prayer over the Offerings: This prayer highlights the Eucharistic exchange present at Mass. The "offering" goes up and the "blessing" comes down. It is a "sacred" offering by virtue of being placed on the altar and thus "set apart" from all else. It is also sacred because it will be united to the self-offering of Christ, the source of our holiness. The "blessing" is not for wealth, physical health, or earthly power, but for "salvation." In other words, it is not for this world at all, but to safeguard us from this world for the next. Our Eucharistic offering

The space below is for your notes.

Refer to pages viii–x for an explanation of the pointing of the chants and to page xii for the Tones for the Presidential Prayers from *The Roman Missal.*

Pointed Text

Collect

A God of might, giver of every good **gift**,
B put into our hearts the love **of** your name,
C so that, by deepening our sense of reverence,
you may nurture in us what is good
and, by your watchful care,
keep safe what you have nur***tured***.
Through our Lord Jesus Christ, your Son,
who lives and reigns with you in the unity of the Holy Spirit,
one God, for ever and ever.

Prayer over the Offerings

A May this sacred offering, O **Lord**,
B confer on us always the blessing **of** salvation,
C that what it celebrates in mystery
it may accomplish in po***wer***.
Through Christ our Lord.

Prayer after Communion

A Renewed by this bread from the heavenly table,
we beseech you, **Lord**,
B that, being the **food** of charity,
C it may confirm our hearts
and stir us to serve you in our neigh***bor***.
Through Christ our Lord.

prepares us not for the world of earthly business, but for the world of the heavenly kingdom. We celebrate (the Latin is *agit*, "do" or "enact") that salvation, that kingdom, "in mystery," that is, in signs and symbols. The signs and symbols communicate the reality, but in our earthly state, we are only able to receive the Sacrament. The mystery works within to prepare us for the glorified existence that awaits us. In glory, we can receive Christ "in power."

Prayer after Communion: Before the Eucharistic Prayer, the Church placed natural bread on an earthly altar; in Holy Communion, she receives supernatural bread from "the heavenly table." In the Roman Canon, the Priest Celebrant prays that the Lord's Angel carry the gifts to the "altar on high." An exchange is effected, and what returns to us is "the food of charity" through which our hunger to give ourselves away in service is "stirred." (The nature of divine "charity" is to give itself away in service.) The word "confirm" means to make firm by adding strength and encouragement. The "heart" is the point of entry for the Spirit of God. It is where we are encouraged or disheartened, inspired or deflated, depending on to whom we open our hearts. The Spirit will stir up and strengthen whatever flame for good is in our hearts. As the image of Christ grows within us, we will recognize that image in others and will be eager to reverence it in them.

TWENTY-THIRD SUNDAY IN ORDINARY TIME

Collect

Pause briefly after **O God**. Raise the voice in emphasis for **redeemed**, pausing briefly before continuing. Proclaim **graciously** with reverence and **beloved** with solemn joy. Give equal stress to **Christ** and **true**. Proclaim **everlasting inheritance** with the mind set on heaven.

O God, by whom we are redeemed and receive adoption,
look graciously upon your beloved sons and daughters,
that those who believe in Christ
may receive true freedom
and an everlasting inheritance.
Through our Lord Jesus Christ, your Son,
who lives and reigns with you in the unity of the Holy Spirit,
one God, for ever and ever.

Prayer over the Offerings

Pause briefly after **O God**. Emphasize **true prayer** and **peace**. Pause briefly after **grant**. Proclaim **fitting homage** slowly and reverently and **divine majesty** with joyful veneration. Proclaim **sacred mystery** with dignity. Pause briefly after **united**.

O God, who give us the gift of true prayer and of peace,
graciously grant that, through this offering,
we may do fitting homage to your divine majesty
and, by partaking of the sacred mystery,
we may be faithfully united in mind and heart.
Through Christ our Lord. *

Prayer after Communion

Proclaim **nourish** and **endow with life** with equal energy and with gratitude. Place parallel emphasis on **Word** and **Sacrament**. Stress **so benefit**, **beloved**, and **great**. Pause briefly after **merit** and stress **eternal**.

Grant that your faithful, O Lord,
whom you nourish and endow with life
through the food of your Word and heavenly Sacrament,
may so benefit from your beloved Son's great gifts
that we may merit an eternal share in his life.
Who lives and reigns for ever and ever.

* Select from Prefaces I–VIII of the Sundays in Ordinary Time in the Order of Mass. Commentary, and proclamation and chant tips, for the Preface can be found at *www.StudyThePresidentialTexts.com/Prefaces* and in *The Order of Mass: A Roman Missal Study Edition and Workbook*, pages 62–77.

Collect: Redemption frees us from slavery to sin. In redemption, we become a free people, though not yet tied to God. Left untethered, we would be blown down by the winds of this world. Adoption cannot be bestowed on slaves, but only upon the free. When the Father looks upon us with grace ("graciously"), he sees his Son, who is "beloved" to him. The image of "true freedom" is Christ on the Cross. No one took his life from him. He laid it down freely. Freely, he turned aside from the powers and pleasures of this world. Freely he embraced all of our sins to nail them to his Cross. The deeper our faith in Christ grows, the closer we draw to our own "cross" and the more ready we are to give our lives in freedom back to God. The "everlasting inheritance" is the result of this kind of freedom, wherein we open (and empty) ourselves so fully that the Spirit is able to penetrate every part of us, raising the "whole man" to the glory where all delight in such self-gift.

Prayer over the Offerings: The phrase "who give us the gift of true prayer" is a translation of *auctor sincerae devotionis*, which means, literally, "author of sincere devotion." Devotion is what makes our prayer personal. Unfortunately, sometimes even devotion can be forced and more the product of showmanship or wishful thinking than "sincere" investment of one's real self. This is what is meant by "true prayer." Peace will flow from a sincere (honest!) offering of self in prayer. The Eucharistic Sacrifice (i.e., the "offering") is a "fitting

Pointed Text

Collect

A O God, by whom we are redeemed and receive adop**tion**,
B look graciously upon your beloved **sons** and daughters,
C that those who believe in Christ
may receive true freedom
and an everlasting inher***i***tance.
Through our Lord Jesus Christ, your Son,
who lives and reigns with you in the unity of the Holy Spirit,
one God, for ever and ever.

Prayer over the Offerings

A O God, who give us the gift of true prayer and of **peace**,
B graciously grant that, **through** this offering,
C we may do fitting homage to your divine majesty
and, by partaking of the sacred mystery,
we may be faithfully united in mind and ***heart***.
Through Christ our Lord.

Prayer after Communion

A Grant that your faithful, O Lord,
whom you nourish and endow with life
through the food of your Word and heavenly Sa**cra**ment,
B may so benefit from your beloved **Son's** great gifts
C that we may merit an eternal share in his ***life***.
Who lives and reigns for ever and ever.

The space below is for your notes.

Refer to pages viii–x for an explanation of the pointing of the chants and to page xii for the Tones for the Presidential Prayers from *The Roman Missal.*

homage" to God, but only when done with "devotion." Even when our homage is lacking such devotion, the graciousness of God still transforms our offering into the "sacred mystery." God's fidelity remains despite our fickleness. In Holy Communion, we receive another chance to enter with true devotion, and if we do so, we can benefit from God's fidelity and be "united in mind and heart." This is a sharing of substance in the Body of Christ.

Prayer after Communion: The food from the heavenly gifts received in the Eucharistic food strengthens us for the next world. This food also "endows with life" (*vivificas*). One of the titles given to the Holy Spirit in the Creed is "giver of life." The food of Communion fills us with life through the Spirit. The word for food (*pabulum*) refers to food for grazing animals. This kind of food must be chewed over and over again in order to extract its full nourishment. God's Word and heavenly Sacrament, likewise, are not exhausted from one hearing or reception. We can meditate on this food over and over again, and it will continually bear new fruit. The petition of the prayer is that the faithful may benefit in this ongoing way from the Eucharistic gifts of Word and Sacrament. The prayer ends with a second mention of life. The first mention implied the Spirit; the second time refers to the life of Christ. The Spirit bestows life by communicating Christ to us and giving us a share in his life.

TWENTY-FOURTH SUNDAY IN ORDINARY TIME

Collect

Proclaim **Look upon us** humbly, and the next line with quiet confidence. Do not overstress **feel**. Emphasize **working**. Proclaim **mercy** with gentleness. Pause briefly after **serve you**. Proclaim **all our heart** with strength.

Look upon us, O God,
Creator and ruler of all things,
and, that we may feel the working of your mercy,
grant that we may serve you with all our heart.
Through our Lord Jesus Christ, your Son,
who lives and reigns with you in the unity of the Holy Spirit,
one God, for ever and ever.

Prayer over the Offerings

Proclaim **look with favor** in humble pleading. Pause briefly after **kindness**. Put emphasis on **each** and **honor**, and pause briefly after **offered**. Finish strong on **all**.

Look with favor on our supplications, O Lord,
and in your kindness accept these, your servants' offerings,
that what each has offered to the honor of your name
may serve the salvation of all.
Through Christ our Lord. *

Prayer after Communion

Pause briefly after **gift** and again after **possession**. Go slowly with **minds and bodies**. Pause after **effects**. Place a parallel emphasis on **effects** and **desires**. Stress **always**.

May the working of this heavenly gift, O Lord, we pray,
take possession of our minds and bodies,
so that its effects, and not our own desires,
may always prevail in us.
Through Christ our Lord.

* Select from Prefaces I–VIII of the Sundays in Ordinary Time in the Order of Mass. Commentary, and proclamation and chant tips, for the Preface can be found at *www.StudyThePresidentialTexts.com/Prefaces* and in *The Order of Mass: A Roman Missal Study Edition and Workbook*, pages 62–77.

Collect: Because the Lord is our Creator, he knows how we are made. Because he is our ruler, he knows what is best for us. In both of these ways, when we ask the Lord to "look upon us," we are giving him permission to perceive deeply how we are and where we need healing or help. The word translated as "mercy," *propitiatio*, literally means to draw near (*prope* = near). We ask the Lord to gaze into our very being and then pray that we will sense or feel his nearness at work in us. This interior work that God effects in us, makes it possible to serve him "with all our heart." Normally, our hearts are divided and distracted. We may feel focused for a time, then "lose heart" and turn aside from our path. Oftentimes, it is only for a "break" that we feel we've earned. The Lord's gaze illumines our shortcomings and the "working of his mercy" purifies and renews us. Such working may be painful, but that pain is the sign that the Spirit is refashioning us to live as we were created to live.

Prayer over the Offerings: "Look with favor" (*propitiare*) means that we ask the Lord to perceive with divine power not only the spoken words of our "supplications," but to respond to the needs of our hearts of which we may not be aware. The "supplication" of the assembly immediately before this prayer is: "May the Lord accept the sacrifice at your hands . . . ." The prayer here makes those words of the assembly its own. In one regard, this is the "supplication" that the assembly makes throughout the Eucharistic Prayer. It is

Pointed Text

Collect

A Look upon us, O God,
Creator and ruler of all **things**,
B and, that we may feel the working **of** your mercy,
C grant that we may serve you with all our ***heart***.
Through our Lord Jesus Christ, your Son,
who lives and reigns with you in the unity of the Holy Spirit,
one God, for ever and ever.

Prayer over the Offerings

A Look with favor on our supplications, O **Lord**,
B and in your kindness accept these, your **ser**vants' offerings,
C that what each has offered to the honor of your name
may serve the salvation of ***all***.
Through Christ our Lord.

Prayer after Communion

A May the working of this heavenly gift, O Lord, we **pray**,
B take possession of our **minds** and bodies,
C so that its effects, and not our own desires,
may always prevail in ***us***.
Through Christ our Lord.

The space below is for your notes.

Refer to pages viii–x for an explanation of the pointing of the chants and to page xii for the Tones for the Presidential Prayers from *The Roman Missal*.

upon that prayer that we beseech the Lord to "look with favor." Divine acceptance of our offerings is the key to receiving the necessary grace in return. In some places in the early Church, the faithful brought bread for the offering. Still today, though we no longer bring bread, each is expected to lay some aspect of his or her heart upon the sacrificial offerings. With the Lord's blessing, they are returned to us to strengthen us so that we might help others.

Prayer after Communion: The "heavenly gift" (singular) is Christ. Saint Paul wrote that we are to have the "mind" of Christ (Philippians 2:5) in the sense of "emptying" ourselves and not "grasping" after a dignity that is not ours to take but only to receive. Saint Paul also wrote that he carried within his body the dying of Christ that he might also have a share in his Resurrection. These are the effects of letting the "heavenly gift" that is Christ "take possession of our minds and bodies." Our "own desires" would take us down a different path. The "effects" of Christ are to empty ourselves and die to ourselves. These are the workings that should "prevail" in us. It is significant that the action of the "heavenly gift" is described as a "working." The sacrificial action of Christ on the Cross is often referred to as the "work" of our redemption. This work is Christ's and not ours. Our work is submission. It is the *fiat* of the Blessed Virgin.

TWENTY-FIFTH SUNDAY IN ORDINARY TIME

Collect

Pause briefly after **O God**. Place strong emphasis on the verb **founded** and proclaim **sacred Law** with reverence, keeping the voice raised with **Law**. Stress **you** and pause briefly. Pause briefly after **that** and stress **eternal**.

O God, who founded all the commands of your sacred Law
upon love of you and of our neighbor,
grant that, by keeping your precepts,
we may merit to attain eternal life.
Through our Lord Jesus Christ, your Son,
who lives and reigns with you in the unity of the Holy Spirit,
one God, for ever and ever.

Prayer over the Offerings

Pause briefly after **favor**. Stress **offerings**. Proclaim **devotion and faith** slowly and deliberately. Pause briefly after **theirs** and stress **heavenly**.

Receive with favor, O Lord, we pray,
the offerings of your people,
that what they profess with devotion and faith
may be theirs through these heavenly mysteries.
Through Christ our Lord. *

Prayer after Communion

Lift the voice slightly with **raise up**. Proclaim **come to possess** with sincere desire. Pause after **mystery** and proclaim it reverently. Proclaim **manner of our life** with hope.

Graciously raise up, O Lord,
those you renew with this Sacrament,
that we may come to possess your redemption
both in mystery and in the manner of our life.
Through Christ our Lord.

* Select from Prefaces I–VIII of the Sundays in Ordinary Time in the Order of Mass. Commentary, and proclamation and chant tips, for the Preface can be found at *www.StudyThePresidentialTexts.com/Prefaces* and in *The Order of Mass: A Roman Missal Study Edition and Workbook*, pages 62–77.

Collect: This prayer reminds us that the Old Testament and its "commands" were given by God as a source of revelation. This revelatory character is what enables us to call the Law "sacred." The definitive revelation of Christ is the key, however, for correctly interpreting and understanding that revelation. Even the summary of the Law in "love of God and of neighbor" is most clearly understood when we look at the example Christ left of obedience. A "precept" is an order or command given before an event or mission to enable one to fulfill the mission or successfully deal with the event. The twofold command of love is the essential precept of Christianity, which enables Christians to fulfill their mission. While the Law is considered a grace to us, Christians also believe that grace is needed to carry out that Law. Our efforts do not "merit" heaven in the sense that we can get there with or without God. Rather, God's grace makes us worthy (*meritorious*) to receive yet another gift: eternal life.

Prayer over the Offerings: Implicit in this prayer is an exhortation to be ready in return to "receive" from the Lord. The Lord is asked to receive "with favor" (*propitiatus*), meaning to draw near with his transforming, cleansing power. By contrast, any receiving on our part should be done with humility; one could borrow from the prayer to say "with devotion and faith." The prayer does not specify "what" God's people profess, though it implies that the "offerings" are the expression or profession of devotion and faith. In this sense, the

Pointed Text

Collect

A O God, who founded all the commands of your sacred Law
upon love of you and of our neigh**bor**,
B grant that, by keep**ing** your precepts,
C we may merit to attain eternal ***life***.
Through our Lord Jesus Christ, your Son,
who lives and reigns with you in the unity of the Holy Spirit,
one God, for ever and ever.

Prayer over the Offerings

A Receive with favor, O Lord, we pray,
the offerings of your peo**ple**,
B that what they profess with devo**tion** and faith
C may be theirs through these heavenly mys***ter***ies.
Through Christ our Lord.

Prayer after Communion

A Graciously raise up, O Lord,
those you renew with this Sa**cra**ment,
B that we may come to possess **your** redemption
C both in mystery and in the manner of our ***life***.
Through Christ our Lord.

The space below is for your notes.

Refer to pages viii–x for an explanation of the pointing of the chants and to page xii for the Tones for the Presidential Prayers from *The Roman Missal*.

prayer presumes that, in the course of the Eucharist, we make the offerings our own by laying upon them our heart's desires. When the prayer prays that "what they profess . . . may be theirs," the understanding is that the offerings may return to us and Christ may indeed "be ours." The word devotion (*pietate*) here means the duty of filial affection. Faith teaches that God is our Father, which means that we, his children, owe him our filial love.

Prayer after Commmunion: The prayer implies a twofold action of the Lord toward us. First, he "renews" us with the "Sacrament" (the Latin is in the plural, implying a reference to the whole Paschal Mystery that is communicated in "this Sacrament"). The Latin for "renew" is literally to "remake." The mystery of Christ acts in us to make of us a new creation ready for his heavenly kingdom. The second action is that God "raises us up." After our nature has been purified and the integrity of body and soul is restored, we still need God's Spirit to "raise us up" to the glorified life of the "risen" Christ. In this glory, we are made to share in divine life. Interior renewal can perfect human nature—the "manner of our life," but resurrection brings a divine perfection to humanity that is beyond our ordinary nature. We glimpse this renewal and resurrection already "in mystery," that is, in the symbol and sacrament of ritual. We also anticipate its fullness in "the manner of our life."

TWENTY-SIXTH SUNDAY IN ORDINARY TIME

Collect

Pause briefly after **O God**. Keep the voice raised slightly at **power**. Stress **above all** and pause briefly. Pause briefly after **we pray**. Proclaim **abundantly** with energy. Stress **hastening** and **heirs**. Proclaim **treasures of heaven** with awe.

O God, who manifest your almighty power
above all by pardoning and showing mercy,
bestow, we pray, your grace abundantly upon us
and make those hastening to attain your promises
heirs to the treasures of heaven.
Through our Lord Jesus Christ, your Son,
who lives and reigns with you in the unity of the Holy Spirit,
one God, for ever and ever.

Prayer over the Offerings

Stress **merciful**. Proclaim **may find acceptance** with gentle confidence. Pause briefly after **through it**. Emphasize **wellspring** and **all**.

Grant us, O merciful God,
that this our offering may find acceptance with you
and that through it the wellspring of all blessing
may be laid open before us.
Through Christ our Lord. *

Prayer after Communion

Stress **heavenly**.

Pray **coheirs in glory with Christ** with awe and reverent energy. Proclaim **suffering** somberly and keep the voice raised with **united**. Speak **proclaim his Death** with determination.

May this heavenly mystery, O Lord,
restore us in mind and body,
that we may be coheirs in glory with Christ,
to whose suffering we are united
whenever we proclaim his Death.
Who lives and reigns for ever and ever.

* Select from Prefaces I–VIII of the Sundays in Ordinary Time in the Order of Mass. Commentary, and proclamation and chant tips, for the Preface can be found at *www.StudyThePresidentialTexts.com/Prefaces* and in *The Order of Mass: A Roman Missal Study Edition and Workbook*, pages 62–77.

Collect: It is easy to be afraid to show mercy out of fear that the one set free will harm us. God "manifests" his omnipotence in that he cannot be harmed by someone he pardons. Power is most absolute when it need not exercise force. This power has no need of coercion. It is eternal invitation—to forgiveness, to grace, to a new life. The request to bestow grace abundantly is both petition and confession that we are willing to receive those graces, which is the more important part of the equation. God is profligate with his graces. Humanity is miserly in receiving them. The prayer implies that for the Christian, there should be a sense of urgency to leave behind the world and "hasten" (the Latin is literally "running") to the promised life of heaven. The most important grace that we receive is that of a sonship in Baptism because it makes us "heirs" to all the "treasures" that God has lavished upon Christ. God's "promises" were fulfilled in Christ. Through Christ, they are fulfilled in us, too.

Prayer over the Offerings: In seeking God's acceptance of our offering, we name him "merciful." His mercy is always invitation to something more. The prayer paints an evocative Trinitarian image. The offering ("through it") is the sacrament of Christ. The "wellspring" is the eternal source of all, including the Trinity, and as such it refers to the Father. This is the image of a well from which fresh and crystal-clear water rises (Revelation 22:1–2). Blessing can often be understood as synonymous with grace or gift. This "blessing,"

Pointed Text

Collect

A O God, who manifest your almighty power
above all by pardoning and showing mer**cy**,
B bestow, we pray, your grace abundantly upon us
and make those hastening to at**tain** your promises
C heirs to the treasures of hea***ven***.
Through our Lord Jesus Christ, your Son,
who lives and reigns with you in the unity of the Holy Spirit,
one God, for ever and ever.

Prayer over the Offerings

A Grant us, O merciful **God**,
B that this our offering may find accep**tance** with you
C and that through it the wellspring of all blessing
may be laid open before ***us***.
Through Christ our Lord.

Prayer after Communion

A May this heavenly mystery, O Lord,
restore us in mind and bo**dy**,
B that we may be coheirs in glo**ry** with Christ,
C to whose suffering we are united
whenever we proclaim his ***Death***.
Who lives and reigns for ever and ever.

The space below is for your notes.

Refer to pages viii–x for an explanation of the pointing of the chants and to page xii for the Tones for the Presidential Prayers from *The Roman Missal.*

which flows from the Father and through the Son, is the gift of the Holy Spirit, who is the river of life flowing from the throne and the Lamb (Revelation 22:1–2). It was the self-offering of Christ on the Cross this "opened" the graces (blessings) of the divine wellspring to us. Through the sacramental offering of the Eucharistic Prayer, this opened wellspring is brought to us, and the infinite and unfathomable blessing of the Spirit pours from it to renew us all.

Prayer after Communion: The offerings which we have presented (bread, wine, and personal interior sacrifices) have been transformed to become a "heavenly mystery," which has power to cleanse and strengthen us. Such is the work of restoration "in mind and body." In rooting out sin, the Sacrament effects an ever greater integration of our mind and body. This work of integration, which is begun in Baptism, makes us capable of inheriting "glory with Christ." One of the purposes of suffering is to empty us of our worldly concerns and distractions. By celebrating the Eucharist, we effect the sacramental presence of the entire Paschal Mystery, including the Passion. This is why Saint Paul could call the Eucharist a proclamation of the Death of Christ. When we receive Holy Communion, we are united with his whole mystery. When we model or preach Christ to others outside of the liturgy, we can't neglect his suffering, which is an essential road to glory.

TWENTY-SEVENTH SUNDAY IN ORDINARY TIME

Collect

Pause briefly after **Almighty**. Stress **abundance**. Proclaim **surpass** with energy. Speak **the merits and the desires** slowly, pausing briefly after **desires**. Proclaim **pour out your mercy** with confident pleading. Capture the rhythm of the last two lines.

Almighty ever-living God,
who in the abundance of your kindness
surpass the merits and the desires of those who entreat you,
pour out your mercy upon us
to pardon what conscience dreads
and to give what prayer does not dare to ask.
Through our Lord Jesus Christ, your Son,
who lives and reigns with you in the unity of the Holy Spirit,
one God, for ever and ever.

Prayer over the Offerings

Pause briefly after **Accept**. Place some emphasis on **instituted** and **your**. Proclaim **sacred mysteries** with reverence and **dutiful service** with a sense of responsibility. Proclaim **graciously** with gentleness and **sanctifying work** with energy. Stress **pleased**.

Accept, O Lord, we pray,
the sacrifices instituted by your commands
and, through the sacred mysteries,
which we celebrate with dutiful service,
graciously complete the sanctifying work
by which you are pleased to redeem us.
Through Christ our Lord. *

Prayer after Communion

Proclaim **refreshed and nourished** slowly but lightly and crisply.

Stress **Sacrament**. Proclaim **transformed** with energy.

Grant us, almighty God,
that we may be refreshed and nourished
by the Sacrament which we have received,
so as to be transformed into what we consume.
Through Christ our Lord.

* Select from Prefaces I–VIII of the Sundays in Ordinary Time in the Order of Mass. Commentary, and proclamation and chant tips, for the Preface can be found at *www.StudyThePresidentialTexts.com/Prefaces* and in *The Order of Mass: A Roman Missal Study Edition and Workbook*, pages 62–77.

Collect: "Kindness" (*pietas*) refers to the devotion that exists between parent and child. As Father, God acts toward his children with an abundance of *pietas*, "surpassing" both the "merits" of their behavior and the "desires" (*vota*) of their hearts. Our desires often are swayed by others' opinions. Having formed our nature, God knows what will satisfy the deepest "desires" of our heart. In this regard, he acts as a loving Father who gives what will satisfy. We should always be full of humility, if not a little fear, when we "entreat" God, because we may be asking for something that will not be helpful in the long run. Conscience, weighed down by our fallen nature, often reacts to God in fear ("dread") as did Adam and Eve, who hid themselves from God after their sin. Christ has taught us not only to trust in God's mercy but to live by it. This should lead not to presumption but to humility. It is our sinfulness that holds us back from seeking God's pardon, not our humility.

Prayer over the Offerings: The prayer makes a distinction between "sacrifices" and "sacred mysteries." The sacrifices are the self-offerings of the assembly, symbolized by the bread and wine. The "commands" to offer such sacrifices were expressed during the Last Supper: take and eat; take and drink; and do this in memory of me. We do "this" in multiple ways. We imitate Jesus in offering and consuming bread and wine in consecrated thanksgiving. We also imitate Jesus in offering ourselves in sacrifice. The "sacred

The space below is for your notes.

Refer to pages viii–x for an explanation of the pointing of the chants and to page xii for the Tones for the Presidential Prayers from *The Roman Missal.*

Pointed Text

Collect

A Almighty ever-living God,
who in the abundance of your kindness
surpass the merits and the desires of those who entreat **you**,
B pour out your mercy upon us
to pardon what **con**science dreads
C and to give what prayer does not dare to ***ask***.
Through our Lord Jesus Christ, your Son,
who lives and reigns with you in the unity of the Holy Spirit,
one God, for ever and ever.

Prayer over the Offerings

A Accept, O Lord, we pray,
the sacrifices instituted by your com**mands**
B and, through the sacred mysteries,
which we celebrate with dut**i**ful service,
C graciously complete the sanctifying work
by which you are pleased to redeem ***us***.
Through Christ our Lord.

Prayer after Communion

A Grant us, almighty **God**,
B that we may be refreshed and nourished
by the Sacrament which we **have** received,
C so as to be transformed into what we con***sume***.
Through Christ our Lord.

mysteries" refer to the transcendent action of Christ. We fulfill God's "commands" when we enact the sacred mysteries in sign and symbol, rendering their saving and "sanctifying" action present to us. Fulfilling these commands is "service" for the sanctification of the people of God. Through this service, God "completes" the work of redemption. This is the work of making the mysteries of Christ come alive in the baptized. In our way, we live Christ.

Prayer after Communion: The word translated as "refreshed" (*inebriemur*) literally means inebriated. The Church prays that the "Sacrament" may permeate our existence in such a way that we are led to act under the influence of the Spirit of Christ. This is more than simply to be "refreshed." The word "nourished" (*pascamur*) refers to the care of a shepherd pasturing his sheep on lush and secure meadows. In one sense, it reinforces the understanding that our "inebriation" is under the influence of the Good Shepherd. The word "received" (*perceptis*) means to be thoroughly grasped. We are not simply to receive in an external way the divine Sacrament (the word "Sacrament" is in the plural, which implies "mysteries" without definite reference to one of the seven Sacraments). We receive these mysteries into the core of who we are. In so doing, the mystery we consume becomes more and more integrated into our identity, but without compromising our uniqueness.

TWENTY-EIGHTH SUNDAY IN ORDINARY TIME

Collect

Pause briefly after **grace**. Proclaim the rhythm of **before us** with rising voice and **follow after** with declining voice. Stress **always** and **good**.

May your grace, O Lord, we pray,
at all times go before us and follow after
and make us always determined
to carry out good works.
Through our Lord Jesus Christ, your Son,
who lives and reigns with you in the unity of the Holy Spirit,
one God, for ever and ever.

Prayer over the Offerings

Pause briefly after **O Lord**. Stress **prayers** and keep the voice raised for **faithful**. Proclaim **sacrificial offerings** with reverence. Give a parallel emphasis to **acts of devotedness** and **glory of heaven**. Pause briefly after **pass over**.

Accept, O Lord, the prayers of your faithful
with the sacrificial offerings,
that, through these acts of devotedness,
we may pass over to the glory of heaven.
Through Christ our Lord. *

Prayer after Communion

Pause briefly after **majesty**, proclaiming it with reverence and **most humbly** in a subdued manner. Keep the voice raised with **nourishment**. Proclaim each word of **most holy Body and Blood** slowly and deliberately. Stress **sharers** and pause briefly after it.

We entreat your majesty most humbly, O Lord,
that, as you feed us with the nourishment
which comes from the most holy Body and Blood of your Son,
so you may make us sharers of his divine nature.
Who lives and reigns for ever and ever.

* Select from Prefaces I–VIII of the Sundays in Ordinary Time in the Order of Mass. Commentary, and proclamation and chant tips, for the Preface can be found at *www.StudyThePresidentialTexts.com/Prefaces* and in *The Order of Mass: A Roman Missal Study Edition and Workbook*, pages 62–77.

Collect: Before we can accomplish a good act, God already has done several things. He has created our human nature to be capable of the good, and he has planted within us a desire for the good and a restlessness until we effect it. Both of these are examples of "grace" that come before our acting. Additionally, God strengthens our hearts to persevere in seeking the good despite hardships. Lastly, after we accomplish some good deed, God's grace works to keep us from growing proud or content and to lead us into deeper awareness of God's action. The most important contribution we make to living a "good" life and carrying out "good works" is our determination. Success should not be measured by achievement, but by our striving or our determination of will. The goal is less the accomplishment of external acts of goodness than the perfection of interior goodness that cooperates ever more fully with God's grace.

Prayer over the Offerings: Prayer and sacrifice are at the heart of Christian religion. Prayer is the relationship that a baptized person maintains and develops with God. Sacrifice is the consequence of a developed relationship and symbolizes the care and devotion that one has come to have for God. Both prayer and "sacrificial offerings" are referred to as "acts of devotedness." The word for "acts" (*officia*) refers to acts of duty or responsibility based on one's job or office. The word "devotedness" is a translation of *piae devotionis*, which

Pointed Text

Collect

A May your grace, O Lord, we **pray**,
B at all times go before us and follow after
and make us al**ways** determined
C to carry out good ***works***.
Through our Lord Jesus Christ, your Son,
who lives and reigns with you in the unity of the Holy Spirit,
one God, for ever and ever.

Prayer over the Offerings

A Accept, O Lord, the prayers of your faithful
with the sacrificial of**fer**ings,
B that, through these acts **of** devotedness,
C we may pass over to the glory of hea***ven***.
Through Christ our Lord.

Prayer after Communion

A We entreat your majesty most humbly, O **Lord**,
B that, as you feed us with the nourishment
which comes from the most holy Body and Blood **of** your Son,
C so you may make us sharers of his divine na***ture***.
Who lives and reigns for ever and ever.

The space below is for your notes.

Refer to pages viii–x for an explanation of the pointing of the chants and to page xii for the Tones for the Presidential Prayers from *The Roman Missal*.

may be more literally translated as filial devotion. *Piae* encompasses the relationship of respect and obedience on the part of children and of care and duty on the part of parents. *Devotionis* means that these acts should be personal and heartfelt. When we act toward God sincerely, even if we fail in word or deed at times, God will act as the caring and dutiful Father who longs to raise us to the same glory as his beloved Son.

Prayer after Communion: The object of this prayer is to seek a share for humanity in the divine nature. We invoke God as "majesty," which calls to mind the supreme heights of divinity. This address is significantly contrasted with the adverb marking the manner of our address: "most humbly." God the Son descended to the most humble nature of humanity. In his Resurrection and Ascension, he raised our lowly humanity to the supreme height of divinity. This prayer asks that we may join in the upward ascent of his humanity by our participation in the Eucharist. The prayer implies that the nourishment that comes from the "most holy," that is, the risen and glorified Body and Blood of Christ, can strengthen us for a similar ascent. It was necessary for Christ to submit to complete abasement, the total emptying out of his humanity, to open his humanity to the fullness of divinity. We will need to embrace his abasement if we hope to be embraced by his divinity.

TWENTY-NINTH SUNDAY IN ORDINARY TIME

Collect

Pause briefly after **Almighty**. Give a parallel emphasis between **our will** and **to yours**. Proclaim **your majesty** with humble reverence and pause briefly.

Almighty ever-living God,
grant that we may always conform our will to yours
and serve your majesty in sincerity of heart.
Through our Lord Jesus Christ, your Son,
who lives and reigns with you in the unity of the Holy Spirit,
one God, for ever and ever.

Prayer over the Offerings

Pause briefly after **Grant us** and proclaim **sincere respect** with a straightforward confidence and desire. Proclaim **purifying action of your grace** slowly and reverently. Stress **cleansed** and pause briefly after it. Proclaim **very mysteries** with slow emphasis.

Grant us, Lord, we pray,
a sincere respect for your gifts,
that, through the purifying action of your grace,
we may be cleansed by the very mysteries we serve.
Through Christ our Lord. *

Prayer after Communion

Stress **heavenly things**. Pause briefly after **helped**. Proclaim a parallel rhythm for **by what you give in this present age** (keeping the voice raised for it) and **for the gifts that are eternal**.

Grant, O Lord, we pray,
that, benefiting from participation in heavenly things,
we may be helped by what you give in this present age
and prepared for the gifts that are eternal.
Through Christ our Lord.

* Select from Prefaces I–VIII of the Sundays in Ordinary Time in the Order of Mass. Commentary, and proclamation and chant tips, for the Preface can be found at *www.StudyThePresidentialTexts.com/Prefaces* and in *The Order of Mass: A Roman Missal Study Edition and Workbook*, pages 62–77.

Collect: In this prayer, obedience and service are intricately connected, with service following upon obedience. We ask the Lord to bring our will into conformity with his. A more literal translation of this line would be "we may always bring a devout will to you." A devout will for God is one that is devoted to him in a personal and prayerful way. In other words, for God to "conform" our will to his, we must be open to it and longing for it. This conforming could involve the letting go of personal convictions to be raised to the divine perspective and resolve. The more we are united to God's will, the more we will live lives of service, because God is eternally giving himself away in service, in sacrificial love. The prayer juxtaposes serving God's "majesty" with the necessary manner of doing so, "in sincerity of heart." Flattery does not work with the divine majesty. The Latin word for "sincere" means to be without any theatrical kind of mask. We stand in service with complete humility.

Prayer over the Offerings: The "gifts," for which the prayer asks a "sincere respect," are the *mysteriis* that cleanse us and through which grace acts on us to purify. They are, in the first place, the bread, wine, and intentional offerings on the altar. Through the action of the Eucharistic Prayer, they become the mysteries of Christ. "Sincere respect" (mind made free would be more literal to the Latin) is deemed important if one is to be cleansed by grace. If our hearts and minds are bound to selfish or worldly pursuits, we

Pointed Text

Collect

A Almighty ever-living **God**,
B grant that we may always conform our **will** to yours
C and serve your majesty in sincerity of ***heart***.
Through our Lord Jesus Christ, your Son,
who lives and reigns with you in the unity of the Holy Spirit,
one God, for ever and ever.

Prayer over the Offerings

A Grant us, Lord, we pray,
a sincere respect for your **gifts**,
B that, through the purifying action **of** your grace,
C we may be cleansed by the very mysteries we ***serve***.
Through Christ our Lord.

Prayer after Communion

A Grant, O Lord, we **pray**,
B that, benefiting from participation in hea**ven**ly things,
C we may be helped by what you give in this present age
and prepared for the gifts that are eter***nal***.
Through Christ our Lord.

The space below is for your notes.

Refer to pages viii–x for an explanation of the pointing of the chants and to page xii for the Tones for the Presidential Prayers from *The Roman Missal*.

will have, at best, a superficial respect for the central role that Christ and his mysteries have in our lives. When the distractions of this life no longer have their hold on us, we begin to see the importance of relationships over control, of charity over greed, of discipleship over power and prestige. We need the grace of the Spirit who flows from the mysteries of Christ that we encounter in the Eucharist. Being truly cleansed, we will begin truly to serve.

Prayer after Communion: This prayer asks for grace to ensure that the Eucharist is never an "activity" from which we become distracted. Our hearts and minds are to be engaged by heavenly things, that is, things that endure beyond this life—relationships both human and divine, as well as the virtues that enable us to live such a heavenly life fully. The heavenly things in which we participate through the Eucharist are helps in the present age. The Sacraments, for example, are of heaven but packaged for earth, so to speak. They prepare us (*erudiamur*) for the life we hope to live in eternity. *Erudiamur* is normally used in the context of education to mean the removal of all that is uncouth or all that hinders us from taking advantage of life's opportunities. In this sense, sacramental things work both to remove sin and to instill in us the discipline and self-gift so necessary for life in the kingdom. They are an essential part of our education and preparation for heaven.

THIRTIETH SUNDAY IN ORDINARY TIME

Collect

Pause briefly after **Almighty**. Proclaim **faith**, **hope and charity** slowly and deliberately. Give a parallel emphasis to **love** and **command**, as well as to **merit** and **promise**.

Almighty ever-living God,
increase our faith, hope and charity,
and make us love what you command,
so that we may merit what you promise.
Through our Lord Jesus Christ, your Son,
who lives and reigns with you in the unity of the Holy Spirit,
one God, for ever and ever.

Prayer over the Offerings

Pause very briefly after **Look**. Proclaim **your majesty** with reverence.
Keep the voice raised with **service**. Proclaim a parallel rhythm with **in your service** and **to your glory**.

Look, we pray, O Lord,
on the offerings we make to your majesty,
that whatever is done by us in your service
may be directed above all to your glory.
Through Christ our Lord. *

Prayer after Communion

Pause briefly after **Sacraments** and after **in us**. Place emphasis on **us** and **them**. Find the parallel rhythm by stressing **now** and **signs** with **one** and **truth**.

May your Sacraments, O Lord, we pray,
perfect in us what lies within them,
that what we now celebrate in signs
we may one day possess in truth.
Through Christ our Lord.

* Select from Prefaces I–VIII of the Sundays in Ordinary Time in the Order of Mass. Commentary, and proclamation and chant tips, for the Preface can be found at *www.StudyThePresidentialTexts.com/Prefaces* and in *The Order of Mass: A Roman Missal Study Edition and Workbook*, pages 62–77.

Collect: This prayer lays out the basic essentials for life in the kingdom of heaven. First is that the heavenly king must bestow the virtues of faith, hope, and charity. These virtues are called "theological" because they are directly connected to our ability to know, love, and serve God. These three virtues are bestowed in Baptism and nourished in the Eucharist, which is why this prayer requests their "increase." If our faith is strong enough and we are willing to exercise it, then it will not be difficult to love what God commands. Faith teaches us to trust God that his commands are not only good for us, but the best for us. To love his commands is to love all that is Good, True, and Beautiful. This is also to be open to the working of the Holy Spirit in our lives. It is the work of the Spirit alone that can enable us to merit God's promise of eternal life. Our merit is not our achievements, but the gifts of God that we accept and embrace. Our achievement, in this case, is to love rightly.

Prayer over the Offerings: In all that we do, especially in the liturgy, it is good to keep our eyes directed to what is greater, to where the things of earth point. God's majesty is known best in the way in which it came to earth in the lowliness of our humanity. Christ was a man like us in all things but sin. The majesty of divinity is present to everything that the Son of God assumed in the Incarnation. From our daily experiences, we look up to this majesty and trust that God is looking at us and the humble offerings we bring.

Pointed Text

Collect

A Almighty ever-living **God**,
B increase our faith, **hope** and charity,
C and make us love what you command,
so that we may merit what you pro***mise***.
Through our Lord Jesus Christ, your Son,
who lives and reigns with you in the unity of the Holy Spirit,
one God, for ever and ever.

Prayer over the Offerings

A Look, we pray, O **Lord**,
B on the offerings we make **to** your majesty,
C that whatever is done by us in your service
may be directed above all to your glo***ry***.
Through Christ our Lord.

Prayer after Communion

A May your Sacraments, O Lord, we **pray**,
B perfect in us what **lies** within them,
C that what we now celebrate in signs
we may one day possess in ***truth***.
Through Christ our Lord.

The space below is for your notes.

Refer to pages viii–x for an explanation of the pointing of the chants and to page xii for the Tones for the Presidential Prayers from *The Roman Missal*.

The service that we give to God is, first of all, the service of prayer and the Sacraments. It also must include our service to one another in charity, whether at work, at school, or home. When God looks upon such acts of service, the light of his face raises whatever good is present in our weak and often selfish attempts to serve him and others. He blesses that goodness, fostering and enriching it, and directs it to glory.

Prayer after Communion: To be a Christian, it is necessary to believe that humanity is lacking something fundamental that only God can supply. Many seek what they lack in the beautiful things of the world rather than the Beauty behind and beyond the world. In the Sacraments, the Lord, who is the Beauty that we all seek, communicates himself to us. In the Sacrament of Holy Communion, the perfected presence of Christ comes to the imperfect image of Christ in us to bring us to his perfection. We received the image of Christ in our Baptism, but it is not yet come to full maturity, and whenever we sin, we both do it damage and hinder its maturation. Our carrying out of sacramental celebrations is necessarily done with "signs" in this temporal world, but this breaks the truth of the mystery into pieces that can be communicated. When we come to full stature in Christ in the glory of heaven, our nature will grasp the whole in reality, that is, in truth.

THIRTY-FIRST SUNDAY IN ORDINARY TIME

Collect

Pause briefly after **Almighty** and similarly after **gift**, but give no significant pause after **offer you**. Proclaim **right and praiseworthy service** slowly. Stress **hasten** but raise the voice for **without stumbling**.
Proclaim **things you have promised** with joyful anticipation.

Almighty and merciful God,
by whose gift your faithful offer you
right and praiseworthy service,
grant, we pray,
that we may hasten without stumbling
to receive the things you have promised.
Through our Lord Jesus Christ, your Son,
who lives and reigns with you in the unity of the Holy Spirit,
one God, for ever and ever.

Prayer over the Offerings

Proclaim **sacrificial offerings** with humble dignity.
Proclaim **pure oblation** and **holy outpouring** with vibrant energy. Catch the rhythm between **for you** and **for us**.

May these sacrificial offerings, O Lord,
become for you a pure oblation,
and for us a holy outpouring of your mercy.
Through Christ our Lord. *

Prayer after Communion

Place equal emphasis on **working** and **power**. Pause briefly after **so that** and proclaim **renewed** with energy and **heavenly Sacraments** with delight. Give parallel emphasis between **prepared by your gift** and **receiving what they promise**.

May the working of your power, O Lord,
increase in us, we pray,
so that, renewed by these heavenly Sacraments,
we may be prepared by your gift
for receiving what they promise.
Through Christ our Lord.

* Select from Prefaces I–VIII of the Sundays in Ordinary Time in the Order of Mass. Commentary, and proclamation and chant tips, for the Preface can be found at *www.StudyThePresidentialTexts.com/Prefaces* and in *The Order of Mass: A Roman Missal Study Edition and Workbook*, pages 62–77.

Collect: The translation "by whose gift your faithful offer" would be more accurately translated from the Latin as "from whose gift comes" (*de cuius munere venit*). The subtle shift from "by" to "from" can communicate, perhaps, a subtle point that the "service" we render is able to be "right and praiseworthy" because it "comes from" the one perfect "gift" of service rendered by Christ on the Cross. Christ alone has offered truly "right and praiseworthy service" to the Father. His is the reality to be posited and in which to participate.

When we open our eyes and hearts to that reality, we are changed by the Love and the Beauty we encounter. This would explain the energy we request to "hasten without stumbling" (the Latin is to "run," much as Peter and John did on the morning of the Resurrection). In this context, to stumble means to hesitate, doubt, sin. The vision of God's promises to us in Christ is necessary to keep us moving toward the goal without stumbling.

Prayer over the Offerings: The "sacrificial offerings" refer to the Eucharistic Sacrifice about to be offered on the altar. Each gift (the spiritual sacrifice) brought by the assembly is included in this one sacrifice. According to the Old Testament regulations, nothing unclean could be placed upon the altar, which is why every animal had to be without blemish. The word translated here as "pure" (*munda*) actually means "cleansed." Pure refers to someone or thing that has never been touched by sin. Cleansed means that one who was sin-

Pointed Text

Collect

A Almighty and merciful God,
by whose gift your faithful offer you
right and praiseworthy ser**vice**,
B grant, we pray,
that we may hasten **with**out stumbling
C to receive the things you have pro***mised***.
Through our Lord Jesus Christ, your Son,
who lives and reigns with you in the unity of the Holy Spirit,
one God, for ever and ever.

Prayer over the Offerings

A May these sacrificial offerings, O **Lord**,
B become for you a **pure** oblation,
C and for us a holy outpouring of your mer***cy***.
Through Christ our Lord.

Prayer after Communion

A May the working of your power, O Lord,
increase in us, we **pray**,
B so that, renewed by these hea**ven**ly Sacraments,
C we may be prepared by your gift
for receiving what they pro***mise***.
Through Christ our Lord.

The space below is for your notes.

Refer to pages viii–x for an explanation of the pointing of the chants and to page xii for the Tones for the Presidential Prayers from *The Roman Missal*.

ful has been made clean. When united to Christ, the offerings become washed clean. We carry our past with us, just as Christ carries the marks of the Cross with him, but through Christ, we believe that our sinful past will be transformed into marks of glory. This can occur because God has promised us a "holy outpouring of his mercy." The holy outpouring is none other than the Holy Spirit, who sanctifies the offerings and, through them, sanctifies us.

Prayer after Communion: The Holy Spirit is often called the "power" (*virtus*) of God. In the Eucharistic Prayer, the sacramental gifts were consecrated by the "working of the Holy Spirit." If we receive those gifts with faith, then assuredly the Holy Spirit will increase within us. This power's purpose is to overcome the temptations and sins which fight within us for mastery. We cannot do this by ourselves. For this to happen our fallen nature must be remade or "renewed." This begins in Baptism and is strengthened with all the Sacraments, which are called "heavenly" because they fill us with the "power" of the Spirit to make us a new creation in Christ. The Sacraments already contain the reality that "they promise," but we will not be able to grasp that reality fully until our renewal is completed in the resurrection. This is why each Catholic can have a more or less intense experience with the Sacraments, depending on inner readiness.

THIRTY-SECOND SUNDAY IN ORDINARY TIME

Collect

Pause briefly after **Almighty**. Stress **all adversity**. Pause after **unhindered**. Proclaim **mind and body alike** slowly. Proclaim **freedom of heart** with grateful joy and **things that are yours** with humble reverence.

Almighty and merciful God,
graciously keep from us all adversity,
so that, unhindered in mind and body alike,
we may pursue in freedom of heart
the things that are yours.
Through our Lord Jesus Christ, your Son,
who lives and reigns with you in the unity of the Holy Spirit,
one God, for ever and ever.

Prayer over the Offerings

Pause briefly after **favor**. Stress **sacrificial gifts**. Pause briefly after **mystery**. Proclaim **Passion of your Son** with reverent energy. Proclaim **honor it with loving devotion** with humble desire.

Look with favor, we pray, O Lord,
upon the sacrificial gifts offered here,
that, celebrating in mystery the Passion of your Son,
we may honor it with loving devotion.
Through Christ our Lord. *

Prayer after Communion

Stress **sacred gift**. Pause briefly after **thanks**. Proclaim **beseech your mercy** with gentle pleading. Speak **pouring forth** slowly and deliberately. Proclaim **grace of integrity** with confidence and with parallel rhythm to **heavenly power**.

Nourished by this sacred gift, O Lord,
we give you thanks and beseech your mercy,
that, by the pouring forth of your Spirit,
the grace of integrity may endure
in those your heavenly power has entered.
Through Christ our Lord.

* Select from Prefaces I–VIII of the Sundays in Ordinary Time in the Order of Mass. Commentary, and proclamation and chant tips, for the Preface can be found at *www.StudyThePresidentialTexts.com/Prefaces* and in *The Order of Mass: A Roman Missal Study Edition and Workbook*, pages 62–77.

Collect: This prayer does not ask the Lord to destroy adversity but to keep it from us (*exclude nobis*). The idea is that God created all things good, but when they are not used in accord with their purpose, they become an adversity to us. The phrase translated as "in freedom of heart" (*liberis mentibus*) is literally "with free minds." This raises an interesting question as to why the prayer seeks for us to be unhindered "in mind and body alike," but to pursue divine things with only free minds. In this life, the body has a key role in communicating to the mind and heart both good things and temptations. We are not machines. We believe that what we do in the body affects our spiritual and mental health. On the other hand, our body is mortal and will not, at least in its present form, participate in the "things that are yours." The things that we should pursue in this life are the things of the mind and heart that find favor with God, that belong to him, and that will endure into eternity.

Prayer over the Offerings: When God looks with favor upon us, it means God is drawing near to us with his power to cleanse and save. We must be willing and able to present "sacrificial gifts" that need his cleansing and saving power. We come to the Eucharist to present to God our encounters that need his perfecting and transforming power. We engage this power by opening ourselves to the mystery of Christ's Passion. To celebrate "in mystery" means to do so in sign and Sacrament. Now, we do not have the

Pointed Text

Collect

A Almighty and merciful **God**,
B graciously keep from us **all** adversity,
C so that, unhindered in mind and body alike,
we may pursue in freedom of heart
the things that are ***yours***.
Through our Lord Jesus Christ, your Son,
who lives and reigns with you in the unity of the Holy Spirit,
one God, for ever and ever.

Prayer over the Offerings

A Look with favor, we pray, O **Lord**,
B upon the sacrificial gifts **off**ered here,
C that, celebrating in mystery the Passion of your Son,
we may honor it with loving devo***tion***.
Through Christ our Lord.

Prayer after Communion

A Nourished by this sacred gift, O **Lord**,
B we give you thanks and be**seech** your mercy,
C that, by the pouring forth of your Spirit,
the grace of integrity may endure
in those your heavenly power has en***tered***.
Through Christ our Lord.

The space below is for your notes.

Refer to pages viii–x for an explanation of the pointing of the chants and to page xii for the Tones for the Presidential Prayers from *The Roman Missal.*

means to communicate the fruits of Christ's Passion in their full reality. We hope to participate in those fruits in the glory of heaven, where Christ makes an eternal offering. On earth, we "honor" that Passion by celebrating the ritual in mystery "with loving devotion" (*pio affectu*). This refers to the affectionate loyalty and responsibility children owe their parents. This is how we honor the Father's gift of his Son's life sacrificed for us.

Prayer after Communion: In the Eucharistic Prayer, we gave thanks for the presence of the Paschal Mystery, and after reception of Holy Communion, we give thanks that so great a Mystery has come to dwell in us. This indwelling Mystery is called the "heavenly power" (*caelestis virtus*). The Spirit is poured forth and the heavenly power enters. The Spirit is pure divine action. Whenever God acts, it is in the pouring forth action of the Spirit: in creation, in the prophets, in the anointing of kings, in the Incarnation, in the Resurrection, and with the Church. This prayer seeks that the "grace of integrity may endure." This implies that such grace has already been bestowed. Integrity (*sinceritatis*) means wholeness. Sin works to create divisions within the individual. With the gift of Holy Communion, the light of Christ shines within us, revealing the person who sometimes acts in contradictory ways. Embracing this light, we can begin to walk by it with integrity.

THIRTY-THIRD SUNDAY IN ORDINARY TIME

Pause briefly after **Grant us** and **gladness**. Proclaim **constant gladness** with joyful energy and **devoted to you** with tenderness. Speak **full and lasting** slowly and confidently. Stress **constancy** and keep the voice raised. Proclaim **all that is good** with contentment.

Collect

Grant us, we pray, O Lord our God,
the constant gladness of being devoted to you,
for it is full and lasting happiness
to serve with constancy
the author of all that is good.
Through our Lord Jesus Christ, your Son,
who lives and reigns with you in the unity of the Holy Spirit,
one God, for ever and ever.

Proclaim **in the sight of your majesty** with reverent awe. Pause briefly after **for us**. Stress **grace** and proclaim **devoted to you** with tenderness. Pause briefly after **gain us**. Stress **prize** and proclaim **everlasting happiness** with energy.

Prayer over the Offerings

Grant, O Lord, we pray,
that what we offer in the sight of your majesty
may obtain for us the grace of being devoted to you
and gain us the prize of everlasting happiness.
Through Christ our Lord. *

Speak the first line deliberately, with emphasis on **partaken**, **gifts**, and **sacred mystery**. Proclaim **commanded** with gentle firmness. Do not pause after **to do**. Stress **memory**. Proclaim **growth in charity** slowly and peacefully.

Prayer after Communion

We have partaken of the gifts of this sacred mystery,
humbly imploring, O Lord,
that what your Son commanded us to do
in memory of him
may bring us growth in charity.
Through Christ our Lord.

* Select from Prefaces I–VIII of the Sundays in Ordinary Time in the Order of Mass. Commentary, and proclamation and chant tips, for the Preface can be found at *www.StudyThePresidentialTexts.com/Prefaces* and in *The Order of Mass: A Roman Missal Study Edition and Workbook*, pages 62–77.

Collect: When two people love each other sincerely, each takes delight in performing acts of devotion for the other. This is the idea behind the "constant gladness" the faithful seek in serving God with personal and heartfelt attention. This kind of service-love is an imitation of Jesus, who washed the feet of his disciples. It is divine self-emptying love for others. This is why it is called "full and lasting happiness" to serve God. Happiness (*felicitas)* is not an end in itself or the satisfaction of our desires. God alone can satisfy the desires of the human heart. Happiness is the consequence of living for others. The root of the word *felicitas* means to bear fruit and be productive. When we bear fruit for others, we will experience the consequent feeling of happiness. God is the ultimate "source" of anything that bears good fruit, of anything "that is good." For these reasons, "full and lasting happiness" is found in imitating God in constant service.

Prayer over the Offerings: The gift or sacrifice offered on the altar is done "in the sight" of God's majesty. We do not hide the Passion of the Cross but proclaim it to all for at least two reasons: first, as a perpetual memorial of what a Christian must never do to another; and second, as a constant witness to what a Christian must be willing to suffer. The suffering and Death of Christ was endured for each of us with the invitation to respond with similar devotion. When we hear the words of institution in the Eucharistic Prayer, "given up for you"

Pointed Text

Collect

A Grant us, we pray, O Lord our **God**,
B the constant gladness of being devo**ted** to you,
C for it is full and lasting happiness
to serve with constancy
the author of all that is ***good***.
Through our Lord Jesus Christ, your Son,
who lives and reigns with you in the unity of the Holy Spirit,
one God, for ever and ever.

Prayer over the Offerings

A Grant, O Lord, we **pray**,
B that what we offer in the sight **of** your majesty
C may obtain for us the grace of being devoted to you
and gain us the prize of everlasting hap***pi***ness.
Through Christ our Lord.

Prayer after Communion

A We have partaken of the gifts of this sacred mys**ter**y,
B humbly implor**ing**, O Lord,
C that what your Son commanded us to do
in memory of him
may bring us growth in char***i***ty.
Through Christ our Lord.

The space below is for your notes.

Refer to pages viii–x for an explanation of the pointing of the chants and to page xii for the Tones for the Presidential Prayers from *The Roman Missal.*

and "poured out for you," we should hear them proclaimed personally. The grace to return such devotion is given by the Holy Spirit, the fire of divine charity. The "prize" (*effectum*) of everlasting happiness would be the overcoming of fear related to death. This is a prize that we can experience fully only in the next life. The phrase translated as "everlasting happiness" (*beatae perennitatis*—blessed immortality) strengthens our hope in life without death.

Prayer after Communion: The sacred mystery is the fullness of Christ in glory, but present to his Body the Church in time and on earth. Mystery is the translation of transcendent eternity into the immanence of time. The effects of such a translation are the Sacraments, and in this prayer they are the "gifts" of Holy Communion. The prayer draws a direct connection between obedience to the Son and growth in charity (*caritas*), which is the self-gift of divine love. Christ's memorial at the altar is the re-presentation of his supreme act of *caritas*, of sacrifical gift. The two words "humbly imploring" are key here. The charity of Christ celebrated at the altar will grow in us only if we act with humility, that is, with awareness of our failures and need for help, and only if we resolve to desire and accept it, that is, implore the gift of charity. Our obedience to the command of the Lord is a measure of our interior freedom. With true freedom, his commands come to be experienced as desires of our heart.

The Solemnities of the Lord during Ordinary Time

First Sunday after Pentecost

THE MOST HOLY TRINITY

Solemnity

To allow an understanding of the theology in the Collect, proclaim the Collect slowly and clearly, respecting the commas.

Tie together lines one, two, and three, clearly enunciating the Persons names in line two. In line four, make a slight drop in the voice for **we pray**. Treat **that** as if a comma followed. Pause slightly at **faith**, holding the word slightly. Pray lines 5 and 6 slowly, but tie the two lines together. Parallel **Trinity . . . glory** and **Unity . . . majesty**.

Collect

God our Father, who by sending into the world
the Word of truth and the Spirit of sanctification
made known to the human race your wondrous mystery,
grant us, we pray, that in professing the true faith,
we may acknowledge the Trinity of eternal glory
and adore your Unity, powerful in majesty.
Through our Lord Jesus Christ, your Son,
who lives and reigns with you in the unity of the Holy Spirit,
one God, for ever and ever.

Line two is parenthetical, so drop the voice slightly.
Enunciate carefully **oblation** and **service**. Make a very slight pause after **it**, to give more impact to the petition that follows. Accent both **eternal** and **offering**.

Prayer over the Offerings

Sanctify by the invocation of your name,
we pray, O Lord our God,
this oblation of our service,
and by it make of us an eternal offering to you.
Through Christ our Lord.

Prayer after Communion

May receiving this Sacrament, O Lord our God,
bring us health of body and soul,
as we confess your eternal holy Trinity and undivided Unity.
Through Christ our Lord.

Collect: Calling God "Father" is to imitate Jesus (cf. Matthew 11:25–27, Luke 22:42, and 23:34–46) and his followers in the early Church. We find in the letters to Saint Paul the greeting: "Grace to you and peace from God our Father and the Lord Jesus Christ" (Romans 1:7).

The name of Christ as "Word," of course, is strong in Saint John's writings, beginning with the Prologue in the Gospel according to John (cf. John 1:1); and in Jesus's prayer to the Father, in John 17:17: "Consecrate" them in truth; your word is truth"). The name "Spirit of sanctification" is in the writings of Saint Paul and Saint John. In 1 Corinthians 6:19, Paul says: ". . . your body is a temple of the holy Spirit . . . ." Saint John calls the Holy Spirit "the Spirit of truth" (1 John 4:6, 5:7).

The Collect prays that we, who have accepted the truths from the Councils and proclaim their Creeds at Mass, will continue to acknowledge the Trinity of God (in Persons), but also the unity of God (in substance).

Prayer over the Offerings: Calling on the name of the Lord results in transformation—so says the New Testament tradition. Thus, Acts 2:21: "[E]veryone shall be saved who calls on the name of the Lord." Of course, in scriptural and ancient Christian terms, "name" means "person." So to call upon the Lord's name is to invoke the presence of his Person. That Presence, which by definition means "the Holy," is needed if our gifts are to be made holy.

The term "oblation of our service" is found in the most ancient Sacramentary

The space below is for your notes.

Refer to pages viii–x for an explanation of the pointing of the chants and to page xii for the Tones for the Presidential Prayers from *The Roman Missal.*

Pointed Text

Collect

A God our Father, who by sending into the world
the Word of truth and the Spirit of sanctifica**tion**
B made known to the human race your **won**drous mystery,
C grant us, we pray, that in professing the true faith,
we may acknowledge the Trinity of eternal glory
and adore your Unity, powerful in ma***jes***ty.
Through our Lord Jesus Christ, your Son,
who lives and reigns with you in the unity of the Holy Spirit,
one God, for ever and ever.

Prayer over the Offerings

A Sanctify by the invocation of your name,
we pray, O Lord our **God**,
B this oblation **of** our service,
C and by it make of us an eternal offering to ***you***.
Through Christ our Lord.

Prayer after Communion

A May receiving this Sacrament, O Lord our **God**,
B bring us health of bo**dy** and soul,
C as we confess your eternal holy Trinity and undivided Un***i***ty.
Through Christ our Lord.

that we know (Verona; Mohlberg, 951). The original Latin of the Missal uses almost the same words, speaking of the "service of the sacred Gift/Offering." The prayer addresses the offering of material elements and ourselves. We join our poor gift to that of Jesus, during Mass. We can hope that the offering, made here of ourselves, will go on for all eternity, by our arriving in heaven to worship the Trinity.

Prayer after Communion: The opening petition of the prayer is all-encompassing. It asks not just for salvation for the communicant's soul, but also for health of body. We know that what the *Catechism of the Catholic Church* (CCC) says is true: "Communion with the flesh of the risen Christ, a flesh 'given life and giving life through the Holy Spirit,' preserves, increases, and renews the life of grace received at Baptism" (CCC, 1392). That is, the redemption that Jesus won for us and that comes to us through Baptism is renewed profoundly whenever we receive Holy Communion. But this petition wants the body to experience some of that life-giving power that certainly is available to the soul. The Church hopes that its intimate union with Jesus through this holy Sacrament will affect the whole person.

We confess God as eternal holy Trinity and undivided Unity—one last restatement of the dogma on which this solemnity is based. And it is this confession we carry out from Mass, on our lips and in our hearts, to be a vital reality in our lives.

Bring out the accent on **be** in **The Lord be with you.** In the response, accent **spirit**, by slightly holding both syllables. In the next phrase, make a strong accent on **Lift**, and slow both notes of **hearts**. In the third dialogue, move to the word **thanks** before accenting, and hold that word slightly to give it emphasis. Broaden both notes of **Lord** and hold **God**.

Sing this proclamation cursively in a reciting tone. In **salvation**, do not hold **-va**; only broaden the two notes slightly. Hold **-tion**. **Always** and **everywhere** require a slight broadening and clear enunciation. The accent of the phrase falls on **thanks**, which should be held briefly. Clearly make three phrases of the next part of the text, by respecting the commas after **Lord** and **Father**.

Do not pause at the word **Spirit**. Clear articulation will probably call for a break for the comma after **God**, thus setting off both **one God** and **one Lord**. Since the sense of the sentence continues, **Lord** should be lengthened but a real pause should not be made there, only a slight break in the voice to indicate the colon.

Hold **-ry** of **glory**; also **Son** and **-it** of **Spirit**.

Pause slightly after **that** to set off the coming clause. A breath will be needed after **Godhead**, the latter syllable of which is to be held briefly. Pause after **Person** and **substance** to

Preface: The mystery of the Most Holy Trinity

In the body of the Preface, the text immediately restates the main elements of the dogma, chiseled out of the efforts of Councils and Fathers of the Church; therefore all Three Persons are mentioned within two lines. Reiterated also is the understanding that the unity of God is in substance, while the Trinity of God is in Persons. Thus, we begin the Eucharistic Prayer with a strong Trinitarian reference, just as we shall end it in the final doxology.

The next paragraph makes the belief of the Church clear: by this extraordinary revelation, God has revealed something of his glory, the marvelous reality that in the Old Testament usually meant God's presence (cf. Exodus 16:7–10, Isaiah 35:2).

This Preface proclaims that all Three Persons are the revelation of God, and that we believe this of all Three Persons equally.

This is delineated a little more, as this great song of praise mentions the details of the dogma yet once again: in confessing the unity of the Godhead, we also adore what belongs to each of the Persons. Not only is their unity in substance reiterated, but a new description of the unity of the Persons is added: their equality in majesty. What is wonderful indeed is that such majesty is infinitely above our human persons, and yet, God has condescended to reveal it to us. It is this marvelous gift of God that leads the Church then to join the whole heavenly chorus in a paean of praise, Holy, Holy, Holy . . . .

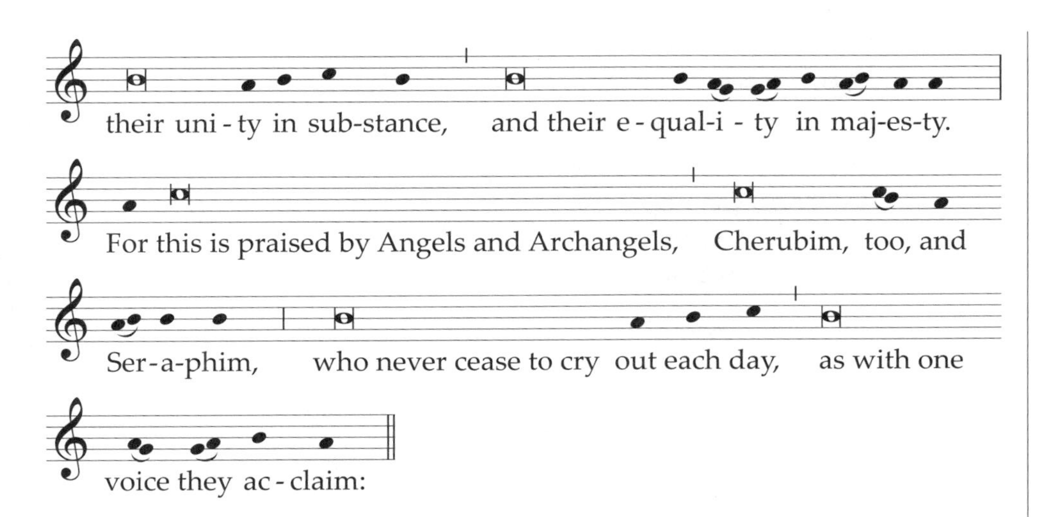

clearly enunciate the dogmas. Broaden **equality in majesty**.

Slow **they ac-**, and put emphasis on **-claim**, so as to evoke the response **Holy, Holy, Holy . . . .**

Holy, Holy, Holy Lord God of hosts . . .

Text without music:

V. **The Lord be with you.**
R. And with your spirit.

V. **Lift up your hearts.**
R. We lift them up to the Lord.

V. **Let us give thanks to the Lord our God.**
R. It is right and just.

It is truly right and just, our duty and our salvation,
always and everywhere to give you thanks,
Lord, holy Father, almighty and eternal God.

For with your Only Begotten Son and the Holy Spirit
you are one God, one Lord:
not in the unity of a single person,
but in a Trinity of one substance.

Tie together lines one and two. Slight pause after **God** and a clearer pause after **Lord**. Accent **not** and **single person**. Emphasize **Trinity** and enunciate clearly **one substance**.

For what you have revealed to us of your glory
we believe equally of your Son
and of the Holy Spirit,
so that, in the confessing of the true and eternal Godhead,

Emphasize **revealed** and **glory**. Tie together the first three lines. Accent **Son** and **Holy Spirit**. Emphasize **confessing**, **true**, **eternal**, and **Godhead**, and then pause briefly.

(The following explores our belief that the unity of God is in substance. It was excerpted from *Preparing Your Parish for the Revised Roman Missal: Homilies and Reproducibles for Faith Formation* © 2010, Liturgy Training Publications.)

The Meaning of Consubstantial

Daniel Merz, SLD

One of the more interesting changes in the new translation of the Missal occurs in the Creed. In the second paragraph of the Creed, the phrase "consubstantial with the Father" has replaced "one in Being with the Father." Some may wonder why such an unfamiliar word needs to be used. On the other hand, it may just as easily be asked, whether we understand the phrase, "one in Being with the Father"? Both options attempt to put into words one of the great mysteries of our faith, that Jesus Christ is equal to the Father.

The Nicene Creed originally was composed in Greek; the Greek word used in the phrase is *homoousios*. This is a compound formed from two words: *homo* (same) and *ousia* (essence, being). The use of this word in the Creed was revolutionary in its day because it is not a scriptural but a philosophical term. The greatest heresy of that day, Arianism, argued the Christ was not of the same substance of the Father but of a similar substance (*homoiousios*) and, therefore, was not equal to the Father. The Church Fathers wanted to be precise in the language used for such a great mystery, and the debates at the time were long and often acrimonious. From the beginning, the Latin Creed translated this Greek word

Accent **adored**, **proper**, **each**, and **Person**. After **Person**, lift the voice slightly as if in expectancy (as if there were a colon there), and continue without a pause, tying lines six and seven together. Parallel **unity in substance** and **equality in majesty**.

you might be adored in what is proper to each Person,
their unity in substance,
and their equality in majesty.

For this is praised by Angels and Archangels,
Cherubim, too, and Seraphim,
who never cease to cry out each day,
as with one voice they acclaim:

Holy, Holy, Holy Lord God of hosts . . .

as *consubstantialem*, for similar precise philosophical and theological reasons. By breaking down the word con-sub-stantial, we can understand it a little better.

The root word "substance" (sub = under; stans = standing) is also a technical, philosophical term that refers to the most real part of a being. Literally, it refers to that which "stands under," the base of a person or thing, that which is at the heart of someone or something. This is fine as long as we don't equate substance with the mere physical or external dimension.

Today, we can use the word substance in reference to the essential, for example, "the substance of the matter," but we can also use it in a rather mundane and materialistic sense. Within the liturgy, of course, the Church is thinking of the former. In the Eucharist, we say that bread and wine are transubstantiated into the Body and Blood, Soul and Divinity of Jesus Christ. The form or appearance of the bread and wine remains the same, but their inner substance, the reality underneath the appearance, is changed. This is why we don't say the bread and wine are just transformed, but transubstantiated.

The other part of consubstantial is the first three letters "con." It comes from the Latin preposition *cum*, meaning "together with." In the Creed, consubstantial means that Christ was of one substance with the Father but also implies one substance with our humanity. He is co-substantial, referring therein to the two natures of Christ—human and divine.

The previous translation "one in Being" does not portray this multivalence.

Also, most would assert that this phrase is not as precise. The English word "Being" has a broader meaning than the philosophical term "substance." "Being" commonly refers to all that is, which would include the appearance or form of a thing, and in relation to the Trinity, could mistakenly include Personhood. God the Son is not the same Person as God the Father, but they share the same inner being or substance. Both phrases, "one in Being" and "consubstantial," are accurate when properly understood. In translating the Creed, however, it is important to be as precise as possible, and the Church believes that the term "consubstantial" is a better choice in naming the Great Mystery that is the relationship of Jesus Christ to God the Father and to us, his adopted sons and daughters.

[In the Dioceses of the United States]
Sunday after the Most Holy Trinity

THE MOST HOLY BODY AND BLOOD OF CHRIST (CORPUS CHRISTI)

Solemnity

Collect

Tie together lines one and two, while respecting that **who . . . Passion** is a parenthetical phrase calling for a slight pause after **God** and a lowering of the voice. Broaden **Body and Blood**, and without a pause, go to **always**, tying together that line with the next.

O God, who in this wonderful Sacrament
have left us a memorial of your Passion,
grant us, we pray,
so to revere the sacred mysteries of your Body and Blood
that we may always experience in ourselves
the fruits of your redemption.
Who live and reign with God the Father
in the unity of the Holy Spirit,
one God, for ever and ever.

Prayer over the Offerings

Lower the voice slightly for the parenthetical, **O Lord,** and **we pray**, pausing after **Lord**. Tie together lines one and two. Enunciate clearly **unity** and **peace.** Tie together lines three and four, enunciating clearly **in mystery**.

Grant your Church, O Lord, we pray,
the gifts of unity and peace,
whose signs are to be seen in mystery
in the offerings we here present.
Through Christ our Lord.

Prayer after Communion

Lower voice slightly for **O Lord, we pray**. Tie together lines two and three. Accent **delight**, **all**, and **eternity**. Enunciate carefully **that share** and **divine life**. A very brief pause may be made there, but remember that the sense calls for going on to **which is**. Accent **present age**. Do not pause there, but tie together that line with the next. Slow and broaden **precious Body and Blood**.

Grant, O Lord, we pray,
that we may delight for all eternity
in that share in your divine life,
which is foreshadowed in the present age
by our reception of your precious Body and Blood.
Who live and reign for ever and ever.

Collect: The opening statement of the prayer expresses an important part of our faith in the Holy Eucharist. Because it contains so much grace and salvific power, this Sacrament is wonderful; it leaves us full of wonder—more than any other. This is so because the Sacrament contains the memorial of the Lord's Passion. When the word "memorial" is used in the liturgy (Greek *anamnesis*), it refers to something—whether word, gesture, or thing—that contains the reality signified. Thus, the "memorial of the Lord's Passion" contains everything that the suffering and Death of Jesus contained, that is, salvation for the whole world.

His once-for-all redeeming Death is made completely present again sacramentally. Revering/adoring the Sacred Mysteries of the Body and Blood of Christ opens us up, then, to experience all the results (fruits) of redemption again. And that makes this a very joy-filled solemnity indeed.

Prayer over the Offerings: The petition begins immediately, with no prefacing phrase. What the Church desires is the fruits the Holy Eucharist brings: unity and peace. The unity comes from our reception of the Sacred Species in Holy Communion. Coming to us under the signs of bread and wine, transformed by his Word and the power of the Holy Spirit, Jesus brings us into union with him. Jesus is our unity.

Peace, another fruit of Holy Communion, was a special gift of the risen Lord to his disciples: "Peace I leave with

The space below is for your notes.

Refer to pages viii–x for an explanation of the pointing of the chants and to page xii for the Tones for the Presidential Prayers from *The Roman Missal.*

Pointed Text

Collect

A O God, who in this wonderful Sacrament
have left us a memorial of your Pas**sion**,
B grant **us**, we pray,
C so to revere the sacred mysteries of your Body and Blood
that we may always experience in ourselves
the fruits of your redemp***tion***.
Who live and reign with God the Father
in the unity of the Holy Spirit,
one God, for ever and ever.

Prayer over the Offerings

A Grant your Church, O Lord, we pray,
the gifts of unity and **peace**,
B whose signs are to be **seen** in mystery
C in the offerings we here pre***sent***.
Through Christ our Lord.

Prayer after Communion

A Grant, O Lord, we **pray**,
B that we may delight for all eternity
in that share in your **di**vine life,
C which is foreshadowed in the present age
by our reception of your precious Body and ***Blood***.
Who live and reign for ever and ever.

you . . . . Not as the world gives . . ." (John 14:27). Peace is, in effect, the Risen Jesus's gift of himself. In Holy Communion, we receive the same Reality that the first disciples received.

In the bread and wine that is lifted up in offering to God, the Church sees the signs of what these elements will become. The Body and Blood of Christ is seen "in mystery," that is, in sign and sacrament, that will soon carry heavenly Reality and grace.

Prayer after Communion: The Body and Blood is described as "precious"—which in the Latin carries as strong a connotation as does the English: of great price. That, of course, is precisely what the Body and Blood of Christ are: because they were the means, in Jesus's Passion, Death, and Resurrection, by which God would save the world, they are of inestimable value to people of faith. Our Communion, just as the liturgy we are completing now, has put us into intimate contact with that "precious" reality that is Jesus.

But we recognize that this contact is earthly. Although delightful to persons of faith, it holds only earthly delight, since our hearts cannot yet share the fullness of delight that Holy Communion foreshadows. And so the Church turns its mind and heart toward that place of fullness, heaven. The prayer then petitions that what we share in now through Sacraments, God's "divine" life, we may share for all eternity. Then we will see God face to face (cf. 2 Corinthians 3:18) and have perfect union with the Trinity (Ephesians 1:10–13).

Bring out the accent on **be** in **The Lord be with you.** In the next phrase, make a strong accent on **Lift**, and slow both notes of **hearts**. In the third dialogue, move to the word **thanks** before accenting, and hold that word slightly to give it emphasis. Broaden both notes of **Lord**, and hold **God**.

Sing this proclamation cursively in a reciting tone. In **salvation**, do not hold **-va**; only broaden the two notes slightly. Hold **-tion**. **Always** and **everywhere** require a slight broadening and clear enunciation. The accent of the phrase falls on **thanks**, which should be held briefly. Clearly make four phrases of the next part of the text, by respecting the commas after **Lord**, **Father**, and **God**.

From **For at the Last** to **praise** is one thought. Because of the melodic development on **Apostles**, it might be best to take a breath here. Do not hold **come** in the next phrase, but continue to **the saving**.
Hold **Cross** and take a short breath there.
Hold **Lamb**. Do not pause for breath, but go on to **the acceptable**. Accent **Nour-** in **Nourishing**, although this is hard to do because of the rise in the melody that follows. Hold **-y** of **mystery**. It would be best to breathe quickly there. Do not stop at or hold **race**, but continue to **bounded**. Hold **world** slightly, but try not to breathe there but continue the sense of **may be enlightened**.

Preface: The fruits of the Most Holy Eucharist
The body of the Preface begins by placing the source of this solemntiy at the Last Supper. The special Passover celebration with the Apostles contained the reality of what Jesus was to do on Good Friday: Jesus did on Holy Thursday in mystery what he would do, a day later, on Good Friday, in history. Again, "memorial" means re-presentation of the event, actual presence at and within the original event, rather than a mere mental recalling. On the Cross, Jesus fulfilled what the Passover was intended to do: he offered himself to God as the new Lamb for the redemption of God's people. Such a gift to God gave him perfect praise, because it was given by God's own Son.

When we eat the Body and Blood of Christ, the Holy One of God (Mark 1:24), we actually become what we eat—which makes us holy, too. The goal of sharing this Sacrament is to extend our unity with Christ to the entire world, witnessing faith in Jesus, and living in the charity of God. The last sentence of the body of the text proclaims how the grace of the Holy Eucharist actually prepares us to begin a new Passover into the heavenly realities which we know here in Sacrament.

(The following homily, written for this solemnity for the Year A readings, is among the homilies at www.RevisedRomanMissal.org.)

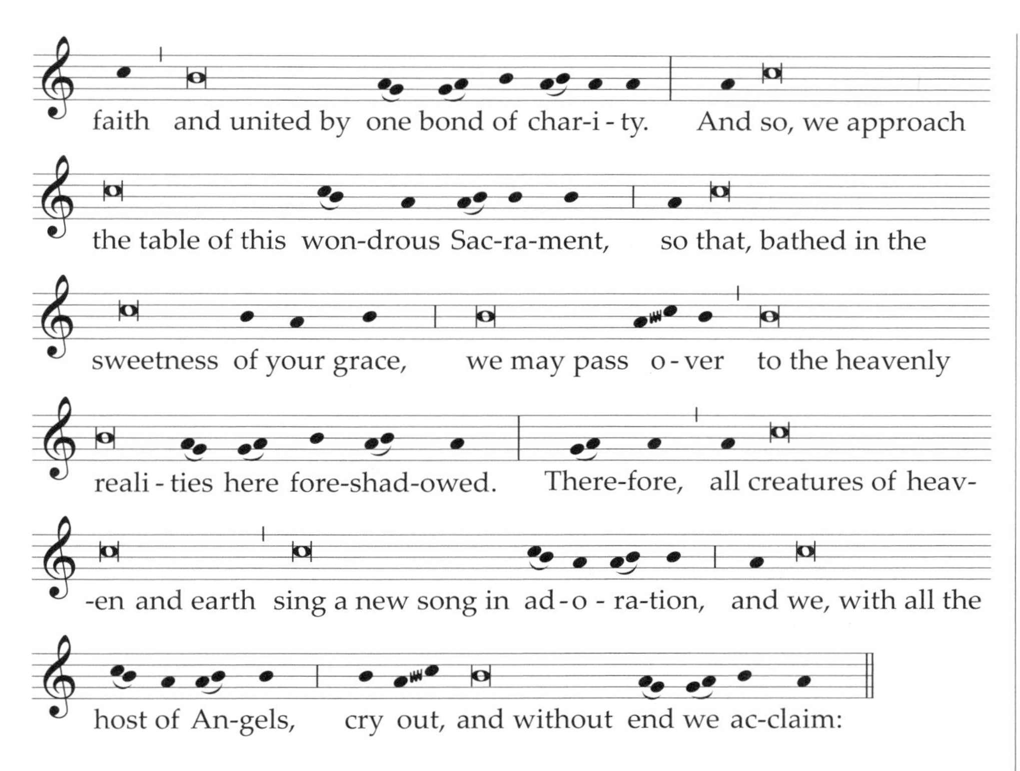

Hold **faith** briefly but try not to breathe, so as to tie this phrase to that which ends with **charity**. Hold **so** and pause briefly there. Hold **-ment** in **Sacrament** and pause briefly. In the next phrase, hold **that** and pause briefly. If possible, do not breathe after **grace**, but continue on to **we may pass**. Again, do not hold **-ver** in **over** but connect it to **to the heavenly**.

Broaden **here foreshadowed**.

Slight pause after **Therefore**. Respect the commas, but try to keep this section together, without big breaks for breaths.

Slow **we ac-**, and put emphasis on **-claim**, so as to evoke the response **Holy, Holy, Holy . . . .**

Holy, Holy, Holy Lord God of hosts . . .

Text without music:

V. **The Lord be with you.**
R. And with your spirit.

V. **Lift up your hearts.**
R. We lift them up to the Lord.

V. **Let us give thanks to the Lord our God.**
R. It is right and just.

It is truly right and just, our duty and our salvation,
always and everywhere to give you thanks,
Lord, holy Father, almighty and eternal God,
through Christ our Lord.

Food for the Journey
Msgr. Joseph DeGrocco

One of the most important preparations before a long trip has to do with making sure there will be enough food. Whether it's packing snacks for a car trip or doing research about rest stops and restaurants along the road, making provisions for food for the journey is an essential element for an enjoyable excursion. The readings for the Solemnity of the Most Holy Body and Blood of Christ (Deuteronomy 8:2–3b, 14b–16a; 1 Corinthians 10:16–17; and John 6:51–58) also speak about food for a journey, but, of course, much more important food for a much more significant journey.

The Old Testament reading from the book of Deuteronomy recalls the trials that the Israelites faced in their wanderings in the desert. They had to deal with hunger, thirst, fiery serpents, and scorpions. The reading also recalls, however, the relief they were provided: God gave them manna, a kind of bread-like substance. God provided them this life-giving bread to eat to strengthen them as they continued on their journey to the Promised Land.

The Gospel reading also refers to the gift of life-giving bread come down from heaven. This reading, from the sixth chapter of the Gospel according to John, is called the Bread of Life discourse. Eucharistic themes run throughout chapter six, which begins with the story of the multiplication of the loaves. A key passage is ". . . unless you eat the flesh of the Son of Man and drink his blood, you do not have life within you. Whoever eats my flesh and

Clearly enunciate **Last Supper** but without pausing. Pause very briefly after **Apostles**. Tie together the phrases **establishing . . . come** and **the saving . . . Cross**. Briefly pause.

Enunciate carefully **Lamb**.

Pause very briefly for the sense at **mystery**. Pause with **holy**. Respect the commas setting off **bounded . . . world**, but do not pause. Continue with **may be enlightened . . .** through **charity**. Put together the phrase together: **And so we approach . . .** pausing slightly after **Sacrament**. Hold slightly the **that** in **so that**, and without breaking the voice, continue with **bathed . . . .** Lengthen slightly **grace** but without a break or breath continue with **we may . . . foreshadowed**, at which point a breath may be taken.

For at the Last Supper with his Apostles,
establishing for the ages to come the saving memorial of the Cross,
he offered himself to you as the unblemished Lamb,
the acceptable gift of perfect praise.

Nourishing your faithful by this sacred mystery,
you make them holy, so that the human race,
bounded by one world,
may be enlightened by one faith
and united by one bond of charity.

And so, we approach the table of this wondrous Sacrament,
so that, bathed in the sweetness of your grace,
we may pass over to the heavenly realities here foreshadowed.

Therefore, all creatures of heaven and earth
sing a new song in adoration,
and we, with all the host of Angels,
cry out, and without end we acclaim:

Holy, Holy, Holy Lord God of hosts . . .

drinks my blood has eternal life . . . . For my flesh is true food and my blood is true drink."

The Gospel writer is showing us that Christ himself is our Eucharistic bread, the bread come down from heaven. Jesus is the food for our journey: our journey toward eternal life—"Unlike your ancestors who ate and still died, whoever eats this bread will live forever"—but also our journey here and now.

The journey we make here and now to Jesus and with Jesus is not one we make alone. Saint Paul reminds us of this in the Second Reading, taken from his first letter to the Corinthians: "Because the loaf of bread is one, we, though many, are one body, for we all partake of the one loaf." Recall that the Corinthians held too much of an individualistic attitude toward the Eucharist. They thought that participating in Eucharist, and receiving the Body and Blood of Christ, was just a matter of their own personal salvation, "Jesus and me." That's a misguided emphasis that still plagues us today. Paul is very strong in teaching that the Eucharist unites us not only to Christ but also to our brothers and sisters in the Christian community. With that unity comes the obligation of love. Such unity in love is what it really means to be united to Jesus and what it really means to participate in the Body and Blood of Christ.

That is the heart of what we celebrate on the Solemnity of the Most Holy Body and Blood of Christ. As the bread and wine are transformed into the Body and Blood of the Lord, they become food for our journey. The journey is that of living in union with Jesus by living his life; the journey is the lifelong project of doing what he did, namely, offering our life to God. That's what we remember in every celebration of the Eucharist—the Paschal Mystery of Jesus's offering of himself to the Father, passing through death into new and resurrected life. Our journey is a journey of offering our life with Jesus.

That's the heart of participation at Mass: offering. The action of the Mass involves everyone's full, conscious, and active participation in offering themselves through Christ, with him and in him. We concretize that unity-in-offering by receiving back, in Holy Communion, the gifts we have offered, which have been transformed. That act of receiving, however, is not a passive reception but an active promise, as it is food that strengthens us as we seek to pour out our life in love and service to one another as Jesus did for us. That journey is undertaken every day as we empty ourselves of ourselves and give our life away to each other. It's a journey, however, that we can only do together, as many parts of the one loaf, one body.

Friday after the Second Sunday after Pentecost

THE MOST SACRED HEART OF JESUS

Solemnity

Collect

Lower the voice slightly to treat **we pray, almighty God** as parenthetical. Accent **we**, with a slight lengthening to show that the next phrase is parenthetical. Emphasize **glory**, **Heart**, and **beloved Son**. Tie together lines two and three, pausing briefly after **for us**. Tie together the next three lines, accenting **worthy**, **overflowing**, and **grace**. Carefully enunciate **fount of heavenly gifts**.

Grant, we pray, almighty God,
that we, who glory in the Heart of your beloved Son
and recall the wonders of his love for us,
may be made worthy to receive
an overflowing measure of grace
from that fount of heavenly gifts.
Through our Lord Jesus Christ, your Son,
who lives and reigns with you in the unity of the Holy Spirit,
one God, for ever and ever.

Or:

Enunciate carefully **Heart of your Son**. Treat **wounded by our sins** as parenthetical. Tie together the first four first lines. Enunciate carefully **in mercy**. Emphasize **boundless**, **treasures**, **love**.
Make **that** sound as though a colon is after it. Pronounce **our** as "ow-were." Tie **that** to **reparation**, accenting **worthy** and **reparation**.

O God, who in the Heart of your Son,
wounded by our sins,
bestow on us in mercy
the boundless treasures of your love,
grant, we pray,
that, in paying him the homage of our devotion,
we may also offer worthy reparation.
Through our Lord Jesus Christ, your Son,
who lives and reigns with you in the unity of the Holy Spirit,
one God, for ever and ever.

Prayer over the Offerings

Enunciate clearly **charity** and **Heart**.

Look, O Lord, we pray, on the surpassing charity
in the Heart of your beloved Son,
that what we offer may be a gift acceptable to you
and an expiation of our offenses.
Through Christ our Lord.

Collect: The Church glories in the Heart of God's beloved Son, since the heart stands for the whole Person's love. Glorying in the Heart, then, goes together with recalling the wonders of God's love, expressed so vividly through the suffering and Death of Jesus. The paschal reality in Jesus brought us the greatest gift of love possible, that is, salvation from sin and death, with the possibility of living forever with Jesus in the glory of heaven.

In the light of that great mystery, which this solemnity celebrates, the Church begs an "overflowing measure" of the grace that comes from Jesus's redemptive love. He is the "fount of heavenly gifts," thanks to his obedience to the Father's will that led to his Death. When we pray about the Heart being the fount, we are speaking of the Heart as representative of the entire Person. This Solemnity puts into a new and very human perspective what we celebrated on Good Friday and Easter Sunday.

Optional Collect: This Collect comes from the older edition of the Missal/Sacramentary. It concentrates on our role in causing suffering to the Heart of Christ. The prayer makes it clear that Christ's wounds have come from our sins. It is Christ's same wounded Heart that brings us God's mercy and opens us to the limitless treasure of God's love. The Heart of Jesus is the sign of his whole Person loving us, even to dying for us sinners.

Now the Church, having turned away from sin, and beginning with the vows we

Pointed Text

Collect

A Grant, we pray, almighty **God**,
B that we, who glory in the Heart of your beloved Son
and recall the wonders of his **love** for us,
C may be made worthy to receive
an overflowing measure of grace
from that fount of heavenly ***gifts***.
Through our Lord Jesus Christ, your Son,
who lives and reigns with you in the unity of the Holy Spirit,
one God, for ever and ever.

Or:

A **O** God, who in the Heart of your Son,
wounded by our **sins**,
B bestow on us in mercy
the boundless treasures **of** your love,
C grant, we pray,
that, in paying him the homage of our devotion,
we may also offer worthy repara***tion***.
Through our Lord Jesus Christ, your Son,
who lives and reigns with you in the unity of the Holy Spirit,
one God, for ever and ever.

Prayer over the Offerings

A Look, O Lord, we pray, on the surpassing charity
in the Heart of your beloved **Son**,
B that what we offer may be a gift accepta**ble** to you
C and an expiation of our offen***ses***.
Through Christ our Lord.

made in Baptism, turns to Jesus with all the "devotion" (the word finds its source in a Latin word that speaks of vows) she can muster, and gives him homage. The Church hopes that her proper response to Jesus's gift will offer him "worthy reparation." That is, because our homage truly is coming from the heart, it will be "worth" something, and will indeed be worthy.

Prayer over the Offerings: The love in Jesus, symbolized by the Heart, was beyond all other loves. Thus, it was a "charity" that would give even to the point of dying for the beloved. In this case, the beloved was the whole world, afflicted with sin and death. But Christ's love was so deep that it could transform the situation—for it was God's love that was being given to us. As Saint Paul said, "It is precisely in this that God proves his love for us, that while we were still sinners, Christ died for us" (Romans 5:8). This prayer wants God to look again, during this celebration, at the love that was in Christ.

Our offering of the gifts at Mass is a sign of our desire to love God. Those gifts stand for our hearts and lives, and thus for the kind of love we have for God. The Church hopes that the offering of this holy Sacrifice will prove to be an "expiation" of our sins. If God looks on such a sacrifice, the Church believes, God will be pleased, as he was with the sacrifice of his Son.

Bring out the accent on **be** in **The Lord be with you.** In the next phrase, make a strong accent on **Lift**, and slow both notes of **hearts**. In the third dialogue, move to the word **thanks** before accenting, and hold that word slightly to give it emphasis. Broaden both notes of **Lord**, and hold **God**.

Sing this proclamation cursively in a reciting tone. In **salvation**, do not hold **-va**; only broaden the two notes slightly. Hold **-tion**. **Always** and **everywhere** require a slight broadening and clear enunciation. The accent of the phrase falls on **thanks**, which should be held briefly. Clearly make four phrases of the next part of the text, by respecting the commas after **Lord**, **Father**, and **God**.

Tie together **Cross** and **he gave** without a hold or pause. Hold **love** at the end of the next phrase and take a breath.

Try to keep together **pierced side** and **the well-spring**, broadening the words **Church's Sacraments** and then pausing for a breath. In the next phrase, hold slightly and pause after **that**.

Hold **-ior** of **Savior** slightly and continue on to **all**. There should not be a pause after **joyfully**. Slow and broaden **springs of salvation**.

Preface: The boundless charity of Christ
Jesus's stretching out his hands on the Cross was an *orantes* gesture, the prayer of offering his life for the life of the world. His love was selfless and total, in a way that it is almost beyond the Church's capacity to give fitting praise and thanksgiving.

The image of the Roman soldier piercing Jesus's side with a lance is invoked, so that the imagery that so entranced teachers and Fathers of the Church (Saints Chrysostom, Augustine, and Bonaventure) might express a deeper reality. That is, the blood and water pouring out of Christ's side were interpreted as the founts for the Sacraments of Eucharist and Baptism.

The Preface draws a conclusion from these two premises (that Jesus gave himself for us; that he is the source of the Sacraments): first, that we might draw from the fountain of grace and salvation coming from the Heart of Christ, the very salvation he came to bring and which is available in his open Heart. And, second, that we might do so joyfully.

(The following excerpt from the November/December 2008 *Pastoral Liturgy* article "The Eucharist Changes the World: Effects on Society and Culture," by Rev. Ronald Lewinski and Andrew Liaugminas, considers how living charity witnesses the Eucharist to the world.)

Living as a Eucharistic People in the World
What does our eucharistic form of life look like in the midst of our world overall? What is the eucharistic quality of life that we, as a whole, are called to live? Above all, the mark of our eucharistic quality of life as a

Text without music:

V. **The Lord be with you.**
R. And with your spirit.

V. **Lift up your hearts.**
R. We lift them up to the Lord.

V. **Let us give thanks to the Lord our God.**
R. It is right and just.

It is truly right and just, our duty and our salvation,
always and everywhere to give you thanks,
Lord, holy Father, almighty and eternal God,
through Christ our Lord.

For raised up high on the Cross,
he gave himself up for us with a wonderful love
and poured out blood and water from his pierced side,
the well-spring of the Church's Sacraments,
so that, won over to the open heart of the Savior,
all might draw water joyfully from the springs of salvation.

And so, with all the Angels and Saints,
we praise you, as without end we acclaim:

Holy, Holy, Holy Lord God of hosts . . .

Pause after **For**, treating the rest of the line as parenthetical. Tie together the first two lines. Enunciate carefully **wonderful love**. Tie together lines three and four and treat line four as parenthetical. A brief pause may be made after **Sacraments**. Treat **won over . . . Savior** as parenthetical. Do not pause after **over** but continue to the next line. Carefully enunciate **all**. Emphasize **joyfully**. Broaden **springs of salvation**.

Church must be charity. In the papal exhortation *Sacramentum Caritatis*, Pope Benedict XVI stresses the role charity plays in being a eucharistic people. Charity starts in our interactions with fellow members of the body of Christ. By simply living charity toward each other, we give witness to the Sacrament of charity to the world.

The eucharistic sacrifice gives us the mandate to be disciples of the Sacrament of charity. At Mass we hear the words of Jesus to take and eat and then to "Do this in memory of me." Thus, in the same action, Jesus not only gives himself to us, but mandates us to do the same for others. We must not let his words become routine. If they do, we may become immune to the power of Jesus's mandate. Lest that happen, the Pope reminds us:

Our communities, when they celebrate the Eucharist, must become ever more conscious that the sacrifice of Christ is for all, and that the Eucharist thus compels all who believe in him to become "bread that is broken" for others, and to work for the building of a more just and fraternal world (SacCar, 88).

We thus cannot say "Amen" to the Eucharistic Prayer and "Amen" when we partake of the consecrated bread and wine and fail to see that we are being asked to commit ourselves to being bread broken and wine poured out for others. Any who catch the radical nature of what they are being asked to do should find the Mass truly invigorating.

These insights into the Eucharist lie at the heart of the Church's social apostolate.

Treat **O Lord** with a slight lowering of the voice, but continue without break to line two. Emphasize **fervent**, **fire**, and **holy love**. Lengthen **that** to prepare for the statement of the consequence/conclusion. In that line, accent **always** as well as **drawn** and **Son**. Accent **neighbor**.

Prayer after Communion

May this sacrament of charity, O Lord,
make us fervent with the fire of holy love,
so that, drawn always to your Son,
we may learn to see him in our neighbor.
Through Christ our Lord.

The image of the servant Christ washing his disciples' feet at the Last Supper and instructing them, "I have given you a model to follow, so that as I have done for you, you should also do" (John 13:15), serves as a lens through which we can penetrate the meaning and social implications of the eucharistic mystery. This mandate to serve others is not just addressed to us individually, but to us corporately as we are, in reality, a community of disciples.

The social dimensions of the liturgical reform fell into the background immediately after Vatican II, because of the pressing need for a response to the Council's mandate to revise the Church's rites. Preoccupied with the reform and translation of the liturgical books, many people lost the social implications of the Eucharist. In the eucharistic writings of Pope John Paul II, and now those of Pope Benedict XVI, there is happily a recovery of this social dimension to the Eucharist. And, in that vein, the concluding paragraphs of *Sacramentum Caritatis* challenge us to "transform unjust structures and to restore respect for the dignity of all men and women" and to commit ourselves "to peacemaking in our world scarred by violence and war, and today in particular, by terrorism, economic corruption and sexual exploitation" (89).

The bridge from the Lord's table reaches to the poor who live below the poverty level, to children deprived of a legitimate claim to happiness, to refugees, to victims of certain forms of globalization that widen the gap between the wealthy and the poor (90). Global issues, such as

Pointed Text

Prayer after Communion

A May this sacrament of charity, O **Lord**,
B make us fervent with the fire of **ho**ly love,
C so that, drawn always to your Son,
we may learn to see him in our neigh***bor***.
Through Christ our Lord.

The space below is for your notes.

Refer to pages viii–x for an explanation of the pointing of the chants and to page xii for the Tones for the Presidential Prayers from *The Roman Missal.*

the huge sums spent on armaments or the neglect of the environment, expand the implications of the Eucharist to all creation (92). What Pope Benedict calls "the food of truth and human need" (90) calls us corporately to live a radically different way of approaching our presence in this world; it "demands that we denounce inhumane situations in which people starve to death because of injustice and exploitation, and it gives us renewed strength and courage to work tirelessly in the service of the civilization of love" (90).

Prayer after Communion: That Holy Communion is called a "sacrament of charity" needs to be understood from several viewpoints. First of all, it is a sign of God's immense love that he would make it possible for us to share intimately in the life of Christ, in divine life, while still living our earthly lives. Secondly, by coming to Communion, we show our love for God, especially in Jesus, by doing what Jesus asked us to do ("Take . . . eat . . . drink," cf. Matthew 26:26–27 and parallel texts). But because we are members of the same body of Christ partaking of this Holy Communion, we need to have a spirit of true charity toward our fellow communicants and all members of Christ's body. Hence the Church prays to become "fervent" with holy love (the Latin underlying this word means burning), so that we can love all the ways God desires.

The last phrase of the prayer makes it clear that we need to be drawn to Jesus always. That, in turn, will help us to see him in "our neighbor." The love of Jesus at the ritual moment will necessarily extend outward.

Last Sunday in Ordinary Time

OUR LORD JESUS CHRIST, KING OF THE UNIVERSE

Solemnity

Collect

Tie together lines two and three, treating **the King . . .** as parenthetical, but not lowering the voice. Accent **whole** and **creation**. Treat the next words within the commas as parenthetical, lowering the voice slightly. Continue without a break to the next line. Tie together lines six and seven. Emphasize **service** and **praise**. Carefully enunciate **ceaselessly**.

Almighty ever-living God,
whose will is to restore all things
in your beloved Son, the King of the universe,
grant, we pray,
that the whole creation, set free from slavery,
may render your majesty service
and ceaselessly proclaim your praise.
Through our Lord Jesus Christ, your Son,
who lives and reigns with you in the unity of the Holy Spirit,
one God, for ever and ever.

Prayer over the Offerings

Tie lines one and two together. Emphasize **sacrifice** and **reconciled**. Tie together lines four and five, accenting **himself**. Broaden **unity and peace**.

As we offer you, O Lord, the sacrifice
by which the human race is reconciled to you,
we humbly pray
that your Son himself may bestow on all nations
the gifts of unity and peace.
Through Christ our Lord.

Prayer after Communion

Carefully enunciate **food of immortality**. Lower the voice slightly. for **we . . . Lord**. Pause very briefly after **that**. Tie the rest of that line to the next line, respecting the commas after **Christ** and **universe** in the latter. (A quick breath may be needed after **universe**.) Emphasize **eternally** and **heavenly Kingdom**.

Having received the food of immortality,
we ask, O Lord,
that, glorying in obedience
to the commands of Christ, the King of the universe,
we may live with him eternally in his heavenly Kingdom.
Who lives and reigns for ever and ever.

Collect: The opening phrase modifying God cites the encyclical of Pope Pius XI (*Quas primas*, 1925), whose goal was "to restore all things in Christ" as an answer to the crumbling of civilization that he saw taking place. The Pope felt that only by returning to Christ as the true King would the world come to know peace and freedom. This vision was in accord with that of the book of Revelation, which sees Christ as "the Alpha and Omega, the first and the last, the beginning and the end" (22:13).

But the prayer goes on to an even larger vision: that the entirety of creation might come to Jesus, as Lord and King, rendering him the service due such an exalted Ruler, and constantly giving him praise. Only by entering the service of Christ will creation be set free from the slavery that has characterized it since the fall of Adam and Eve. In other words, serving Christ is not a new slavery, but an authentic liberation. The Church prays for that kind of gift.

Prayer over the Offerings: The letter to the Colossians states, "For in him all the fullness was pleased to dwell, / and through him to reconcile all things for him, / making peace by the blood of his cross / [through him], whether those on earth or those in heaven." (1:20). The paschal sacrifice of Jesus accomplished this great act of reconciling, thus lifting the curse of sin and death from the human race. Our sacrifice has value only because it is inserted into that all-encompassing and once-for-all sacrifice of Christ. Our ritual at Mass opens

The space below is for your notes.

Refer to pages viii–x for an explanation of the pointing of the chants and to page xii for the Tones for the Presidential Prayers from *The Roman Missal.*

Pointed Text

Collect

A Almighty ever-living God,
whose will is to restore all things
in your beloved Son, the King of the un**i**verse,
B grant, we pray,
that the whole creation, set free from slavery,
may render your ma**jes**ty service
C and ceaselessly proclaim your ***praise***.
Through our Lord Jesus Christ, your Son,
who lives and reigns with you in the unity of the Holy Spirit,
one God, for ever and ever.

Prayer over the Offerings

A As we offer you, O Lord, the sacrifice
by which the human race is reconciled to **you**,
B we humbly pray,
that your Son himself may bestow **on** all nations
C the gifts of unity and ***peace***.
Through Christ our Lord.

Prayer after Communion

A Having received the food of immortal**i**ty,
B we ask, O Lord,
that, glorying in obedience
to the commands of Christ, the King **of** the universe,
C we may live with him eternally in his heavenly king***dom***.
Who lives and reigns for ever and ever.

anew this window to the Infinite, to make available in a new contemporary way the saving gift that Jesus's sacrifice brought to the world by his death on Calvary.

Because the event of Calvary achieved peace for all those reconciled to God by means of it, we pray for that peace to be given to all nations. We also pray for the gift of unity. We want the whole world to come to unity, gathered around Christ, its true king.

Prayer after Communion: Holy Communion is seen here as partaking in the food of "immortality." This phrase is another way of expressing Jesus's teaching in John 6:51—"I myself am the living bread come down from heaven. If anyone eats this bread he shall live forever; the bread I will give is my flesh, for the life of the world." And three verses later: "He who feeds on my flesh and drinks my blood has life eternal."

Our prayer has a special application of the eucharistic truth because of today's solemnity. The image of Christ the King appears as the culmination of the petition. By uniting to Christ intimately in Holy Communion, we are promising to keep such union by obedience to our King's commands. Indeed, our obedience is cause for "glorying," since it brings us into union with Christ. Sharing Communion with him, and obeying our King, leads the Church to ask that we may live with him eternally.

Bring out the accent on **be** in **The Lord be with you.** In the next phrase, make a strong accent on **Lift**, and slow both notes of **hearts**. In the third dialogue, move to the word **thanks** before accenting, and hold that word slightly to give it emphasis. Broaden both notes of **Lord**, and hold **God**.

Sing this proclamation cursively in a reciting tone. In **salvation**, do not hold **-va**; only broaden the two notes slightly. Hold **-tion**. **Always** and **everywhere** require a slight broadening and clear enunciation. The accent of the phrase falls on **thanks**, which should be held briefly. In the next phrase, clearly make three phrases of the text, by respecting the commas after **Lord** and **Father**.

Pause very briefly at **gladness** because it needs the phrase that starts with **as** to complete the thought. Slow and broaden the entire phrase **as eternal . . . creation**. Hold slightly and pause at **that**. Do not pause at or hold **Cross** but continue through the next phrase. If at all possible do not pause, after a short hold of **peace**, but finish the thought with the phrase he **might**, slowing **human redemption**, holding the last syllable, and then taking a breath. In the next phrase, hold briefly **and**. Do not hold and pause at **rule**, but rather continue with **he might**. This phrase is very

Preface: Christ, King of the Universe
The body of the Preface begins with an image from Psalm 45:8: "God, your God, has anointed you / with the oil of gladness above your fellow kings." The same phrase is repeated by the author of the letter to the Hebrews (1:9) in describing Jesus.

That Jesus is the Anointed One is explicit in Luke's account of the Gospel. Jesus's reading of the passage from Isaiah 61:1, "The Spirit of the Lord is upon me, / because he has anointed me . . ." (Luke 4:18) is followed with his statement: "Today this scripture passage is fulfilled in your hearing" (Luke 4:21). Both priests and kings are anointed in the tradition of the Old Testament. The Preface applies the anointing from God to Jesus, as both eternal Priest and King of all creation—which this solemnity celebrates in a particular way.

The next phrase capitalizes on Jesus as priest. The Cross is seen as an altar, and the victim is Jesus. Using the biblical image, these lines speak of Jesus as a "spotless" sacrifice. Some of the earliest Bible texts address the need for Israel's sacrifices to be of animals without blemish. Thus, the first Passover required a lamb without blemish: "The Lord said to Moses and Aaron in the land of Egypt . . . 'Tell the whole community of Israel: On the tenth of every month every one of your families must procure for itself a lamb . . . . The lamb must be a year-old male without blemish" (Exodus 12:5).

The same imagery is found in the New Testament, very notably in the letter to the Hebrews, 9:14: ". . . how much more will the blood of Christ, who through the eter-

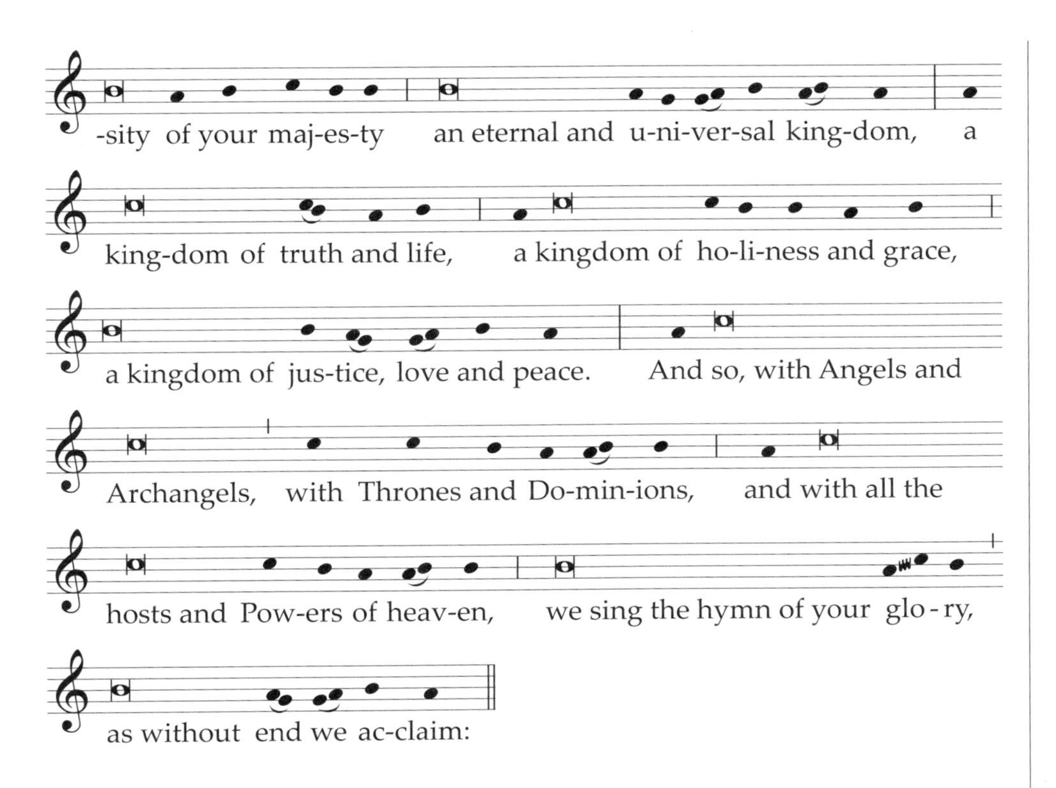

long, so it will be necessary to make a short break at **majesty** and get a good breath there. Hold briefly the **-ty** of **majesty**. The melody has been written so as to emphasize **universal kingdom**, so that is the place to slow slightly and take a good breath at the end. But if at all possible, try to articulate the phrases so that **an eternal . . . kingdom** is seen to go with the following three phrases, each beginning with **a kingdom**. Slow and broaden **justice**, **love and peace**.

Slight pause after **And so**. Respect the commas, but try to keep this section together, without big breaks for breaths. Broaden the last phrase, especially on **glory**.

Slow **we ac-**, and put emphasis on **-claim**, so as to evoke the response **Holy, Holy, Holy . . . .**

Text without music:

V. **The Lord be with you.**
R. And with your spirit.

V. **Lift up your hearts.**
R. We lift them up to the Lord.

V. **Let us give thanks to the Lord our God.**
R. It is right and just.

It is truly right and just, our duty and our salvation,
always and everywhere to give you thanks,
Lord, holy Father, almighty and eternal God.

For you anointed your Only Begotten Son,
our Lord Jesus Christ, with the oil of gladness
as eternal Priest and King of all creation,
so that, by offering himself on the altar of the Cross
as a spotless sacrifice to bring us peace,

Tie together the first three lines, while respecting the commas with a slight lengthening of the word at the comma.

Emphasize **Priest** and **King**.
Pause slightly after **that**.

Tie together lines four and five.

nal spirit offered himself up unblemished to God . . . ." The result of the sacrifice of Jesus is peace, that is, reconciliation of humanity with God. Peace, thus, means union with God—which is not completely possible without the offering of Christ.

By this offering, states the Preface, Jesus accomplishes the mysteries of our redemption, for which all of humanity has been longing since the fall from paradise. At the same time, this sacrifice of Jesus places him in such an exalted state that all creation comes under his rule. The body of the Preface ends with a listing of nine of the attributes of the kingdom of Jesus. It is eternal and universal, because that is the extent that Christ's divine and human nature encompasses. It is of truth and life—while this world's kingdoms are so often built on lies and spiritual death. It is of holiness and grace—in contrast to the secularism and godlessness that so often characterize the kingdoms of earth. And it is of justice, love, and peace—attributes that go beyond the emotional content of those words, because Jesus's kingdom participates in God's kind of virtues.

In the reading from Isaiah 9:1–6 that is proclaimed at the Mass during the Night on the Nativity of the Lord, we hear that the Messiah is called the "Prince of Peace" and has a vast peaceful kingdom: "For a child is born to us, a son is given us; / upon his shoulder dominion rests. / They name him Wonder-Counselor, God-Hero, / Father-Forever, Prince of Peace. / His dominion is vast / and forever peaceful, / from David's throne, and over his kingdom, / which he

Broaden **mysteries of human redemption**. Treat **making . . . rule** as parenthetical, so slightly lower the voice but also carefully enunciate each word in the phrase. Tie together lines eight and nine. Sustaining **kingdom** as if it had a colon will link the three following phrases. Pause after each of the phrases, proclaiming the whole of each phrase slowly and solemnly. Make a clear conclusion with **peace**. But do not pause too long before continuing with the concluding phrase. Emphasize and lengthen **And so**.

he might accomplish the mysteries of human redemption
and, making all created things subject to his rule,
he might present to the immensity of your majesty
an eternal and universal kingdom,
a kingdom of truth and life,
a kingdom of holiness and grace,
a kingdom of justice, love and peace.

And so, with Angels and Archangels,
with Thrones and Dominions,
and with all the hosts and Powers of heaven,
we sing the hymn of your glory,
as without end we acclaim:

Holy, Holy, Holy Lord God of hosts . . .

confirms and sustains / by judgment and justice . . . ."

Both Christ's kingship and holiness were part of Angel Gabriel's announcement to Mary that she would bear the Messiah. "He will be great . . . and the Lord God will give him the throne of David his father, and he will rule over the house of Jacob forever, and of his kingdom there will be no end" (Luke 1:32–33). "Therefore the child to be born will be called holy, the son of God" (Luke 1: 35).

In reflecting on this Preface, we may want to consider how we work toward a kingdom of justice, love and peace. Do our lives reflect holiness? Are we a source of grace to others? Saint Paul spoke of how God builds the kingdom in people who strive for holiness. We should consider Paul's words: "Mend your ways, encourage one another, agree with one another, live in peace, and the God of love and peace will be with you. Greet one another with a holy kiss. All the holy ones greet you" (2 Corinthians 5:11–12).

The vision of this universal kingdom where all live in peace leads the Church to joyful proclamation: Holy, Holy, Holy . . . .

Proper of Saints

February 2

THE PRESENTATION OF THE LORD

Feast

The Blessing of Candles and the Procession

These prayers are prayed after either the First Form: The Procession or the Second Form: The Solemn Entrance. Please refer to The Presentation of the Lord in *The Roman Missal.*

Dear brethren (brothers and sisters),
forty days have passed since we celebrated the joyful feast
of the Nativity of the Lord.
Today is the blessed day
when Jesus was presented in the Temple by Mary and Joseph.
Outwardly he was fulfilling the Law,
but in reality he was coming to meet his believing people.
Prompted by the Holy Spirit,
Simeon and Anna came to the Temple.
Enlightened by the same Spirit,
they recognized the Lord
and confessed him with exultation.
So let us also, gathered together by the Holy Spirit,
proceed to the house of God to encounter Christ.
There we shall find him
and recognize him in the breaking of the bread,
until he comes again, revealed in glory.

Carefully enunciate and pause after **Today**.

Contrast **Outwardly** and **in reality**. Slight emphasis on **Holy Spirit** each time it is mentioned.

Slightly emphasize **Prompted** and **Enlightened**. The same holds true for the two verbs describing their reaction to Jesus: **recognized** and **confessed**. Articulate carefully **So let us also** with slight emphasis on **us**.

Emphasize **gathered** and **proceed** and **find him** and **recognize him**.

After the address the Priest blesses the candles, saying, with hands extended:

Let us pray.

O God, source and origin of all light,
who on this day showed to the just man Simeon
the Light for revelation to the Gentiles,
we humbly ask that,
in answer to your people's prayers,
you may be pleased to sanctify with your blessing ✠ these candles,
which we are eager to carry in praise of your name,

Make the Blessing slowly with a large gesture, so as to be seen throughout the worship space. Carefully articulate the expressions of **light**. Emphasize **this day**. Treat the phrase, **in answer . . . prayers** clearly as a parenthetical phrase, so as not to lose the sense of the petition. While practicing before the liturgy, put the petition together without the parenthetical phrase: **we humbly ask that . . . you may be pleased to sanctify** to understand the sense. Tie together the phrases **which . . . so that . . .** as the sense demands.

Overview of the Feast of the Presentation of the Lord

This feast has had multiple emphases over the centuries and in different parts of the Church. In the Eastern Rites, the emphasis from a very early period was on the symbolism of Christ coming to the Temple in Jerusalem (see Egeria, ca. 400). Christ's meeting with Simeon and Anna is a sign of his meeting his people. Thus, by 450, it is called the Feast of the Meeting.

We see in this feast an extension and echo of the Christmas mystery, the celebration of the Incarnation of God coming not only to meet human beings but also to be in humanity, in the flesh. In the Roman Rite, the feast was seen as a kind of Christian answer to the pagan ritual of Lupercalia. In time, special emphasis came to be placed on Christ the Light, dispelling the darkness of pagan ignorance and sin. From this came an emphasis on candles (Candlemas), which are symbols of Christ the Light, highlighted both at Christmas and at Easter.

In a way, the feast straddles the celebrations of Christmas and Easter, with Christ the Light of the World at the center. The texts of the liturgy bring out this profound and grace-filled reality.

Address: The first thematic looks back to the Nativity. We see, in line seven, the Eastern Rite emphasis of the meeting of Christ and his people. This theme of meeting extends to Simeon and Anna and culminates toward the end of the address with the invitation to all to go to God's house to meet with ("encounter") Christ.

so that, treading the path of virtue,
we may reach that light which never fails.
Through Christ our Lord.
R. Amen.

Or:

O God, true light, who create light eternal,
spreading it far and wide,
pour, we pray, into the hearts of the faithful
the brilliance of perpetual light,
so that all who are brightened in your holy temple
by the splendor of these candles
may happily reach the light of your glory.
Through Christ our Lord.
R. Amen.

No sign of blessing is indicated in the text of the second option, but it may be made at the words **these candles**. Respect the commas in **true light** and **who . . . eternal** to show that they are descriptive. Lower the voice for **we pray** so as to keep the sense of the petition together. Pause after **light** and again after **so that**, as if there were a comma there. The next pause in the voice is not until the word **candles**. The culminating phrase should be slowed to emphasize the point of the coming procession and liturgy: **reach the light of your glory**.

This encounter takes place especially at the Eucharist, which the earliest Church called "the breaking of the bread." Important in the spiritual vision presented in this prayer is the role of the Holy Spirit. The Spirit who overshadowed Mary in the Incarnation (Matthew 1:20; Luke 1:35) "prompted" Simeon and Anna to go to the Temple and "enlightened" them to recognize Christ in their "meeting." The address sees the action of the Holy Spirit in gathering us, so that we can "meet" Jesus in a new and profound way.

Blessing of candles: As creator, God is the "source" of light. As eternal Light, God is the "origin" of light (Genesis 1:3–5; cf. also, Eucharistic Prayer IV: "dwelling in unapproachable light"). In the Temple, the "Light," in Christ, came to Simeon, the symbol and representative of both Jews and Gentiles (although this text emphasizes the latter (cf. Luke 2:30–32). Our candles are in that line of illumination passed down from Christ's time to ours. They are to be symbols of the interior light within us (virtue), shining thanks to grace.

Because the candles are to be signs of the inner holiness or sanctity that Sacred Scripture identifies with light, the Church prays that God, by divine blessing, would sanctify the candles to be carried and burned in praise of God and service of the Church that gathers precisely to praise God's name. It is the combination of liturgy and of life that leads to God. "Treading the path of virtue" is the same as living in God's light on earth, of being sacraments of that light. Praying and living thus will strengthen us until we reach the eternal Light.

THE PRESENTATION OF THE LORD

At the Mass

Collect

Respect the comma after **that** and join this and the next two lines. Carefully enunciate **on this day**. Pause slightly at the contrasting words **our flesh** and **your grace**. Parallel **presented** in lines four and seven. Careful enunciation is needed to show that **we may be presented** is the culmination of **we humbly implore your majesty**. Slightly pause after the contrasting words **our flesh** and **your grace.**

Almighty ever-living God,
we humbly implore your majesty
that, just as your Only Begotten Son
was presented on this day in the Temple
in the substance of our flesh,
so, by your grace,
we may be presented to you with minds made pure.
Through our Lord Jesus Christ, your Son,
who lives and reigns with you in the unity of the Holy Spirit,
one God, for ever and ever.

Prayer over the Offerings

Slightly contrast **offering . . . Church** and **Son . . . offered**. Drop the voice slightly at **we pray**. Without unduly emphasizing, show the importance of **willed** and **offered**. Bring out **Lamb** clearly.

May the offering made with exultation by your Church
be pleasing to you, O Lord, we pray,
for you willed that your Only Begotten Son
be offered to you for the life of the world
as the Lamb without blemish.
Who lives and reigns for ever and ever.

Prayer after Communion

The culmination of the first part of the petition is **grace to perfection within us** and so the line needs to be articulated carefully, with a slight stress on **perfection**. Pause slightly after **and**. Try to keep this and the next two lines together with one breath. Pause slightly after **so may we** and **Lord**. Slow the text **going forth to meet**. Slightly emphasize **gift**. Slightly pause after **and**. Try to keep this and the next two lines together with one breath. Pause slightly after **we** and Lord, to set off this descriptive phrase.

By these holy gifts which we have received, O Lord,
bring your grace to perfection within us,
and, as you fulfilled Simeon's expectation
that he would not see death
until he had been privileged to welcome the Christ,
so may we, going forth to meet the Lord,
obtain the gift of eternal life.
Through Christ our Lord.

Optional blessing: This blessing begins with the vision of "light eternal," calling God the "true" light. The text is a prayer of blessing for the candles that will symbolize the Light of God in the midst of the Church today, on the feast commemorating the presentation of Jesus, the Light of the world (Luke 1:78–79: "daybreak from on high"; cf. also, John 8:12). We pray that the Light, which is eternal, perpetual, will be poured into our hearts. Thus, we bless and carry candles in procession here. In the light of the biblical text of Jesus's being presented in the Jewish temple, the text speaks of the church building as a "temple." We desire to bless the candles because they then become signs of the transformation in our hearts by God's light. Such transformation will help us to carry God's light as we proceed through this world (the liturgical procession is a symbol of the life procession), until we reach the eternal Light which was and is forever, because it is God's glory.

Collect: God is addressed at the outset as "almighty" and "ever-living," because those attributes were particularly important to Israel: first, in the creation of light and its extension to the world; second, in God's Presence in the Temple, although both the Old and New Testaments use the titles often when speaking about God (e.g., Deuteronomy 32:40; Revelation 4:9, 15:7). As the core of the petition begins, a fundamental doctrine tied to the Incarnation of Jesus is highlighted. The prayer states that Jesus had the substance of our human

Pointed Text

Collect

A Almighty ever-living **God**,
B we humbly implore your majesty
that, just as your Only Begotten Son
was presented on this day in the Temple
in the substance **of** our flesh,
C so, by your grace,
we may be presented to you with minds made ***pure***.
Through our Lord Jesus Christ, your Son,
who lives and reigns with you in the unity of the Holy Spirit,
one God, for ever and ever.

Prayer over the Offerings

B May the offering made with exultation by your Church
be pleasing to you, O **Lord**, we pray,
C for you willed that your Only Begotten Son
be offered to you for the life of the world
as the Lamb without blem***ish***.
Who lives and reigns for ever and ever.

Prayer after Communion

A By these holy gifts which we have received, O Lord,
bring your grace to perfection within **us**,
B and, as you fulfilled Simeon's expectation
that he would not see death
until he had been privileged to wel**come** the Christ,
C so may we, going forth to meet the Lord,
obtain the gift of eternal ***life***.
Through Christ our Lord.

flesh, although he was God's Only Begotten Son and, therefore, fully divine. Although liturgy's primary purpose is not to propound dogma, in fact it does that. This phrase could have been lifted from the Council of Chalcedon (*Definitio fidei: Deum vere et hominem vere*).

The Collect contrasts the coming of God's Son and his presentation in the Temple with our presentation back to God (by "grace") after being transformed by the Light of Christ ("minds made pure").

Prayer over the Offerings: The "joy" of which this prayer speaks is related to Christmas (though Christmas Time ended at the Baptism of the Lord, the day is still connected to that period). More explicitly, the Church's joy stems from God's willing that her offering be one with that of Jesus, as the Lamb of sacrifice. The presumption (as is brought out in the blessings of God in the Preparation of the Gifts) is that God offered to us first, his Son, for the life of the world. Thus, this feast looks forward to the celebration of the Paschal Mystery in the Holy Triduum. Calling Jesus the "Lamb" emphasizes the connection to Passover—so important in the Hebrew dispensation, but taken over and re-interpreted in the light of Jesus's teachings and salvific action. Very important, however, is the phrase that Jesus was offered for the "life of the world." This reflects the hymn that Simeon proclaims as he takes the child in his arms, and speaks of him as a light of revelation to the Gentiles, but also the glory of God's people, Israel (Luke 2:32).

Bring out the accent on **be** in **The Lord be with you**. In the response, accent **spirit** by holding slightly both syllables. In the next phrase, make a strong accent on **Lift**, and slow both notes of **hearts**. In the third dialogue, move to the word **thanks** before accenting, and hold that word slightly to give it emphasis. Broaden both notes of **Lord**, and hold **God**.

Sing this proclamation cursively in a reciting tone. Do not hold -**va** in **salvation**; only broaden the two notes slightly. The -**tion** should be held. Slightly broaden **always** and **everywhere**. The accent of the phrase falls on **thanks**. In the next part of the text, clearly make three phrases, by respecting the commas after **Lord** and **Father**.

Emphasize **Son**.
Hold -**ple** of **Temple** slightly.

Slow slightly **glory of Israel**, but if possible, do not breathe after **Israel** but continue with **and Light**. Be clear about adding the **t** to **Light**. Slow **na-** in **nations** and hold the second syllable. In the concluding phrase, make a slight pause after **so**, and respect the comma after **forth**. Hold **-tion** of **Salvation**. Broaden the last phrase, especially on **praise**. If possible, do not breathe between **you** and **as**. Slow **we ac-** and put emphasis on -**claim**, so as to evoke the **Holy, Holy, Holy . . . .**

Preface: The mystery of the Presentation of the Lord.

Holy, Holy, Holy Lord God of hosts . . .

Prayer after Communion: We come, in another procession, to receive the gifts that Jesus brings to us in Holy Communion. In the Eucharist, the grace already received in Christian initiation is moved toward its fulfillment ("perfection"). Our meeting with Jesus in Holy Communion was prefigured by the meeting with Simeon. This prayer sees the events in Simeon's life (his desire to see the Messiah before he died and the meeting at the Presentation) as foreshadowing the event that we have celebrated in the Sacred Liturgy. We, having welcomed Christ personally in Holy Communion, are concerned now with the ultimate in welcomes, when we "meet" the Lord at the gate of eternal life. In fact, the gift of Communion has prepared our hearts for the everlasting gift of heaven, eternal life. We have celebrated the beginning of Jesus's earthly life, by calling to mind his Presentation in the Temple as a child. The prayer's petition concerns the end of our lives—and the coming of Jesus "to meet" his people is at the center of the prayer.

Preface: The mystery of the Presentation of the Lord

The body of the Preface begins by stating the fact of the feast celebrated this day, the presenting of Jesus in the Temple. The Presentation in the Temple equals a revelation to men and women of faith (thanks to the Holy Spirit's gift and action) (cf. Luke 2:32). The text of the Preface, staying close to the biblical text, is clear that this revelation was both for the Jews ("Israel") and the Gentiles ("nations"). Simeon says of the child he holds, "a light for revelation to the

Text without music:

V. **The Lord be with you.**
R. And with your spirit.

V. **Lift up your hearts.**
R. We lift them up to the Lord.

V. **Let us give thanks to the Lord our God.**
R. It is right and just.

It is truly right and just, our duty and our salvation,
always and everywhere to give you thanks,
Lord, holy Father, almighty and eternal God.

For your co-eternal Son was presented on this day in the Temple
and revealed by the Spirit
as the glory of Israel and Light of the nations.

And so, we, too, go forth, rejoicing to encounter your Salvation,
and with the Angels and Saints
praise you, as without end we acclaim:

Holy, Holy, Holy Lord God of hosts . . .

Treat **our duty . . . salvation** as parenthetical, while still articulating **duty** and **salvation**. Carefully articulate **always** and **everywhere**. The voice drops slightly at **thanks**. Note **on this day**. Without rushing, the entire phrases from **For your co-eternal . . . Light of the nations** should be tied together. In the conclusion, it will help the sense to articulate carefully **And so** while also drawing out **go forth**, but without breaking up the sense until **Salvation**. The last phrase, **as . . . acclaim** should be slowed so that the people have the sense that it is time to come in on the **Holy, Holy, Holy . . . .**

Gentiles, / and glory for your people Israel." This revelation in the temple in Jerusalem comes not long after the revelation to the shepherds who returned home, "glorifying and praising God for all they had heard and seen" (Luke 2:20). The shepherds were given the message first in the fields. The same message—that God had come in human form—was given to Simeon in the entirely different setting of the temple in Jerusalem. In this revelation, it was understood that the Messiah was not only for the covenanted people of Israel but for all the world. It is easy to see how the Presentation of the Lord is linked with Christmas Time. The message is still being revealed. This time it is given to a man who was "righteous and devout awaiting the consolation of Israel, and the holy Spirit was upon him" (Luke 2:25).

This text emphasizes again the "meeting," or "encounter," of God's people with God's salvation. This encounter took place in history, and it takes place again today in the liturgy. This meeting, which takes place at this Holy Eucharist, leads the Church to praise and acclamation of God's holiness, now brought to earth. And that rejoicing in the Church is the lead-in to the acclamation with which every Preface ends: Holy, Holy, Holy . . . .

March 19

SAINT JOSEPH, SPOUSE OF THE BLESSED VIRGIN MARY

Solemnity

Collect

Treat **we pray** as subordinate, so as to bring out clearly **almighty God**. Treat **that** as if it had a comma after it, and do the same for **intercession**. Pray the next two lines slowly, but without a break in the text. Slightly emphasize on the words **constantly**, **unfolding**, and **mysteries**. Pause briefly after **salvation**. Slow the ending, and thus bring out clearly **faithful care**.

Grant, we pray, almighty God,
that by Saint Joseph's intercession
your Church may constantly watch over
the unfolding of the mysteries of human salvation,
whose beginnings you entrusted to his faithful care.
Through our Lord Jesus Christ, your Son,
who lives and reigns with you in the unity of the Holy Spirit,
one God, for ever and ever.

Prayer over the Offerings

Emphasize **Saint Joseph**. Do not pause at **care**, but rather continue the sense with **your Only . . . .** Treat the phrase **born . . . Mary** as descriptive of **Son**, by a slight lowering of the voice. Emphasize **we**. Put the text of **to minister with a pure heart** together.

We pray, O Lord,
that, just as Saint Joseph served with loving care
your Only Begotten Son, born of the Virgin Mary,
so we may be worthy to minister
with a pure heart at your altar.
Through Christ our Lord.

Prayer after Communion

Accent **defend**, **unfailing**, and **protection**. Tie together, accenting slightly **family** and **food**. Highlight **rejoice** and **Saint Joseph**. Parallel **rejoice** and **keep safe your gifts**.

Defend with unfailing protection,
O Lord, we pray,
the family you have nourished
with food from this altar,
as they rejoice at the Solemnity of Saint Joseph,
and graciously keep safe your gifts among them.
Through Christ our Lord.

Collect: The beginning of salvation is characterized as the coming of Jesus in human form. Jesus's coming, though, was the culmination of a great deal of salvation history. The Collect also sees the mysteries of salvation continuing in our day, thus extending forward as well as back in time. The Church, the inheritor of the promises and redemptive gift of Jesus, continues to unfold these mysteries, which are renewed every time the Church gathers to celebrate the liturgy.

Faith was an essential component in Saint Joseph's love and solicitude of God's Only Begotten Son and the Mother of God. Surely, God had chosen him because of that very faith, and has given him a place in the unfolding of the mysteries of salvation.

So too, the Church watches over those mysteries unfolding. Because of Saint Joseph's role in the life of Jesus, we pray for his intercession to aid the Church in presenting the mysteries, or the sacraments. And thus Joseph's role is perpetuated in a new way and will continue until the end of time.

Prayer over the Offerings: Our prayer first recognizes the type of service that Joseph offered Mary and Jesus. This was a loving man who did what was required, not calling attention to himself.

Secondly, our prayer includes the service that we give God the Father, through Jesus, and in the Holy Spirit, when celebrating the Holy Eucharist ("at your altar").

Significantly, our service is put in terms of "to minister," a word that combines a Latin word meaning "less" and a Greek word also meaning "less." Ministry

The space below is for your notes.

Refer to pages viii–x for an explanation of the pointing of the chants and to page xii for the Tones for the Presidential Prayers from *The Roman Missal.*

Pointed Text

Collect

A Grant, we pray, almighty **<u>God</u>**,
B that by Saint Joseph's intercession
your Church may constantly watch over
the unfolding of the mysteries of hu**man** salvation,
C whose beginnings you entrusted to his faithful ***care***.
Through our Lord Jesus Christ, your Son,
who lives and reigns with you in the unity of the Holy Spirit,
one God, for ever and ever.

Prayer over the Offerings

A We pray, O **<u>Lord</u>**,
B that, just as Saint Joseph served with loving care
your Only Begotten Son, born of the **Vir**gin Mary,
C so we may be worthy to minister
with a pure heart at your al***tar***.
Through Christ our Lord.

Prayer after Communion

A Defend with unfailing protection,
O Lord, we **<u>pray</u>**,
B the family you have nourished
with food **from** this altar,
C as they rejoice at the Solemnity of Saint Joseph,
and graciously keep safe your gifts among ***them***.
Through Christ our Lord.

demands that the individual be "less-less." The Priest Celebrant allows the Word and the Sacrifice to have attention, keeping his personality in the background. He strives for a pure heart, a heart undivided by other agendas or by sin, which blocks the possibility of authentic service/ministry. Saint Joseph modeled purity of heart, being devoted to less, so that Jesus and Mary might be all. We bring our gifts and pray that we will offer them with an undivided heart.

Prayer after Communion: The prayer, in this translation, is structured in what musicians and poets consider "the A-B-A" form. We see: A) Defend with . . . protection; B) the family fed with divine food; A) keep safe your gifts.

The content of this prayer rests in the image of Saint Joseph. It was he who defended and protected Jesus and Mary, (cf. Matthew, chapters one and two, especially, 2:13ff.). It was Joseph who saw to their care and nourishment. The example of Saint Joseph puts into a certain context our reception of the Body and Blood of the Lord and brings cause to "rejoice."

In the joy of the Gospel example and imagery surrounding this Saint, the Church begs God to keep safe the family who has just been nourished with Communion. The request that God "defend" conjures imagery of an army protecting a city from attack. But the concluding request to "keep safe your gifts" suggests another kind of defense, such as a defense *inside* a city's walls to repel danger from the outside.

Bring out the accent on **be** in **The Lord be with you**. In the response, accent **spirit**, by holding slightly both syllables. In the next phrase, make a strong accent on **Lift**, and slow both notes of **hearts**. In the third dialogue, move to the word **thanks** before accenting, and hold that word slightly to give it emphasis. Broaden both notes of **Lord**, and hold **God**.

Sing this proclamation cursively in a reciting tone. Do not hold **-va** in **salvation**; only broaden the two notes slightly. The **-tion**, should be held. Slightly broaden **always** and **everywhere**. The accent of the phrase falls on **thanks**. In the next part of the text, clearly make three phrases, by respecting the commas after **Lord** and **Father**.

Try to tie together the three phrases, starting with **and on the Solemnity of Saint Joseph** and concluding with **bless you**. Slow slightly on the last phrase, so as to enunciate clearly **-fy you** and **bless**. Hold only the final **you**. Tie together without a breath the next two phrases, from **For this just man** through **Mother of God**. Do not pause at **servant**, but continue in one breath through **household**, pausing slightly there. If taking a breath at the end of the next phrase, at **Son**, make it very short, so as to keep the thought together with the next phrase, beginning with **who was conceived**. Similarly, after a short hold on **-it** of **Spirit,** go right on to **our Lord**, slowing these last four words in the phrase.

Preface: The mission of Saint Joseph.

Preface: The mission of Saint Joseph
The opening section of this Preface is greatly extended, nearly double the usual opening of Prefaces. The Church always gives thanks in the Preface and the Eucharistic Prayer, but this opening adds the need of giving "fitting praise," to glorify and bless God, on the Solemnity of Saint Joseph, Spouse of the Blessed Virgin Mary.

Saint Joseph, in accord with Sacred Scripture, is called a "just man" ("Joseph her husband, since he was a righteous man" [Matthew 1:19]; flowing from texts of the Old Testament, such as "The just shall flourish like a palm tree" (Psalm 92:13). Because of that grace in him, which is truly a share in God's righteousness, he could play several roles: (1) spouse of the Virgin Mother; (2) servant in charge of God's household—thus anticipating his role as intercessor for the Church, which will later be called "the household of God," [Ephesians 2:19]; (3) a father to God's Son, conceived not by his own action, but by the Holy Spirit.

Joseph led a life pleasing to God. He had a faith that allowed him completely to put his trust in God. His was a life directed toward God. With such faith, he took a wife that he had planned to divorce and fled to Egypt when the Angel told him to do so. He sought to be oriented to God. (The following is an excerpt of an article examining *Sacramentum Caritatis* from the November/December 2008 *Pastoral Liturgy, www.PastoralLiturgy.org*. It explains that the Eucharist reorients our lives to be directed to God).

If possible, sing the next three phrases with one breath, with a short lengthening on **-ty** of **majesty** and on **-dore** of **adore**, and on **you**. Take a good breath in the next phrase making only a short lengthening of **-phim** in **Seraphim**, so as to go right on to **worship**. But slow slightly the double notes at **with exultation**, lengthening the last and taking a good breath after it. Slow the entire last phrase, tying together **praise** and **as** and slowing clearly the last three words, so that the people sense to come in on **Holy, Holy, Holy . . . .**

Holy, Holy, Holy Lord God of hosts . . .

Text without music:

V. **The Lord be with you.**
R. And with your spirit.

V. **Lift up your hearts.**
R. We lift them up to the Lord.

V. **Let us give thanks to the Lord our God.**
R. It is right and just.

It is truly right and just, our duty and our salvation,
always and everywhere to give you thanks,
Lord, holy Father, almighty and eternal God,
and on the Solemnity of Saint Joseph
to give you fitting praise,
to glorify you and bless you.

Articulate very clearly **Solemnity of Saint Joseph**, and then in the next line, accent **fitting**. Accent slightly **glorify** and **bless**.

The Eucharist Changes the World: Effects on the Person

Ron Lewinski and Andrew Liaugminas

No one can encounter the living God and remain the same. And no person transformed profoundly by an encounter with God can continue to interact with others just as before. As the Eucharist affects the life of the individual, it thereby affects the broader community. This twofold eucharistic transformation forms the heart of Pope Benedict XVI's third part (#70–97) of his 2007 papal exhortation on the Eucharist *Sacramentum Caritatis*. In this reflection on that part, our focus is on the Holy Father's discussion of the Eucharist's effects on the life of the individual.

One of the primary themes Pope Benedict XVI emphasizes in the final part of *Sacramentum Caritatis* (SacCar) is that the Eucharist renews the life of the individual through a reorientation to God in an all-inclusive way. The Eucharist transforms the whole of our lives because it transforms us into an ever more alive and alert companion of God in the world. Incorporating the whole of our lives, it brings us into an intimate communion with the living God, a communion that does not merely endure only while we are in sacred space. God-with-us accompanies us as we go into the world to labor and live our everyday lives.

Christ enters our life to transform it at its very core. This theme is the foundation for the concluding part of *Sacramentum Caritatis*. The Eucharist, since it embraces the concrete, everyday existence of the believer, makes possible, day by day, the

Articulate very carefully the description of Saint Joseph, **just man**, and accent **spouse** so as to tie it with **just man**. Broaden (and thus slow slightly) **Virgin Mother of God**. Articulate clearly **wise and faithful servant**, but the line continues without a break through lines four and five, the accent in the latter falling on **father**—a kind of parallel to **servant** and also on **Son**. **Who was . . . Spirit** is descriptive of **Son**, and so the voice carries the text forward until it can rest on **our Lord Jesus Christ**.

For this just man was given by you
as spouse to the Virgin Mother of God
and set as a wise and faithful servant
in charge of your household
to watch like a father over your Only Begotten Son,
who was conceived by the overshadowing of the Holy Spirit,
our Lord Jesus Christ.

Through him the Angels praise your majesty,
Dominions adore and Powers tremble before you.
Heaven and the Virtues of heaven and the blessed Seraphim
worship together with exultation.
May our voices, we pray, join with theirs
in humble praise, as we acclaim:

Holy, Holy, Holy Lord God of hosts . . .

progressive transformation of all those called by grace to reflect the image of the Son of God. "There is nothing authentically human—our thoughts and affections, our words and deeds—that does not find in the sacrament of the Eucharist the form it needs to be lived to the full" (SacCar, 71). We should note the uniquely Catholic nature of this claim in all its parts: that we can be transformed in who we are, that our reception of the Eucharist is essential to that transformation, and that the Eucharist fulfills our lives—beliefs that Christians do not universally hold. It is a distinctively Catholic worldview.

After affirming how the Eucharist enables the fulfillment of all that makes up our lives, Benedict identifies that process with the "spiritual worship acceptable to God" that Saint Paul speaks of in Romans 12:1. The Holy Father, thereby, links our authentic human fulfillment with the "making holy"—the "sanctification"—of the whole of our lives. And indeed, these two effects—fulfillment and sanctification—are two sides of one transformation the Eucharist works in our lives. As the Eucharist encompasses the whole of our being, we begin to order all that we do in life for God's glory. "Worship pleasing to God thus becomes a new way of living our whole life, each particular moment of which is lifted up, since it is lived as part of a relationship with Christ and as an offering to God" (SacCar, 71).

As Christian worship is ultimately oriented to the Resurrection commemorated on the Lord's Day, so does the reorientation of our lives around the Eucharist likewise center us on the weekly Sabbath. This is an important point to the Holy Father: "Sunday is thus the day in which Christians rediscover the eucharistic form which their lives are meant to have" (SacCar, 72). Since what is celebrated on the Lord's Day is Christ's triumph over sin and death, Sunday thus "gives rise to the Christian meaning of life and a new way of experiencing time, relationships, work, life and death" (SacCar, 73).

Along with a recovery of the authentic meaning of time, the Pope teaches that the Sabbath day, being a day of freedom from our work, "relativizes work and directs it to the person" (SacCar, 74). In this context, Benedict XVI acknowledges Pope John Paul II's apostolic letter, *Dies Domini*, for reminding us about the true significance of Sunday for the Christian. It is the discipline of Sunday rest that renews us and readies us to return to our daily labor. Without the Lord's Day, work and leisure become inordinate. Rather than making our observance of the Lord's Day revolve around our duties or our leisure, both Pontiffs remind us that it is our duties and our leisure that must revolve around the Lord's Day. That is the right ordering of a Christian's life, not the reverse. This is a prime example of how the Eucharist gives us a form of life that leads to our personal fulfillment and sanctification.

March 25

THE ANNUNCIATION OF THE LORD

Solemnity

Collect

Note the alliteration in **willed**, **Word**, and **womb**. Do not pause until **Mary**. Slow **that . . . man**. Pronounce **our** as **ow-were**. Accent **partakers** and slightly accent **even**. Slowing down and emphasizing **divine nature** is also important.

O God, who willed that your Word
should take on the reality of human flesh
in the womb of the Virgin Mary,
grant, we pray,
that we, who confess our Redeemer to be God and man,
may merit to become partakers even in his divine nature.
Who lives and reigns with you in the unity of the Holy Spirit,
one God, for ever and ever.

Prayer over the Offerings

Bring out **pleased** to set off the address, **almighty God**. Be careful to pronounce **accept** with the first syllable sounding like **ack**. **Offering** has three syllables, so it should be slowed and a slight pause made after praying it. Bring out **she**, and treat the next phrase with a slight lowering of the voice, but with emphasis on **Incarnation** and **Son**. In the final phrase, **may rejoice** should sound like it really follows **she** in line three. Broaden the entire line.

Be pleased, almighty God,
to accept your Church's offering,
so that she, who is aware that her beginnings
lie in the Incarnation of your Only Begotten Son,
may rejoice to celebrate his mysteries on this Solemnity.
Who lives and reigns for ever and ever.

Prayer after Communion

Accent **Confirm**, **mysteries**, and **true faith**. Continue the sense with **we pray** before breaking. Pause after **so that** in order to set off the clear statement of the dogma. Both **true God** and **true man** need to be emphasized. Treat **saving power** as if one word. Broaden at the end of the phrase, **Resurrection**. The accent in line six clearly falls on the end, **eternal joy**.

Confirm in our minds the mysteries of the true faith,
we pray, O Lord,
so that, confessing that he who was conceived of the Virgin Mary
is true God and true man,
we may, through the saving power of his Resurrection,
merit to attain eternal joy.
Through Christ our Lord.

Collect: The prayer makes it clear at the outset that it was God's will that the Word should become flesh and that the reality of the Incarnation should happen in the womb of the Virgin Mary. What people believed about Jesus as the Word of God, was already true of him in the Incarnation: begotten not by blood, nor by carnal desire, nor by man's willing it, but by God (John 1:13).

Jesus is referred to as Redeemer, thus providing the point of the Incarnation in a nutshell. He came precisely to die for the redemption of the world. The prayer uses the term "confess" while describing the action of the Church in relation to Jesus on this solemnity. Confessing Jesus means declaring faith in the mystery of God becoming incarnate and lifting up our voices in praise, giving thanks and glory to God for the wonderful works of salvation.

Corresponding to that great mystery and gift of God, the Church prays that we might become sharers in his divinity. We do that through Baptism, by sharing the Word, and in Holy Communion.

Prayer over the Offerings: The Prayer states that the Church recognizes its beginnings in the Incarnation of Jesus. The history of the New Testament and of our salvation is summed up in the mysteries of the life, Death, and glorification of Christ. Christ chose disciples to carry on the mission, sending his Holy Spirit upon them; and as members of his Church, we are the descendants of that chosen group.

The prayer begs for our offering to be accepted by God. By making such an offering, the Church enters into the once-for-all

The space below is for your notes.

Refer to pages viii–x for an explanation of the pointing of the chants and to page xii for the Tones for the Presidential Prayers from *The Roman Missal.*

Pointed Text

Collect

A O God, who willed that your Word
should take on the reality of human flesh
in the womb of the Virgin Ma**ry**,
B grant, we pray,
that we, who confess our Redeemer to be **God** and man,
C may merit to become partakers even in his divine na***ture***.
Who lives and reigns with you in the unity of the Holy Spirit,
one God, for ever and ever.

Prayer over the Offerings

A Be pleased, almighty God,
to accept your Church's of**fer**ing,
B so that she, who is aware that her beginnings
lie in the Incarnation of your Only Be**got**ten Son,
C may rejoice to celebrate his mysteries on this Solem***ni***ty.
Who lives and reigns for ever and ever.

Prayer after Communion

A Confirm in our minds the mysteries of the true faith,
we pray, O **Lord**,
B so that, confessing that he who was conceived of the Virgin Mary
is true God **and** true man,
C we may, through the saving power of his Resurrection,
merit to attain eternal ***joy***.
Through Christ our Lord.

offering that Jesus made. When God accepted His Son's offering, he, in effect, showed a willingness to accept the offering of his disciples, of us, the Church. This exchange is celebrated in the solemnity today: God's giving the world his Son as Savior, and our giving the world his Son as Savior, and our giving God that Son back, in a sacramental manner, through our Eucharistic liturgy.

Prayer after Communion: We have just celebrated "the Mystery of Faith," the Holy Eucharist, culminating with the reception of the Body and Blood of the Lord in Holy Communion. In the light of this celebration, the Church prays that the mysteries of our faith might be confirmed in us. The reason given spans the whole New Testament dispensation. The confession of the Church begins with the mystery of this day, the conception / Incarnation of God's Son in the womb of the Virgin Mary. The faith of the Church defined in numerous Councils is restated: in his earthly conception, he remains true God, while also becoming true man.

The confession of the Church goes further, the prayer begs that through the salvation that we have received, may we one day come to share everlasting joy in heaven. Where Christ has gone, we hope to follow. The span of the New Testament vision is complete: beginning with the Incarnation of Jesus, passing through his Death and Resurrection, and arriving at the attainment of heaven itself.

Bring out the accent on **be** in **The Lord be with you**. In the response, accent **spirit**, by holding slightly both syllables. In the next phrase, make a strong accent on **Lift**, and slow both notes of **hearts**. In the third dialogue, move to the word **thanks** before accenting, and hold that word slightly to give it emphasis. Broaden both notes of **Lord**, and hold **God**.

Sing this proclamation cursively in a reciting tone. Do not hold **-va** in **salvation**; only broaden the two notes slightly. The **-tion** should be held. Slightly broaden **always** and **everywhere**. The accent of the phrase falls on **thanks**. In the next part of the text, clearly make four phrases, by respecting the commas after **Lord**, **Father**, and **God**.

Lengthen slightly **faith**. Continue without a breath until **that the Christ**. Do not lengthen or breathe at **men**. Continue directly with **and for men's sake**. Lengthen slightly **sake**, and take a quick breath. Slow and broaden **power**. Continue without a break with **of the Holy**. Lengthen **-it** of **Spirit** and take a breath. Accent **Lov-** in **Lovingly**. Lengthen **womb**. Make a slight break in the voice before continuing with **that the promises**. Lengthen slightly **-bout** in **about**. If necessary, take a quick breath to complete the next phrase without breathing or breaking. Broaden **hope of nations**, but do not lengthen the last syllable. Continue with **be accomplished**. Broaden the last five syllables of the phrase,

Preface: The mystery of the Incarnation

The body of the Preface brings out the primary elements of this solemnity. It begins with noting the Virgin Mary's hearing with faith the voice of the Angel's announcing the incarnation of God's Son (Luke 1:26–38). The liturgical text emphasizes that it was by the "overshadowing power of the Holy Spirit" that this miracle could happen. It also summarizes the meaning of the Incarnation: he was to be born among men, but for the sake of saving all men and women in the world. Once again, the liturgical text links the Incarnation with the Paschal Mystery of redemption.

Returning to Mary, the prayer describes the Mother of God as bearing Christ in her immaculate womb ("How can this be since I do not know man?" Luke 1:34). Like any mother, she bears this pregnancy with love for her Son. However, she is filled with love for him for another and deeper reason than human maternal emotion. She bears him with love because of her faith: for she knows that through him, as the Angel said, the promises to Israel would be fulfilled. Further, she knows that, through him, the hope of the nations will finally be answered and fulfilled, and in a way beyond what anyone could possibly have imagined. All of this is the basis for Mary's extraordinary love.

(The following homily explores the meaning of God's becoming "incarnate of the Virgin Mary," as stated in the Creed. It is excerpted from the CD *Preparing Your Parish for the Revised Roman Missal,* © 2010, Liturgy Training Publications.)

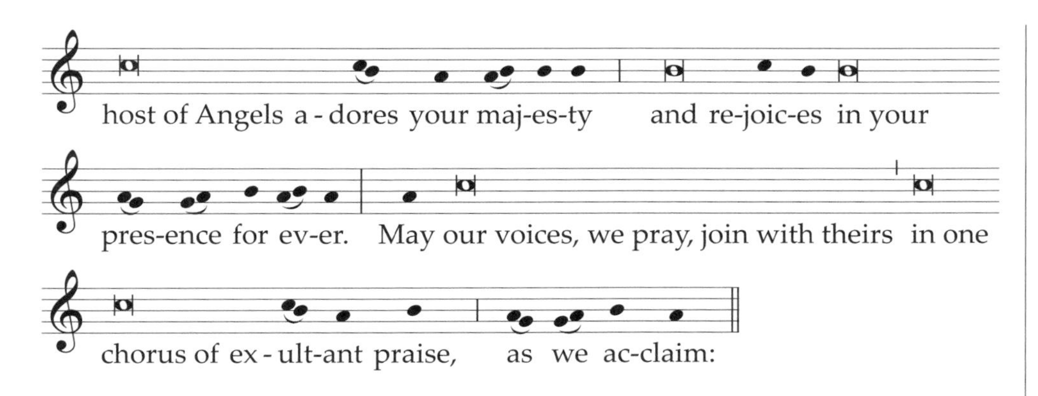

holding the last and taking a breath there.

Slow **we ac-** and put emphasis on **-claim**, so as to evoke the response **Holy, Holy, Holy . . . .**

Text without music:

V. **The Lord be with you.**
R. And with your spirit.

V. **Lift up your hearts.**
R. We lift them up to the Lord.

V. **Let us give thanks to the Lord our God.**
R. It is right and just.

It is truly right and just, our duty and our salvation,
always and everywhere to give you thanks,
Lord, holy Father, almighty and eternal God,
through Christ our Lord.

For the Virgin Mary heard with faith
that the Christ was to be born among men and for men's sake
by the overshadowing power of the Holy Spirit.
Lovingly she bore him in her immaculate womb,
that the promises to the children of Israel might come about
and the hope of nations be accomplished beyond all telling.

Through him the host of Angels adores your majesty
and rejoices in your presence for ever.
May our voices, we pray, join with theirs
in one chorus of exultant praise, as we acclaim:

Holy, Holy, Holy Lord God of hosts . . .

Accent slightly **faith**. At the end of line two, slow the descriptive words about Christ's birth, **among men and for men's sake**, but the voice should continue without pause to **by the . . . Spirit**. Articulate carefully **overshadowing power**. Treat **Lovingly** as if a comma were after it. Articulate very carefully **immaculate womb**. Parallel and contrast **children of Israel** and **hope of nations**. Parallel **might come about** and **be accomplished**.

In the conclusion, note in the third line the word **our**. Pronounce it as **ow-were**.

The Creed
Daniel J. Merz, SLD
The Creed is our communion in the faith that enables us to share in Communion in the Eucharist. It serves as key and summary of the Word, as well as introduction to, and criterion for, Communion.

In the first part of the Creed, we profess God the Father as Creator. He is "maker of heaven and earth, / of all things visible and invisible." God is the maker of what is visible, such as the earth and the stars and you and me; he is maker not only of "unseen" things (as the former translation has it) but also of "invisible" things, such as angels. He is also maker of what is invisible, such as our immortal souls.

The main point of the second part of the Creed is our affirmation that Jesus Christ is both divine and human. The same man who became flesh, "incarnate of the Virgin Mary" (in other words, who received our human nature from her), and who suffered death on the cross—this man is also "God from God, Light from Light." John's first letter tells us that God is light (1 John 1:5–7), so Jesus is divine light. The holy ones, the saints, dwell in this light. They dwell in the presence of this eternal light, in the presence of Jesus. Thus, we pray that our deceased loved ones may dwell forever in this light!

Let's be mindful of how this Creed opens up the correct understanding of the Bible, and how it calls us to communion in faith so that we can approach the altar to receive Communion.

June 24

THE NATIVITY OF SAINT JOHN THE BAPTIST

Solemnity

At the Vigil Mass

This Mass is used on the evening of June 23, either before or after First Vespers (Evening Prayer I) of the Solemnity.

Collect

Pause at all commas, so that the people have time to hear the prayer. Slow on **way of salvation**, as it is the culmination of the first thought. After the pause at **and**, lower the voice for the parenthetical/descriptive phrase. Emphasize **safely** and **One**, and slow for **our Lord Jesus Christ**.

Grant, we pray, almighty God,
that your family may walk in the way of salvation
and, attentive to what Saint John the Precursor urged,
may come safely to the One he foretold,
our Lord Jesus Christ.
Who lives and reigns with you in the unity of the Holy Spirit,
one God, for ever and ever.

Prayer over the Offerings

Try to go from the beginning through line three without a pause or breath. Pause very briefly, for emphasis, after **grant**. Emphasize and parallel **mystery** and **devoted service**.

Look with favor, O Lord,
upon the offerings made by your people
on the Solemnity of Saint John the Baptist,
and grant that what we celebrate in mystery
we may follow with deeds of devoted service.
Through Christ our Lord. *

Prayer after Communion

Although proclaiming slowly, try to pray the first three lines without a break. Proclaim **our** as **ow-were**. Lower voice slightly in the parenthetical phrase of **since . . . sins**. Set off **now** by accenting it clearly.

May the marvelous prayer of Saint John the Baptist
accompany us who have eaten our fill
at this sacrificial feast, O Lord,
and, since Saint John proclaimed your Son
to be the Lamb who would take away our sins,
may he implore now for us your favor.
Through Christ our Lord.

*The Preface for the Vigil Mass is found in the spread for At the Mass during the Day; see pages 288–289.

Collect: The prayer asks first for the grace of God to be given to the Church—here called "the family (of God)"—to walk in the way of salvation. The latter phrase is what an inhabitant of Philippi claimed to be the content of what Saint Paul and his companions preached (Acts 16:17). But the prayer also hearkens back to the Exodus event, in which God leads his people to their salvation (e.g., Numbers 10:34–36; cf. also, Psalms 68:20; 74:12; 91:16).

To walk the way of salvation means not to deviate from the path God wants for us: the Baptist's message was at the core to "prepare / make straight the way of the Lord" (Matthew 3:3 and parallels, which cite Isaiah 40:3).

The Church asks to come "safely" to Jesus, the One foretold by the Baptist. We ask this, because we want to arrive at our salvation, which is union with Jesus. To do so, the Church intends to be attentive to the teaching of the Baptist; thus, while keeping vigil for the Solemnity, we will prepare for the coming of Christ into our hearts in a new way.

Prayer over the Offerings: The offerings that we bring to the altar, as God's people, are a response to the love we have received from God. John the Baptist made a similar offering when he answered God's call to the office and actions of prophet. The Church desires to see its offerings as breathing the spirit of surrender and response which Saint John gave to the Lord's call and grace.

John the Baptist called for deeds, that is, a life responding to what had been received from God. His opposition and

The space below is for your notes.

Refer to pages viii–x for an explanation of the pointing of the chants and to page xii for the Tones for the Presidential Prayers from *The Roman Missal*.

Pointed Text

Collect

A Grant, we pray, almighty God,
that your family may walk in the way of salva**tion**
B and, attentive to what Saint John the Precursor urged,
may come safely to the One **he** foretold,
C our Lord Jesus ***Christ***.
Who lives and reigns with you in the unity of the Holy Spirit,
one God, for ever and ever.

Prayer over the Offerings

A Look with favor, O Lord,
upon the offerings made by your people
on the Solemnity of Saint John the Bap**tist**,
B and grant that what we cele**brate** in mystery
C we may follow with deeds of devoted ser***vice***.
Through Christ our Lord.

Prayer after Communion

A May the marvelous prayer of Saint John the Baptist
accompany us who have eaten our fill
at this sacrificial feast, O **Lord**,
B and, since Saint John proclaimed your Son
to be the Lamb who would take a**way** our sins,
C may he implore now for us your fa***vor***.
Through Christ our Lord.

reaction to excess religious verbiage and little surrender of the heart led the prophet to call the Pharisees a "brood of vipers" (Matthew 3:7) and to demand that lives begin to evidence the spirit of reform. So, too, with this prayer, the Church hopes to make our celebration not merely lip-service to God, but rather life-service. This will happen when our deeds, in accord with John's challenging teaching, show that our hearts match the externals of the rituals we perform.

Prayer after Communion: This prayer of the Church begins by invoking the Baptist's prayer that accompanied Jesus's baptism for reform, and that led to the heavens being opened at Jesus's baptism (Matthew 3:16–17). We want to be associated with the Baptist's prayer, since it will lead us to the experience of heavenly marvels.

The text of the prayer recalls the Baptist's hailing Jesus as the Lamb of God (John 1:29) as it subtly proclaims his paschal vocation for the redemption of the world. That redemption means that Jesus is the One who takes away our sins. Since John, by his preaching, proclaimed this role for Jesus, the Church begs that he might intercede with God for us, that we might know the divine "favor" / "promise" (cf. Psalm 89:2; Isaiah 49:8). We have known such favor in the Holy Communion just shared. This prayer is that such favor might accompany us now as we leave the church and return to daily life.

THE NATIVITY OF SAINT JOHN THE BAPTIST

At the Mass during the Day

Collect

Emphasize the end of the first and second lines to bring out the contrast between **Saint John** and **Christ**.

Set off lines three and four by vocally connecting **give** and **joys**.

Pause after **and** to set off the second petition.

O God, who raised up Saint John the Baptist
to make ready a nation fit for Christ the Lord,
give your people, we pray,
the grace of spiritual joys
and direct the hearts of all the faithful
into the way of salvation and peace.
Through our Lord Jesus Christ, your Son,
who lives and reigns with you in the unity of the Holy Spirit,
one God, for ever and ever.

Prayer over the Offerings

The first three lines go together, but it is probably too long for one breath. Make a slight pause at **honor**, setting off **the nativity**. Don't pause too long after **Savior**, because the phrase is not finished until the fourth line.

We place these offerings on your altar, O Lord,
to celebrate with fitting honor the nativity of him
who both foretold the coming of the world's Savior
and pointed him out when he came.
Who lives and reigns for ever and ever.

Prayer after Communion

Treat the first line as the subordinate clause it is. To understand the structure, while practicing, drop the line and start with **We pray, O Lord**. Emphasize the second line by praying it slowly and with clear enunciation. Drop the voice slightly for the subordinate clause **finding joy . . . Baptist**. Emphasize **author** to match the emphasis on **Christ**.

Having feasted at the banquet of the heavenly Lamb,
we pray, O Lord,
that, finding joy in the nativity of Saint John the Baptist,
your Church may know as the author of her rebirth
the Christ whose coming John foretold.
Who lives and reigns for ever and ever.

Collect: Making a "nation fit" for the Lord (words the Angel used in telling Zechariah of John the Baptist's birth [Luke 1:17]), requires repentance and reform. John the Baptist had been called by God precisely to make ready such a people, for God's coming to earth. Because Israel had not listened to the voice of earlier prophets, that voice was all but stilled. Israel had been deaf to earlier prophets because it had its own agenda, not the Lord's. God allowed them to engage in wars and lose freedom to their conquerors.

The Church prays for "the grace of spiritual joys." This is in contrast to those who saw the repentance John the Baptist preached and the austerity he practiced as contrary to joy. It is also in contrast to those who saw an Israelite triumph over political foes as the greatest source of joy. Receiving the grace of spiritual joys will "make straight the way of the Lord" (Matthew 3:3ff) in the hearts of people with authentic faith. This alone is the way to "salvation" and "peace"—from the Canticle of Zechariah (Luke 1:77, 79).

Prayer over the Offerings: Bringing offerings to the altar is a sign of the repentance and turning to God that John preached. The offerings symbolize a turning to the Lord, a return of God's gifts to their Source. Hence, it is a ritual action that fulfills precisely what Saint John preached to his contemporaries, and thus is a way of truly honoring him. John the Baptist's birth showed God's infinite power to work miracles in any circumstance (even the impossible one of a woman too old for bearing children to give birth; Luke 1:24–25).

The space below is for your notes.

Refer to pages viii–x for an explanation of the pointing of the chants and to page xii for the Tones for the Presidential Prayers from *The Roman Missal.*

Pointed Text

Collect

A O God, who raised up Saint John the Baptist
to make ready a nation fit for Christ the **Lord**,
B give your people, we pray,
the grace of spir**i**tual joys
C and direct the hearts of all the faithful
into the way of salvation and ***peace***.
Through our Lord Jesus Christ, your Son,
who lives and reigns with you in the unity of the Holy Spirit,
one God, for ever and ever.

Prayer over the Offerings

B We place these offerings on your al**tar**, O Lord,
C to celebrate with fitting honor the nativity of him
who both foretold the coming of the world's Savior
and pointed him out when he ***came***.
Who lives and reigns for ever and ever.

Prayer after Communion

A Having feasted at the banquet of the heavenly Lamb,
we pray, O **Lord**,
B that, finding joy in the nativity of Saint **John** the Baptist,
C your Church may know as the author of her rebirth
the Christ whose coming John fore***told***.
Who lives and reigns for ever and ever.

This matches the sign value of John the Baptist's life and preaching, pointing out the coming of God's Son as the world's Savior. Thus everything about John pointed to Christ, and made him much more than a mere prophet in the Israelite tradition—but rather the "forerunner," the one who understood the world-transforming call and action of his cousin, the humble Lamb of God, and who did not hesitate to point Jesus out to his disciples and contemporaries (Luke 3:15–18; Matthew 3:13–17).

Prayer after Communion: We have just partaken of "the supper of the Lamb" (Revelation 19:9) in the Holy Communion we have received and shared. Just before that ritual moment, the Priest Celebrant lifted the Body and Blood of the Lord, saying, "Behold the Lamb of God." In John 1:29, John the Baptist said these words as he heralded Jesus. The prophet was proclaiming, already at the beginning of Jesus's ministry, the Paschal conclusion of that same ministry (the Lamb was at the center of the Passover meal, and its blood was salvific for the people of Israel, just as Jesus's Blood was salvific for the world).

Celebrating the birth of this prophet brings the Church "joy," in the same way that knowing Jesus intimately brings deep joy. John the Baptist's identity was in leading people to Jesus. He saw himself as "A voice of one crying out in the desert, / . . . / 'make straight his paths'" (Luke 3:4). This communion with Jesus is the fulfillment of Saint John's preaching ministry and hope. The Church prays that the celebration brings people to know Christ.

Bring out the accent on **be** in **The Lord be with you.** In the response, accent **spirit**, by holding slightly both syllables. In the next phrase, make a strong accent on **Lift**, and slow both notes of **hearts**. In the third dialogue, move to the word **thanks** before accenting, and hold that word slightly to give it emphasis. Broaden both notes of **Lord**, and hold **God**.

Sing this proclamation cursively in a reciting tone. Do not hold **-va** in **salvation**; only broaden the two notes slightly. The **-tion** should be held. Slightly broaden **always** and **everywhere**. The accent of the phrase falls on **thanks**. In the next part of the text, clearly make four phrases, by respecting the commas after **Lord**, **Father**, and **God**.

Respect the commas around **Saint John the Baptist**. Place a slight hold on **-ry** in that phrase.

Broaden **honor** but do not pause after it. Hold **-en** in **women** and breathe. Take a quick breath after **rejoicing**, but treat the semicolon more as a colon, showing that the next phrase parallels **rejoicing**. Hold **joy** but only slightly, as it must be kept together with **at the coming**. Hold **-tion** of **salvation** and breathe. Do not pause after **-ets** of **prophets**. Hold **-tion** in **redemption**.

Preface: The mission of the Precursor

The body of the Preface, in three paragraphs, summarizes the joy of the Church this day, as it recalls the role of John the Baptist in salvation history. The first paragraph calls him the "Precursor"—the one who runs before an important person to awaken people to the coming event. The Church recognizes that it was the hand of God that made Saint John's birth so special—and that is why the text praises God for his great glory, rather than concentrating on praise of the Saint. The Baptist was consecrated from the womb with singular honor, according to the prophetic words of the Angel to Zechariah (Luke 1:14–15). Further, it was Jesus who called him "the greatest born of women" (Matthew 11:11).

The second paragraph highlights that John's nativity would be cause for great rejoicing—certainly for his aged parents, but also for all those awaiting the redemption of Israel (cf. Luke 1:14; 1:68ff; 2:25–32). Even in the womb, the Baptizer responded to the presence of Jesus during Mary's visit to her cousin, Elizabeth (Luke 1:44). This paragraph also brings out John's preaching, that pointed to Jesus as the paschal Lamb to bring redemption to the whole world (and not just to Israel), by forgiveness of sin and the end of death (rather than merely freedom from slavery in Egypt).

The third paragraph mentions the baptism of Jesus, which rather than making Jesus holy made the waters for Baptism holy (Matthew 3:15–17). And this paragraph culminates in the mention of the

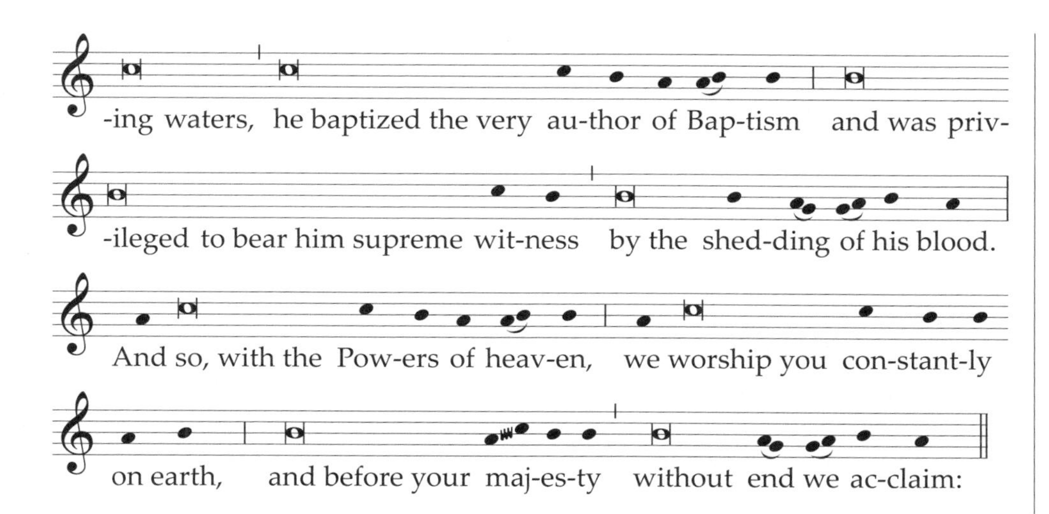

Pause after **waters** only to respect the comma. Take a short breath after **-tism** of **Baptism**.

Do not pause or hold **-ness** of **witness**. Hold **blood**, and then breathe. Pause in the next line after **so**. But make only a slight pause at **-en** of **heaven**, with the same for **earth**. Broaden **maj-** of **majesty**. Slow down proclaiming the text on these last words, but sing the entire phrase, **and before . . . acclaim** without taking a breath.

Holy, Holy, Holy Lord God of hosts . . .

Text without music:

V. **The Lord be with you.**
R. And with your spirit.

V. **Lift up your hearts.**
R. We lift them up to the Lord.

V. **Let us give thanks to the Lord our God.**
R. It is right and just.

It is truly right and just, our duty and our salvation,
always and everywhere to give you thanks,
Lord, holy Father, almighty and eternal God,
through Christ our Lord.

In his Precursor, Saint John the Baptist,
we praise your great glory,
for you consecrated him for a singular honor
among those born of women.

Accent **your**.
Accent **consecrated** and **singular**, with the natural accent falling on **honor**. Do not pause after **honor**, but continue with **among . . . .**

martyrdom which John was to undergo at the hands of Herod (Matthew 14:1–12).

(John the Baptist heralded Jesus with the words "Behold, the Lamb of God." Those words are used in the Invitation to Communion. The following excerpt of a Homily explores the words of John the Baptist as used at Mass The Homily was excerpted from the CD *Preparing Your Parish for the Revised Roman Missal: Homilies and Reproducibles for Faith Formation*, © 2010, Liturgy Training Publications.)

The Lamb of God: Our Way to Redemption
Daniel J. Merz, SLD

"Behold the Lamb of God, / behold him who takes away the sins of the world."

With the revised translation of *The Roman Missal*, the priest will say these words as he holds up the consecrated host just before Holy Communion. It is interesting that the liturgy puts this quotation from John the Baptist adjacent to the words "Blessed are those called to the supper of the Lamb," which alludes to Revelation 19:9 (NAB). The lamb is the most frequent image for Christ in the book of Revelation, and, perhaps more significantly, the "supper of the lamb" in Revelation refers to the wedding feast of Christ and his Bride, the Church. What is interesting is that, in a passage a little beyond the one quoted above from the Gospel according to John, John the Baptist calls himself the friend of the Bridegroom, and then later is beheaded because he protested the illicit marriage of King Herod. The beauty is that the Baptist,

Tie together lines two and three and four and five. Accent **womb**.

His birth brought great rejoicing;
even in the womb he leapt for joy
at the coming of human salvation.
He alone of all the prophets
pointed out the Lamb of redemption.

Articulate carefully **pointed out**.

Broaden **flowing waters**, but pause only after **Baptism**. Articulate carefully **supreme witness**, since it summarizes Saint John's special place in salvation history. Emphasize **blood**.

And to make holy the flowing waters,
he baptized the very author of Baptism
and was privileged to bear him supreme witness
by the shedding of his blood.

And so, with the Powers of heaven,
we worship you constantly on earth,
and before your majesty
without end we acclaim:

Holy, Holy, Holy Lord God of hosts . . .

who was a celibate, gave his life defending the sanctity of marriage. The liturgy delights in this type of wordplay. Eucharist is the foretaste of the heavenly wedding feast, and so we have a celibate priest speaking the words of the celibate John the Baptist to the Bride of Christ the Church—you, the assembly—and pointing to Christ, the Bridegroom. The previous translation stated, "Happy are those called," but the revised translation states that those called are "blessed." Regardless of whether we feel happy or sad when we come to Church, we are all "blessed" in being called to Holy Communion with our Bridegroom. And we hope always that this Communion increases our longing all the more for the heavenly feast.

As we continue to look at the liturgy, we see that the assembly's response to the priest just before Holy Communion comes from Matthew 8:8 and Luke 7:6–7. The revised translation is more faithful to the scripture that underlies this prayer. Many may never have realized that they were quoting the words of the Roman centurion in Luke's account of the Gospel. The centurion had asked Jesus to heal his servant, and when Jesus agreed, saying that he would come to the house, the centurion replied, "Lord, I am not worthy to have you enter under my roof; only say the word and my servant shall be healed" (NAB). Jesus responds to the centurion's words by saying that never in all of Israel had he found such faith, and he heals the servant from a distance. The liturgy asks us to call to mind the faith, humility, and reverence of this centurion, who sought the healing power of Jesus, but felt unworthy to have Jesus come under the roof of his house. The Christian who approaches the altar should have the same faith, humility, and reverence in preparing to receive the Holy Eucharist under the "roof" of our body. Just as the roof is the external shelter for what is most important to us as social beings—our family—so too is our body the "roof" or external shelter for that which is most precious to us as individuals—our soul.

The Church places three scripture readings side by side in the liturgy and communicates so much with so little. We are reminded of the mutual support that celibates and married people can provide for each other: the celibate defending the sanctity of marriage and married people providing support and friendship to the celibate—the friend of the Bridegroom. We are reminded that our Communion derives from the sacrifice of the Lamb who has taken away our sins. We are reminded that this banquet meal is a foretaste of the heavenly wedding feast. We are reminded that in coming to Holy Communion, we are to have the attitude of the centurion in Luke's account of the Gospel, a man of faith, humility, and reverence. And we are reminded that we are also in need of healing, just as the centurion's servant was.

In this Eucharist, may we indeed find the healing and forgiveness we need and the eternal love and commitment of the Bridegroom, whom we need above all else.

June 29

SAINTS PETER AND PAUL, APOSTLES

Solemnity

At the Vigil Mass

This Mass is used on the evening of June 28, either before or after First Vespers (Evening Prayer I) of the Solemnity.

Collect

Pause appropriately to bring out the contrast between **that** and **so**.

Grant, we pray, O Lord our God,
that we may be sustained
by the intercession of the blessed Apostles Peter and Paul,
that, as through them you gave your Church
the foundations of her heavenly office,
so through them you may help her to eternal salvation.
Through our Lord Jesus Christ, your Son,
who lives and reigns with you in the unity of the Holy Spirit,
one God, for ever and ever.

Prayer over the Offerings

Drop the voice slightly for **O Lord**, but without pause continue with the next two lines of text **as we glory**. Parallel **the more** in the successive lines. Tie together **the more . . . loving kindess**.

We bring offerings to your altar, O Lord,
as we glory in the solemn feast
of the blessed Apostles Peter and Paul,
so that the more we doubt our own merits,
the more we may rejoice that we are to be saved
by your loving kindness.
Through Christ our Lord. *

Prayer after Communion

Articulate carefully **heavenly Sacrament**, and then drop the voice slightly for **O Lord, we pray**. Parallel **strengthen your faithful** and **enlightened with the teaching** by accenting the two verb forms at the beginning of these words and the two noun forms at the end of them.

By this heavenly Sacrament, O Lord, we pray,
strengthen your faithful,
whom you have enlightened with the teaching of the Apostles.
Through Christ our Lord. **

* The Preface for the Vigil Mass is found in the spread for At the Mass during the Day; see pages 296–297.

** You may use the Solemn Blessing for Saints Peter and Paul in the Order of Mass; also in *The Order of Mass: A Roman Missal Study Edition and Workbook*, page 174.

Collect: God gave the Church the Apostles Peter and Paul for its foundation. Saint Peter was part of the foundation because Jesus had given him the keys—since it would be his calling to open the gates of heaven to those of faith (Matthew 16:15–19). Saint Paul was part of the foundation of the Church, as Jesus had given him the task of founding, building up, and caring for local churches. This task entailed bringing those churches to Jesus, through preaching and teaching (Acts 13:26, 32–33; 2 Corinthians 5:19–20).

As has been indicated, both vocations came from Jesus directly, and so they are said to have a "heavenly office"—the means for the Church, the living body of Jesus, to attain heaven. The Church once needed these Apostles' physical presence and preaching to lay the foundations of the Church as sign and vehicle of eternal salvation. Now we need their intercession to arrive at that salvation, and it is for this that the Collect prays.

Prayer over the Offerings: The Church brings "offerings" to the altar at Mass, and this surrender of gifts is a sign that we are bringing to God what we are and have—which is what Saints Peter and Paul did. That is why we can "glory" in the solemn feast we celebrate in their honor. They knew their lives did not merit God's love: Saint Peter, because he betrayed his Lord at the crucial moment of his arrest and trial (Matthew 26:69–75 and parallels); Saint Paul, because he persecuted the Church with great zeal (Acts 9:1–2; Philippians 3:6).

The space below is for your notes.

Refer to pages viii–x for an explanation of the pointing of the chants and to page xii for the Tones for the Presidential Prayers from *The Roman Missal.*

Pointed Text

Collect

A Grant, we pray, O Lord our God,
that we may be sustained
by the intercession of the blessed Apostles Peter and **Paul**,
B that, as through them you gave your Church
the foundations of her hea**ven**ly office,
C so through them you may help her to eternal salva***tion***.
Through our Lord Jesus Christ, your Son,
who lives and reigns with you in the unity of the Holy Spirit,
one God, for ever and ever.

Prayer over the Offerings

A We bring offerings to your altar, O **Lord**,
B as we glory in the solemn feast
of the blessed Apostles Pe**ter** and Paul,
C so that the more we doubt our own merits,
the more we may rejoice that we are to be saved
by your loving kind***ness***.
Through Christ our Lord.

Prayer after Communion

A By this heavenly Sacrament, O Lord, we **pray**,
B streng**then** your faithful,
C whom you have enlightened with the teaching of the Apos***tles***.
Through Christ our Lord.

So too, the Prayer reminds those celebrating this liturgy of sacrifice and communion that the rite itself doesn't earn, or make us merit, salvation. Rather, it is the occasion for us, sinners all, simply to open up to give God our all, and then receive God's gratuitous "gift" more profoundly. We can hope to have God's loving kindness, that is salvation, because our gifts are united and assumed into the gift of Jesus. The model for this surrender to God, in Jesus, is particularly strong in Saints Peter and Paul.

Prayer after Communion: Enlightenment comes from receiving the Word of God, which was the content of the teaching of the Apostles we honor today. Jesus identified himself as the light that would provide the way. He told the Pharisees: "I am the light of the world. Whoever follows me will not walk in darkness but will have the light of life" (John 8:12). So all the faithful have received the enlightenment of Jesus, beginning with their Baptism and Confirmation, and anew, in reception of the Holy Eucharist.

We pray here that the light of faith already received may be made strong, through this new contact with Jesus's Body and Blood in the Sacrament of Holy Communion. Thus, we are prepared, thanks to God's strength, to leave the physical structure of the church after this ritual celebration and to take the strength of our faith to transform our lives and the life of the world. The Prayer after Communion usually has this double structure: back to the action of Communion and forward to bring Christ to the world.

SAINTS PETER AND PAUL, APOSTLES

At the Mass during the Day

Collect

Articulate clearly **Apostles Peter and Paul**. Enunciate carefully **noble** and **holy joy**.

Set off **in all things**, as if the words were surrounded by commas. Pray **follow . . . religion** within one phrase and breath, broadening **those** in the phrase.

O God, who on the Solemnity of the Apostles Peter and Paul
give us the noble and holy joy of this day,
grant, we pray, that your Church
may in all things follow the teaching
of those through whom she received
the beginnings of right religion.
Through our Lord Jesus Christ, your Son,
who lives and reigns with you in the unity of the Holy Spirit,
one God, for ever and ever.

Prayer over the Offerings

Accent **prayer** and **gift**. Tie together lines two and three, and four and five.

Slow **celebration of the sacrifice** for emphasis.

May the prayer of the Apostles, O Lord,
accompany the sacrificial gift
that we present to your name for consecration,
and may their intercession make us devoted to you
in celebration of the sacrifice.
Through Christ our Lord.

Prayer after Communion

Tie together lines four and five to echo Acts 2:42.
Articulate clearly **one heart** and **one soul**. Emphasize **your love**.

Grant us, O Lord,
who have been renewed by this Sacrament,
so to live in the Church,
that, persevering in the breaking of the Bread
and in the teaching of the Apostles,
we may be one heart and one soul,
made steadfast in your love.
Through Christ our Lord. *

* You may use the Solemn Blessing for Saints Peter and Paul in the Order of Mass; also in *The Order of Mass: A Roman Missal Study Edition and Workbook*, page 174.

Collect: The opening phrase of the prayer states that the celebration of this solemnity provides the Church a joy that is both "noble" and "holy." This is so because of the participation in the heavenly and eternal liturgy and feast that the two Apostles are celebrating now in glory. Our feast is a sacramental sharing on earth of theirs in the glory of heaven. Our liturgy, so to speak, "pulls back the curtain" on the heavenly liturgy, and makes it present in our midst.

Celebrating Saints Peter and Paul brings us back to the foundation of our faith, the "beginnings of right religion." Both Apostles called their countrymen to recognize the Messiah. They also called Gentiles to let go of the empty ritual actions of pagan worship, to turn to Christ for salvation. This Collect prays that the Church may always follow the teaching it has received from these Apostles and thus remain close to Jesus, whom they preached and for whom they died.

Prayer over the Offerings: The presentation of good words on one's behalf by someone important always helps one's cause, at least psychologically. That is why the Church desires that the "good prayer" of the two Apostles we honor today will go to God along with our gifts; thus we can be assured of a hearing by God. It is not a merely external offering that is at stake here (to "your name" means, "to the Person of God"). Rather it is that the action of the Holy Spirit and the words of Jesus will

The space below is for your notes.

Refer to pages viii–x for an explanation of the pointing of the chants and to page xii for the Tones for the Presidential Prayers from *The Roman Missal.*

Pointed Text

Collect

A O God, who on the Solemnity of the Apostles Peter and Paul
give us the noble and holy joy of this **day**,
B grant, we pray, that your Church
may in all things fol**low** the teaching
C of those through whom she received
the beginnings of right reli***gion***.
Through our Lord Jesus Christ, your Son,
who lives and reigns with you in the unity of the Holy Spirit,
one God, for ever and ever.

Prayer over the Offerings

A May the prayer of the Apostles, O **Lord**,
B accompany the sacrificial gift
that we present to your name for **con**secration,
C and may their intercession make us devoted to you
in celebration of the sac***ri***fice.
Through Christ our Lord.

Prayer after Communion

A Grant us, O Lord,
who have been renewed by this Sacrament,
so to live in the **Church**,
B that, persevering in the breaking of the Bread
and in the teaching of **the** Apostles,
C we may be one heart and one soul,
made steadfast in your ***love***.
Through Christ our Lord.

transform and consecrate our gifts into the Body and Blood of Jesus.

Thus, we hope that the Apostles' intercession will help us to transform our hearts with true devotion and love. Both Saints Peter and Paul made a sacrifice in union with Christ, showing complete devotion to their Lord. Peter was crucified and Paul was beheaded. Such an example is what the Church needs and can rejoice in this day, as it tries to sacrifice its all in a ritual and sacramental manner, in union with the redemptive sacrifice of Jesus.

Prayer after Communion: We have been brought into an intimate communion with Christ. Our Communion leads to true renewal—a "making new" of each communicant disposed to receiving the grace of the Eucharist. We pray now for the grace to live our calling to be Church. We will do that by firmly adhering to the teaching of the Apostles, especially Saints Peter and Paul, and to the celebration of Mass (known in the early Church as "the breaking of the bread"). The terminology is taken from the account in the Acts of the Apostles that described the early Church's life and practice: "They devoted themselves to the apostles' instruction and the communal life, to the breaking of the bread and the prayers . . . (they) had all things in common . . . " (Acts 2:42, 44).

We petition that our Communion may sustain us, and keep us united as Church ("one in heart and soul"), united with God, and with one another as Church. Thus, we will be "steadfast" in God's love, so lavishly poured out in the liturgy we have just celebrated.

Bring out the accent on **be** in **The Lord be with you.** In the response, accent **spirit**, by holding slightly both syllables. In the next phrase, make a strong accent on **Lift**, and slow both notes of **hearts**. In the third dialogue, move to the word **thanks** before accenting, and hold that word slightly to give it emphasis. Broaden both notes of **Lord**, and hold **God**.

Sing this proclamation cursively in a reciting tone. Do not hold **-va** in **salvation**; only broaden the two notes slightly. The **-tion** should be held. Slightly broaden **always** and **everywhere**. The accent of the phrase falls on **thanks**. In the next part of the text, clearly make three phrases, by respecting the commas after **Lord** and **Father**.

Beginning with **For by your . . .**, hold taking a breath until **joy**—and then the breath needs to convey the colon, that is, not too long of a hold or pause. Pause at the comma after **Peter**, and hold **faith**. But continue without a breath (if possible), pausing after **Paul**, and slowing on **preacher**, holding the last syllable. Repeat that pattern in the next phrase. Be sure to accent **Pe-** in **Peter** and not the second syllable.

Enunciate carefully **Gentiles** and hold **call** with a breath afterward. Hold **so**, but without a breath. Slow slightly at **family** and hold **Christ**, taking a short breath afterwards.

Preface: The twofold mission of Peter and Paul in the Church

At the outset, the Preface tells of the "joy" that Apostles Peter and Paul bring to the Church. The text unpacks that statement to get at its deeper meaning. Joy comes from reflecting on Saint Peter, who by his confession of Jesus as Messiah, merited Christ's strong approval and blessing (Matthew 16:16–19), and became a constant model of how all of us should confess our faith in Jesus. Joy comes from reflecting on Saint Paul also, as he was an extraordinary preacher of the faith that he received from Jesus so miraculously (Acts 9:3–19). Thus, both were men of faith, confessing it and preaching it even to martyrdom. By their faith, they became founders of the Church—as the descendant of Israel (for whom Peter is the great symbol) and for the revelation of Jesus to the Gentiles (for whom Paul is the great symbol).

The summary of their lives and work, as well as their death by martyrdom, was that they gathered both Jew and Gentile into one family of Christ. That has led to their being revered wherever there is the Church—which means throughout the world.

(Peter followed Jesus throughout the Lord's ministry. Paul never knew the earthly Jesus. The following excerpt of a Homily, by Monsignor Joseph DeGrocco, considers how we come to know Jesus. The Homily has been excerpted from the CD *Preparing your Parish for the Revised Roman Missal: Homilies and Reproducibles for Faith Formation,* © 2010; Liturgy Training Publications.)

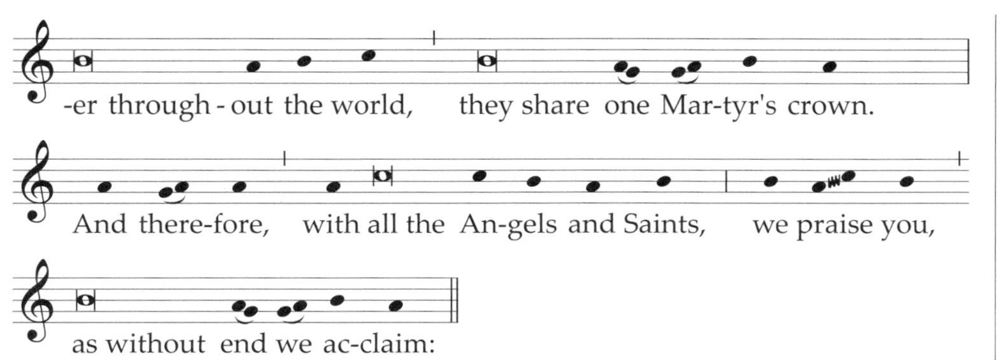

Slow at **-out the world**, with a slight hold on **world**. Slow the next phrase so that it is clearly enunciated.

For the concluding phrase, hold **-fore** of **therefore** but without taking a breath. Broaden **Angels and Saints**, as well as **praise.**

Holy, Holy, Holy Lord God of hosts . . .

Text without music:

V. **The Lord be with you.**
R. And with your spirit.

V. **Lift up your hearts.**
R. We lift them up to the Lord.

V. **Let us give thanks to the Lord our God.**
R. It is right and just.

It is truly right and just, our duty and our salvation,
always and everywhere to give you thanks,
Lord, holy Father, almighty and eternal God.

For by your providence
the blessed Apostles Peter and Paul bring us joy:
Peter, foremost in confessing the faith,
Paul, its outstanding preacher,
Peter, who established the early Church from the remnant of Israel,
Paul, master and teacher of the Gentiles that you call.

Contrast the names **Peter** and **Paul** in lines three and four, and five and six.

And so, each in a different way
gathered together the one family of Christ;
and revered together throughout the world,
they share one Martyr's crown.

Pause after **so** and also slightly after **each** and **way**. Tie together the first two lines.
Slightly pause after **and**. Lengthen slightly **world** and continue without a break to **they share . . . crown**.

And therefore, with all the Angels and Saints,
we praise you, as without end we acclaim:

Holy, Holy, Holy Lord God of hosts . . .

How Do We Come to Know Jesus in the Liturgy?

As Catholics rooted in a rich sacramental and liturgical tradition, we cannot overlook the truth that in our celebration of the Eucharist the risen Jesus is most powerfully present to us.

This truth is brought home to us in the Gospel story of the appearance of the risen Jesus to the two disciples on the road to Emmaus (Luke 24:13–35). This story reflects the structure of the eucharistic liturgy throughout the centuries. Notice how Jesus is present in the dual aspects of word and sacrament, that is, through the telling of the story and the sharing of the meal. At Mass, the Liturgy of the Word and the Liturgy of the Eucharist are so intimately connected that they form but one act of worship. Reflecting on the elements in the Emmaus story can help us recognize the various ways the risen Jesus is present in our eucharistic celebrations.

First, notice how Jesus joins the disciples. The Lord has promised that wherever two or three are gathered in his name, he is present. Our arrival at Mass is more than just a casual coming together; rather, it is a visible sign of the unity and communion we should be sharing as we walk with the Lord all week. By the way we greet each other and make each other feel welcome, we show that we are the body of Christ.

Next, notice in the Emmaus story that the Lord is actively present to the disciples as he explains the scriptures. When the readings are proclaimed at Mass, we are called to open ourselves to the ways God speaks to us.

August 6

THE TRANSFIGURATION OF THE LORD

Feast

Collect

The first four lines belong together. If a breath is needed, it should be short. Articulate clearly **Transfiguration**.

O God, who in the glorious Transfiguration
of your Only Begotten Son
confirmed the mysteries of faith by the witness of the Fathers
and wonderfully prefigured our full adoption to sonship,
grant, we pray, to your servants,
that, listening to the voice of your beloved Son,
we may merit to become co-heirs with him.
Who lives and reigns with you in the unity of the Holy Spirit,
one God, for ever and ever.

Pause after **that**. Emphasize **listening**, **co-heirs**, and **him**.

When this Feast falls on a Sunday, the Creed is said.

Prayer over the Offerings

Drop the voice for **O Lord, we pray**, so that the sense of **Sanctify these offerings** comes through clearly. Pause very briefly after **here**. Tie together the rest of line two and line three. Accent **radiant splendor** and **stains of sin**.

Sanctify, O Lord, we pray,
these offerings here made to celebrate
the glorious Transfiguration of your Only Begotten Son,
and by his radiant splendor
cleanse us from the stains of sin.
Through Christ our Lord.

Prayer after Communion

Drop the voice for **O Lord, we pray**. No significant pause after **Lord**. Emphasize **transform**, **likeness**, and **Son**. Only a brief pause after **Son**.

May the heavenly nourishment we have received,
O Lord, we pray,
transform us into the likeness of your Son,
whose radiant splendor you willed to make manifest
in his glorious Transfiguration.
Who lives and reigns for ever and ever.

Introduction: This feast is very ancient, being celebrated in the Eastern Churches already in the fifth century. Only in the medieval period did it take root in the West, and was extended to the universal Western Church only in the sixteenth century. The feast's theological richness is revealed in the euchologies of the liturgy. The significance of the Transfiguration explains why each synoptic Gospel account reports the event (Matthew 17:1–9; Mark 9:2–10; Luke 9:28–36). We should note also that all three synoptic accounts have Jesus predicting his Passion and Death, as well as the Resurrection, just before the story of the Transfiguration (Matthew 16:21–23; Mark 8:31; Luke 9:22). This "scandal" of suffering and Death on the Cross (which disturbed Peter especially, and earned him a strong reprimand from Jesus; cf. Mark 8:32–33) is remedied and transformed by the Transfiguration. This message will appear in the euchologies of the feast more than once.

Collect: At the opening of the prayer, the Transfiguration is called "glorious," because it displayed Jesus to his disciples as full of glory. This is the glory he has as Only Begotten Son; it is the glory that is his forever in heaven. It gave a vision of heaven to the three disciples. Thus, the faith of the disciples was confirmed as they recognized God's glory in Jesus. This recognition by the disciples happened shortly after Jesus's prediction of his Passion and suffering. Second, the Transfiguration was intended to confirm and orient the faith of

The space below is for your notes.

Refer to pages viii–x for an explanation of the pointing of the chants and to page xii for the Tones for the Presidential Prayers from *The Roman Missal.*

Pointed Text

Collect

A O God, who in the glorious Transfiguration
of your Only Begotten Son
confirmed the mysteries of faith by the witness of the Fathers
and wonderfully prefigured our full adoption to son**ship**,
B grant, we pray, to your servants,
that, listening to the voice of your be**lov**ed Son,
C we may merit to become co-heirs with ***him***.
Who lives and reigns with you in the unity of the Holy Spirit,
one God, for ever and ever.

When this Feast falls on a Sunday, the Creed is said.

Prayer over the Offerings

B Sanctify, O Lord, we pray,
these offerings here made to celebrate
the glorious Transfiguration of your Only Be**got**ten Son,
C and by his radiant splendor
cleanse us from the stains of ***sin***.
Through Christ our Lord.

Prayer after Communion

A May the heavenly nourishment we have received,
O Lord, we **pray**,
B transform us into the likeness **of** your Son,
C whose radiant splendor you willed to make manifest
in his glorious Transfigur***a***tion.
Who lives and reigns for ever and ever.

Israel, the people who followed Moses and Elijah (the Fathers). Third, this miracle confirms the faith of all followers of Jesus. In effect, we go up the mountain through our celebration of the liturgy, with the understanding that God is calling us to glory. He does this by making us disciples. Baptism initiated us into the life of Christ, and made us adopted children of God. The Transfiguration prefigured the end result of this adoption, when we share fully God's glory in heaven.

The petition speaks of us as God's "servants," because we are called to do his will. On the Mount, God said, "This is my beloved Son, with whom I am well pleased; listen to him" (Matthew 17:5). Submission to God's will starts with listening to his Son and proceeds to the obedience of good servants. In this way we hope to merit being fully sons and daughters of God, co-heirs with Jesus of heavenly glory. What God has given Jesus, manifested in the Transfiguration, we desire for all of us.

Prayer over the Offerings: The gifts we have brought to the altar have been made holy (sanctified) by putting them in contact with God, the all-holy. Today, these offerings are put into contact with the transfigured Christ. (The original Latin of this prayer asks that the sanctification of the gifts occur by means of that very Transfiguration.) Therefore, as God's glory can and did transfigure the earthly flesh of Jesus, so the transfigured Christ can and does sanctify the earthly bread and wine we have placed on the altar. Those elements

Bring out the accent on **be** in **The Lord be with you.** In the next phrase, make a strong accent on **Lift**, and slow both notes of **hearts**. In the third dialogue, move to the word **thanks** before accenting, and hold that word slightly to give it emphasis. Broaden both notes of **Lord**, and hold **God**.

Sing this proclamation cursively in a reciting tone. Do not hold -**va** in **salvation**; only broaden the two notes slightly. The -**tion** should be held. Slightly broaden **always** and **everywhere**. The accent of the phrase falls on **thanks**. In the next part of the text, clearly make four phrases, by respecting the commas after **Lord**, **Father**, and **God**.

Take a quick breath after **witnesses**.

No pause at **bodily form** but continue immediately with **which**. Hold -**ty** of **humanity** and take a breath.

No pause at **removed** but continue immediately with **from**.

No pause between **Church** and **is**, and between -**filled** of **fulfilled** and **what**.

will be "transfigured" (transubstantiated) into the Body and Blood of Christ at this Holy Eucharist.

The second petition is that we be transformed from people whose interiors are darkened by sin to a people cleansed of sin. This sacrifice that is to be offered participates sacramentally in Jesus's Sacrifice on Calvary. In this prayer, the cleansing results from contact with that very lightsome splendor that shone forth in Jesus on the mountain, and which we want to shine forth in us.

Prayer after Communion: Holy Communion is called "heavenly nourishment" because we share in a sacramental way the very Body and Blood of Christ that has ascended into heaven. As we have lifted up our small gifts in sacrifice to the Father and in union with the gift that the paschal Christ gave his Father, those gifts have been transformed into his Body and Blood, and that is what we receive anew in Holy Communion.

The petition culminates in the request that by consuming his Body and Blood, we may become what we eat, that is, that we may be transformed into the likeness of Jesus, a sort of icon (*eikon*) of the Lord, representing his image, his mind and heart, to everyone we meet when we leave this liturgy. This means also that we are praying to share in the glory (radiant splendor) that belongs by right to Jesus in his heavenly state, and which shone forth from him and was thus manifest in the event of the Transfiguration.

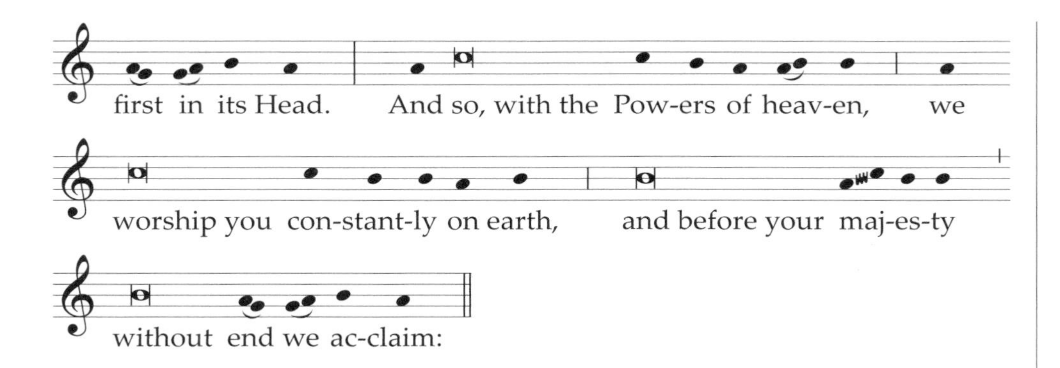

Holy, Holy, Holy Lord God of hosts . . .

Text without music:

V. **The Lord be with you.**
R. And with your spirit.

V. **Lift up your hearts.**
R. We lift them up to the Lord.

V. **Let us give thanks to the Lord our God.**
R. It is right and just.

It is truly right and just, our duty and our salvation,
always and everywhere to give you thanks,
Lord, holy Father, almighty and eternal God,
through Christ our Lord.

For he revealed his glory in the presence of chosen witnesses
and filled with the greatest splendor that bodily form
which he shares with all humanity,
that the scandal of the Cross
might be removed from the hearts of his disciples
and that he might show
how in the Body of the whole Church is to be fulfilled
what so wonderfully shone forth first in its Head.

And so, with the Powers of heaven,
we worship you constantly on earth,
and before your majesty
without end we acclaim:

Holy, Holy, Holy Lord God of hosts . . .

The first three lines go together, but a brief pause at the end of the first line, at **witnesses**, is okay. Articulate clearly **greatest splendor**. Enunciate well the three words **that bodily form**. Tie together lines four and five. Think of **how** as having a comma, and thus set off the prepositional phrase, **in the . . . Church**. Enunciate clearly **forth first**, accenting **first** slightly. Hold **Head** and take a breath.

Hold and pause slightly at **so**. Take just a small pause after **heaven** and **earth**. Broaden the final words, from **majesty** to the end, slowing the last three words noticeably.

Preface: The mystery of the Transfiguration

The body of the Preface reviews the event that makes this day celebratory. It begins by mentioning the revelation of God's glory in Jesus before his three chosen disciples. It is significant that God's splendor and glory shine forth from Jesus's body, the very flesh that he shares with all of us. This is not an accident, but has very real purpose in the mind of Christ.

The first purpose was to remove the scandal of the Cross. In the Gospel accounts, Jesus is shown as alerting the disciples to the necessity of his suffering and Death, and this communication is placed just before the recounting of the event of the Transfiguration (Matthew 16:21–28; Mark 8:31–9:1; Luke 9:22–27). Seeing the flesh of Jesus filled with glory should help the followers who love him to deal with the horror which would unfold at his Passion and Death. The second purpose was to show how the body of every member of the Church will appear in the end. The bodies of the faithful will be glorious in eternal life just as was the body of the Church's Head at the Transfiguration. Through the Transfiguration, the disciples' faith in the face of Jesus's Death had an opportunity to be strengthened. The event graced Peter, James, and John with hope so they would carry on after Christ's Resurrection.

August 15

THE ASSUMPTION OF THE BLESSED VIRGIN MARY

Solemnity

At the Vigil Mass

Collect

Contrast **lowliness** and **raised**.

Articulate carefully **this day** and emphasize **surpassing glory**.

Drop the voice slightly for **saved . . . redemption**, so that **that** goes with **we may merit**.

O God, who, looking on the lowliness of the Blessed Virgin Mary,
raised her to this grace,
that your Only Begotten Son was born of her according to the flesh
and that she was crowned this day with surpassing glory,
grant through her prayers,
that, saved by the mystery of your redemption,
we may merit to be exalted by you on high.
Through our Lord Jesus Christ, your Son,
who lives and reigns with you in the unity of the Holy Spirit,
one God, for ever and ever.

Prayer over the Offerings

Drop the voice slightly on **we pray, O Lord**, so that **Receive . . . the sacrifice** go together. Tie together lines two and three. Do not pause at **praise**. Briefly pause after **God**. Emphasize **pardon** and **thanksgiving**.

Receive, we pray, O Lord,
the sacrifice of conciliation and praise,
which we celebrate on the Assumption of the holy Mother of God,
that it may lead us to your pardon
and confirm us in perpetual thanksgiving.
Through Christ our Lord. *

Prayer after Communion

Drop the voice at **table** and continue without pausing until **God**.

Drop the voice slightly for **who . . . God**.

Having partaken of this heavenly table,
we beseech your mercy, Lord our God,
that we, who honor the Assumption of the Mother of God,
may be freed from every threat of harm.
Through Christ our Lord. **

* The Preface for the Vigil Mass is found in the spread for At the Mass during the Day, see pages 306–307.

** You may use the Solemn Blessing for The Assumption of the Blessed Virgin Mary in the Order of Mass; also in *The Order of Mass: A Roman Missal Study Edition and Workbook*, page 174.

Collect: At the outset, the prayer establishes the contrast between Mary's self-proclaimed lowliness (the text of the "Magnificat" Canticle is proclaimed in the Gospel today; cf. Luke 1:48), and the grace to which she has been raised. This "raising" was for two reasons: first, because she was Mother of God's Son in the flesh; second, because she was given heaven's glory at her death. It is particularly the latter point that is made present sacramentally in the liturgy celebrated today.

The petition makes clear that saving redemption comes only from God. The Church begs that the Blessed Virgin will intercede for the rest of us redeemed in Christ, so that we might also be exalted on high—just as we celebrate Mary's exaltation. In the structure of this prayer, there is a parallel between "raised" (speaking of Mary), and "exalted" (speaking of the Church's future). This matches the parallelism between "lowliness" and "saved." These parallels are a way of uniting the Church to Blessed Mary on this special day.

Prayer over the Offerings: Sacrifice, in the history of religion, has always had an aspect of placating God (or, the gods) for sin and disobedience. The greatest satisfaction possible was given by Jesus in the Sacrifice of his very Self, in obedience to the Father's will, and for the salvation of the world.

Our liturgy inserts our sacrifice into that of Jesus. Eucharistic Prayer III states this by asking God to look upon our sacrifice, now transformed by the power of the Holy Spirit and the consecrating Word of

The space below is for your notes.

Refer to pages viii–x for an explanation of the pointing of the chants and to page xii for the Tones for the Presidential Prayers from *The Roman Missal.*

Pointed Text

Collect

A O God, who, looking on the lowliness of the Blessed Virgin Mary,
raised her to this **grace**,
B that your Only Begotten Son was born of her according to the flesh
and that she was crowned this day with sur**pass**ing glory,
C grant through her prayers,
that, saved by the mystery of your redemption,
we may merit to be exalted by you on ***high***.
Through our Lord Jesus Christ, your Son,
who lives and reigns with you in the unity of the Holy Spirit,
one God, for ever and ever.

Prayer over the Offerings

A Receive, we pray, O **Lord**,
B the sacrifice of conciliation and praise,
which we celebrate on the Assumption of the holy Mo**ther** of God,
C that it may lead us to your pardon
and confirm us in perpetual thanksgiv***ing***.
Through Christ our Lord.

Prayer after Communion

A Having partaken of this heavenly table,
we beseech your mercy, Lord our **God**,
B that we, who honor the Assumption of the Mo**ther** of God,
C may be freed from every threat of ***harm***.
Through Christ our Lord.

Jesus, and to see "the Victim by whose death / you willed to reconcile us to yourself." This is the "conciliation" spoken of in this prayer.

We praise God for the wonders he has worked in Mary, which culminated in her bodily assumption into heaven.

We petition that this celebrative sacrifice might enable us to experience God's pardon for our sins. That, in turn, should lead us to constant gratitude, not just here within the ritual of Eucharistic thanksgiving.

Prayer after Communion: The first line is a proclamation of faith. Although what we consume in Holy Communion looks, tastes, and seems like mere bread and wine, we recognize that it is food from heaven, the very Body and Blood of the Lord. Only faith can result in such recognition. Because God has allowed us this Holy Communion with the divine, we have the courage to petition for God's mercy, his loving kindness (the Hebrew covenant used the term *hesed*) to be the fruit of the meal in us.

The second petition is made in the light of our celebration of the Assumption. Mary was preserved always from sin, and that grace and privilege led to her exaltation in body and soul in heaven. In that light, we beg not for preservation from sin as such, but rather freedom from all the evils that threaten us in daily life (evils which can be moral, intellectual, or emotional). These are actually the result of sin. These evils damage us on a much deeper level than does physical harm.

THE ASSUMPTION OF THE BLESSED VIRGIN MARY

At the Mass during the Day

Collect

Do not make a significant pause until after **glory**.

Pause after **that** to set off the phrase **always . . . above** as preparing for the climax of the prayer, **sharers of her glory**.

Almighty ever-living God,
who assumed the Immaculate Virgin Mary, the Mother of your Son,
body and soul into heavenly glory,
grant, we pray,
that, always attentive to the things that are above,
we may merit to be sharers of her glory.
Through our Lord Jesus Christ, your Son,
who lives and reigns with you in the unity of the Holy Spirit,
one God, for ever and ever.

Prayer over the Offerings

Drop the voice for **our tribute of homage**, to keep the sense between **oblation** and **rise up**.
Tie together lines three and four while respecting the comma after **Mary**. Emphasize **aflame**, **fire**, and **love**, while conveying the sense **our hearts . . . constantly long . . . .**

May this oblation, our tribute of homage,
rise up to you, O Lord,
and, through the intercession of the most Blessed Virgin Mary,
whom you assumed into heaven,
may our hearts, aflame with the fire of love,
constantly long for you.
Through Christ our Lord.

Prayer after Communion

Drop voice slightly for **we . . . Lord**.

Tie together lines three and four.
Connect **Mary** and **whom**.
Emphasize **glory** and **resurrection**.

Having received the Sacrament of salvation,
we ask you to grant, O Lord,
that, through the intercession of the Blessed Virgin Mary,
whom you assumed into heaven,
we may be brought to the glory of the resurrection.
Through Christ our Lord. *

* You may use the Solemn Blessing for The Blessed Virgin Mary in the Order of Mass; also in *The Order of Mass: A Roman Missal Study Edition and Workbook*, page 174.

Introduction: Very early (the fifth century) this feast was present in the liturgical calendars of the East. In Jerusalem, it was called the "birthday" of the Blessed Virgin, meaning her birthday into heaven. That is why it is known in Jerusalem also as the Dormition, or the "Falling Asleep" of Mary. In the West, the feast was celebrated on different days until August 15 was the date settled upon. The Assumption was declared a dogma in 1950 by Pope Pius XII (*Munificentissimus Deus*).

Collect: The opening statement of the prayer places a number of dogmas about Mary before the praying community: she is "Immaculate" (preserved from original sin); "Virgin" (her motherhood of Jesus was by the overshadowing of the Holy Spirit); and "Mother of your Son" (from the declaration of the Council of Ephesus in 431, declaring Mary the Mother of God, since she was mother of God's divine Son).

That "body and soul" were assumed into heavenly glory is from the apostolic constitution of 1950. As Pope Pius XII said: "Since Mary was joined so intimately to Jesus—immaculate in her conception . . . one who gained full triumph over sin and its consequences, and in death attained the highest crown . . . she should also be immune from the corruption of the tomb . . . and be taken body and soul into the supernal glory of heaven."

The statement turns minds and hearts to the glory in which Mary resides. The Church's petition is that, as we remain concentrated on those heavenly things, we may arrive at the same glory Mary enjoys.

The space below is for your notes.

Refer to pages viii–x for an explanation of the pointing of the chants and to page xii for the Tones for the Presidential Prayers from *The Roman Missal.*

Pointed Text

Collect

A Almighty ever-living God,
who assumed the Immaculate Virgin Mary, the Mother of your Son,
body and soul into heavenly glo**ry**,
B grant, we pray,
that, always attentive to the things that **are** above,
C we may merit to be sharers of her glo***ry***.
Through our Lord Jesus Christ, your Son,
who lives and reigns with you in the unity of the Holy Spirit,
one God, for ever and ever.

Prayer over the Offerings

A May this oblation, our tribute of homage,
rise up to you, O **Lord**,
B and, through the intercession of the most Blessed Virgin Mary,
whom you assumed **in**to heaven,
C may our hearts, aflame with the fire of love,
constantly long for ***you***.
Through Christ our Lord.

Prayer after Communion

A Having received the Sacrament of salvation,
we ask you to grant, O **Lord**,
B that, through the intercession of the Blessed Virgin Mary,
whom you assumed **in**to heaven,
C we may be brought to the glory of the resurrec***tion***.
Through Christ our Lord.

Prayer over the Offerings: The image of the opening petition is that of the ancient gesture of prayer and offering, the lifting up of hands (cf. Psalm 141:2) as a sign of the interior gift of the heart and person to God. Thus, the offering of the Eucharistic gifts is an authentic sign of tribute, of interior homage, because these gifts stand for something far greater than ourselves.

The second part of the petition seeks an intercession from Mary as it states the belief that she was "assumed into heaven." The Church hopes that the Virgin will intercede for the rest of us, still struggling. The goal of the intercession is that our hearts, which the offering of our gifts shows are aflame with love of God, will constantly be set to "long for you." (Colossians 3:12: "Set your hearts on the things that are above.") We pray that our hearts will continue to be inflamed with love and longing for God (cf. Psalm 63:2–3), that is, for our entrance into glory where Mary now reigns as Queen.

Prayer after Communion: The prayer begins with a statement that we have received in Communion the Sacrament of the Death, Resurrection, and Ascension of Jesus, with all the consequences of being placed in intimate contact with those mysteries of our redemption. We are saved from sin, given intimate union with Jesus, renewed in our baptismal life for a new unity as Church, and provided with a pledge of future glory. This happens at every Communion, if our hearts are open in faith to receive such profound grace.

Bring out the accent on **be** in **The Lord be with you.** In the response, accent **spirit**, by holding slightly both syllables. In the next phrase, make a strong accent on **Lift**, and slow both notes of **hearts**. In the third dialogue, move to the word **thanks** before accenting, and hold that word slightly to give it emphasis. Broaden both notes of **Lord**, and hold **God**.

Sing this proclamation cursively in a reciting tone. Do not hold **-va** in **salvation**; only broaden the two notes slightly. The **-tion** should be held. Slightly broaden **always** and **everywhere**. The accent of the phrase falls on **thanks**. In the next part of the text, clearly make four phrases, by respecting the commas after **Lord**, **Father**, and **God**.

Emphasize **today** and pause slightly afterward (but do not hold). If necessary, take a very short breath after **heaven**. The goal is to tie together **heaven . . . perfection** into one large statement.

Slow and broaden by careful enunciation **hope** and **comfort**, and at the end of the phrase, hold **-ple** of **people** and take a good breath. A slight pause after singing **rightly** would be appropriate.

Take only a quick breath at **tomb**, but hold the word slightly.

Do not respect the comma after **Son** as a sign for a breath, but rather only as a slight hold.

Having been renewed in the mysteries of salvation, the Church turns its eyes again to Mary. Today we celebrate that the pledge of future glory has been fulfilled in her, since she was taken into the glory of heaven. The key petition of this prayer is that we might arrive at the same destination when we are called to the final resurrection of the dead. The movement of the imagery underlying the prayer is from the Cross to the Resurrection ("sacrament of salvation") and from Communion to resurrection and glory in the Church.

Preface: The Glory of Mary assumed into heaven

The body of the Preface states, "For today the Virgin Mother of God was assumed into heaven." The use of the word "today" is typical of the liturgy. What we celebrate on a given day telescopes the actual event, so that we are present at the event, in a sacramental manner, as if we were present on the historical date of its occurrence.

The last four lines of the body of the Preface echo the words of Pope Pius XII in his declaration of the dogma in 1950: God would not allow Mary's body to corrupt in the tomb, since that very body was the graced and pure means by which God's Son, the author of perpetual life, was made incarnate. The graces Mary had received earlier in her life came to completion and fruition when she was taken into heaven, to reign always in glory.

But the three lines preceding this last part turn the praying community's mind away from the person of Mary, who otherwise has received full attention. These lines look to the Church and the meaning of the

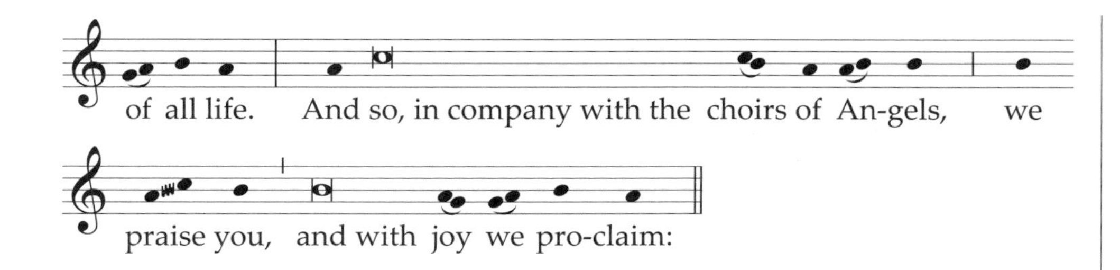

Enunciate **all life** and hold the latter. Pause after **And so**, and hold **so**.

Take only a quick breath after **Angels**. Broaden **praise**. Tie together **you** and **and**. Slow the last three words.

Holy, Holy, Holy Lord God of hosts . . .

Text without music:

V. **The Lord be with you.**
R. And with your spirit.

V. **Lift up your hearts.**
R. We lift them up to the Lord.

V. **Let us give thanks to the Lord our God.**
R. It is right and just.

It is truly right and just, our duty and our salvation,
always and everywhere to give you thanks,
Lord, holy Father, almighty and eternal God,
through Christ our Lord.

For today the Virgin Mother of God
was assumed into heaven
as the beginning and image
of your Church's coming to perfection
and a sign of sure hope and comfort to your pilgrim people;
rightly you would not allow her
to see the corruption of the tomb
since from her own body she marvelously brought forth
your incarnate Son, the Author of all life.

And so, in company with the choirs of Angels,
we praise you, and with joy we proclaim:

Holy, Holy, Holy Lord God of hosts . . .

Enunciate clearly **today**, but continue with **the Virgin . . . .** The first five lines go together, but a quick breath may need to taken after **perfection**.

A slight pause after **heaven** would be appropriate. Clearly enunciate **beginning** and **image**, as well as **sure hope** (both words should receive an accent) and **comfort**. A slight pause after **rightly**, at the beginning would be helpful to bring out the sense of the following phrase. **Tomb** can be held briefly and a short breath may be taken. **Own** and **body** deserve an accent. Tie this line together with the next line. Pause slightly at **Son**.

Assumption of Mary for us. Since Mary is the first member of the Church, the disciple of Jesus, her reaching this state of perfection in the glory of heaven is surely the beginning for our arrival at that point. Further, the "image" is a kind of signal of what is to happen to all who are faithful to Jesus in his Church. Mary is the image of the "Church's coming to perfection." In Mary's glory, we can see the Church's future glory. We may know our imperfections too well, but one day, we will be in the state of glory that Mary is in now. This image, the Preface proclaims, gives the Church, God's "pilgrim people," on the way to our final homeland, "sure hope." Such solace is needed since the pilgrim's trek often tests one's hope, and the road may seem long and arduous at times. But Mary's triumph does more than give the Church hope: it also provides comfort. For no matter the vicissitudes we face in this life, including sin, suffering, and sorrow, one of us—the first of us in the Church—has "made it." What a comfort that must be to a people of faith. This hope and comfort, renewed at the liturgy, lead us now to join our voices to the heavenly choir in a foretaste of the everlasting praise we will give God, as we sing/say: Holy, Holy, Holy . . . .

September 14

THE EXALTATION OF THE HOLY CROSS

Feast

Collect

Do not pause at **Cross**, so as to tie together **which . . . Cross and canceled . . . world**. Contrast **mystery on earth** and **redemption in heaven**.

O God, who willed that your Only Begotten Son
should undergo the Cross to save the human race,
grant, we pray,
that we, who have known his mystery on earth,
may merit the grace of his redemption in heaven.
Through our Lord Jesus Christ, your Son,
who lives and reigns with you in the unity of the Holy Spirit,
one God, for ever and ever. *

Prayer over the Offerings

Carefully enunciate **this oblation**, since it is in the following text tied so closely to the oblation of the **Cross**. Tie together lines two and three. Do not break too long at **world**, as the sense demands moving forward.

May this oblation, O Lord,
which on the altar of the Cross
canceled the offense of the whole world,
cleanse us, we pray, of all our sins.
Through Christ our Lord. **

Prayer after Communion

The opening is a parenthetical phrase. The petition begins with **we beseech you**. Keep lines two to five together, but by inflection of the voice set off **those you . . . life-giving Cross**. The culmination of the petition is **glory of the resurrection**.

Having been nourished by your holy banquet,
we beseech you, Lord Jesus Christ,
to bring those you have redeemed
by the wood of your life-giving Cross
to the glory of the resurrection.
Who live and reign for ever and ever.

* Sing or recite the Creed if this feast falls on a Sunday.

** The Preface for the Victory of the Glorious Cross may be used and is found on pages 310–311. Priests may also use Preface I of the Passion of the Lord in the Order of Mass. Commentary, and proclamation and chant tips, for the Preface can be found at *www.StudyThePresidentialTexts.com/Prefaces* and in *The Order of Mass: A Roman Missal Study Edition and Workbook*, pages 44–45.

Collect: The prayer immediately states what is central to the story of salvation—that it was the Father's will that Christ die on the Cross. The prayer's petition is premised by the fact that we have known the mystery of Christ and his Cross while living on earth in a number of ways.

First, we have known this mystery through Baptism, by which we have died and risen with Christ, already in the hope of sharing his exaltation.

Secondly, we have known the Cross through the vicissitudes of life, in which we see the Cross in the suffering of the poor and the sick, as well as in ourselves. No one can escape the reality of the Cross.

Finally, we know the Cross through our celebration of this Eucharist, for the saving action of Christ on the Cross, as well as the exalted glory of his Resurrection, are made present here sacramentally.

Given that we know the mystery of the Cross in these multiple ways, we pray that the redemption which it brought might truly be ours, when we are called home to heaven.

Prayer over the Offerings: The vision of the Cross as the means of the redemption ("canceled the offense") of the world is at the center of this prayer. Our offering at the altar puts us in touch with that salvific offering of Jesus on the Cross. In fact, through this sacramental action, the very offering of Jesus on the Cross is represented in sign. The text here is phrased so that those making the offerings will see the parallel with the offering of Jesus—thus his Cross is called an altar.

The space below is for your notes.

Refer to pages viii–x for an explanation of the pointing of the chants and to page xii for the Tones for the Presidential Prayers from *The Roman Missal.*

Pointed Text

Collect

A O God, who willed that your Only Begotten Son
should undergo the Cross to save the human **race**,
B grant, we pray,
that we, who have known his myster**y** on earth,
C may merit the grace of his redemption in hea***ven***.
Through our Lord Jesus Christ, your Son,
who lives and reigns with you in the unity of the Holy Spirit,
one God, for ever and ever.

Prayer over the Offerings

A May this oblation, O **Lord**,
B which on the altar of the Cross
canceled the offense of **the** whole world,
C cleanse us, we pray, of all our ***sins***.
Through Christ our Lord.

Prayer after Communion

A Having been nourished by your holy ban**quet**,
B we beseech you, Lord **J**esus Christ,
C to bring those you have redeemed
by the wood of your life-giving Cross
to the glory of the resurrec***tion***.
Who live and reign for ever and ever.

The petition asks that what Jesus did on the Cross long ago (forgiveness of and purification of sins) for all humanity might be applied to us at this altar. For here the sacrifice of Jesus on Golgotha is presented anew in a sacramental way. Eucharistic Prayer III sums this up well: "Look, we pray, on the oblation of your Church / and, recognizing the sacrifical Victim by whose death / you willed to reconcile us to yourself."

Prayer after Communion: The ritual of Holy Communion is the culmination of the entire Eucharistic action of Mass. As such, it encompasses and makes present sacramentally the Death and Resurrection of Jesus for the redemption of the world. The nourishment we have received, then, is not primarily for the body, but rather for the reception of what alone will satisfy the soul, Jesus, in his Paschal Mystery. Holy Communion brings us into intimate contact with this mystery of Jesus's saving Death and Resurrection.

That spiritual reality being presumed, the petition asks God to bring to completion in the Church the saving action begun in the liturgy. We have been redeemed by the Cross (redeemed = bought back, from sin and death) which brings life to us, thanks to the saving Death of Jesus. We ask that our Holy Communion may bring us another step closer to the culmination of the Paschal Mystery, that is, to the glory of the Resurrection.

Bring out the accent on **be** in **The Lord be with you.** In the response, accent **spirit**, by holding slightly both syllables. In the next phrase, make a strong accent on **Lift**, and slow both notes of **hearts**. In the third dialogue, move to the word **thanks** before accenting, and hold that word slightly to give it emphasis. Broaden both notes of **Lord**, and hold **God**.

Sing this proclamation cursively in a reciting tone. Do not hold **-va** in **salvation**; only broaden the two notes slightly. The **-tion** should be held. Slightly broaden **always** and **everywhere**. The accent of the phrase falls on **thanks**. In the next part of the text, clearly make three phrases, by respecting the commas after **Lord** and **Father**.

Hold briefly **Cross**. Slow on **death arose** but continue on to **life**. Hold and pause briefly at **forth**. Respect the comma after **evil one**, but do not pause at **tree**, but rather continue on with **might**.

Clearly enunciate **conquered**; however, do not pause there, but continue with **through Christ our Lord**, slowing on these words. Slow and enunciate **majesty** carefully; similarly at the end of the next part of the phrase, **tremble before you**. Hold **you** and pause for breath. Emphasize **Heav-** rather than **-en**.

Preface: The victory of the glorious Cross

The body of the Preface restates the theology underlying the liturgical celebration today. Once again the fundamental purpose of the Cross in God's plan is stated, and this, at the very outset of this central part of the Preface, for the salvation of the whole world. The two related reasons for the Cross being so central to God's plan are then presented.

First, the Cross is a means of death made from a tree, and it was a tree which brought death to the human race through the sin of Adam and Eve in the garden, and which might now bring life to the same race. Thus, a new creation of life through what happened on a tree in a different form, that is, the wood of the Cross.

Secondly, the Cross is central to God's plan so that the evil one, who was victorious over the human race by enticing Adam and Eve to sin by means of a tree in the garden might be conquered by means of another tree, in the form of the Cross.

(The following excerpt of a Homily, by Monsignor Joseph DeGrocco, examines Christ's self-emptying on the Cross. The Homily has been excerpted from the CD *Preparing Your Parish for the Revised Roman Missal: Homilies and Reproducibles for Faith Formation*, © 2010, Liturgy Training Publications.)

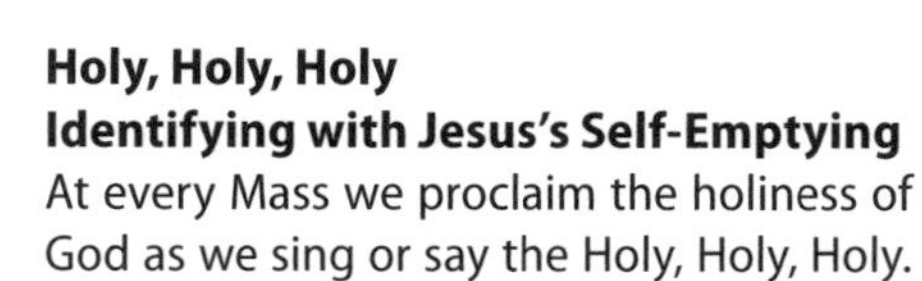

Holy, Holy, Holy

Identifying with Jesus's Self-Emptying

At every Mass we proclaim the holiness of God as we sing or say the Holy, Holy, Holy.

Hold **-phim** of **Seraphim**. Do not take a breath there, but continue on to **worship**. Slow and broaden **exultation**. Set off **we pray** in the last phrase, with due respect for the commas around it. Tie together **praise** and **as**, with no pause there.

Slow **we ac-** and put emphasis on **-claim**, so as to evoke the response **Holy, Holy, Holy . . . .**

Holy, Holy, Holy Lord God of hosts . . .

Text without music:

V. **The Lord be with you.**
R. And with your spirit.

V. **Lift up your hearts.**
R. We lift them up to the Lord.

V. **Let us give thanks to the Lord our God.**
R. It is right and just.

It is truly right and just, our duty and our salvation,
always and everywhere to give you thanks,
Lord, holy Father, almighty and eternal God.

For you placed the salvation of the human race
on the wood of the Cross,
so that, where death arose,
life might again spring forth
and the evil one, who conquered on a tree,
might likewise on a tree be conquered,
through Christ our Lord.

Tie together lines one and two.

Significant pause after **that**. Contrast **death** and **life**.

Contrast **tree** in **who conquered on a tree** with **tree** in **on a tree be conquered**.

Through him the Angels praise your majesty,
Dominions adore and Powers tremble before you.
Heaven and the Virtues of heaven and the blessed Seraphim
worship together with exultation.
May our voices, we pray, join with theirs
in humble praise, as we acclaim:

Holy, Holy, Holy Lord God of hosts . . .

The triple acknowledgment of God's holiness echoes the words of scripture, as found in the sixth chapter of the book of the prophet Isaiah and also the fourth chapter of the book of Revelation. Whenever we proclaim the Holy, Holy, Holy we are proclaiming God's dominion over heaven and earth. To say that God is the God "of hosts" affirms that the power and majesty of God is beyond anything we could imagine. It's a power and a holiness that, we know, was fully revealed in Jesus's death and Resurrection, and therefore, it is a power and a holiness that is most clearly manifested whenever God raises up those who are empty, broken, and even dead.

The Holy, Holy, Holy acknowledges, "Blessed is he who comes in the name of the Lord. Hosanna in the highest." These words echo the acclamation with which the crowds greeted Jesus at his entry into Jerusalem—an entry that would lead to his handing over his life. To be blessed and to be acknowledged as one who "comes in the name of the Lord" involves handing over one's life to the Father.

The heavenly powers know that the Paschal Mystery of dying and rising is the very life of God, insofar as it is the journey the Son of God underwent and, as they acknowledge the holiness of that journey, we join in their song when we celebrate the Eucharist. The acclamation "Holy, Holy, Holy" should be made with the recognition that holiness only comes from being in union with Jesus Christ, who handed himself over and emptied himself completely, and so was raised from the dead. It is an identification we are asked to make.

November 1

ALL SAINTS

Solemnity

Collect

Do not pause from **by** to **Saints**, so as to tie the lines together. The sense of the petition is **bestow on us . . . an abundance of the reconciliation**, so do not emphasize the intervening phrases.

Almighty ever-living God,
by whose gift we venerate in one celebration
the merits of all the Saints,
bestow on us, we pray,
through the prayers of so many intercessors,
an abundance of the reconciliation with you
for which we earnestly long.
Through our Lord Jesus Christ, your Son,
who lives and reigns with you in the unity of the Holy Spirit,
one God, for ever and ever.

Prayer over the Offerings

Tie together **grant that** and **so**, with a clear emphasis on the latter.

May these offerings we bring in honor of all the Saints
be pleasing to you, O Lord,
and grant that, just as we believe the Saints
to be already assured of immortality,
so we may experience their concern for our salvation.
Through Christ our Lord.

Prayer after Communion

Clearly enunciate **holy** and **wonderful**.

Emphasize **perfect**.

Contrast **pilgrim table** and **banquet of our heavenly**.

As we adore you, O God, who alone are holy
and wonderful in all your Saints,
we implore your grace,
so that, coming to perfect holiness in the fullness of your love,
we may pass from this pilgrim table
to the banquet of our heavenly homeland.
Through Christ our Lord. *

* You may use the Solemn Blessings for All Saints in the Order of Mass, page 175 in *The Order of Mass: A Roman Missal Study Edition and Workbook.* The Votive Mass of All Saints may also be used.

Introduction: This feast was celebrated in the Eastern Churches already in the fourth century to honor the Martyrs. In the early seventh century, Pope Boniface IV ordered a great many of the relics of the catacombs outside of Rome to be transferred into the city, and placed in the ancient Roman temple of the Pantheon, thus designating it as a church in honor of Mary and all the martyrs. A century later, the feast was extended to all the saints and transferred from the spring to November 1.

Collect: The texts at Mass (for those Saints for whom formularies have been provided) highlight an aspect of that particular Saint's life that merited the glorious crown of heaven for him or her. At the opening of this Collect, the Church sees it as a gift from God that we could honor the varied merits and extraordinary lives of all the Saints, in a single celebration.

The Church concentrates in this prayer on the spiritual vision of the feast. Thus, we look to the Saints' individual lives, so united to the life and Death of Jesus, and see that those lives were spent in bringing Christ to their fellow members of the Church, and reconciling the world to God. Looking at the selfless work of the Saints while they were on earth, we recognize that they are just as selfless now. This is why, as members of the Church triumphant, they are intercessors for the rest of us in the Church militant.

The petition is that God will listen to their intercession and grant us a fullness of reconciliation with him, which our hearts, filled with longing for God, so desire.

The space below is for your notes.

Refer to pages viii–x for an explanation of the pointing of the chants and to page xii for the Tones for the Presidential Prayers from *The Roman Missal.*

Pointed Text

Collect

A Almighty ever-living God,
by whose gift we venerate in one celebration
the merits of all the **Saints**,
B bestow on us, we pray,
through the prayers of so many **in**tercessors,
C an abundance of the reconciliation with you
for which we earnestly ***long***.
Through our Lord Jesus Christ, your Son,
who lives and reigns with you in the unity of the Holy Spirit,
one God, for ever and ever.

Prayer over the Offerings

A May these offerings we bring in honor of all the Saints
be pleasing to you, O **Lord**,
B and grant that, just as we believe the Saints
to be already assured of **im**mortality,
B so we may experience their concern for our salva***tion***.
Through Christ our Lord.

Prayer after Communion

A As we adore you, O God, who alone are holy
and wonderful in all your **Saints**,
B we implore your grace,
so that, coming to perfect holiness in the fullness **of** your love,
C we may pass from this pilgrim table
to the banquet of our heavenly home***land***.
Through Christ our Lord.

Prayer over the Offerings: Our offerings are brought to God, in a special way honoring all the Saints today, for they brought God their offerings—symbols of the surrender of their lives—before us. As the ancient mosaics on the walls of the church of Saint Apollinaris in Ravenna graphically show, the Saints were in the procession with the gifts long before us, and are still in the procession with us. We believe that with the culminating offering of their lives, they achieved immortality, for they brought to God the greatest gift they could, their own earthly existence. They achieved immortality not just by bringing such a profound offering to the sanctuary of a church during the celebration of Mass, but by entering into the sanctuary of heaven, to their everlasting joy.

Our petition is similar to that prayed in the Collect: that they will not forget us but rather be deeply concerned that we arrive where they are, in heaven. We would like them to look after us that we may achieve fully our salvation.

Prayer after Communion: At the outset, as we conclude the liturgy celebrating the holy ones of the Church's history, this prayer proclaims God as the one who alone is holy. This leads the Church to adoration. We have just entered a Holy Communion with God by sharing the Body and Blood of Jesus. The Saints also participated in the sharing of the Eucharist, which is why the holiness of God can be seen in their lives and deaths. The Church is filled with wonder and joy that God has made his holiness so evident in his holy ones.

Bring out the accent on **be** in **The Lord be with you.** In the response, accent **spirit**, by holding slightly both syllables. In the next phrase, make a strong accent on **Lift**, and slow both notes of **hearts**. In the third dialogue, move to the word **thanks** before accenting, and hold that word slightly to give it emphasis. Broaden both notes of **Lord**, and hold **God**.

Sing this proclamation cursively in a reciting tone. Do not hold -**va** in **salvation**; only broaden the two notes slightly. The -**tion** should be held. Slightly broaden **always** and **everywhere**. The accent of the phrase falls on **thanks**. In the next part of the text, clearly make three phrases, by respecting the commas after **Lord** and **Father**.

Pause slightly at **today** for emphasis.

Tie together without pause, **city, the heavenly**. Take a quick breath after **mother**, but continue right on to **where**.

Broaden **brothers** and **sisters** to enunciate these words clearly, but, without pause, continue to **already**.

Pause at **her** and hold briefly. **Faith** could be held slightly so as not to lose the sense of the continuing thought.

Hold **Church**; however, do not take a breath but continue on to **through**.

This vision of the relationship of God to the Saints leads to the petition for God's grace (which is also his holiness) to be given to the Church. This is to bring us who have just received Jesus, the Holy One of God (which even the demons recognized: "I know who you are—the Holy One of God! Jesus rebuked him and . . . the unclean spirit . . . came out of him." Mark 1:24) to a state of perfect holiness—achievable only by receiving the fullness of God's love.

The petition expands to beg for transition from the earthly/sacramental ("pilgrim") table of Holy Communion in this liturgy, to the heavenly and eternal banquet of God's love, where we will be in union with God, face to face, forever.

Preface: The glory of Jerusalem, our mother

The body of the Preface continues the praise offered in the protocol. When this part of the Preface begins, the Church, with typical sacramental perspective, sees itself as already celebrating in heaven the festival of the Jerusalem on high. In this way, we are joining all those who have gone before us and are spending all eternity giving praise to God. It is right and just that we should explicitly allude to what is going on, in heaven today, as we join that

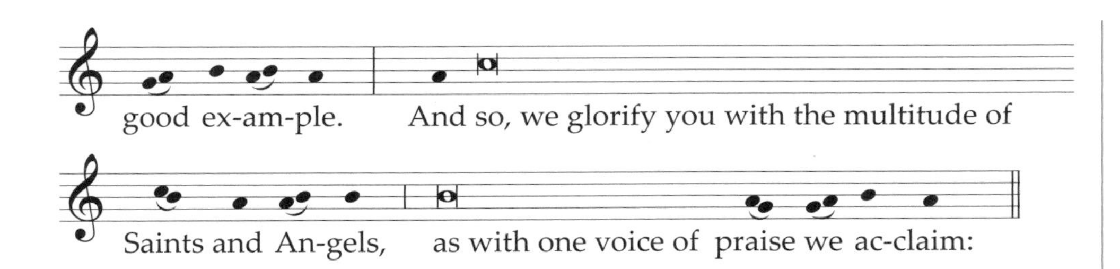

Slow to enunciate **good example**; hold the last syllable there, and take a breath. Pause at **so**, then slow to enunciate clearly **Saints** and **Angels**. If possible, go on to **as** without a breath (if not possible, make the breath very brief so as not to break the sense of the sentence). Slow and broaden **praise we acclaim**.

Holy, Holy, Holy Lord God of hosts . . .

Text without music:

V. **The Lord be with you.**
R. And with your spirit.

V. **Lift up your hearts.**
R. We lift them up to the Lord.

V. **Let us give thanks to the Lord our God.**
R. It is right and just.

It is truly right and just, our duty and our salvation,
always and everywhere to give you thanks,
Lord, holy Father, almighty and eternal God.

Emphasize **truly**, **duty**, **salvation**.

For today by your gift we celebrate the festival of your city,
the heavenly Jerusalem, our mother,
where the great array of our brothers and sisters
already gives you eternal praise.

Towards her, we eagerly hasten as pilgrims advancing by faith,
rejoicing in the glory bestowed upon those exalted members of the Church
through whom you give us, in our frailty, both strength and good example.

And so, we glorify you with the multitude of Saints and Angels,
as with one voice of praise we acclaim:

Holy, Holy, Holy Lord God of hosts . . .

Emphasize **today**. Treat **by your gift** as if it were set off by commas. Tie together lines one and two, while respecting the commas. Similarly, join lines three and four. Pronounce **our** as two syllables. Accent **already**. Enunciate clearly both **rejoicing** and **exalted members**. Lower the voice in the last line before the doxology, for the phrase **in our frailty**. Accent both **strength** and **good example.**

heavenly choir through this sacramental action of praise and thanksgiving.

The second part of the body of the Preface returns the vision to earth ("we eagerly hasten as pilgrims advancing by faith"). We recognize that, although we can join heaven in a sacramental manner, we still are pilgrims on the way, not fully there yet in our whole persons, but definitely advancing, thanks to faith (it is the Mystery of Faith that we are celebrating).

Looking at the vision of so many of our (once) fellow pilgrims who have attained the exalted state of heaven, the Church can and does rejoice at their victory From this celebration, we—weak though we may be—are renewed in strength, thanks to God's grace. Their good example also inspires us to keep striving: this feast makes it clear that the goal is attainable.

November 2

THE COMMEMORATION OF ALL THE FAITHFUL DEPARTED

(All Souls' Day)

The Masses that follow may be used at the discretion of the celebrant.

Even when November 2 falls on a Sunday, the Mass celebrated is that of the Commemoration of All the Faithful Departed.

1

Collect

Pray the text very slowly, befitting the somberness of the day. Respect the commas while keeping lines two and three together. Similarly, keep together lines four and five.

Listen kindly to our prayers, O Lord,
and, as our faith in your Son,
raised from the dead, is deepened,
so may our hope of resurrection for your departed servants
also find new strength.
Through our Lord Jesus Christ, your Son,
who lives and reigns with you in the unity of the Holy Spirit,
one God, for ever and ever.

Prayer over the Offerings

Pause briefly after **Lord**.
Tie together lines two and three.
Enunciate carefully **great mystery of love**.
Emphasize **united**.

Look favorably on our offerings, O Lord,
so that your departed servants
may be taken up into glory with your Son,
in whose great mystery of love we are all united.
Who lives and reigns for ever and ever. *

Prayer after Communion

Lower the voice at **for . . . Sacrament**. The petition is: **Grant . . . that . . . servants . . . may pass over**. Parallel **paschal** and **pass over.** Slow the ending, with broadening of **light** and **peace**.

Grant we pray, O Lord, that your departed servants,
for whom we have celebrated this paschal Sacrament,
may pass over to a dwelling place of light and peace.
Through Christ our Lord. **

* Select from Prefaces I–V for the Dead in the Order of Mass. Commentary, and proclamation and chant tips, for the Preface can be found at *www.StudyThePresidentialTexts.com/Prefaces* and in *The Order of Mass: A Roman Missal Study Edition and Workbook*, pages 114–123.

** You may use the Solemn Blessings in Celebrations for the Dead in the Order of Mass; also on page 176 in *The Order of Mass: A Roman Missal Study Edition and Workbook*.

Collect: This prayer begins with the plea that God "kindly" listen to our prayers. This particular word is a translation of what is found often in Sacred Scripture, speaking of God's "loving kindness" (e.g., Jeremiah 9:23; Romans 2:4 and 11:22; Ephesians 2:7, et al.). The prayer makes it clear that our approach to death and dying—and thus, to the dead—is not based on emotion or psychological reactions. Rather, it is based on faith. We believe what the texts of Saint Paul in the Entrance Antiphon state: that the dead will rise to life, in Christ (1 Thessalonians 4:14; 1 Corinthians 15:22). This prayer begs God for a deepening of faith, since in the face of death, it is easy for emotion to take over.

If our faith in the Resurrection of Jesus is strong, then so too is our hope that all those who have striven to live in Christ also will know resurrection to eternal life. The Church's prayer shows that this day, although traditionally dedicated to prayer for and thoughts of, the dead, is really about life, risen life in the risen Christ for all eternity.

Prayer over the Offerings: The offerings of the Church stand for ourselves, our entire body-persons, as well as all creation being brought back to God from whom it came. Our departed brothers and sisters, all servants of God, made similar offerings while they were alive, and in the same way, using earthly elements as symbols of their very beings lifted up to God. By identification with the departed at this moment in Mass, the Church can petition that they be taken up into glory with Jesus, and that our gifts be transformed by being intimately

The space below is for your notes.

Refer to pages viii–x for an explanation of the pointing of the chants and to page xii for the Tones for the Presidential Prayers from *The Roman Missal.*

Pointed Text

1

Collect

A Listen kindly to our prayers, O **Lord**,
B and, as our faith in your Son,
raised from the **dead**, is deepened,
C so may our hope of resurrection for your departed servants
also find new ***strength***.
Through our Lord Jesus Christ, your Son,
who lives and reigns with you in the unity of the Holy Spirit,
one God, for ever and ever.

Prayer over the Offerings

A Look favorably on our offerings, O **Lord**,
B so that your departed servants
may be taken up into glory **with** your Son,
C in whose great mystery of love we are all uni***ted***.
Who lives and reigns for ever and ever.

Prayer after Communion

A Grant we pray, O Lord, that your departed ser**vants**,
B for whom we have celebrated this **pas**chal Sacrament,
C may pass over to a dwelling place of light and ***peace***.
Through Christ our Lord.

united with the sacrificial offering of Jesus lifted up to the Father.

Jesus, the mediator of God's love, comes to us as gift at Mass. This gift is then returned to the Father. Into this dynamic of love-gift, both the living, now celebrating Eucharist, and the deceased, departed from this life, are embraced and united. We ask that the glory of Jesus in heaven may encompass and surround (and transform) our gifts on this day, and also do the same for our deceased brothers and sisters.

Prayer after Communion: A single and simple petition forms the heart of this prayer. We have celebrated Mass for the deceased, because as the Prayer over the Offerings states, we are "united in love" with them. This union stems from God's initiative to unite us, through the Death and Resurrection of his Son, Jesus. Because of our unity in Christ with the deceased, the Church has the courage to make its petition.

The petition seeks that the deceased, because of Jesus's passing over (paschal Sacrament), also may pass over—from darkness and death to light and peace in the dwelling place of heaven. Jesus came to bring divine light to the world (cf. John 8:12), which was suffering from the darkness of sin. He also came to bring his special peace to the world through his disciples (John 14:27). The peace he came to bring stems not primarily from the cessation of hostilities, but from achieving at-one-ment with God. The Church wants its beloved deceased to experience such light and peace, in fullness, in heaven.

2

Collect

Parallel **glory of the faithful** with **life of the just**. Take a short breath after **just**. Tie together **by** to **redeemed**. Short pause after **redeemed**. The heart of the petition is **look . . . servants**. Emphasize **mystery . . . resurrection** (be careful of **our**) and **joys of eternal happiness**.

O God, glory of the faithful and life of the just,
by the Death and Resurrection of whose Son
we have been redeemed,
look mercifully on your departed servants,
that, just as they professed the mystery of our resurrection,
so they may merit to receive the joys of eternal happiness.
Through our Lord Jesus Christ, your Son,
who lives and reigns with you in the unity of the Holy Spirit,
one God, for ever and ever.

Prayer over the Offerings

Tie together lines two through four, while dropping voice slightly for **we pray**. Parallel and contrast **purify unceasingly** with **once cleansed**.

Almighty and merciful God,
by means of these sacrificial offerings
wash away, we pray, in the Blood of Christ,
the sins of your departed servants,
for you purify unceasingly by your merciful forgiveness
those you once cleansed in the waters of Baptism.
Through Christ our Lord. *

Prayer after Communion

Having received the Sacrament of your Only Begotten Son,
who was sacrificed for us and rose in glory,
we humbly implore you, O Lord,
for your departed servants,
that, cleansed by the paschal mysteries,
they may glory in the gift of the resurrection to come.
Through Christ our Lord. **

* Select from Prefaces I–V for the Dead in the Order of Mass. Commentary, and proclamation and chant tips, for the Preface can be found at *www.StudyThePresidentialTexts.com/Prefaces* and in *The Order of Mass: A Roman Missal Study Edition and Workbook*, pages 114–123.

** You may use the Solemn Blessings in Celebrations for the Dead in the Order of Mass, page 176 in *The Order of Mass: A Roman Missal Study Edition and Workbook*.

Collect: All who live faith-filled lives (the faithful) have a relationship with God, who already is sharing his glory with them and thus preparing them for the everlasting glory yet to come. Similarly, the faithful live justly because God has placed his divine life in them. In other words, Christian Initiation has placed us in a special relation with God the Father, which has consequences of glory and life.

The Paschal Mystery, places us in a unique relationship with the Son of God, for we are his redeemed disciples. In the light of this profound reality, the Church asks that God look with love (a word identified with God's mercy) on those who have departed this life, because they were already in a special relationship with the Father and Son. Because of that relationship, they believed in their resurrection, in union with the risen Christ. The Church asks that through Jesus's gift, the faithful may know eternal joy (the text doubles "joy" and "happiness" to describe the indescribable in heaven).

Prayer over the Offerings: The New Testament sees the Blood of Christ as the agent of purification from sin. This is evident in Romans 5:9 ("How much more then, since we are now justified by his blood, will we be saved through him from the wrath") and also in 1 Corinthians 11:25, Ephesians 1:7, Hebrews 9:14. We see it, too, in the the words of Institution, when the Priest says, "for this is the chalice of my Blood . . . , which will be poured out for you and for many / for the forgiveness of sins."

2

Collect

A O God, glory of the faithful and life of the just,
by the Death and Resurrection of whose Son
we have been re**deemed**,
B look mercifully on your de**part**ed servants,
C that, just as they professed the mystery of our resurrection,
so they may merit to receive the joys of eternal hap***pi***ness.
Through our Lord Jesus Christ, your Son,
who lives and reigns with you in the unity of the Holy Spirit,
one God, for ever and ever.

Prayer over the Offerings

A Almighty and merciful **God**,
B by means of these sacrificial offerings
wash away, we pray, in the Blood of Christ,
the sins of your de**part**ed servants,
C for you purify unceasingly by your merciful forgiveness
those you once cleansed in the waters of Bap***tism***.
Through Christ our Lord.

Prayer after Communion

A Having received the Sacrament of your Only Begotten Son,
who was sacrificed for us and rose in glo**ry**,
B we humbly implore you, O Lord,
for your de**part**ed servants,
C that, cleansed by the paschal mysteries,
they may glory in the gift of the resurrection to ***come***.
Through Christ our Lord.

The space below is for your notes.

Refer to pages viii–x for an explanation of the pointing of the chants and to page xii for the Tones for the Presidential Prayers from *The Roman Missal.*

With our sacrificial offerings soon to partake of the power of redemption in the Blood of Christ, our petition is that this redemption might cleanse the departed of their sins.

Since each time Mass is offered the purification begun in Baptism continues, God's mercy and forgiveness are unceasing in our lives. That is one of the gifts of the Paschal Mystery. Today, we petition for the full cleansing of the sins of the deceased, so they will merit the joys and blessedness of heaven.

Prayer after Communion: If we are open, our Holy Communion brings us into intimate union with Jesus, uniting us with the Paschal Mystery. The union depends not only on God's action but our faith-filled response.

The reality of our faith gives the Church the courage to pray for our beloved deceased brothers and sisters who shared that faith. They too, if they acted in faith, experienced the cleansing from sin made possible in the Lord's Paschal Mystery. In a very real sense, the faithful departed have been purified through their celebration of the various Sacraments of faith throughout their lives. We believe that they have also been affected by the celebration of the paschal sacrifice today at this altar—so deep is our solidarity in faith with them. Therefore, we pray that the Paschal Mystery, which they have begun to share in this life, may be complete in them now in the next. We pray, thus, that they may know fully God's gift of resurrection, and spend all eternity glorying in that gift.

3

Collect

Tie together lines one through three, while lowering the voice for **having conquered death**.
Slow slightly the words **pass over**.
Pause slightly after **that**. The phrase completing this line is parenthetical. The heart of the petition is: **that . . . they may gaze . . . .** Broaden both **Creator** and **Redeemer**.

O God, who willed that your Only Begotten Son,
having conquered death,
should pass over into the realm of heaven,
grant, we pray, to your departed servants
that, with the mortality of this life overcome,
they may gaze eternally on you,
their Creator and Redeemer.
Through our Lord Jesus Christ, your Son,
who lives and reigns with you in the unity of the Holy Spirit,
one God, for ever and ever.

Prayer over the Offerings

Tie together the first three lines while dropping the voice slightly for **in your kindness**. Pause briefly after **that** and tie together the rest of the line with the fifth line, pausing slightly after **sacrifice**.
Broaden **eternal life**.

Receive, Lord, in your kindness,
the sacrificial offering we make
for all your servants who sleep in Christ,
that, set free from the bonds of death
by this singular sacrifice,
they may merit eternal life.
Through Christ our Lord. *

Prayer after Communion

Tie together the first two lines, setting off **O Lord** at the end of the second line. Slow down and broaden **your great mercy** at the end of line three. Pause briefly after **and**. Parallel **grace of Baptism** with **fullness of eternal joy**.

Through these sacrificial gifts
which we have received, O Lord,
bestow on your departed servants your great mercy
and, to those you have endowed with the grace of Baptism,
grant also the fullness of eternal joy.
Through Christ our Lord. **

* Select from Prefaces I–V for the Dead in the Order of Mass. Commentary, and proclamation and chant tips, for the Preface can be found at *www.StudyThePresidentialTexts.com/Prefaces* and in *The Order of Mass: A Roman Missal Study Edition and Workbook*, pages 114–123.

** You may use the Solemn Blessings in Celebrations for the Dead in the Order of Mass; also on page 176 in *The Order of Mass: A Roman Missal Study Edition and Workbook.*

Collect: God's mysterious will is stated at the outset of this prayer: that his Only Begotten Son should conquer Death and pass over to the fullness of life in heaven. This statement of the basic vision of the Paschal Mystery sets up the parallel of the petition. The Church prays that our departed brothers and sisters, all servants of God, have also passed through and beyond death. Because of their actions as God's servants while in this life, and because of our intercession and faith, the Church prays that the death they have undergone might be overcome, that it might not be the last word. Our prayer is that their death is a "passing over" into heaven, where they may gaze forever on the Holy Trinity. The Father, the Creator of all, and the Son, the Redeemer of all, are mentioned explicitly because of their relation to human mortality.

Prayer over the Offerings: We beg God to receive our sacrificial offering with "kindness"—a word often used in Sacred Scripture to describe God's benign action toward his people and the world. The heart of Jesus, opening up to receive humanity into his sacrifice, gives the Church courage to lift up the intentions of its beloved deceased as it makes its sacrifice.

The prayer of the Church is that our sacrifice will, thanks to God's mercy, set the deceased free from death (described like a prison, with bonds tying up the dead) and

3

Collect

A O God, who willed that your Only Begotten Son,
having conquered death,
should pass over into the realm of hea**ven**,
B grant, we pray, to your departed servants
that, with the mortality of this life **o**vercome,
C they may gaze eternally on you,
their Creator and Redee***mer***.
Through our Lord Jesus Christ, your Son,
who lives and reigns with you in the unity of the Holy Spirit,
one God, for ever and ever.

Prayer over the Offerings

A Receive, Lord, in your kindness,
the sacrificial offering we make
for all your servants who sleep in **Christ**,
B that, set free from the bonds of death
by this sing**u**lar sacrifice,
C they may merit eternal ***life***.
Through Christ our Lord.

Prayer after Communion

A Through these sacrificial gifts
which we have received, O **Lord**,
B bestow on your departed servants **your** great mercy
C and, to those you have endowed with the grace of Baptism,
grant also the fullness of eternal ***joy***.
Through Christ our Lord.

The space below is for your notes.

Refer to pages viii–x for an explanation of the pointing of the chants and to page xii for the Tones for the Presidential Prayers from *The Roman Missal*.

enable them to merit eternal life. This petition rests on the power of our "singular sacrifice." This sacrifice represents the sacrifice of Jesus on the Cross in a sacramental manner and it unites the sacrifice of the Church to that of Jesus, in such a way that the Church is not so much offering a new sacrifice as participating sacramentally in the one single sacrifice that has saved the world and brought it at-one-ment with God (which is what we desire for our beloved deceased.

Prayer after Communion: The gifts that we have received in Holy Communion were offered in a way that they sacramentally became Jesus. Because our gifts have become the gift pleasing to the Father, the Church longs that it may become an everlasting gift to the Father in union with Jesus (cf. Eucharistic Prayer III). This gift is renewed in us sacramentally in Holy Communion.

Because of our union with the deceased in love, as members of the Church, we have courage to ask God, in the light of his great mercy (a word that has appeared repeatedly in today's prayers) to grant eternal joy to them. This petition rests on the fact that they have known God's election in Baptism, which grace has incorporated them into Christ and, hence, into Christ's Church. In this way they were given a share in the Paschal Mystery of Jesus. For that reason, the Church prays that what was begun in Baptism in these beloved deceased may reach fullness in eternity, with the joy that only can be known in heaven.

November 9

THE DEDICATION OF THE LATERAN BASILICA

Feast

Collect

O God, who from living and chosen stones
prepare an eternal dwelling for your majesty,
increase in your Church the spirit of grace you have bestowed,
so that by new growth your faithful people
may build up the heavenly Jerusalem.
Through our Lord Jesus Christ, your Son,
who lives and reigns with you in the unity of the Holy Spirit,
one God, for ever and ever.

Emphasize **living** and **chosen**. Tie together lines one and two. Emphasize **eternal**. Slow down **increase . . . bestowed**. Emphasize **new growth**, and tie together this line and the next. Emphasize **heavenly** and **Jerusalem**.

Or:

O God, who were pleased to call your Church the Bride,
grant that the people that serves your name
may revere you, love you and follow you,
and may be led by you
to attain your promises in heaven.
Through our Lord Jesus Christ, your Son,
who lives and reigns with you in the unity of the Holy Spirit,
one God, for ever and ever. *

Articulate very carefully **your Church the Bride**, accenting **Bride**.

Pray slowly, pausing after **revere you**, **love you**, and **follow you**. Pray slowly, **be led by you** and tie together this line and the next.

Prayer over the Offerings

Accept, we pray, O Lord, the offering made here
and grant that by it those who seek your favor
may receive in this place
the power of the Sacraments
and the answer to their prayers.
Through Christ our Lord.

Be sure to pronounce **Accept** correctly (ack). Pause after **here**. Slow **by it**. Tie together **and** to **Sacraments**. Parallel **power** and **Sacraments** with **answer** and **prayers**.

* Recite or sing the Creed if this feast falls on a Sunday.

Introduction: The Lateran complex with basilica in Rome, which was a gift to the Pope by Constantine the Great, became the home of the Popes of the first millennium. The basilica was dedicated first to the Savior in the fourth century, but in the medieval period it also was given the name St. John the Baptist. The original baptistry next to the church had been dedicated to the prophet from the beginning. From this time on, the church tended to be called John Lateran. As the first basilica of the Popes, it is the mother-church of the other Catholic churches in Rome and throughout the world. Five ecumenical Councils were held in this church during the medieval period.

Collect: The dedication of the external basilica church leads the author of this prayer to think of the spiritual church, the mystical body of Christ. Thus, looking at the material stones at the outset of the celebration, the author considers 1 Peter, which speaks of Christ as the living Stone on which the Church is built. He goes on to assert that all disciples of Christ are living and chosen stones (cf. 1 Peter 2:5, 9). This reflects the Gospel according to John: "From his fullness we have all received, grace in place of grace" (1:16).

The space below is for your notes.

Refer to pages viii–x for an explanation of the pointing of the chants and to page xii for the Tones for the Presidential Prayers from *The Roman Missal.*

Pointed Text

Collect

A O God, who from living and chosen stones
prepare an eternal dwelling for your ma**<u>jes</u>**ty,
B increase in your Church the spirit of grace you **have** bestowed,
C so that by new growth your faithful people
may build up the heavenly Jeru***sa***lem.
Through our Lord Jesus Christ, your Son,
who lives and reigns with you in the unity of the Holy Spirit,
one God, for ever and ever.

Or:

A O God, who were pleased to call your Church the **<u>Bride</u>**,
B grant that the people that serves your name
may revere you, love **you** and follow you,
C and may be led by you
to attain your promises in hea***ven***.
Through our Lord Jesus Christ, your Son,
who lives and reigns with you in the unity of the Holy Spirit,
one God, for ever and ever.

Prayer over the Offerings

A Accept, we pray, O Lord, the offering made **<u>here</u>**
B and grant that by it those who seek your favor
may receive in this place
the power **of** the Sacraments
C and the answer to their ***prayers***.
Through Christ our Lord.

The second line speaks of a dwelling place for God's majesty. In the Hebrew dispensation, the Temple in Jerusalem was seen as that (Psalm 76:3; 84:2–3; 132:5, 7). In the New Testament, Jesus is viewed as the primary dwelling place of God (cf. John 1:14). But we too, his disciples and members, are the place where God resides (cf. 2 Corinthians 5:2). Our churches are a kind of sacrament of the living Church, and in them we also find the Presence of God dwelling.

The Collect petitions an increase of the grace already bestowed in Baptism, which made us Church. This grace was entirely gratuitous on God's part (Romans 3:24; 5:15–17). The last part of the petition speaks of growth of God's faithful. Perhaps it is a reference to what occurs in baptistries or to the Baptistry of John Lateran. It speaks of a growth that will not end until the entire Church arrives in heaven (cf. 2 Corinthians 5:2).

Optional Collect: The image with which this Collect begins is that of the Church as Bride of Christ. The image is strong in the book of Revelation: "Let us rejoice and be glad / and give him glory. / For the wedding day of the Lamb has come, / his bride has made herself ready. / She has been allowed to wear / a bright, clean linen garment" [This represents the righteous deeds of the holy ones.] (Revelation 19:7–8; cf. also, Revelation 21:2 and 2 Corinthians 11:2). It was God's choice to call the Church

Preface: The mystery of the Church, the Bride of Christ and the Temple of the Spirit.

Bring out the accent on **be** in **The Lord be with you**. In the response, accent **spirit**, by holding slightly both syllables. In the next phrase, make a strong accent on **Lift**, and slow both notes of **hearts**. In the third dialogue, move to the word **thanks** before accenting, and hold that word slightly to give it emphasis. Broaden both notes of **Lord**, and hold **God**.

Do not lengthen or pause after **benevolence**, but continue with **you are pleased**. Lengthen slightly **prayer**, but do not hold long, for the sense requires going on to **in order to**. Broaden **Holy Spirit**. It probably will be necessary to take a quick breath there, to sustain for the next two phrases. At the end of the next phrase, hold **grace** slightly, and then go on with **and resplendent**. Lengthen and slow the melodic development on **glory**, but do not pause there; continue with **of a life**, but broaden the ending syllables. In the next phrase, even though the melody moves up to "doh" on **by**, do not accent or emphasize that word. This might best be done by lengthening slightly the two uses of **Year**. At the end of the phrase, hold **Christ** slightly, and, if possible, continue with **foreshadowed**

thus, not something that the Church could take upon herself in any other way.

The people "that serves your name" are those called by God. The scriptural sense of "name" is the same as "person." Serving the name is the same as serving God's Person. The Hebrews were dedicated to this, as is seen in Psalm 2:11, "Serve the LORD with fear / . . . bow down in homage." We are baptized "in the name" of the Trinity, and in particular, of Jesus Christ. This calls for a response of service to these Persons with dedicated lives.

The petition is that we might first "revere" God—which is very logical, since we have been called by a God who is infinite and unfathomable and yet wants to draw us near. All brides need to begin their relationship with their husbands with reverence. But then, and this Collect reflects this, that spirit moves on to love. And it is out of such love that we are committed to following the Lord, of allowing ourselves to be led by God. That leading affects our daily life here, and ends with everlasting life in heaven.

Prayer over the Offerings: The physical church as a sacramental reality stands at the heart of this prayer. That is, church (with a small "c") stands for Church (with a capital "C"), or the body of Christ. At this point in Mass, the prayer begins directly with the petition that the Church's offering of bread and wine be accepted by the Lord. The next line gives the second petition: that God be receptive to the offering of our very selves. Our offering is not made so as to manipulate God, but rather to receive God's favor, his responsive love. We

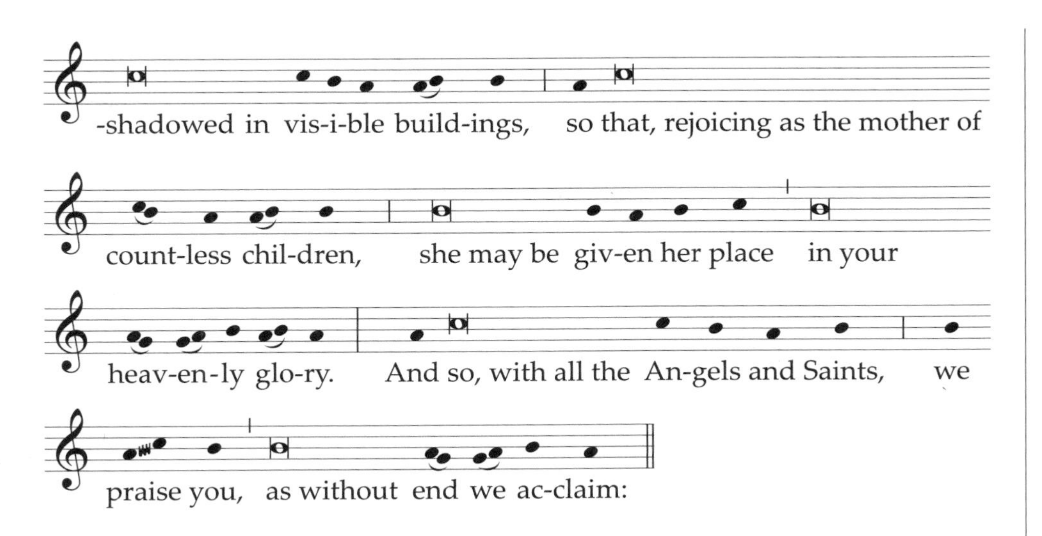

without a breath. Take a short breath after **buildings**, holding the last syllable slightly. Respect the comma after **so that**, by broadening the word, and then continuing without a break with **rejoicing**. Broaden the end of that phrase, **countless children**, holding the last syllable slightly. But try to continue without a breath, with **she may**. Hold slightly **place**, not breaking there, but rather continuing with **in your**. Articulate carefully **heavenly glory**, which will slow it somewhat, and hold **-ry** and take a breath.

Holy, Holy, Holy Lord God of hosts . . .

Text without music:

V. **The Lord be with you.**
R. And with your spirit.

V. **Lift up your hearts.**
R. We lift them up to the Lord.

V. **Let us give thanks to the Lord our God.**
R. It is right and just.

It is truly right and just, our duty and our salvation,
always and everywhere to give you thanks,
Lord, holy Father, almighty and eternal God.

For in your benevolence you are pleased
to dwell in this house of prayer
in order to perfect us as the temple of the Holy Spirit,
supported by the perpetual help of your grace
and resplendent with the glory of a life acceptable to you.

Stretch out **For**. Tie together lines one and two. Slight emphasis on **this**. Carefully enunciate **perfect us**, **temple**, and **Holy Spirit**. Short pause after **Spirit**, so as to continue to the next lines. Slightly emphasize **perpetual help**. Carefully enunciate **resplendent**. Emphasize **glory**, **life**, **acceptable**, and **you**.

do not come before the Lord from a position of strength, but rather as beggars (the Latin original carries that sense).

The heart of the petition follows: that through this Mass and the offering we make here, we might receive back from God the power of the Sacraments. This refers not only to the Eucharist but also to all the other Sacraments that are conferred in the Church. Note that the prayer mentions explicitly "in this place"—the actual physical church stands for the deeper interior Church. For it is we who desire the grace and power of the Sacraments to come into our beings and lives. Further, the physical church is a place of prayer, and the interior reality of Church should be that also. To receive a favorable answer to our prayers is to know in a profound way the favor of the Lord that we seek.

Preface: The mystery of the Church, the Bride of Christ and the Temple of the Spirit

As the body of the Preface explores the core theology and meaning of a feast in honor of a church, it notes first the indwelling Presence of God in the church, here called a "house of prayer." (The Real Presence in the Holy Eucharist preserved in our churches was defined by the Fourth Lateran Council, 1215, Const. 1—a special connection of this church with the phrase in the Preface.) God's indwelling in the

Stretch out slightly **Year by year** and pause. Accent **sanctify**, **Church**, **Bride**, and **Christ**. Do not pause after **Christ** but continue the sense, enunciating carefully **visible buildings**. Pause slightly after **so that**. Accent **rejoicing**, **mother**, and **countless children**. Carefully enunciate **her place** and emphasize **heavenly glory**.

Year by year you sanctify the Church, the Bride of Christ,
foreshadowed in visible buildings,
so that, rejoicing as the mother of countless children,
she may be given her place in your heavenly glory.

And so, with all the Angels and Saints,
we praise you, as without end we acclaim:

Holy, Holy, Holy Lord God of hosts . . .

Prayer after Communion

Tie together the first three lines. Emphasize **foreshadow**, **heavenly**, and **sign**. Take care with pronouncing **our**. Accent both **partaking** and **Sacrament**, pausing briefly there.

Parallel **temple . . . grace** with **dwelling place . . . glory**.

O God, who chose to foreshadow for us
the heavenly Jerusalem
through the sign of your Church on earth,
grant, we pray,
that, by our partaking of this Sacrament,
we may be made the temple of your grace
and may enter the dwelling place of your glory.
Through Christ our Lord. *

* You may use the Solemn Blessings for the Dedication of a Church in the Order of Mass; also on page 176 in *The Order of Mass: A Roman Missal Study Edition and Workbook.*

Church perfects it as a bearer of the Holy Spirit, here symbolized as a temple, a reality strongly emphasized by Saint Paul: "Do you not know that you are the temple of God, and that the Spirit of God dwells in you?" (1 Corinthians 3:16). Also: "Do you not know that your body is a temple of the holy Spirit within you, whom you have from God, and that you are not your own?" (1 Corinthians 6:19). To "perfect" us as a bearer of the Holy Spirit is to bring us to the fullness of the Presence which God wants in us.

The next phrase proclaims that the gift of being God's temple cannot be sustained except by the constant help of God's grace. He calls us to be his temple; he sustains us to be so. And this leads to a spiritual beauty in the Church that is unsurpassed by any other (cf. Revelation 19:7–8) — that of living in virtue. This gift of God's grace comes to the Church constantly ("year by year"), and it means sanctification (making holy) for the Church as God's Bride. All of this beauty is sacramentalized in a physical church building such as St. John Lateran. The last phrases evoke again the baptistry, where the Church gives birth to "countless children." But even the earthly beauty of a basilica such as the Lateran is nothing compared to the glory of the heavenly temple—for which the body of the Preface petitions in the final phrase.

The space below is for your notes.

Refer to pages viii–x for an explanation of the pointing of the chants and to page xii for the Tones for the Presidential Prayers from *The Roman Missal*.

Prayer after Communion

A O God, who chose to foreshadow for us
the heavenly Jerusalem
through the sign of your Church on **earth**,
B grant, we pray,
that, by our partaking **of** this Sacrament,
C we may be made the temple of your grace
and may enter the dwelling place of your glo***ry***.
Through Christ our Lord.

Prayer after Communion: We have seen that other euchologies on this feast view the physical church of the Lateran basilica as a sacrament for the whole Church itself. This Prayer opens with the sacramentality pointing the other way: the physical church and the Mystical Body of Christ, the Church, for which the building is a sacrament—both point beyond themselves to the Church of heaven, the eschatological vision of eternal life. Heaven here is called, symbolically, Jerusalem, since the ancient city was seen as God's special dwelling place on earth. ("Remember your flock that you gathered of old, / the tribe that you redeemed as your very own. / Remember Mount Zion where you dwell" [Psalm 74:2].)

The Church has just received the Sacrament of the Body and Blood of Christ, in Holy Communion. That is, Jesus has come to dwell within us, as God did of old in Jerusalem. The Presence for us is the same as grace. Therefore, we pray that Jesus's coming to us in this act of Communion make us more completely the "temple" of that Presence in our daily lives. Living in the Presence will, in turn, make it possible for us to enter the eternal "dwelling place" of God's glory, heaven itself. This is the petition of the final phrase.

December 8

THE IMMACULATE CONCEPTION OF THE BLESSED VIRGIN MARY

PATRONAL FEASTDAY OF THE UNITED STATES OF AMERICA

Solemnity

Collect

O God, who by the Immaculate Conception of the Blessed Virgin
prepared a worthy dwelling for your Son,
grant, we pray,
that, as you preserved her from every stain
by virtue of the Death of your Son, which you foresaw,
so, through her intercession,
we, too, may be cleansed and admitted to your presence.
Through our Lord Jesus Christ, your Son,
who lives and reigns with you in the unity of the Holy Spirit,
one God, for ever and ever.

Carefully enunciate **worthy dwelling**.

Tie together lines four and five without a pause. Drop the voice slightly at **which you foresaw** and also with **through her intercession**. Accent and enunciate carefully **we**, **too**, **cleansed**, **admitted,** and **presence**.

Prayer over the Offerings

Graciously accept the saving sacrifice
which we offer you, O Lord,
on the Solemnity of the Immaculate Conception
of the Blessed Virgin Mary,
and grant that, as we profess her,
on account of your prevenient grace,
to be untouched by any stain of sin,
so, through her intercession,
we may be delivered from all our faults.
Through Christ our Lord.

Tie together the first two lines, with a slight lowering of the voice at **O Lord**. Short pause at **Lord**, to go on to the next two lines.

Treat **on . . . grace** as parenthetical. Slightly accent **your**, **prevenient**, and **grace**. Slightly accent **untouched** and **sin**. Drop the voice slightly for **through her intercession**, but tie together this line and the final line. In that last line, accent **delivered**, **all,** and **faults** (paying attention to the pronunciation of **our**).

Collect: With joy we celebrate God's gift that preserved Mary from all sin, so that her person might be worthy to host the presence of God's Only Begotten Son. This preservation from sin was a gift that came from the saving Death of Jesus, extending back to the moment of Mary's conception. We have a kind of double miracle underlying this feast. First, the Death of Jesus was to be the saving grace and redemption of all. Anyone who responded to God's grace and call would be awarded the gift of salvation. Secondly, the Death of Jesus was a saving grace in a unique way for Mary, preserving her from any taint of sin from the first moment of her conception.

Meditating on Mary's gift of being conceived without sin, the Church petitions for Mary's intercession that her prayer brings us the grace of cleansing from sin too. We make this request so that we may be admitted to God's presence in heaven, a presence which the Mother of God experienced in a way unlike others.

Prayer over the Offerings: The Church petitions at the outset of this prayer for God to accept the sacrifice that we are about to offer. This sacrifice is "saving," because it shares sacramentally in the sacrifice that Jesus made on Calvary. The first recipient of this "saving" was Mary. She had the grace to be completely pure, untouched by sin, from the first moment of her conception—the special gift of God in her that we celebrate at this Mass. Because she received this gift from God, the Church asks to be delivered from all sin. Since all

The space below is for your notes.

Refer to pages viii–x for an explanation of the pointing of the chants and to page xii for the Tones for the Presidential Prayers from *The Roman Missal.*

Pointed Text

Collect

A O God, who by the Immaculate Conception of the Blessed Virgin
prepared a worthy dwelling for your **Son**,
B grant, we pray,
that, as you preserved her from every stain
by virtue of the Death of your Son, which **you** foresaw,
C so, through her intercession,
we, too, may be cleansed and admitted to your pre***sence***.
Through our Lord Jesus Christ, your Son,
who lives and reigns with you in the unity of the Holy Spirit,
one God, for ever and ever.

Prayer over the Offerings

A Graciously accept the saving sacrifice
which we offer you, O Lord,
on the Solemnity of the Immaculate Conception
of the Blessed Virgin Ma**ry**,
B and grant that, as we profess her,
on account of your prevenient grace,
to be untouched by any **stain** of sin,
C so, through her intercession,
we may be delivered from all our ***faults***.
Through Christ our Lord.

human beings are sinners, this is an important request.

Though we were not conceived without sin, we can still hope that our lives, thanks to her intercession and through this sacrificial celebration, might end up being without faults. We pray for this because of the grace of deliverance provided by Jesus's sacrifice, to which we are about to join ours.

Bring out the accent on **be** in **The Lord be with you.** In the response, accent **spirit**, by holding slightly both syllables. In the next phrase, make a strong accent on **Lift**, and slow both notes of **hearts**. In the third dialogue, move to the word **thanks** before accenting, and hold that word slightly to give it emphasis. Broaden both notes of **Lord**, and hold **God**.

Sing this proclamation cursively in a reciting tone. Do not hold **-va** in **salvation**; only broaden the two notes slightly. The **-tion** should be held. Slightly broaden **always** and **everywhere**. The accent of the phrase falls on **thanks**. In the next part of the text, clearly make three phrases, by respecting the commas after **Lord** and **Father**.

Carefully articulate both **you** and **preserved**.

Hold briefly **sin**. Pause briefly at **that** and **her**.

A brief pause at **grace** would be appropriate, but without taking a breath. Hold **Son**, then take a quick breath before continuing with **and signify**. Hold **Church**, but without pause or taking a breath, continuing on to **his**. Broaden and slow **-out** of **without** and the next three words. Pause after **She** and **Virgin**, but without taking a breath. Hold **Son** a little. Carefully enunciate and hold slightly **Lamb** but without pausing or

Preface: The mystery of Mary and the Church.

V. The Lord be with you. R. And with your spir-it.

V. Lift up your hearts. R. We lift them up to the Lord.

V. Let us give thanks to the Lord our God. R. It is right and just.

It is truly right and just, our duty and our sal-va-tion, al-ways and everywhere to give you thanks, Lord, holy Father, almighty and e- -ter-nal God. For you preserved the most Blessed Virgin Mary from all stain of o-rig-i-nal sin, so that in her, endowed with the rich fullness of your grace, you might prepare a worthy Mother for your Son and signify the beginning of the Church, his beautiful Bride with-out spot or wrin-kle. She, the most pure Virgin, was to bring forth a Son, the in-no-cent Lamb who would wipe a-way

Preface: The mystery of Mary and the Church

As the beginning of the text provides the reason for the Blessed Virgin's preservation from sin, we hear the voice of her cousin Elizabeth: "Most blessed are you among women, and blessed is the fruit of your womb" (Luke 1:42). Not only do we hear of the grace that fills the Mother of God, but also of her *fiat*. We hear of the strength of her belief. "Blessed are you who believed that what was spoken to you by the Lord would be fulfilled" (Luke 1:45).

In this Preface, we see another dimension of the solemnity: "signify the beginning of the Church, / his beautiful bride without spot or wrinkle." Those words recall Ephesians 5:27: "that he might present to himself the church in splendor, without spot or wrinkle or any such thing that she might be holy without blemish."

The content is repeated in the first line of the second paragraph of the body of the Preface, in terms of Mary being "most pure" (immaculate, in her conception) in order to become the Mother of God's Son. The Son himself was immaculate (innocent) in order to offer the pure sacrifice (as an unblemished Passover Lamb) that would take away the world's sin. But an even further dimension is then stated, in the light of this solemnity: Mary was given such an exalted state so she could be an intercessor (advocate of grace) and a model that we could follow as we strive for holiness.

(Mary gave herself over to God's will. The following Homily explores how we are to do likewise. The Homily was excerpted

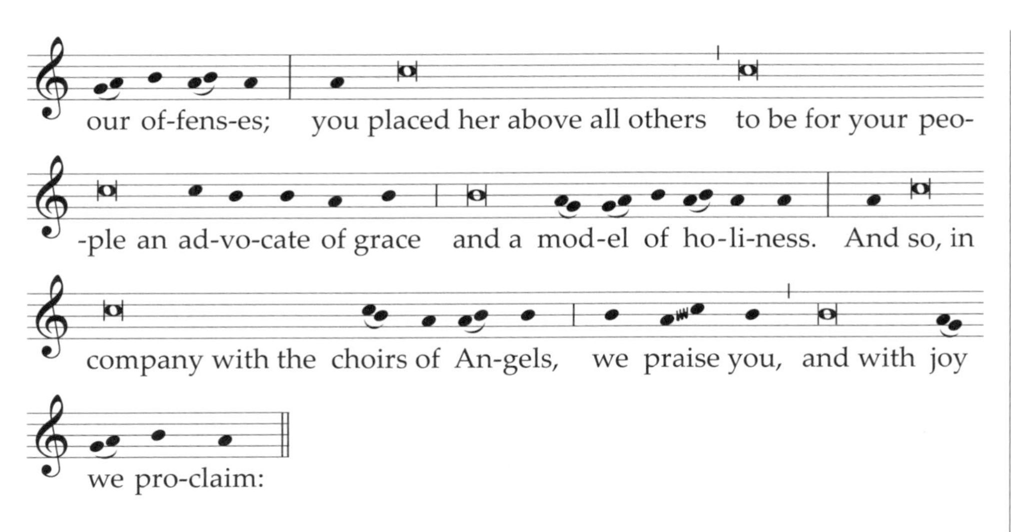

taking a breath. Hold **-es** of **offenses** and pause. In the next phrase, tie together **others** and **to be**. Hold **grace** slightly but take no breath. Enunciate carefully **model of holiness**. In the final sentence, pause at **so**. Hold **-gels** of **Angels** slightly, but continue on to **we**. Broaden **praise** and do not pause at **you** but rather continue with **and with**. Slow, and enunciate carefully, **joy**, and **-claim** of **proclaim**.

Holy, Holy, Holy Lord God of hosts . . .

Text without music:

V. **The Lord be with you.**
R. And with your spirit.

V. **Lift up your hearts.**
R. We lift them up to the Lord.

V. **Let us give thanks to the Lord our God.**
R. It is right and just.

It is truly right and just, our duty and our salvation,
always and everywhere to give you thanks,
Lord, holy Father, almighty and eternal God.

For you preserved the most Blessed Virgin Mary
from all stain of original sin,
so that in her, endowed with the rich fullness of your grace,
you might prepare a worthy Mother for your Son
and signify the beginning of the Church,
his beautiful Bride without spot or wrinkle.

Tie together the first two lines without a pause.
Drop the voice slightly for the parenthetical phrase **endowed . . . your grace**. Clearly enunciate **worthy** and **Mother**. Very brief pause after **Son** and also **Church**. Broaden the words **beautiful Bride** but do not pause after them. Slight accent to both **spot** and **wrinkle**.

from the CD *Preparing Your Parish for the Revised Roman Missal: Homilies and Reproducibles for Faith Formation* © 2010, Liturgy Training Publications.)

The Lord's Prayer
Daniel J. Merz, SLD

In Pope Benedict XVI's excellent commentary on the Our Father (see his book, *Jesus of Nazareth*), he writes that it is significant that the Gospel according to Luke places the Our Father in the context of Jesus's own praying. "Jesus thereby involves us in his own prayer" (p. 132). The Our Father, when prayed after the Eucharistic Prayer, draws us ever deeper, then, into the heart of Jesus and his interior dialogue with his Father.

Pope Gregory the Great gave the Our Father its current place in Mass in the sixth century. He wrote, "It seemed to me quite inappropriate, on the one hand, to say over the offering a prayer composed by one or other writer and, on the other, not to say over the redeemer's body and blood the prayer which he himself composed and which tradition has preserved for us" (IX, 12, PL 77, col. 956 s). The Pope felt the need to balance the words composed by human beings with words composed by Christ himself. The Our Father introduces the Communion Rite, which is the high point and goal of the whole liturgy: our communion with the Lord. Reciting the prayer of the Lord is understood as perhaps the best way to prepare ourselves for that intimate communion.

From earliest times, Christians have felt a mixture of confidence and trepida-

Pause after **She**. Treat the next phrase as parenthetical. Accent and lengthen slightly **Son**, but do not pause. Pause after **offenses**. Accent **her**, so as to bring out the contrast with **all others**. Continue to line four, accenting **people**, **advocate**, and **grace**. Tie together lines four and five, accenting **model** and **holiness**.

She, the most pure Virgin, was to bring forth a Son,
the innocent Lamb who would wipe away our offenses;
you placed her above all others
to be for your people an advocate of grace
and a model of holiness.

And so, in company with the choirs of Angels,
we praise you, and with joy we proclaim:

Holy, Holy, Holy Lord God of hosts . . .

Prayer after Communion

Treat **O . . . God** as parenthetical, with a slight drop in the voice. Carefully enunciate **wounds**. Tie together **heal . . . Conception**. Treat **in a singular way** as if commas were around it. Slowly enunciate **Immaculate Conception**.

May the Sacrament we have received,
O Lord our God,
heal in us the wounds of that fault
from which in a singular way
you preserved Blessed Mary in her Immaculate Conception.
Through Christ our Lord. *

* You may use the Solemn Blessings for The Blessed Virgin Mary in the Order of Mass; also on page 174 in *The Order of Mass: A Roman Missal Study Edition and Workbook*.

tion at joining in with Jesus's prayer, especially his address to God: "Father!" Are we really that intimate with our Creator? The words of introduction to the Our Father at Mass reflect this mingled trepidation and confidence: "At the Savior's command / and formed by divine teaching, / we dare to say . . . ." To call God "Father" is daring! And we do so only because he commanded and taught us to do so. To prepare us for the intimacy of Holy Communion, the Our Father reminds us that through our Baptism we have become children of God.

Holy Communion is a foretaste of the heavenly banquet feast of the kingdom. The petition "thy kingdom come" serves both to ready us for the foretaste we are about to receive, and to make us long for its fulfillment in heaven.

Holy Communion implies that we are striving for union with God. The petition, "thy will be done / on earth as it is in heaven," reminds us of the concrete implications of union with God, namely, letting his will become sovereign in our lives.

Many Church Fathers and scholars assert that the petition, "give us this day our daily bread," was coined specifically for the Eucharist. The Greek word that we translate here as "daily" is unique. It refers to a special kind of bread, the bread that alone will satisfy. One could almost paraphrase, "Give us this day that mysterious bread, which alone is enough for us today." Bread, of course, has always been used to stand for whatever is most necessary to survive. For the Christian, to survive means to be alive in Christ, and the most impor-

The space below is for your notes.

Refer to pages viii–x for an explanation of the pointing of the chants and to page xii for the Tones for the Presidential Prayers from *The Roman Missal.*

Prayer after Communion

A May the Sacrament we have received,
O Lord our **God**,
B heal in us the wounds **of** that fault
C from which in a singular way
you preserved Blessed Mary in her Immaculate Concep***tion***.
Through Christ our Lord.

tant way we do that is by sharing in the bread that is his body.

Saint Paul tells us that we should examine our conscience to be able to receive the body of the Lord worthily (see 1 Corinthians 1:27). The Our Father helps us to do this with the petition: "forgive us our trespasses, / as we forgive those who trespass against us." I shouldn't approach the sacramental body of the Lord while holding a grudge against another member of the Mystical Body of the Lord. This petition helps us to cleanse our conscience.

Prayer after Communion: Even as the Church has intimate communion with God, through our reception of the Body and Blood of Christ, we recognize ourselves as sinners. This is in contrast to Mary, so singularly preserved from Original Sin and all other sin in her Immaculate Conception.

Therefore, the Church begs that the holy Sacrament we have received might also be for the healing of our sinfulness. This is a petition that Mary never needed to make, but we know that all of us have to. Sinfulness is like a wound, maiming us so we are not the true selves we are intended to be, after the transforming grace of Baptism. So we pray for healing of the wound(s). In doing so, we are not asking for Mary's unique and wonderful privilege, but rather for a restoration of what Baptism gave us, when we first professed to follow Christ and be faithful members of the Church. If God gives such a grace, thanks to our Holy Communion with Jesus, our daily lives will be transformed and will end up witnessing Jesus to the world.

[In the Dioceses of the United States]

December 12

OUR LADY OF GUADALUPE

Feast

Collect

Drop voice for **Father of mercies** and continue on to next line, tying it with line three. Slow down and enunciate clearly **Son's most holy Mother**. Treat **with ever more lively faith** as parenthetical. The sense is **may seek . . . the progress**. Slow **the progress . . . of peace**.

O God, Father of mercies,
who placed your people under the singular protection
of your Son's most holy Mother,
grant that all who invoke the Blessed Virgin of Guadalupe,
may seek with ever more lively faith
the progress of peoples in the ways of justice and of peace.
Through our Lord Jesus Christ, your Son,
who lives and reigns with you in the unity of the Holy Spirit,
one God, for ever and ever.

Prayer over the Offerings

Tie together first two lines. Emphasize **this** and **sacrifice**. Make a very slight pause after **strengthen us**. Tie together **to fulfill . . . Virgin Mary**.

Accept, O Lord, the gifts we present to you
on this feast of Our Lady of Guadalupe,
and grant that this sacrifice
may strengthen us to fulfill your commandments
as true children of the Virgin Mary.
Through Christ our Lord.

Prayer after Communion

Tie together lines one and two, treating the latter as parenthetical. Enunciate carefully **always**, and accent **reconcile** and **love**. Tie together lines four and five, accenting **united** and **peace**. Slightly pause after **world** before going on to **until**. Broaden **dawns in glory**.

Lord God, may the Body and Blood of your Son,
which we receive in this sacrament,
reconcile us always in your love;
and may we who rejoice in Our Lady of Guadalupe
live united and at peace in this world
until the day of the Lord dawns in glory.
Through Christ our Lord.

Collect: The Blessed Virgin's apparition, in 1531, to Juan Diego was a special blessing. The prayer notes the "singular protection" the Blessed Mother offers. As *Lumen Gentium*, 60, explains: "Mary is our mother in the order of grace."

The petition notes three virtues: a lively faith, justice, and peace. We cannot underestimate the importance of the latter two virtues for "the progress of peoples." This phrase is surely taken from the 1967 Encyclical Letter of Pope Paul VI (*Populorum Progressio*). Justice and peace was also a passion of Pope John Paul II. In his January 1, 1998, message, he said: "Justice goes hand in hand with peace and is permanently and actively linked to peace . . . (#1). Peace for all of us comes from the justice of each of us" (#7).

The hope of the petition in this Collect is that those who love and invoke the Blessed Virgin Mary will take to heart the prayer implicit in her Canticle (Luke 1:52–53) that the lowly will be lifted up and the hungry filled. This happens when there is true justice and peace.

Prayer over the Offerings: Offering this holy sacrifice is a liturgical and sacred way of showing God that we are offering him our lives. Our action of sacrifice is especially fitting on a feast of the Blessed Virgin Mary, as she is—after her Son—the most perfect model of self-sacrifice to the will of God ("Behold, I am the handmaid of the Lord. May it be done to me according to your word" [Luke 1:38]).

That is why the Church prays that the sacrifice it is about to offer, with the inner spirit of surrender to and union with God,

The space below is for your notes.

Refer to pages viii–x for an explanation of the pointing of the chants and to page xii for the Tones for the Presidential Prayers from *The Roman Missal.*

Pointed Text

Collect

A O God, Father of mercies,
who placed your people under the singular protection
of your Son's most holy Mo**ther**,
B grant that all who invoke the Blessed Virgin of **Guad**alupe,
C may seek with ever more lively faith
the progress of peoples in the ways of justice and of ***peace***.
Through our Lord Jesus Christ, your Son,
who lives and reigns with you in the unity of the Holy Spirit,
one God, for ever and ever.

Prayer over the Offerings

A Accept, O Lord, the gifts we present to you
on this feast of Our Lady of Guadalu**pe**,
B and grant that this sacrifice
may strengthen us to fulfill **your** commandments
C as true **children** of the Virgin Ma***ry***.
Through Christ our Lord.

Prayer after Communion

A Lord God, may the Body and Blood of your Son,
which we receive in this sa**cra**ment,
B reconcile us always **in** your love;
C and may we who rejoice in **Our Lady** of Guadalupe
live united and at peace in this world
until the day of the Lord dawns in glo***ry***.
Through Christ our Lord.

will help her always to live by God's direction (fulfill your commandments), always to respond positively to God's will in its life. Such a spirit would make us true children of Mary, because it reflects her interior spirit. "Do whatever he tells you," (John 2:5), her words to the waiters at Cana, could well be her urging to us. Fulfilling what God commands us can only be done with God's grace. But we also want Mary's intercession to help us respond to that divine grace.

Prayer after Communion: We pray immediately to be reconciled in God's love. This reconciliation is first to be with God, which the paschal Christ has achieved for us (2 Corinthians 5:18–19; Ephesians 2:16; Colossians 1:20), and secondly with other human beings, from whom we become easily estranged.

Our Lady is again our model. Always living in union with God, she was chosen to be the most wonderful instrument of human and divine unity, by her being the mother of Jesus, who was both her son and the Son of God. As we rejoice in her on this feastday, we pray for the grace of unity and peace with God and with our fellow human beings. The petition prays that this double grace of God be extended all through our daily lives to which, Mass now concluding, we are about to return. The Church also asks that this grace remain in us until the end of the world, when the Lord will come again in glory.